ἔφην. οὐ δεὶ ἀπολεῖζου ὑμῖν μάχεσαι δυἀσμαι ἃ ἀνὺς,
ἣ ἡμᾶων νόμῳ τῶ δγ ταύτης τῆς ὁ νοῦ δὶ ὁσαται πύι
ἐντρόπον γνως, πάντω ϑ αὐτὶ ἡμῖν ὁμοια ποιῆσητ ε
τὸ ἡμῶν εἶναιτῶν χὴ τοῦ θ ῦ †

· ·: ← ἀ τ π πρὸς τοὺ ἀ ν α λου μαχ   αχ   ᾳ ·
· : ι του ου αι μου ·
· ·: ·ου ἀ τοῦ τ ιου ιου αιμου † ι λοσο ισ συν ν ι ὠ
τι ρ ο ι ι πο λογια ι π ρ εὶ ει εν ἱ εν, τ τιος α
ρ...ι ι νουισ μ λη τ ολ ι †

Καὶ τὰ χολα δὲ καὶ δεφ ημ ἐν τῇ πόλει ὑμῶν Γεγόνον
ἠπούεΓἴκου ἀ ἑωμαῖοι. Θτα ῥμ Γεχοῦ ὁποι εὗ
ὑπὸ τωμ ἡγουμένων δόγω πεχαΤὸ μενά, ἑξημά
παδολμες ἰ∞ι̃φ ὑμῶν. ὁποι ο πε δ ωμ ὄμτων ὦ δ ίδϵλ
φῶν. κὴ μ αΓμοῖ τε και μη δε λητε δγ ατῶ δόξ ὀρν
των γομ ζομένων ἀξι ωμάτων, τῆν πῶν δὲ τῶν μ ἰον
σω αξ ἰμ ποι ήσθαι· πονΓεχοῦ ρφ· ὃς ἀμ σω φεορι
ζηται ῶ πρὸ. ἤ τει τομος. ἤ τκ νου. ἤ φι λου. ἤ ἀ δελ
φῶν· ἤ ἀμ δεος ἤ Γμαικος κατέλει ψί μ χωεισ Τῶν
πει ὠ ένΤων διὸ ἀ δύκοιν ἀ λ κελά σοτο ἐμ αι ωρί ω.
σω εἰ κο χ λεα ῖ σε δται· τοισ δ͂ν δὲ ἔτοισ. Θ ὁ κύ ωος
χω ρίω Γωτζς, ῞Ν ἀ παθ είᾳ. σὺ τομ ε όναι τῶ θε͂ο ἀ μέγο
δξ Των Γ ω ρ ομ μων χείσ ανων διὰ τὸ λὸ μάλς θον καὶ

B 6

Justin Martyr and His Worlds

Justin Martyr
and His Worlds

Edited by

Sara Parvis and Paul Foster

Fortress Press
Minneapolis

JUSTIN MARTYR AND HIS WORLDS

Cover image: Icon of Saint Justin. Photo courtesy of St. Vladimir's Seminary Press.
Cover design: Josh Messner
Book design: The HK Scriptorium

Library of Congress Cataloging-in-Publication Data

Justin Martyr and his worlds / Sara Parvis and Paul Foster, editors.
    p. cm.
  Includes bibliographical references and index.
  ISBN 978-0-8006-6212-7 (alk. paper)
  1. Justin, Martyr, Saint. I. Parvis, Sara. II. Foster, Paul, 1966-
BR65.J86J87   2007
270.1092—dc22

                              2007008175

The paper used in this publication meets the minimum requirements of American National Standard for Information Sciences—Permanence of Paper for Printed Library Materials, ANSI Z329.48-1984.

                    Manufactured in Canada

Contents

Abbreviations   vii

Contributors   xi

Justin Martyr Timeline   xiii

Justin's Writings   xiv

Map: Justin Martyr and His World   xvi

Introduction: Justin Martyr and His Worlds   1
Sara Parvis and Paul Foster

Part One. Justin and His Text

1. Justin Scholarship: Trends and Trajectories   13
   Michael Slusser

2. Justin, Philosopher and Martyr: The Posthumous Creation   22
   of the *Second Apology*
   Paul Parvis

3. The *Rescript* of Hadrian   38
   Denis Minns

Part Two. Justin and His Bible

4. Justin and His Bible   53
   Oskar Skarsaune

5. Justin and Israelite Prophecy   77
   Bruce Chilton

6. Was John's Gospel among Justin's *Apostolic Memoirs?*   88
   C. E. Hill

7. Interpreting the Descent of the Spirit: A Comparison   95
   of Justin's *Dialogue with Trypho* and Luke-Acts
   Susan Wendel

8. The Relationship between the Writings of Justin Martyr and   104
   the So-Called *Gospel of Peter*
   Paul Foster

Part Three. Justin and His Tradition

9. Justin Martyr and the Apologetic Tradition   115
   Sara Parvis

10. "Jesus" as God's Name, and Jesus as God's Embodied Name   128
    in Justin Martyr
    Larry W. Hurtado

11. *Altercatio Jasonis et Papisci* as a Testimony Source for Justin's   137
    "Second God" Argument?
    Will Rutherford

12. Justin and the Pontic Wolf   145
    Sebastian Moll

13. Questions Liturgists Would Like to Ask Justin Martyr   152
    Colin Buchanan

14. Justin and Hellenism: Some Postcolonial Perspectives   160
    Rebecca Lyman

Notes   169

Bibliography   215

Index of Names   235

Index of Ancient Sources   239

Abbreviations

Ancient Writings

Abr.	Philo, *De Abrahamo*
Ad Vig.	Pseudo-Cyprian, *Ad Vigilium Episcopum de Iudaica Incredulitate*
Adv. Haer.	Irenaeus, *Adversus Haereses*
Adv. Jud.	Tertullian, *Adversus Judaeos*
Adv. Marc.	Tertullian, *Adversus Marcionem*
Adv. Prax.	Tertullian, *Adversus Praxean*
Adv. Valentin.	Tertullian, *Adversus Valentinianos*
Agric.	Philo, *De Agricultura*
Ant.	Josephus, *Antiquitates*
Apol.	Justin Martyr, *Apologies*
1 Apol.	*First Apology*
2 Apol.	*Second Apology*
AZ	*Athanasius and Zacchaeus* (Jewish-Christian dialogue)
Cast.	Tertullian, *De Exhortatione Castitatis*
C. Cels.	Origen, *Contra Celsum*
CD	Cairo (Genizah) texts of the *Damascus Document*
Comm. Gal.	Jerome, *Commentarii in Epistulam ad Galatas*
Comm. in Isaiam	Eusebius, *Commentarii in Isaiam*
Comm. Ps.	Hilary, *Commentary on Psalms* (*Tractatus super Psalmos*)
De Test. An.	Tertullian, *De Testimonio Animae*
Dial.	Justin Martyr, *Dialogue with Trypho*
Ep.	Jerome, *Epistulae*
Epid.	Irenaeus, *Epideixis tou apostolikou kērygmatos*
Exc. Th.	*Excerpts from Theodotus* (*Excerpta ex Theodoto*)
G.Pet.	*Gospel of Peter*
G.Tr.	*Gospel of Truth*
H.E.	Eusebius, *Historia Ecclesiastica*
Hom. Ezech.	Origen, *Homiliae in Ezechielem*
Ign. *Magn.*	Ignatius, *Ad Magnesios*
Ign. *Smyrn.*	Ignatius, *Ad Smyrnaeos*
Ign. *Trall.*	Ignatius, *Ad Trallianos*
JP	*Altercatio Jasonis et Papisci* (*Disputation between Jason and Papiscus*)
LR	Long Recension of *Timothy and Aquila*

LXX	Septuagint
Mart. Pol.	*Martyrium Polycarpi*
Mem.	Xenophon, *Memorabilia* of Socrates
Migr.	Philo, *De Migratione Abrahami*
Mon.	Tertullian, *De Monogamia*
Mut. Nom.	Philo, *De Mutatione Nominum*
Paed.	Clement of Alexandria, *Paedagogus*
Pan.	Epiphanius, *Panarion*
Pliny *Ep.*	Pliny, *Epistulae*
Praescr.	Tertullian, *De Praescriptione Haereticorum*
Ps.-Barn.	Pseudo-Barnabas
Pud.	Tertullian, *De Pudicitia*
4Q	Qumran Cave 4
4QTestim	*Testimonia* from Qumran Cave 4
Qu. Hebr. Gen.	Jerome, *Quaestiones Hebraicae in Genesim*
Som.	Philo, *De Somniis*
SR	Short Recension of *Timothy and Aquila*
STh	*Simon and Theophilus* (Jewish-Christian dialogue)
Strom.	Clement of Alexandria, *Stromata*
Supp.	Athenagoras, *Supplicatio pro Christianis*
TA	*Timothy and Aquila* (Jewish-Christian dialogue)
Test.	Cyprian, *Testimonia*
V. Hadr.	Scriptores Historiae Augustae, *Vita Hadriani*
Vit. Mos.	Philo, *De Vita Mosis*

Periodicals, Reference Works, and Serials

AB	Anchor Bible
AGJU	Arbeiten zur Geschichte des antiken Judentums und des Urchristentums
ALBO	Analecta lovaniensia biblica et orientalia
ANF	*Ante-Nicene Fathers,* ed. Alexander Roberts et al.
BEThL	Bibliotheca ephemeridum theologicarum lovaniensium
BHTh	Beiträge zur historischen Theologie
Bib	*Biblica*
BJRL	*Bulletin of the John Rylands University Library of Manchester*
BZNW	Beihefte zur *ZNW*
CH	*Church History*
CSEL	Corpus scriptorum ecclesiasticorum latinorum
ÉtB	Études bibliques
EThL	*Ephemerides theologicae lovanienses*
FRLANT	Forschungen zur Religion und Literatur des Alten und Neuen Testaments

GCS	Griechische christliche Schriftsteller
HDR	Harvard Dissertations in Religion
HTR	*Harvard Theological Review*
ICC	International Critical Commentary
JBL	*Journal of Biblical Literature*
JR	*Journal of Religion*
JRS	*Journal of Roman Studies*
JSJSup	*Journal for the Study of Judaism in the Persian, Hellenistic, and Roman Periods,* Supplements
JSNTSup	*Journal for the Study of the New Testament,* Supplements
JTS	*Journal of Theological Studies*
LD	Lectio divina
NovTSup	*Novum Testamentum,* Supplements
NTS	*New Testament Studies*
POxy	*Oxyrhynchus Papyri*
PTS	Patristische Texte und Studien
RB	*Revue biblique*
RBén	*Revue bénédictine*
RevScRel	*Revue des sciences religieuses*
RHPhR	*Revue d'histoire et de philosophie religieuses*
SANT	Studien zum Alten und Neuen Testaments
SBLDS	Society of Biblical Literature Dissertation Series
SBT	Studies in Biblical Theology
SC	Sources chrétiennes
Scr	*Scripture*
SecCent	*Second Century*
SJLA	Studies in Judaism in Late Antiquity
SMSR	*Studi e materiali di storia delle religioni*
SNTSMS	Society for New Testament Studies Monograph Series
StPat	*Studia Patristica*
StTh	*Studia theologica*
ThH	*Théologie historique*
ThLZ	*Theologische Literaturzeitung*
TLG	*Thesaurus Linguae Graecae*
TU	Texte und Untersuchungen
VC	*Vigiliae christianae*
VCSup	*Vigiliae christianae,* Supplements
VTSUP	*Vetus Testamentum,* Supplements
WMANT	Wissenschaftliche Monographien zum Alten und Neuen Testament
WUNT	Wissenschaftliche Untersuchungen zum Neuen Testament
ZKG	*Zeitschrift für Kirchengeschichte*
ZNW	*Zeitschrift für die neutestamentliche Wissenschaft*

Contributors

COLIN BUCHANAN was bishop of Woolwich in the Church of England diocese of Southwark until he retired in 2004. He is editor of *Justin Martyr on Baptism and Eucharist: Text in English Translation with Introduction and Commentary* (Alcuin/GROW Joint Liturgical Studies 64, forthcoming).

BRUCE CHILTON is Bernard Iddings Bell Professor of Religion at Bard College, executive director of the Institute of Advanced Theology, and general editor of *The Cambridge Companion to the Bible* (2nd ed., Cambridge: CUP, 2007).

PAUL FOSTER is senior lecturer in New Testament language, literature, and theology at the University of Edinburgh. He is the author of *The So-Called Gospel of Peter—An Introduction and Commentary* (Oxford: Oxford University Press, forthcoming).

CHARLES E. HILL is professor of New Testament at Reformed Theological Seminary in Orlando, Florida, and author of *The Johannine Corpus in the Early Church* (Oxford: Oxford University Press, 2004).

LARRY W. HURTADO has been professor of New Testament language, literature, and theology at the University of Edinburgh since 1996. He is the author of *Lord Jesus Christ: Devotion to Jesus and Earliest Christianity* (Grand Rapids: Eerdmans, 2003).

J. REBECCA LYMAN is Samuel Garrett Professor of Church History emerita, the Church Divinity School of the Pacific, Berkeley, California. She is the author of *Christology and Cosmology: Models of Divine Activity in Origen, Eusebius, and Athanasius* (Oxford Theological Monographs; Oxford: Clarendon, 1993).

DENIS MINNS, OP, is lecturer in patristics at Blackfriars, Oxford, and member of the Faculty of Theology, University of Oxford. He is coauthor (with Paul Parvis) of *Justin Martyr's Apologies: A Textual Commentary* (Oxford Early Christian Texts; Oxford: Oxford University Press, forthcoming).

SEBASTIAN MOLL is a doctoral student in Christian origins and patristics at the University of Edinburgh. He is working on the life and thought of Marcion.

PAUL PARVIS is an honorary fellow of the School of Divinity at the University of Edinburgh. He is coauthor of *Justin Martyr's Apologies: A Textual Commentary* (Oxford Early Christian Texts; Oxford: Oxford University Press, forthcoming).

SARA PARVIS is lecturer in patristics at the University of Edinburgh. She is the author of *Marcellus of Ancyra and the Lost Years of the Arian Controversy 325–345* (Oxford Early Christian Studies; Oxford: Oxford University Press, 2006).

WILL RUTHERFORD is a doctoral student in New Testament and Christian origins at the University of Edinburgh. His thesis title is "The Use of Monotheism in the Shaping of Christian Identities vis-à-vis Judaism (70–170 C.E.)."

OSKAR SKARSAUNE is professor of church history at the MF Norwegian School of Theology, Oslo. He is the author of *The Proof from Prophecy: A Study in Justin Martyr's Proof-Text Tradition* (NovTSup 56; Leiden: Brill, 1987).

MICHAEL SLUSSER was chair of the Department of Theology and professor, Duquesne University, Pittsburgh, Pennsylvania, until his retirement in 2006. He is the translator of *St. Gregory Thaumaturgus: Life and Works* (Fathers of the Church 98; Washington: Catholic University of America Press, 1998).

SUSAN WENDEL is a doctoral student at McMaster University. Her thesis title is "The Fate of Israel and the Nations: A Study of the People of God in Luke-Acts and Justin Martyr's *Dialogue with Trypho* and *First Apology*."

Justin Martyr Timeline

98–117	Reign of Trajan
c. 100–110	Birth of Justin in Flavia Neapolis (modern Nablus)
117–138	Reign of Hadrian
Uncertain	Justin's conversion to Christianity
130s	Gnostic Basilides active in Alexandria
132–135	Bar Kokhba revolt
135	Setting of Justin's *Dialogue with Trypho* in Ephesus
138–161	Reign of Antoninus Pius
140s	Marcion and Valentinus teaching in Rome
Uncertain	Justin living in Rome (two separate sojourns)
	Writing of Justin's lost *Syntagma against All the Heresies*
154/155	Composition of *First* and *Second Apologies*
156	Probable date of the martyrdom of Polycarp
c. 160	Writing of the *Dialogue with Trypho*
161–180	Reign of Marcus Aurelius
c. 165	Execution of Justin in Rome under the Urban Prefect Q. Junius Rusticus

Justin's Writings[1]

I. Surviving Genuine Works

First Apology
Second Apology
Dialogue with Trypho the Jew

II. Lost or Unknown Works

Referred to by Justin:

Handbook (Syntagma) Against All the Heresies (cf. *1 Apol.* 26.8)

Referred to by Irenaeus:

Against Marcion (cf. Irenaeus, *Against the Heresies* IV.6.2). (This work could be identical with a section of the above.)[2]

Referred to by Eusebius of Caesarea (*Church History* IV.18.2–6):

Two *Apologies* (not necessarily corresponding to the two surviving apologies)[3]
Against the Pagans (see below)
Against the Pagans, "which he also called *Refutation*" (see below)[4]
On the Sole Rule (see below)
The Harpist (= Psaltes)
On the Soul[5]

---

1. With thanks to Paul Parvis.
2. Irenaeus is a good witness: he probably knew Justin in Rome (cf. Michael Slusser, "How Much Did Irenaeus Learn from Justin?" *StPat* 40 (2006), 515–20).
3. This point is discussed in the chapter by Paul Parvis in this volume.
4. That *Refutation* was another name for the *Exhortation to the Pagans* is suggested by Photius (*Bibliotheca*, codex 232), referring to a citation in a work by the sixth-century Monophysite Stephen Gobar of a passage from *Exhortation to the Pagans (= Cohortatio ad Graecos)*. Gobar seems to have repeatedly described the work as a "refutation."
5. There is no way to tell whether *The Harpist* and *On the Soul* really were writings of Justin: Eusebius says nothing about the former and little about the latter and does not quote from them. It is not even clear that he had actually seen them himself.

III. False Attributions

Parisinus graecus 450, which contains the three surviving genuine works, also contains the following, all attributed to Justin:

> *Letter to Zenas and Serenus*
> *Exhortation to the Pagans (= Cohortatio ad Graecos)* (see above)[6]
> *On the Sole Rule (of God = De Monarchia)*
> *Exposition of the Right Faith*
> *Refutation of Certain Teachings of Aristotle*
> *Questions of the Christians to Pagans*
> *Questions and Answers to the Orthodox*
> *Questions of the Pagans to Christians*
> *On the Resurrection* (ascribed to Athenagoras in the lost manuscript *Argentoratensis graecus* 9)

Argent. gr. 9 also contained two other works that it attributed to Justin:

> *Against the Pagans (= Ad Graecos)*
> *Letter to Diognetus*

Though all of these were often included in early editions of Justin, it is clear on both theological and stylistic grounds that none of them can be his work.

A minority of scholars maintain the authenticity of a set of fragments entitled *On the Resurrection* and transmitted in the anthology known as the *Sacra Parallela* originally compiled by John of Damascus in the first half of the eighth century. This is not the same work as the one normally edited under the name of Athenagoras (despite the fact that *Par. gr.* 450 attributes it to Justin).

All of these works except the "Athenagoras" *On the Resurrection* are edited (as "doubtful" or "spurious") by J. C. T. Otto, *Iustini Philosophi et Martyris Opera Quae Feruntur Omnia* II–III (Corpus Apologetarum Christianorum Saeculi Secundi III–V, 3rd ed; Jena, 1879–81). The *Letter to Diognetus* is now included in editions of the Apostolic Fathers.

---

6. *Parisinus graecus* 451 (the Arethas codex) contains these two work and ascribes them to Justin; it does not contain the genuine works of Justin.

Cramond
Antonine
Wall

*North
Sea*

BRITANNIA

*ATLANTIC
OCEAN*

GALLIAE
Lyons
Vienne

HISPANIAE

Corsica

ITALY
Rome

Sardinia

Sicily

Carthage

AFRICA

Mediterranean

LUCIDITY INFORMATION DESIGN, LLC

Justin Martyr and His World

0   500 Miles

Danube

Black Sea

BITHYNIA AND PONTUS

Sardis   ASIA
Smyrna   Hierapolis
Corinth
Athens   Ephesus
ACHAIA

Antioch

Tigris

Euphrates

SYRIA

Cyprus

Sea

Crete

JUDEA/   Flavia Neapolis
PALESTINE
Jerusalem

Alexandria

ARABIA

EGYPT

Nile

Red
Sea

Justin Martyr and His Worlds

SARA PARVIS AND PAUL FOSTER

JUSTIN, PHILOSOPHER AND CHRISTIAN MARTYR, Samaritan, exegete, apologist, and witness to so many of the intellectual and cultural worlds of the later Roman Empire, surprises every generation of scholars anew with the riches he has to offer them. He is the most generous of subjects, one who wrote openly and at length about the different worlds in which he moved, where the works of so many of his contemporaries are guarded, anonymous, blinkered, undatable, unplaceable, or fragmentary. In his surviving arguments with Diaspora Jews and Roman emperors, he counted among his sources the Law and the Prophets, popular contemporary philosophy, contemporary Roman legal practice, contemporary Christian practice, and the emerging Christian holy writings, giving us invaluable snapshots of all of these in the process. Whether we regard him with the sympathetic reverence of the Christian scholars who followed him, despite their own greater understanding of the philosophical world with which he sought to engage, or the contempt of Celsus, probably one of his earliest critics, he is a veritable mine of information about mid-second-century Christian and even Jewish and Roman theology, attitudes, and practices.

The purpose of the present volume is twofold. We are seeking both to take stock of the current state of Justin scholarship, including by offering significant contributions to some of the Justin debates already in progress, and to open Justin's works to the scrutiny of a new generation of scholars with new concerns and to ask some new questions of him.

Justin is rightly of considerable interest to both Jewish scholars and late Antique scholars, whatever reservations they might have about some of his assumptions, or even those of many of his traditional commentators. We hope that this work will offer a valuable resource for both of these disciplines. But it is in the area of Christian theology and early Christian history that we have focused, above all at the interface between biblical studies and patristics, with the two editors being drawn from these two disciplines.

Given ongoing discussion as to the dates of the later books of the New Testament, which some commentators push well into the second century, biblical scholars find themselves increasingly taking cognizance of extracanonical Christian literature that is or may be from this period. The Apostolic Fathers are now as studied by New Testament scholars as they are by patristics scholars, and Justin is coming to mark the watershed between the two disciplines. Scholars of patristics, used to studying Justin with at least one eye on the theological controversies of the fourth century, are relishing the chance to look backward to the previous century as well.

If Justin moved between many worlds in the second century, he does so again today. Our hope is that he can become a familiar inhabitant of other scholarly milieus also: world Christianity, for example, where his navigation of his own multiple identities, his negotiation of the complex politics of a society with a multilayered colonial history, and his interactions with a partly hostile, partly curious dominant culture ought to belie any assumption that he is simply a representative of "Western" Christianity.

Justin, as Rebecca Lyman points out in this volume's concluding chapter, has often been regarded as either idiotic or duplicitous: an autodidact with ideas above his intellectual station, or conversely a kind of cultural traitor, too seduced by the attractions of philosophy to see that he was adulterating the pure stream of Christianity with its insidious poison. In this volume, we try to show rather that as much for the worlds he opens to us today as for his opening up of his own religion to the worlds in which he lived, Justin was one of the most remarkable early Christians of them all.

Justin and His Text

In our first chapter, "Justin Scholarship: Trends and Trajectories," Michael Slusser sets the scene by examining the current state of Justin scholarship, concentrating on the last fifty years. He outlines the history of the printed critical editions of Justin's works and then looks in detail at two trends he isolates in recent work on Justin: the "Justin of the Apologies" and the "Justin of the Dialogue." The first, sourced by the *Apologies* and the first nine chapters of the *Dialogue with Trypho*, arises in the wake of Carl Andresen's 1955 study of Celsus, *Logos und Nomos*, and concentrates on Justin's philosophical views. The second, which is currently the more lively and, Slusser implies, fruitful, was launched by Oskar Skarsaune's 1987 study of Justin's use of Scripture, *The Proof from Prophecy*. (It will be noted that Skarsaune's fundamentally important work, which stimulated a whole new generation of work on Justin's sources, has provided the impetus for a number of the chapters in the present volume, whether or not they agree with him on all points!) Slusser picks out Skarsaune's examination of apocryphal and intertestamental literature as being particularly important, as well as his conclusion that Justin's education could be located in a Palestinian context, in which many of his implied interlocutors are Jewish.

Slusser next examines the rich debate that has subsequently (and, in part, consequently) sprung up on the topic of Christian and Jewish self-definition in the time of Justin, citing works by Timothy Horner, James Dunn, Judith Lieu, Alan Segal, Marc

Hirshman, and Daniel Boyarin. Slusser comments, "It is getting hard to imagine how Justin can be understood properly without taking this literature into consideration"; indeed, Justin's contribution to this debate is becoming one of the most valuable he has to offer modern scholarship.

Slusser concludes by identifying four areas in which he would like to see more work. First is the demographics of Jewish/Christian interaction in the time of Justin, including of those who identified with both categories or with a general category of *theosebeia*, piety toward God. His second is the world of the Clementine *Recognitions* and *Homilies,* with their rival preachers traveling the same circuits of the Mediterranean, and what they might tell us about Justin's life. Third, he would like to see a rethinking of the category of apology (a task at which this volume has perhaps made a start, though not necessarily in the direction for which he is calling). Finally, he wonders what a new general monograph on Justin might have to offer to a nonexpert reader of today. Rebecca Lyman's chapter may offer him something of an answer.

The chapters by Paul Parvis and Denis Minns reflect a new edition of the text of Justin's *Apologies* that they have jointly prepared, which is with the publisher at the time of writing. This edition enters much more deeply into the problem of the corruption of the one independent manuscript of the *Apologies, Parisinus graecus* 450, than has yet been done, and their papers tease out some of the questions they have worked on in the process.

Paul Parvis addresses the notorious problem of the relation of the apologies to one another: are they two, one, or one and a half (in other words, an apology with some sort of appendix or covering speech or letter)? He argues here that what we currently know as the *Second Apology* was produced by Justin's pupils after his sudden death at the hands of the Roman authorities, from portions that he had himself excised from his first apology, to take account of, among other things, the condemnation of the Valentinians.

Parvis's paper includes an important discussion of the textual history of the *Apologies,* concentrating particularly on two phases: the ancestor manuscript of *Parisinus graecus* 450, which we know to have shed at least one of its leaves (either a folio or a whole bifolium), and the manuscript that Eusebius of Caesarea used for the extracts he gives in the *Ecclesiastical History.* Parvis and Minns believe that the last two chapters of the *Second Apology* are out of place as the result of the shedding of another leaf and that they in fact belong to the end of the *First Apology.* The evidence is set out in detail in this chapter. Parvis also here deals with the original title of the work and how it got the name "apology."

Denis Minns here looks at the problem of the rescript of the emperor Hadrian to Minucius Fundanus, governor of Asia, attached in *Parisinus graecus* 450 to Justin's *First Apology* (which the manuscript calls the *Second Apology*). This legal document, potentially a vital witness to the legal status of Christians in the empire before the mid-third century, is mentioned by Melito of Sardis in his *Apology* and given in Greek by Eusebius of Caesarea in his *Ecclesiastical History,* as well as in Latin by Rufinus in his translation of Eusebius's work. Scholars have often doubted whether the rescript can be genuine, wondered whether Rufinus's translation was the original Latin version or a retroversion of Eusebius's Greek text, and debated whether Justin used the rescript in his original apology, and if so, where.

Minns argues, on the basis of the Minns-Parvis edition of Eusebius's text, Mommsen's edition of Rufinus's Latin text, and Paul Parvis's translation of the Syriac text of the rescript as given in the Syriac version of the *Ecclesiastical History*, that the rescript is indeed genuine but that Rufinus's Latin is a retroversion from Eusebius's Greek and not the original document. He includes a detailed discussion of the key phrases of the rescript on the basis of parallels in the famous Pliny-Trajan correspondence and gives a proposed retroversion of them into Latin. His case is that the rescript represents no advance in treatment of Christians on the Trajanic legislation but "simply tells the governor to get on with his job and not to allow his or the emperor's time to be wasted by petitions seeking action against Christians outside the existing and adequate procedures." Nonetheless, because it demands that an accuser should prove the accused has done "something against the laws" (*contra leges*), a phrase that for Hadrian might well include simply being a Christian, Justin was able to seize on the wording and make his case on the basis of it. Minns argues that Justin therefore did use the petition, that it fits perfectly into his argument, and that it belongs exactly where it is in the manuscript, except that it was then followed by the two final dislocated chapters of the *Second Apology*, restored as the end of the *First Apology* in the Minns-Parvis edition.

Justin and His Bible

Oskar Skarsaune, building on his own seminal earlier work, here focuses on the physical form of the artifact in front of Justin that we would label as the Bible. In his chapter "Justin and His Bible," Skarsaune notes that the terms "Old Testament" and "New Testament" are grossly anachronistic, but for heuristic reasons they are to be retained. He tantalizingly introduces the possibility that Justin may have been acquainted with the collection later labeled as the New Testament. He states that "as far as the New Testament is concerned, he did not know the specific collection of books that later got that name. Or so we used to think."

Although not adopting the overarching theory of David Trobisch, Skarsaune picks up two of his points: namely, that Justin encountered subcollections of New Testament books (such as the Gospels) in codex form and that Paul's letters had been collected and published in a single codex in the same order as occurs in the present-day arrangement. (It is noted that the inclusion of the epistle to the Hebrews in this collection is a complicating factor.) It is further argued that Justin knew scriptural texts in two versions. In the *Apology* the quotations are taken from Christian works that had already separated the citations from their wider contexts. However, in the *Dialogue* Justin betrays a knowledge of the wider Old Testament context from which such citations are drawn. Skarsaune argues that, as corollaries of this, Justin obtained complete biblical scrolls from Jewish scribes and also that he was aware of the process of revising the Septuagint translation in his own day. Skarsaune comes to the conclusion that Justin knew the Jewish Scriptures not in codex form, but as separate scrolls written by

Jewish scribes. This contrasts with his knowledge of writings that later formed the New Testament, which he argues were consulted in codex subcollections of the Gospels or the Pauline epistles. For Skarsaune, Justin is a harbinger of the notions of canonicity that come to fruition a few decades later in the writings of Irenaeus.

In the chapter "Justin and Israelite Prophecy," Bruce Chilton argues that when Justin referenced the prophetic tradition, he was "conceiving of the significance of the prophets of Israel in respect of a stable of favorite passages as expressed in preferred recensions, rather than a fixed set of scriptural proof-texts." Thus Chilton not only shows his disagreement (along with the majority of New Testament scholars) with the theory of a testimonies book, but more importantly argues for a richer, more dynamic use of the prophetic material by Justin. Chilton suggests that Justin asserts four key aspects of his own understanding of the prophetic tradition. First, the prophets, beginning with Moses and including David, attested to Christ. Second, the prophetic tradition inspired the best of Greek philosophy. Third, it forecast the transfer of the prophetic Spirit from Israel to the Christians. And fourth, it supported the contention that the divine *Logos* lies at the heart of human cognition of God. Each of these points is discussed in detail, with Chilton marshalling a range of textual support from Justin's writing. However, the primary aim is not simply to show that such themes are indeed Justin's own. Rather, the themes are introduced to demonstrate how Justin's philosophical arguments are aligned with contemporary Judaism as reflected in the Mishnah and some of the Targumim. By comparing Jewish and Christian use of the prophetic material, Chilton argues that each religious outlook operated with a different systemic center. For Judaism this was the Torah, but for the version of Christianity represented by Justin it was the *Logos*. It was for this reason that both sides in this debate were doomed not to be able to understand each other, because although they disputed the other's interpretation of the same body of texts, they could not agree on the hermeneutical key for unlocking the meaning of the very texts for which both parties claimed to be the legitimate interpreters. By appreciating this disjunction in thought, Chilton better equips scholars to engage in a critical reading of Justin's understanding of the function of the prophetic corpus.

Charles Hill wrestles with issues that overlap with Skarsaune's investigation, but he focuses on a much narrower question. The question is, namely, whether John's gospel is included under Justin's umbrella term "memoirs of the apostles," and what evidence can be presented for showing the use of the Fourth Gospel in the writings of Justin. Hill states that the "only quote, or near quote, of the Fourth Gospel is of Jesus' saying from John 3:5, 7 about being reborn and seeing the kingdom of heaven (of God, in John) (*1 Apol.* 61.4)." Hill, however, argues that the perspectives and theology of the Fourth Gospel have shaped Justin's thinking. In particular, Justin's *Logos* Christology is seen as being dependent on the Johannine prologue. The citation of *Dialogue* 105.1 is highly significant since it appears to link such *Logos* Christology with the apostolic memoirs. Furthermore, describing the trial scene in the Fourth Gospel, Hill notes a number of features that among the canonical Gospels are known only from John's account. Here Hill interacts with Helmut Koester's counterclaim that Justin is referring to "Gospel materials" that refer not to canonical accounts, but to those traditions that were part of the prehistory of the canonical texts. After considering all of the details unique to John known by Justin, Hill comes to the conclusion that the Fourth Gospel was indeed among the collection of writings referred to by the label "memoirs of the apostles." In fact, Hill sees only one theoretical alternative: "the supposition that there once existed another Gospel . . . that contained all of these details that occur in John but not in the Synoptics." Hill continues by noting the absurdity of the view that this otherwise unattested document remained in circulation until the middle of the second century. Hill concludes by acknowledging that Justin's explicit use of the Synoptics is far greater than his use of John, but he also notes the profound way in which Justin's thought-world is shaped by the Fourth Gospel.

Susan Wendel investigates the disputed claims, in this formative period for both Judaism and Christianity, about identity and the inheritance of the mantle of historic Israel. Drawing on Justin's discussion in the *Dialogue*, Wendel observes that Justin states "that Christians had displaced the Jews as the true people of God, the spiritual Israel (*Dial.* 11.5; 123.9), and would become the rightful priests and heirs of Jerusalem in the age to come (82.1; 116.3)." It is noted that such a "replacement theology" may in fact antedate Justin, finding its origins in Luke-Acts. However, Wendel argues that Justin departs from the Lukan account of the fulfillment of the promises to Israel in his discussion of the activity of the Spirit in *Dialogue* 87. Wendel's argument independently develops the third point that Chilton also notes in respect of Justin's understanding of the prophetic tradition. Thus the descent of the Spirit in Luke-Acts is understood, according to Wendel, as a depiction of Jewish restoration, whereas for Justin it is a pivotal assertion of the church in a supersessionary relation to Israel. It is noted that in *Dialogue* 83 Jesus' own baptism is seen as the moment when the potential for the Spirit to be poured out on Jewish prophets ceases. Thus "the Spirit-baptism of Jesus represents a transfer of the very presence and powers of God from the Jewish people to Jesus." It is also noted that both Justin and Luke-Acts cite Joel 3:1-2, which foretells the end-time outpouring of the Spirit. Wendel argues that while this is a promise of restoration in Luke-Acts, for Justin it confirms his perspective that "the Spirit was taken from the Jews and given to Jesus and Christ-believers instead." Therefore, Wendel observes how Justin could rework the theological outlook of New Testament writers to make their perspectives better align with the theological concerns and positions of his own time.

It has often been suggested that Justin drew upon Jesus traditions contained in a wider range of texts than just the canonical Gospels. One of the prime contenders among the noncanonical accounts that has been suggested as a potential source for Justin is the so-called *Gospel of Peter*. Paul Foster assesses the merits of this claim. Prior to undertaking the direct textual comparison, Foster discusses the whole methodology of establishing literary dependence. The spectrum of current thought on the topic is described, from those arguing that "echoes" of scriptural language may have been expected to resonate with readers or hearers of the text, to the more rigorous position requiring demonstrable terminological affinities. Three pieces of evidence are reconsidered, which have formed the basis of the discussion. First, *Dialogue* 106.3, which both refers to Peter and uses the phrase "the memoirs of him" in close proximity, is assessed to see whether this could be an indirect reference to a gospel penned in Peter's name. Close examination reveals that the basis for arguing that Justin is referring to the text we know as the *Gospel of Peter* is tenuous. Second, this chapter considers two suggested literary parallels (*1 Apol.* 35.6//*G.Pet.* 3.6–7 and *Dial.* 97//*G.Pet.* 4.12). In both instances it is argued that the putative points of contact are insignificant and that literary dependence between the writings of Justin and the *Gospel of Peter* cannot be established. It is noted that the tendency to "make" the *Gospel of Peter* a literary source for Justin is not an entirely neutral endeavor but in certain cases arises from a desire to make the dating of noncanonical texts as early as possible.

Justin and His Traditions

Justin's place at the heart of the history of Christian apologetic is well established, but Sara Parvis argues, in her chapter "Justin Martyr and the Apologetic Tradition," that we should go further and recognize Justin as that tradition's founder. She points out that the evidence dating the apologies of Aristides and Quadratus to the reign of Hadrian is by no means secure, arguing that such a dating was the result of the desire of a later editor to provide a reason for the supposed concession to Christians represented by Hadrian's rescript, and that Aristides' apology, in any case, looks to be a doctored general treatise rather than a genuine petition to an emperor.

On the other hand, two further apologies addressed to emperors or magistrates, those of Athenagoras and Tertullian, can be shown to be essentially rewrites of Justin's *Apology* (assuming it was originally one document) to make it more intellectually respectable. The same may be true of the lost apologies of Melito of Sardis, Apolinarius of Hierapolis, and Miltiades (like Athenagoras, Quadratus, and Tertullian all linked to the debates over Montanism of the later second century). Other writings influenced by Justin, such as Tatian's *Against the Greeks*, Theophilus's *To Autolycus*, and later works, which were not termed apologies in antiquity, should not be so now. The apologetic tradition proper, in the precise sense of a defense of Christianity intended as a forensic speech or legal deposition, should be seen as starting with Justin and ending with Tertullian, to be replaced by Christian apology in the looser sense of polemical literary exchanges among individuals of equal intellectual standing. The strength and bravery of Justin's achievement, with all its intellectual faults, will then become clear, the more so because he is a pivotal figure in the move of Christianity out of the ghetto and into the wider Greco-Roman cultural world.

Devotion to Jesus is a well-known phenomenon in early Christian worship. Building on perspectives in his earlier work, Larry Hurtado, in the chapter "'Jesus' as God's Name, and Jesus as God's Embodied Name in Justin Martyr," argues that Justin makes two important claims about the divinity of Jesus. First, Hurtado argues that Justin views the name "Jesus" as being a divine name, and second, he argues that the person Jesus is the embodiment of God's "name." Taking the second of these arguments, Hurtado summarizes Justin's logic in *Dialogue* 76 in the following manner: "(1) God promised a figure who would lead Israel into Canaan and who would bear God's name; (2) in the biblical record the figure who led Israel into Canaan is Joshua; and (3) this figure had been given this name by Moses; therefore, (4) 'Joshua/Ιησους' must be God's name, given to Hoshea to prefigure his greater namesake, Jesus." Discussing the debate between Trypho and Justin in *Dialogue* 65, Hurtado notes Justin's creative exegesis in reinterpreting the apparently monotheistic statement in Isaiah 42:8, "I am the LORD; this is my name; my glory will I not give to another, nor my virtues." Here Justin argues that this statement means that God gives God's glory to Jesus alone and to no other. It is noted that arguments of this type do not occur in the *Apology*. Hurtado suggests that this is because "the category was not so useful or even meaningful to readers unappreciative of Jewish/biblical religious tradition." Hence the growing cultural distance from Judaism in the second half of the second century rendered such arguments redundant (though it might be noted that they still appear as late as the writings of Marcellus of Ancyra), but they are historically interesting in revealing the Semitic elements in early christological formulations.

Will Rutherford ("*Altercatio Jasonis et Papisci* as Testimony Source for Justin's 'Second God' Argument?") takes up Oskar Skarsaune's suggestion that the *Disputation between Jason and Papiscus* might have been identical with what Skarsaune argues to be the "recapitulation source" behind a passage in the *Dialogue with Trypho* (*Dial.* 61–62). Might this text in fact be a source for the whole of Justin's "second God" argument, asks Rutherford?

He lines up and discusses Justin's "second God" proof-texts in *Dialogue* 56–62. *Dialogue* 56–60 deploys the theophanies to Abraham, Jacob, and Moses at Mamre, Sodom, Bethel, Peniel, Luz, Haran, and the burning bush, the "two Lords" texts (Gen. 19:24 and LXX Ps. 109:1), and the "two Gods" text (LXX Ps. 44:7-8). *Dialogue* 61–62 cites proof-texts for a second divine being involved in creation: Proverbs 8:22-36; Genesis 1:26-28; and Genesis 3:22. Rutherford argues that in the absence of close parallels in existing literature, they are likely all to come from the same unknown preexisting tradition.

He then considers the case for seeing them as dependent on the lost *Dialogue of Jason and Papiscus*, building on Frederick Conybeare's proposal to see three fourth- to sixth-century dialogues as independent witnesses for the contents of this work. He examines the tables of parallels constructed by Lawrence Lahey, which show that most of the same texts used by Justin were cited in the three dialogues in question. However, he shows that the order in which the texts are cited in the hypothetically reconstructed *Dialogue of Jason and Papiscus* is not the same as the order in which Justin cites these texts, and the parallels between the three dialogues are not always very close. He concludes that the case for seeing the *Dialogue of Jason and Papiscus* as a source for Justin's "second God" argument cannot be made successfully given the current state of the evidence.

Sebastian Moll, in "Justin and the Pontic Wolf," looks at Justin's relations with one of his most intriguing contemporaries, Marcion. Moll makes the point that scholars often ignore Justin's short discussion of Marcion in the *First Apology* because the information on Marcion available elsewhere seems so much more extensive. However, "it is not Justin who does not provide any additional information on Marcion: if anything, it is the other Fathers who do not provide any additional information compared to Justin."

Moll begins by arguing that the *First Apology* is not a literary fiction, engaging with Lorraine Buck's recent article arguing to the contrary. He goes on to distill a clear portrait of Marcion from Justin's presentation: he has many followers around the Roman world; his followers revere him; he believes in a god who did not create the universe and who is superior to the Demiurge; he believes in a son of this superior god, who is not the Christ predicted by the prophets; his teaching is irrational and without demonstration.

But why mention him in an apology? Moll argues that Marcion's rejection of Christianity's Jewish roots is a liability when Justin is so keen to show that Christianity is not novel, but respectably antique. He argues that the terms in which Justin describes Marcion in the *First Apology* are carefully calculated to alienate the emperors. Moll also looks at what Justin likely knows but does not say about Marcion, arguing that each of the remaining best-attested features of Marcion's theology and practice would have been dangerous to allude to, as they might have made all too much sense to a Hellenistic audience.

Colin Buchanan's chapter, "Questions Liturgists Would Like to Ask Justin Martyr," is something of a *via negativa*: he makes a salutary case for how little Justin actually tells us about early Christian liturgy, despite appearances and despite the extensive use that has been made of his work by liturgical commissions. He outlines the problem thus: liturgists get glimpses of early practice from a handful of second- and third-century texts and extrapolate without pausing to think how much of the landscape remains obscure and how diverse what lies hidden is likely to be in practice. Buchanan nonetheless identifies areas in which Justin has been of help in revising the liturgy, such as his use of the term "presider," and concludes with a series of questions that both reveals how much early liturgical historians owe to Justin of what they currently do know and underlines how much important information about early liturgy is simply not accessible to us.

Finally, Rebecca Lyman takes Justin scholarship in a new and promising direction in "Justin and Hellenism: Some Postcolonial Perspectives." Drawing on subaltern studies, Lyman looks at the way in which individuals at "difficult" times in history can be "doubly colonized"—first by the original imperial discourse and second by the political interests of contemporary scholars, whose views they do not neatly fit (she cites the example of the self-offering of Indian widows). Listening to such voices demands that we hear what we do not already understand and let it challenge our own conceptions of totalities.

The second century has long been fought over in the name of the totalizing discourses of Hellenism, Judaism, and Christianity, but recent scholarship has been insisting on the diversity within and between each of these: Roman imperial power and Greek education did not create a stable cultural synthesis but stimulated writers to define themselves in various relations to these and to more local traditions or beliefs. Within these worlds, ancient Christian authors lived and acted. Lyman argues that we should not see them simply as sources to be mined for narratives of emerging orthodoxies, but look at their own intellectual questions and their strategies of self-presentation within the culture of their time.

Lyman reminds us how rich a source Justin is for any discussion of second-century religion and identity, given his provincial origins and conversion to Christianity through philosophy, as well as his Samaritan links. She points out how often he has been fought over by Christians and classicists, each eager to deny that Christianity and philosophy could have any real common ground and to denigrate him for attempting to live simultaneously in two worlds, clutching at the same time his Bible and his philosopher's cloak. Accusations of "wearing two hats" and having a "double nature" are all too familiar to students of postcolonialism. Hybridity, an "unstable and problematic transgressing of imagined boundaries that robs them of their purity and hence their power," frightens a Harnack as much as it does a Celsus.

Justin, as an "apologist" (itself often a term of abuse), offers us a creative hybridity, Lyman argues, an authentic "doubling" in which the differences between Christianity and Greek philosophy are not denied, for the value of both is necessary to the working of his history of truth or his *Logos* theology. In fact, as she points out, "Greekness" is itself partly a means of resistance to the legitimacy of Roman authority.

The site of Justin's "complicity" with the dominant culture, Lyman concludes, is the site of his resistance, as he constructed a universal philosophy that is Christianity, albeit mimicry and menace to the later colliding worlds of orthodoxy and Neoplatonic Hellenism. Our task in studying him is to appreciate the shifting complexities of second-century religious and philosophical thought as expressed in his Christianity.

Acknowledgments

The conference at which most of the chapters of this book were offered as papers met in Edinburgh in July 2006. We would like to thank the British Academy for their generous grant in support of that event, and consequently of this book, and the School of Divinity at the University of Edinburgh, particularly our colleagues at the Centre for the Study of Christian Origins, and among them particularly Professor Larry Hurtado, for support of various kinds. Our warmest thanks are also due to Will Rutherford, to Kirsty Murray, to Susan Exeter, to Chris Keith, and to Karoline McLean. Professor Stuart Hall generously supplied us with some answers to Colin Buchanan's questions, which we were unfortunately not able to include because the questions changed in the interim. We would also like to thank all those at Fortress Press who worked on this book, above all Joshua Messner.

Finally, our most heartfelt thanks are due, as ever, to Paul Parvis, whose many skills were invaluable to both of the editors in the preparation of this book.

Part One

JUSTIN AND HIS TEXT

CHAPTER ONE

Justin Scholarship

Trends and Trajectories

MICHAEL SLUSSER

JUSTIN SCHOLARSHIP HAS BEEN GROWING and changing in character in recent years. This essay presents an overview of the trends in scholarship and points to some of the directions in which I believe this new work is leading us. It is not an exhaustive survey of the work that has been done on Justin, even in recent years.[1] What I propose is more modest: after reviewing the production of critical editions, I shall present two major trends of the last half century. The first trend emphasized Justin as a philosopher, and one might call it the "Justin of the *Apologies*," even though much attention was also given at that time to the first several chapters of the *Dialogue with Trypho*. That will be followed by a second, more recent trend, in which the emphasis has shifted to the *Dialogue*; this trend has been further stimulated by increased interest in the light that Justin throws on Jewish-Christian relations in the second century. The final section of this paper will propose four issues that still lie ahead on the agenda of Justin scholarship; they are certainly not the only issues, but they seem to me important for further advances.

First, let me make an observation about our texts. It may seem surprising that the works of a writer who had a tremendous influence on later Christian thought are represented by such a slender manuscript tradition. Other second-century writers did not fare much better, and some fared even worse. It is worth recalling that the *Epistle to Diognetus* survived into modern times in only one manuscript and that the sole manuscript perished in the fire that destroyed the library in Strasbourg on August 24, 1870, during the Franco-Prussian War.[2] War, it seems, is dangerous not only to children and other living things, but also to the artifacts by which we are connected to our history. The great *Adversus Haereses* of Irenaeus of Lyon survives only in borrowings by other authors and in ancient translations, apart from two papyrus fragments that seem to

13

represent the direct transmission. The same author's *Demonstration of the Apostolic Preaching* is known to us in Armenian translation, and before the Armenian version of the *Didache* was discovered, we did not recognize its indirect transmission in Greek. Only fragments quoted by other authors survive of the works of Hegesippus, Papias of Hierapolis, Marcion, and many other second-century authors. Of course, there were other named authors from whom not even fragments survive, and we can assume that there were writers of whom we do not know even the names.[3]

The manuscript tradition of Justin, frail as it is, is therefore normal for early Christian texts outside the New Testament. Other papers in this volume address some of the difficult issues in the text of the *Codex Regius Parisinus* 450. Here I wish simply to note some of the history of printed editions. There was a series of "*opera omnia*" editions beginning with Robert Estienne in 1551; I shall not linger over the details, which can be read elsewhere, particularly in Miroslav Marcovich's introductions to his recent editions of the *Apologies* and the *Dialogue with Trypho*.[4] Separate editions of the *Dialogue* and the *Apologies*, however, have not appeared at the same rate: Marcovich lists thirteen separate editions of the *Apologies* prior to his own, but he names only three editions of the *Dialogue* as a separate work.[5] It is not rash to infer from that publishing history that over the years interest in the *Apologies* has been much greater than interest in the *Dialogue*. For an explanation, Oskar Skarsaune aptly quotes Erwin R. Goodenough: "The reason for this comparative neglect is not hard to find. The piece is nearly as long as the four Gospels combined, and as a whole is so astonishingly dull that to a general theological reader it can by no means have the same attraction as the Apologies."[6] But whether one considers the opera omnia or the separate works of Justin, scholarship worked with the same editions for more than seventy years—generally those of J. C. T. Otto, Louis Pautigny,[7] Georges Archambault,[8] A. W. F. Blunt,[9] and Edgar Goodspeed.[10] Recently, however, there has been a burgeoning of new efforts.

The first new attempt at a Justin edition to appear in a long time was André Wartelle's edition of the *Apologies*.[11] That was followed rather quickly by the two volumes, one devoted to the *Apologies*, the other to the *Dialogue*, edited by Miroslav Marcovich, who had earlier reedited some of the pseudo-Justin texts.[12] In 1995, Charles Munier produced an edition of the *Apologies*,[13] which he contends should be viewed as a unified text.[14] More recently, Philippe Bobichon published what can only be described as an *editio maxima* of the *Dialogue with Trypho*.[15] At the end of 2006, Munier's critical edition of the *Apologies*—along the general lines established in his *editio minor*—appeared, with full introduction, notes, and French translation, in the *Sources chrétiennes* series.[16] Another critical edition of the *Apologies*, not yet published, has been prepared by Paul Parvis and Denis Minns.[17] Clearly the drought of editions to Justin's works is over. It remains to be seen what their effect will be on other aspects of Justin scholarship.

Before proposing what I see as the two major trends in Justin scholarship over the last fifty years, I would like to look back to the earlier period. Erwin Goodenough's analytical bibliography of writings about Justin, published in 1923,[18] is helpful in pointing out the areas that received special interest before that date. Particular attention had been given to Justin's use of the New Testament and the New Testament Apocrypha, to his ideas about the *Logos*, and to his invaluable testimony about the sacraments and ritual of his time.[19] Goodenough himself did not dwell much on either Justin's use of Scripture or his account of liturgical usage. He set out instead to show how deeply Justin's theology and cosmology shared both structural ideas and points of detail with the works of Philo: on Goodenough's theory, if Justin was familiar with many themes of Hellenistic philosophy, that was due much more to Jewish influences of the sort represented by Philo rather than to a direct influence from pagan philosophers. In the pre–World War II era, Justin was read either through the traditional eyes of Goodenough's predecessors or with the aid of Goodenough's radical attempt to relocate Justin to the fringes of the Jewish world of his time.

During the past fifty years, two scholars have redirected Justin scholarship in fresh directions and to a great extent set the agenda for the rest of us. The first of them opened the period of what I would like to call the "Justin of the *Apologies*"; the second gave rise to the period of the "Justin of the *Dialogue*." The first of these major influences was, of course, Carl Andresen, first in his long 1952 article on Justin and Middle Platonism,[20] then in his book *Logos und Nomos*,[21] which, although it focused on Celsus, concluded that his opponent must have been Justin. Andresen asks, "How did the first adversary of the Christians come to carry out his polemic against Christianity not simply on the basis of his Platonism but on the basis of a complicated theory of history that was concentrated on the concepts of 'Logos' and 'Nomos'?" The reason, in Andresen's view, must be sought in the opponent against whom Celsus was writing, and of all the Christian apologists whom we know, this fitted Justin best.[22]

These publications by Andresen were followed by a great deal of further scholarship by other scholars who tried to analyze Justin's philosophical views more accurately. Not surprisingly, their analyses, like Andresen's, turned more to the *Apologies* than to the *Dialogue with Trypho*, apart from the first nine chapters of the *Dialogue* in which Justin recounts to Trypho his philosophical search and his conversion. Two of the more famous books of this period argued about how that search narrative should be understood: Niels Hyldahl's *Philosophie und Christentum*[23] and J. C. M. van Winden's reply, *An Early Christian Philosopher*.[24] It would be beyond my task here to try to map all of the scholarly contributions in this period that addressed the issue of Justin's relation to Hellenistic philosophy, but they were many, and nearly all make some reference to Andresen's contributions.[25] For more than a decade, scholars of early patristics continued their reappropriation of the philosophy of the second and third centuries, assisted by studies from writers such as A. H. Armstrong,[26] Michel Spanneut,[27] Ludwig Edelstein,[28] John Rist,[29] Robert Joly,[30] and Cornelia J. De Vogel.[31]

This period that I am calling "Justin of the *Apologies*" also saw studies devoted to other aspects of Justin. A good example would be the effort of Pierre Prigent in 1964 to prove, through a detailed study of how Justin used the Old Testament, that his lost *Syntagma against the Heresies* was the source of both the *First Apology* and the *Dialogue*.[32] Although Prigent did not convince many readers of his theory about the lost *Syntagma* (nor of Justin's authorship of the fragment *De resurrectione*), the way that he addressed Justin's text in search of its sources and how they had been used made a fruitful impression and helped to contribute to later scholarship. Another work in this area was Joost Smit Sibinga's attempt to reconstruct Justin's Old Testament text.[33] I remind you that in 1923 Goodenough had not found enough studies of Justin's use of the Old Testament to warrant a separate category in his extensive bibliography.[34] General books also appeared at this time, such as those by Leslie Barnard[35] and Eric Osborn,[36] which made use of more recent research while at the same time attempting to give an overview of how Justin treated matters commonly dealt with in theology. These authors looked into Justin's writings for answers to questions that modern readers would want to ask. That may have been inevitable, even though Justin's concerns were quite different from those of modern Christians. The authors of general treatments were responding to the book market and to structural problems in scholarship with which we still must wrestle.

I see the second trend, "Justin of the *Dialogue with Trypho*," as fully launched with the publication in 1987 of Oskar Skarsaune's *The Proof from Prophecy*.[37] Granted, it examines Justin's use of prophecy in both the *Apologies* and the *Dialogue with Trypho*. Skarsaune went much deeper than his predecessors in uncovering the traditions upon which Justin drew in the *Dialogue with Trypho*, particularly his use of Old Testament texts. One of the traditions upon which Justin could draw was of course the New Testament, and here Skarsaune reached conclusions somewhat at odds with those of other scholars: he thinks that Justin took over some quotations directly from Paul's letter to the Romans;[38] that he knew Hebrews, though he did not cite it; and that while there are similarities between Justin's works and the book of Acts, he depended far less on Acts than earlier scholars had thought.[39] But where Skarsaune made great advances was in his examination of apocryphal and intertestamental literature derived from Jewish and Christian sources, whether extant or known to us only indirectly. He found that Justin did derive many of his arguments from earlier traditions. Skarsaune noted particularly strong affinities between Justin's use of Scripture texts and that of a few sources whose line of reasoning was not exactly Justin's own. According to Skarsaune, material that he calls the "recapitulation" source probably came from the *Controversy between Jason and Papiscus* by Aristo of Pella; the material that he refers to as coming from a "kerygmatic" source could most fruitfully be compared with the so-called *Anabathmoi Jacobou* section in the pseudo-Clementine *Recognitions*[40] and with the *Testaments of the Twelve Patriarchs*.[41] These are but two of his many findings.

One of the most significant corollaries of Skarsaune's analysis was that Justin's education could be located in a Palestinian context, one in which his implied interlocutors were to a great extent Jewish. He explains:

> If the above analyses of Justin's material have come somewhere near the truth, it seems we are justified in hearing two distinct voices speaking to us through Justin's tradition.
>
> The first is the voice of Jewish Christians addressing their fellow Jews in the distressing years immediately after the Bar Kokhba revolt. Theirs is a message of repentance and salvation for Israel; a presentation of the true Messiah after the frustrating experience with the failure of Bar Kokhba. . . .
>
> The second voice speaking to us from Justin's material is the voice of triumphant Gentile Christianity. It is a Gentile Christianity still in close contact

with rabbinic exegesis, still vitally concerned with Jerusalem and the land. It is a Gentile Christianity which absorbs the Judaeo-Christian tradition described above—while deeply modifying the concept of the people of God, circumcision, and the other rites affecting Jewish identity. The Christological testimonies are left untouched.[42]

While Skarsaune is tentative in his suggestions about how and where Justin acquired this background, he "can see nothing which excludes the possibility that Justin got his fundamental theological 'education' in Palestine," perhaps even in Aelia Capitolina, among "the gentile Christians who occupy Jerusalem after the revolt."[43]

Skarsaune agrees with the general evaluation of Justin as "a 'mainstream' theologian not particularly dependent on any specific branch of early Christian theology," but he adds, "In any case, Justin *became* a mainstream theologian."[44] This process of Justin's becoming a theologian seems to have had as its matrix the area and the demographic context where it would have been impossible for him to avoid coming to terms with the issues that were beginning to constitute the boundaries between rabbinic Judaism and early Christianity.

Subsequently, an increasing number of studies have focused on the Justin of the *Dialogue*; I shall mention only a few.[45] Philippe Bobichon, in his edition mentioned earlier and in a more recent article,[46] argues strongly for the coherence and deliberate plan of the *Dialogue* against those who have criticized it for lacking structure. How does one discover a structure to such a lengthy work? It is hard to avoid coming to the task with preconceived ideas as to what a structure must look like, preferably one drawn from classical literary models. But perhaps Justin had in mind something that we were not expecting and consequently produced a work with a structure that we do not easily recognize. Perhaps it is necessary to approach the analysis from a completely different perspective, and Bobichon attempts to do that.

Timothy Horner tries a completely different approach in his 2001 book, *Listening to Trypho*.[47] Horner's hypothesis is that within the *Dialogue* one may identify "an autonomous text," which he names "the Trypho Text because it is characterized by words or sayings attributed directly to Trypho." Based on this text, Horner believes, one can reach new conclusions about Diaspora Jews in the second century.[48] It is easy to see how far apart are Bobichon's and Horner's theses about the *Dialogue*, but anyone who works with the *Dialogue* now will need to address the issue of its structure and composition with rather more seriousness than was necessary twenty years ago.

Another new study of the *Dialogue* not only treats it as a deliberately composed unity, but also tries to determine its theological intention. Anette Rudolph[49] sees Justin as presenting a universal worship of God and a continuous history of salvation—not a supersessionist theology and likewise not a proposal that there are two ways of salvation, one for Jews and one for Gentiles.[50] Her thesis touches directly a theme important to a growing body of literature by both Christians and Jews on the connections and influences that early Christianity and the Judaism of its time, even rabbinic Judaism, had on each other. It is getting hard to imagine how Justin can be understood properly without taking this literature into consideration.

Though James D. G. Dunn's *The Parting of the Ways* was not the first work on this topic, it has probably done more than others to awaken widespread awareness among Christians of the question of how Christianity and Judaism came to define themselves as different from each other.[51] Dunn's book has been followed by symposia, articles, and other books in which many other scholars have been involved. The roots of this area of study lay in older treatments of so-called Jewish Christianity, in the works of Hans Joachim Schoeps, Jean Daniélou, and especially Marcel Simon. New Testament scholars such as E. P. Sanders[52] and Martin Hengel[53] laid much of the groundwork on which others have built. Other studies compare Jewish and Christian interpretations of the same biblical texts, and there Justin must feature prominently in any discussion of Christian interpretation; a full survey of the literature is quite impossible in this chapter.[54] Judith Lieu's *Neither Jew nor Greek?*—whose very title with its question mark points to the openness of many of the questions in this area—offers a very good, though necessarily not exhaustive, bibliography of more recent publications.[55]

Jewish scholars have also been involved in this area of mutual self-definition, and they, too, use Justin as a Christian point of reference. One long-running discussion is the question of the benediction against the heretics in synagogue prayer (*birkat ha-minim*).[56] When did it come into use? Did it aim at Christians? Can Christian scholars find there any substantiation of the charge that Jewish Christians were excluded from the synagogues, particularly the one in Justin's *Dialogue* 16.3: "You dishonor and curse in your synagogues all those who believe in Christ"? Naturally this charge is of great concern, particularly for the role it has played in forming an anti-Jewish mentality among Christians. So far, no basis in fact has been demonstrated, but in the process a number of other traditional notions have been dismantled, such as the role of a "synod of Javneh (Jamnia)" after the fall of Jerusalem in 70 C.E., where this benediction and other matters might have been legislated.[57]

Even that long-running and, as I would describe it, self-contained discussion about the Twelfth Benediction has been transformed by dramatic developments in recent Jewish scholarship on its own sources. The application of historical-critical and form-critical method to the Mishnah, the Midrash, the Tosefta, and the rest of the Talmudic literature has begun to yield a more nuanced and three-dimensional picture of what was happening in Judaism in the first and second centuries. This untraditional way of reading Jewish sources has not been accepted easily in Jewish scholarly circles, and leading exponents such as Jacob Neusner have not lacked opposition.[58] Still, an increasing number of Jewish scholars are concluding that it may be important for understanding the formation of rabbinic Judaism to pay attention to the Christianity of the time, just as Christian scholars now realize that an adequate understanding of the formative years of Christianity can be reached only when one pays attention to the Jewish context. Examples of this newer Jewish scholarship can be found in the work of Alan Segal, whose *Two Powers in Heaven* laid bare the complexity of which the Jewish monotheistic vision was aware;[59] Marc Hirshman, who studied the exegetical traditions in *A Rivalry of Genius*[60] with extensive attention to Justin Martyr and his *Dialogue with Trypho*; and Daniel Boyarin, whose *Dying for God: Martyrdom and the Making of Christianity and Judaism* has been followed by *Border Lines: The Partition of Judaeo-Christianity*, a book in which Justin figures largely.[61] While it may be an overstatement to say that Jewish scholarship and Christian scholarship have joined forces in study-ing the mutual self-definition of their traditions, there is much more direct discussion and use of each other's findings today than there was even thirty years ago.

If the trend over the last fifty years has been from the "Justin of the *Apologies*" to the "Justin of the *Dialogue with Trypho*"—and I do not claim that that way of portray-ing Justin scholarship is the only possible one—what might one propose as its trajec-tory? For want of a crystal ball, I shall simply point to a few areas where I think that it would be profitable to do more work. Since we have just been discussing Christianity and Judaism, I shall begin there.

1. Demographic categories remain a problem. A nonspecialist in patristics, the sociologist Rodney Stark, in his book *The Rise of Christianity*,[62] entitled his third chapter very provocatively: "The Mission to the Jews: Why It Probably Succeeded." Stark's hypothesis was not that the followers of Jesus persuaded most or even a large percentage of their fellow Jews to join the new movement; on the contrary, he thought that was neither likely nor necessary for his hypoth-esis to be correct. If even a small percentage of the Jews in the Diaspora were drawn to what became Christianity, that would suffice, said Stark, to explain most of the growth of Christianity up to the year 250 C.E.[63]

    The fact that we know so little about how nascent rabbinic Judaism affected Diaspora Jews, who did not share the language in which the Oral Torah was being communicated and discussed in rabbinic circles, is one of the chronic problems in working with Jewish and Christian relations in the time of Justin.[64] Did Diaspora Jewish communities, where daily speech was in Greek or Latin, have a "house of study," and if so, what did they study there? How far could those communities be included into the new universe of discourse that flour-ished in Palestine and Babylon? What degree of assimilation to Greco-Roman culture usually followed upon that linguistic estrangement? I know that the lin-guistic estrangement was not total and that significant numbers of devout Jews no doubt traveled and maintained a network that brought them into contact with houses of study where the Oral Torah was being discussed in Semitic lan-guages. But take Justin himself, for example: he does not identify himself as a Jew, but neither is he very Gentile. Our categories provide maps, but they do not tell us what we need to know about the territory.[65] Shaye J. D. Cohen, in his immensely illuminating *The Beginnings of Jewishness*,[66] asks, "How, then, did you know a Jew in antiquity when you saw one? The answer is that you did not. But you could make reasonably plausible inferences from what you saw."[67] There were many degrees of assimilation to Greco-Roman society, and I would not want to be the rash scholar who would assert that after a specified point, an Antique Jew became a Gentile! In fact, it seems likely to me that even in assim-ilated families it would take generations for the sense of being Jewish rather than Gentile to disappear. A neat dichotomy of Jew or Gentile probably obscures a range of people in the middle; so much energy has been spent on the "God-fearers," so little on people who may have been moving the other direction (or standing still), but without anything that could be described as a conversion.[68] In this connection, it is interesting to see what F. Stanley Jones, in his recent characterization of the religion of the "Circuits of Peter," an early third-century document that he believes is embedded in the pseudo-Clementines, writes: "The *Circuits'* concern . . . is not actually with who should be called a Jew. This writer wants rather to know who is a 'worshiper of God' (*theosebēs*). This term apparently presents the author's self-understanding, and it is notable again . . . that the author does not struggle to be clearly included in the category 'Jew.'"[69] Where, we should ask, did Justin fit, before and after his conversion to Christianity? And where did most of the people he spoke to fit?

2. We do not learn much from Justin himself about how he lived his life, where he worked, and what it meant for him to be a Christian teacher. Because it is almost impossible to discuss Justin without some reference to what we know about Jewish Christians, many studies include references to the pseudo-Clementine *Recognitions* and *Homilies*. I am intrigued by the possibility that those texts could help us understand practically what Justin's life may have looked like, even if theologically they chiefly provide material for comparison. Peter and Simon are portrayed as dogging each other's journeys, showing up in the same cities and towns so as to refute or debate each other. Whatever the pseudo-Clementines tell us about anti-Paulinism, I think that they may offer us a glimpse of what big-time Christian missionary work was like at the time that their putative *Grundschrift* was composed. Can this public rivalry of traveling debaters be simply a novelistic topos, or does it reflect an actual phenomenon? Some of the satires of Lucian of Samosata could be compared with the pseudo-Clementines in this regard. Justin may have followed Marcionite or "Gnostic" preachers around, engaging them in debate in town after town; or perhaps he himself was the one being pursued by defenders of a Jewish Christian construction of Christianity! If Justin did carry on a traveling debating ministry like the ones portrayed in the pseudo-Clementine novel, that might lead us to read him somewhat differently: while he may have "become a mainstream theologian," as Skarsaune says, it was probably difficult in those circumstances to tell what ideas were normative.

3. If, in the period of "Justin of the *Dialogue*," attention has shifted away from Justin as primarily a philosopher, I think that it also has made it less appropriate to call him an "apologist." In fact, the whole category of "apologist" may need to be rethought. There are texts that we should no doubt continue to call "apologies," but perhaps their authors should not be designated in terms of those writings. The fact that their writings have certain shared characteristics ought not to lead us to assume that their authors shared many traits at all. Because of the richness of Justin's writings, we have been able to imagine him in more complex detail. The other writers generally listed under the heading "the apologists" have left us much less to go on, but maybe we could start approaching them with the questions and techniques that we have learned from studying Justin.

4. My final question for future Justin scholarship is one that I have adverted to ear-
    lier in this chapter: How, after the scholarship of the last thirty years, can a gen-
    eral book about Justin be written now? Should the book reflect a particular
    theoretical perspective, like Goodenough's book in 1923? Are the questions to
    which today's readers want to have answers going to dominate, as I think they
    did in Barnard's and Osborn's studies? How will the scholarship since Osborn
    be incorporated into a general account of Justin and his work? One could imag-
    ine a compendium of data of Justin, such as the one that Stefan Heid has pro-
    vided in the *Reallexikon für Antike und Christentum*, but it seems to me that
    such a description tells only part of the story. To all who are dealing with var-
    ious particular aspects of the significance of Justin, I put a general question:
    When we come to tell the overall story of Justin, what do people who are not
    experts in our disciplines need to know about him?

CHAPTER TWO

Justin, Philosopher and Martyr

The Posthumous Creation of the Second Apology

PAUL PARVIS

THE FIRST VISITOR TO EDINBURGH to have taken a serious interest in Justin was probably Q. Lollius Urbicus. At least, Justin took a serious interest in him, which is, of course, not quite the same thing. Between 139 and 142, Urbicus, as governor of Britain, presided over the building of the Antonine Wall running from the Forth to the Clyde. He must, in that capacity, have been a regular visitor to the great Roman naval base at Cramond on the Firth.

A dozen or so years after his recall from Britain, Urbicus—now Urban Prefect—found himself presiding over the trial of a Christian teacher named Ptolemy. That was part of the train of events that, Justin tells us, triggered the writing of the text we know as the *Second Apology*.

But is that what it is? One of the more well-worn problems of Justin scholarship is the question of how many apologies there are. In this chapter I want to look again at that problem, not so much for its own sake as for the sake of the light it might have to shed on the evolution of a difficult and complex work. The question has normally been approached as a literary puzzle, but I think that if we are to get anywhere, we have to try to take into account other aspects of the history of the text as well as the context of the Church of Rome in the crucial decade of the 150s.

That means that we have to try to keep a number of balls in the air at the same time, which certainly does not make things any easier. But if the question is worth pursuing, it is precisely because it may, perhaps, help us to see the text whole. So after (1) trying to set out the problem and some possible solutions, I am going to (2) visit two stages in the history of the text—namely, the leaf-shedding ancestor of *Parisinus graecus* 450 and what Eusebius had in front of him—and then (3) worry about the title of the work. After (4) taking a brief inventory of the motley contents of the *Second Apology*, I will finally (5) offer a tentative, hesitant, and modest proposal.

I. The Problem

Justin's works are, of course, transmitted in only one manuscript of independent standing, *Parisinus graecus* 450, which was completed, the scribe tells us, on September 11, 1364. It presents two documents, a shorter one called in the manuscript "Justin the Philosopher and Martyr's Apology for the Christians, to the Roman Senate," followed by a longer text called "St Justin's Second Apology for the Christians, to Antoninus Pius." Eusebius in his *Historia Ecclesiastica* quotes from both of those documents and says explicitly that Justin wrote two apologies.

So the answer to our question looks blindingly obvious. But nothing is ever as simple as it seems. (Or perhaps I should say, nothing in Eusebius is ever as simple as he seems.) Eusebius never makes it clear that he is quoting from what *he* thinks is the *Second Apology*. And he explicitly attributes quotations from both of our documents to what he calls the *First Apology*.

And the short apology—which comes first in the manuscript—contains a number of back references introduced by "as we have already said" that *do not* refer to things he has already said in that text, but which *can* be matched up with things he says in the long apology.[1] So ever since Thirlby's impish edition of 1722, the two texts have been reversed. What we know as the *First Apology*, then, is what the manuscript calls the *Second Apology*, and what we call the *Second Apology* is the short text that actually comes first in the manuscript.

Inevitably, the waters have been further muddied by centuries of scholarly boots splashing through the problem. So despite the fact that the manuscript presents us with what *appears* to be two texts—a *Second Apology* that is really the *First* and a *First Apology* that is really the *Second*—we still have to ask what the relationship between them is.

There are three traditional and deeply entrenched schools of thought. There are those who think that there are in fact two apologies, those who think that there is really only one, and those who compromise[2] by opting for one and a half—or, rather, for an apology with an appendix.

The first view is that the texts we call the *First* and *Second Apologies* are indeed two separate works. That is, after all, the way they are presented in the manuscript.

But it has often been thought that the *Second Apology* is too insubstantial a text to stand on its own: it begins abruptly; it is very short (under 2,500 words); and the argument—such as it is—hangs largely on the answers to three imagined objections (introduced at *2 Apol.* 3.1, 4.1, and 9.1). So in 1897 Adolf Harnack could say magisterially:

> That the texts transmitted in the sole independent manuscript as Justin's Second and First Apologies are to be transposed and regarded as a single writing is so manifest a result of criticism that, after the demonstrations by Boll, Zahn, myself, and Veil, there is no need of further exposition. [One need only ask] whether the shorter portion is the originally intended conclusion of the Apology or an appendix.[3]

The former answer—that it is the originally intended conclusion—gives us the view that our *First* and *Second Apologies* originally formed a single, continuous text, perhaps divided, as Eduard Schwartz suggested,[4] by a scribe bedazzled by Eusebius's claim that Justin had in fact written two apologies. Three main arguments for this view were developed by F. C. Boll as long ago as 1842.[5] He noted the back references from the *Second Apology* to the *First*. He observed that at the beginning of *1* there are references to piety and philosophy (in the address in 1.1 and in 2.1, 2; 3.2) that form a nice *inclusio* with the end of *2*. And he suggested that there is a natural transition from the end of *1* to the beginning of *2*, for at the end of *1* Justin cites a rescript of the emperor Hadrian (Antoninus Pius's predecessor) to Minicius Fundanus, proconsul of Asia, on the legal status of Christians, while at the beginning of *2* he describes recent trials of Christians in Rome. The train of thought would then be that though Hadrian had insisted (Justin thought) that Christians be tried only on specific criminal charges, in Rome the rescript was being ignored and Christians were being tried for the Name alone.

Harnack's other possibility—that *2* is an appendix to *1*—has an even hoarier pedigree. It was first suggested by Johann Ernst Grabe (the greatest of all Justin's editors) in his Oxford edition of 1700. It was the option that Harnack himself favored, on the grounds that "the so-called First Apology is a complete whole in and of iteslf."[6]

The authority of Harnack helped to elevate the appendix theory to the dizzy and precarious heights of received opinion. Edgar Goodspeed's widely used edition of 1914 actually labeled the two documents "Apologia" and "Appendix," and in 1966 Johannes Quasten's (standard) *Patrology* could say uncomplicatedly "today most scholars agree."[7]

Since then the appendix theory has not had things all its own way. It was strongly attacked by Wolfgang Schmid in 1975,[8] and some recent discussions have gone back to a one-apology theory.[9] And yet in his widely used edition of the apologies, published in 1994, Miroslav Marcovich could claim that "all difficulties disappear as soon as we recognize that 2 A. is only an *Appendix*, Supplement or Postscript ('Nachschrift,' 'Anhang,' 'Begleitschreiben') to 1 A."[10]

Such, then, are the three theories: two apologies, one apology, one apology plus appendix. What are we to make of them? Boll's first and second arguments in particular—the back references from *2* to *1* and the *inclusio*—appear valid and persuasive. But, on the other hand, two apologies corresponds to the evidence of the manuscript (for what that is worth), and *1*, at least, is in some ways a self-contained whole.[11] And, more crucially, a one-apology theory cannot explain the abrupt change in tone and texture that confronts us when we pass from *1* to *2*.

It is worth underlining that fact. Robert Grant, for example, can say that the *Second Apology* "is more favorable to philosophy than the earlier one—there is hardly any Christian theology, in fact."[12] That phrase involves a definition of "Christian theology" at which we might want to cavil. But the point remains. The *Second Apology* alludes to Plato and cites Xenophon but contains not a single quotation from Scripture. And of course the *Logos spermatikos*—so often regarded as one of Justin's key ideas—appears in *2*[13] but not in *1*. So those who stress the positive side of Justin's relationship to pagan philosophy usually start from *2*. They usually allow the *Second Apology*—consciously or unconsciously—to control their reading of the *First*.[14]

That would seem to leave us with the appendix theory, and yet that is a solution that may be more apparent than real.[15] Why was it left simply tacked on to the end of a self-contained text rather than being either worked into it or explicitly introduced for what it is? And why is there so much repetition and overlapping of material? The deploying of a modern category like "appendix" is a sort of three-card trick: it lets us skate over the reality of what was actually going on. And I am bound to say that the plausibility of the theory is not really enhanced by reinforcing the category of "appendix" with the words "Supplement or Postscript ('Nachschrift,' 'Anhang,' 'Begleitschreiben')."

In any event, none of the three theories is trouble-free, though each has something to be said for it. What I would like to suggest is that none of them is right and all of them are right.

Let us begin at the end and look at *2 Apology* 14.1: "And so we ask you to subscribe what seems good to you and to post up this petition" (καὶ ὑμᾶς οὖν ἀξιοῦμεν ὑπογράψαντας τὸ ὑμῖν δοκοῦν προθεῖναι τουτὶ τὸ βιβλίδιον). It has now been widely recognized that Justin is here using the proper, quasi-technical terminology of Roman *libellus* procedure.[16]

An emperor had to be accessible. He was accessible to cities, officials, important personages by letter: they could write to him, and he would write back to them. Pliny's correspondence with Trajan is an obvious example. But humbler folk could approach the emperor through written petition. The texts of a few such petitions to the emperor do survive, of which the best example is that submitted by the inhabitants of the village of Scaptopara in Thrace to Gordian III in 238. But similar petitions in their thousands survive in the papyri, addressed to the prefect or to lower functionaries in Egypt.

There is a recognizable pattern. They normally begin with the name of the recipient and that of the petitioner, the former in the dative and the latter commonly the object of the preposition παρά. The problem is described, and a request—for redress of grievance, for administrative intervention, for a legal ruling—is then made, regularly introduced with the verb ἀξιόω.

The Scaptopareni, for example, begin, "To the Emperor Caesar Marcus Antonius Gordian Pius Felix Augustus, a request from the villagers of Scaptopara." They then explain, in a rather brightly colored narrative, that they suffer from the unwelcome visits of soldiers and others who take it upon themselves to make the most of the amenities of their attractive village. "Therefore, invincible Augustus, we ask [δεόμαι here rather than ἀξιόω] that through your divine rescript you order" them to stop it.

The recipient of such a petition would write his answer at the end of the document: he would subscribe it. And a number of such subscriptions, probably still attached to the original petitions, would then be pasted together and posted in a public place. The petitioner would get his answer simply by looking through the latest batches of posted petitions and waiting until his turn came. If he wanted a certified copy, he then had to arrange for one to be made. There would be others interested in reading through the posted petitions as well, for the rulings they contained could be made to serve as legal precedent.

In the case of the Scaptopareni, it is clear that their petition was actually handed in by a landholder in the village named Aurelius Pyrrus, who was serving in Rome as a soldier of the praetorian guard. It is he who receives the emperor's reply, which begins,

"The Emperor Caesar Marcus Antonius Gordian Pius Felix Augustus to the villagers through Pyrrus the soldier, their fellow land-holder." It was also Pyrrus who had the copy of the subscript made, "copied and checked from the book of petitions answered by our lord the Emperor Marcus Antonius Gordian Pius Felix Augustus and posted in Rome in the portico of the baths of Trajan."

In this case the emperor's answer was abrupt. Gordian told the Scaptopareni (in a Latin response to a Greek petition) that they should have taken their complaint to the governor rather than to him. But the villagers were proud enough of having received an answer from "the divine autocrat" himself to have the texts carved in stone and presumably displayed at the entrance to the village, where the emperor's rescript might serve to deter passing soldiers from tarrying—especially, Theodor Mommsen suggested, those whose Latin was too weak to make out what it actually said.[17]

The normal term for such a petition was *libellus*, most commonly rendered in Greek as βιβλίδιον. To subscribe was *subscribere*/ὑπογράφειν. To post the answer was *proponere*/προθεῖναι. That is exactly the vocabulary we have in *2 Apology* 14.1.

Is the *Second Apology*, then, a petition? If so, what is it a petition for? What is the emperor being asked? Absolutely nothing. The only request in the whole document as it stands is that the answer be posted. Moreover, the *Second Apology* does not begin like a petition, with the names of recipient and petitioner.

The *First Apology*, by contrast, does begin like a petition, with the names of the recipients and of the petitioner—"Justin, son Priscus, son of Baccheios," to the emperor and his sons (*1 Apol.* 1). It also makes a request. In 7.4 Justin asks (ἀξιοῦμεν) that "the deeds of all who have been denounced to you be examined, so that anyone who is found worthy of reproach might be punished as a wrong-doer, but not as a Christian, while if anyone is seen to be irreproachable, he might be released, as a Christian who has done no wrong." The same request is anticipated in 3.1, where Justin asks (ἀξιοῦμεν) that charges against Christians be examined, and is reinforced in 16.14, where he asks (ἀξιοῦμεν) that those who are called Christians but do not live in accordance with Christ's teachings be punished.[18] The *First Apology* also ends, as many of the papyrus *libelli* do, with the citation of a precedent: Justin says that he could have based his request (again using a form of the verb ἀξιόω) simply on Hadrian's rescript to Minicius Fundanus (68.3), which he then cites.

That means that we have two documents, one of which is in form a petition and the other of which is not. But the one that is not refers to "this petition" (τουτὶ τὸ βιβλίδιον) and asks that it be subscribed and posted. So the *First Apology* looks like the petition to which the *Second* refers. How can that anomalous state of affairs be explained? A number of different solutions are possible.

Is it possible, for starters, that *2* is a covering document for *1*—that it is a little speech of presentation designed to accompany the handing in of the petition? Might Justin at least imagine that he is addressing Antoninus Pius and his entourage, introducing his petition and commending it to them? There would, then, be a sort of analogy with the ambassadors' speeches described in the handbook of Menander Rhetor—short presentations introducing a decree of a city council and culminating in a request (ἀξιώσεις) that the emperor receive or hear the decree.[19]

Such a hypothesis might explain a number of things. It might, for example, offer an explanation of the overlap between *2 Apol.* and *1 Apol.*, for the *Second Apology* often repeats or resumes things that have been said in the *First*.[20]

It might also explain why the flavor of *2* is so different from the flavor of *1*. That might be because in *2* Justin is trying to build bridges, to draw his audience on actually to read the petition's long exposition of Christian practice and belief and to wade through its reams of proof-texts. Such a hypothesis might also offer some explanation for the curious contents of the *Second Apology*. It consists of an explanation of the occasion of writing—the story of "a certain woman" (γυνή τις) and her marital troubles—three objections and replies to them, a rousing appeal for moral conversion, and the puzzling request that "this petition" be subscribed and posted. For one who was trying to present and gain a hearing for the *First Apology*, it might make sense to tell the dramatic and rather moving story of recent events and to try to forestall objections, to remove hostile prejudice from the minds of the hearers.

But there is an obvious objection. Is there any reason to think that petitioners were actually able to make covering speeches to the emperor? The candid answer is no. There is some anecdotal evidence for emperor and petitioner speaking face-to-face.[21] Hadrian, we are told, was once approached by a white-haired man asking for something—perhaps presenting a petition (for *petenti* is the verb used). His request was denied, but he turned up again, with his hair dyed, hoping for better luck. Hadrian, recognizing him, said, "I have already refused this to your father." The story is presumably apocryphal; it comes from the *Historia Augusta* (*V. Hadr.* 20.8). But the fact that it is fiction might be regarded as all the more reason for seeing in it the expression of a genuine expectation. It is clear that an emperor—at least a conscientious one—would see and attend to many petitions in person. But, anecdote aside, that he would see and attend to many *petitioners* in person is highly doubtful.

But the *Second Apology* is clearly addressed, in the second person, to the emperor.[22] So if we are to see it as a sort of covering speech, there is a strong element of fantasy on Justin's part, and his manipulation of the *libellus* system loses much of its point and purpose. He has hijacked an established administrative procedure and used it as a way of gaining access to an otherwise closed society.[23] But to attach a covering speech is to slip back into the domain of make-believe, into the pretend world of a text like the *Apology* of Aristides, which lectures the emperor on religion and had not the slightest chance of reaching its ostensible target.

A second possibility might be to deploy some version of the appendix theory. On this reckoning, Justin submitted a petition—our *First Apology*—in the hope that it would be processed and posted. It was not, but events moved on, so he resubmitted the petition shortly afterward with a new account of the trials of Christians before Urbicus and a reminder that it had not been answered. On this theory, as on the covering speech theory, the "this" of the phrase "this petition" in 14.1 is deictic rather than self-referential. That is, when Justin asks for "this petition" to be subscribed and posted, he does not mean "this document you are reading now," but "*this* petition I am pointing to or to which this update is attached."

But whereas in the previous theory—the covering-speech theory—the *Second Apology* at least had a real function in smoothing the way for the *First*, in this version it has little point other than as a convoluted reminder to the imperial secretariat to look in their in-tray.

So in our edition Denis and I have tried to cut the Gordian knot by moving the last two chapters of the *Second Apology*—numbered now as *2 Apology* 14 and 15—to the end of the *First*. The procedure is actually less arbitrary than it sounds. In order to see why that might be so, we have to look at something of what can be reconstructed of the history of the text.

II. The Text and Its History

2.1. The text transmitted by *Parisinus graecus* 450—the sole manuscript of independent standing, known to its friends as A—is self-evidently lacunar. Apart from various sudden jumps in the argument, there is a sizable lacuna in the middle of the *Dialogue,* and there is, above all, a lacuna in *2 Apology* 2, covering most of the story of the unnamed woman whose marital troubles sparked the train of events that led Justin to write. But by a happy chance, that passage is quoted by Eusebius in *Ecclesiastical History* IV.17.2–13. A simple if heroically tedious process yields the conclusion that, counting *nomina sacra* in their contracted form, there are 2,137 letters missing from A.[24] Now, there must be a physical, codicological explanation for that. At some stage in the ancestry of A, there was a leaf-shedding manuscript that had fallen on hard times. 2,137 letters must represent the length of a folio or a bifolium—either is paleographically possible for almost any conceivable period in which the leaf-shedding manuscript might have been written. And so we have a handle on an earlier and clearly difficult stage in the history of the transmission of the text. It is important to realize that we are here dealing not with a theoretical construct, but with a physical object—with an actual manuscript that must once have existed.

If the great lacuna represents a bifolium, each folio would represent on average 1,068 or 1,069 letters. Chapters 15 and 16 of the *Second Apology* contain 1,084 letters. We suggest that this was exactly a folio that became detached in the leaf-shedding manuscript and was moved, by a scribe trying to put the pieces together, from the end of *1 Apology* to the end of *2 Apology*.

Were that so, *1 Apology* would be nicely rounded off. It begins as a *libellus* should, with the names of petitioner and recipient, and would end with the request that "this petition"—self-referential, not deictic this time—be subscribed and posted. And there would be a nice *inclusio* within the one text with the references to piety and philosophy in the address being balanced by the references to piety and philosophy in the very last sentence of the work (the section numbered *2 Apol.* 15.5).

But the *Second Apology* then becomes, if anything, even more of an enigma. It is now a mutilated torso, without a proper beginning or a proper end. It contains the story of the woman and her marital problems and a series of more or less unconnected observations, a number of which have close parallels in the *First Apology*.[25]

The remainder of my argument here coheres with this transposition theory but does not necessarily depend on it.

2.2. But before we move on to the next step, there is one other particular moment in the history of the text about which it is possible to offer some comment other than a groan of despair, and that is the phase represented by Eusebius of Caesarea. The notices in Eusebius have often been discussed and are not luminously clear. Eusebius quotes from both of our *Apologies*—the *First* and the *Second*, the longer and the shorter. The problem is whether he classifies our *Second Apology* as a part of what he calls "the former apology for our doctrine, to Antoninus" (*H.E.* II.13.2) or counts it as a separate work. At IV.17 he cites the story of the woman (*gune tis*), so filling the great lacuna in A—and introduces it by saying that Justin mentions this "in the former apology."[26] But in the previous chapter he has said that Justin, "after delivering a second book on behalf of our doctrines to the rulers we have indicated [in context this means Marcus Aurelius and Lucius Verus],[27] is adorned with holy martyrdom" (IV.16.1), and he supports this by quoting the passage about Crescens the Cynic from *2 Apology* 8(3).1–6, which he introduces by saying, "And this man, most philosophical in truth, clearly signifies ahead of time in the aforementioned apology (τῇ δεδηλωμένῃ ἀπολογίᾳ), as it was about to happen concerning him so soon thereafter, thus in these words" (*H.E.* IV.16.2).

So the question is whether "the aforementioned apology" is the *First Apology* that Eusebius has discussed earlier, or the "second book" that he has just mentioned. I think that here Harnack is right, and Eusebius means the *First Apology*.[28] Too often his references to Justin's works have been collected and analyzed out of context.[29] It is the merit of Harnack's discussion to look at the references in the broader context of what Eusebius is talking about and what he is trying to do.

Here I think we can say that Eusebius is embarrassed. His catalogue of Justin's writings records "a book addressed (λόγος προσφωνητικός) to Antoninus called Pius and his sons and the Roman senate on behalf of our doctrines and another containing a second apology on behalf of our faith, which he wrote for Antoninus Verus [he means Marcus Aurelius], the successor of the aforementioned emperor, who had the same name" (IV.18.2).

So Eusebius thinks that some little time has elapsed between the writing of what he calls the first apology and the writing of what he calls the second. But he chooses to see in the reference to Crescens a clue as to the circumstances of Justin's death—a conclusion to which he is no doubt led both by wishful thinking and by Tatian's claim that it was Crescens who compassed Justin's death.[30] How, then, can it be that the reference to Crescens occurs in the earlier document?

The answer, as so often in Eusebius, is not to lie but to resort to a little sleight of hand. First, he says explicitly that Justin "signifies this ahead of time" and calls his statement a "prophecy" (IV.16.2, 7). Second, he minimizes the time gap by saying that all this was to happen "so soon thereafter"—despite the fact that on his reckoning, Justin was martyred in the next reign, under Marcus rather than under Pius. Third, he covers his back by quoting Tatian to support the connection he wants to make (IV.16.7–9).

And finally, he uses a studiously vague phrase—"in the aforementioned apology"—so as not to draw attention to the problem.

So I think that Harnack must—as usual—be right when he thinks that the "former apology to Antoninus" comprises our *Second Apology* as well. This may shed some light on a curious phrase Eusebius uses in IV.11.11, where he says that Justin "addresses also other discourses (ἑτέρους λόγους) containing apology on behalf of our faith to the Emperor Antoninus, who was called Pius, and the Roman senate." What does he mean by "other discourses" (ἕτεροι λόγοι)?

The plural of λόγος is used in the *Ecclesiastical History* exactly one hundred times.[31] It often means "the divine (or holy) words"—that is, Scripture[32]—and can mean something like "culture" in general.[33] It can refer specifically to oral teaching[34] or to debate.[35] It not infrequently means "words" as opposed to deeds.[36] But most frequently it refers to a literary unit—that is, a "book," either in the specific or in the generic sense. Thus Eusebius speaks of the preface to Papias's *logoi* and of the eight *logoi* of Clement's *Hypotyposeis*. More generally, the "books"/"writings" of Justin were deemed worthy of eager study (IV.18.9), while pagan philosophers submitted their *logoi* to Origen for criticism, and *logos* in this sense can be used as a synonym for σύγγραμμα (IV. pinax 17 and 18) or βιβλίδιον (IV.26.1 and 2). But it never means simply "prose" or "connected bits of discourse" in a way that would make some sense of the phrase "other *logoi* containing an apology" (IV.11.11). So Eusebius's first apology—to Antoninus— is a *logos* (IV.18.2), but one made up of *logoi*.

The situation is roughly the same in the citations included in the *Sacra Parallela*. There our *First Apology* is normally called simply "To Antoninus the Emperor,"[37] while an extract from our *2 Apology* 11 is introduced as coming "from the second part (μέρος) of his *Apology*." So again there is one text, one work, but with some kind of vaguely defined internal articulation.

III. The Title

What was that work called? Whatever Justin called it, it was not *Apology*. In fact, the first of the works of "the apologists" to bear some form of that word in the title must have been Tertullian's *Apologeticus*.[38] The word ἀπολογία itself occurs only twice in the text of the *Apologies*, and in both passages it means "excuse" or "cop-out."[39] When he describes his own work, apart from the reference to "this petition" (βιβλίδιον), he uses the pairs "address and petition" (τὴν προσφώνησιν καὶ ἔντευξιν, *1 Apol.* 1) and "address and explanation" (τὴν προσφώνησιν καὶ ἐξήγησιν, *1 Apol.* 68.3). Now προσφώνησις is fairly rare, though λόγος προσφωνητικός was one of the categories of epideictic oratory analyzed by the rhetoricians. In Menander's words, "An 'address' (προσφωνητικὸς λόγος) is a speech of praise to a governor spoken by an individual. In treatment it is an encomium, but not a complete one, since it does not include all the elements of the encomium. Strictly speaking, the 'address' is produced when the speech draws its amplification from the actual deeds performed by the subject."[40]

Whatever effect Justin's *Apology* would have had on its ostensible recipients, they would hardly have felt buttered up by it. But what is curious is the twin pairs of descriptors. This is the only place in the whole range of Greek literature covered by the *Thesaurus Linguae Graecae* where προσφώνησις and ἔντευξις occur within one line of each other, and the only place where προσφώνησις and ἐξήγησις occur within one line of each other. But whatever the explanation, Justin must have called his work something like "Address and Petition to Antoninus."

What does Eusebius call it? He refers to the apologies on a number of occasions, and we have encountered some of his labels already. He speaks of "the former apology," "the apology to Antoninus," "the former apology to Antoninus on behalf of our doctrine," and—most elaborately of all—"address [λόγος . . . προσφωνητικός] to Antoninus called Pius and his sons and the Roman senate on behalf of our doctrines" (IV.18.2).[41] In all, Justin accounts for eight of the thirty-one occurrences of the word *apologia* in the *Ecclesiastical History*.

Wolfram Kinzig concludes a very useful survey of the way Eusebius describes the work of "the apologists" by observing, "Eusebius' surprisingly consistent terminology allows scarcely a doubt but that the group of writings he adduces and which—at least in part—he had in front of him bore the word *apologia* in their title."[42] But perhaps it is not quite as simple as that might suggest, at least in the case of Justin. Clearly, Eusebius normally called the work an "apology," but the word does not appear as a title in either of his two most formal references—"*logos prosphonetikos* to Antoninus called Pius and his sons and the Roman senate on behalf of our doctrines" in the set-piece catalogue of Justin's writings (IV.18.2)[43] and "discourses containing apology on behalf of our faith (addressed) to the emperor Antoninus, who was called Pius, and to the Roman senate" (IV.11.11), introducing his citation of the opening sentence of *1 Apology*. The element most consistently present is "To Antoninus," *Pros Antoninon*, and another recurring element is a phrase like "on behalf of our doctrine" (II.13.2), "on behalf of our doctrines" (IV.18.2), "on behalf of our faith" (IV.11.11). "Apology" has more the character of a generic description. And the text that Eusebius chooses to regard as the *Second Apology*—whatever it was[44]—is called a "second book (*biblion*) on behalf of our doctrines" (IV.16.2) and another *logos* "containing"—not "being"—"an apology on behalf of our faith" (IV.18.2). The position in the *Sacra Parallela* is, as we have seen, rather similar, for "To Antoninus" is there contrasted with "the second part of the apology."[45]

Of the titles actually found in A, that given to our *Second Apology*—"of the same Saint Justin [ἅγιος Ἰουστῖνος], philosopher and martyr, apology on behalf of Christians, to the Senate of the Romans"—is clearly secondary: there is absolutely nothing in the text to justify an assumption that it is addressed to the Senate. Our *First Apology* is called "of the same ἅγιος Ἰουστῖνος, second apology on behalf of Christians to Antoninus Pius." The latter, with the omission of the word "second," must be what the scribe of A or of one of his exemplars had in front of him.[46]

Next, the author. He is, as we have seen, styled "holy Justin, philosopher and martyr" in the *Sacra Parallela* and in A, but he is already called "*Justinus, philosophus et martyr*" by Tertullian (*Adv. Valentin.* 5), and the same designation may have been known to Eusebius, since he prefaces his quotation from *2 Apology* 8(3)—which he regards as a prophecy of Justin's martyrdom—by calling him "in truth the most philo-sophical" (ὁ ταῖς ἀληθείαις φιλοσοφώτατος; IV.16.2).

The conclusions to be drawn from all of this are, I think, that

1. our *First Apology* consistently bore the title, or a title that included, *Pros Antoninon*;
2. at some stage between Justin himself and Eusebius, the word *apologia* was added, but at least sometimes as a general title covering more than our *First Apology*;
3. some phrase like "on behalf of the doctrines of the Christians" was also added— probably attached to "Apology" rather than to "To Antoninus," since Eusebius uses it both of his first and of his second apologies; and
4. probably as early as the end of the second century, the author was identified as "Justin, philosopher and martyr."

IV. The Contents of Our *Second Apology*

At last we can turn from the wrapping to what is inside the package and look at the oddly assorted contents of the *Second Apology*. It begins, of course, with the story of recent persecution—the unnamed woman (*gune tis*) denounced by her jilted husband and the execution of three Christians by our friend, Q. Lollius Urbicus, the first of whom, the one with whom Justin is most concerned, was her teacher, Ptolemy.

Since Harnack, this Ptolemy—who was "a lover of truth and neither deceitful nor falsely minded" (*2 Apol.* 2.11)—has not infrequently been identified with Ptolemy the Gnostic.[47] One of the somber manifestations of the tendency of scholarship to abhor a vacuum is the assumption that there cannot be two people in the same place at the same time with the same name—even a place as large as Rome. And the temptation to connect all possible dots reaches its logical—or illogical—end in the further conclusion that *gune tis* must be Flora—the Flora to whom Ptolemy the Gnostic wrote—on the grounds that they are both female.[48]

And yet, despite one's ingrained skepticism, the identification of the two Ptolemies does have something to be said for it. Quite apart from the argument that the name is relatively rare, though far from unknown, in contemporary inscriptions from Rome,[49] there is the salient fact that in the *Dialogue with Trypho* Justin bitterly denounces those who "instead of reverencing Jesus, confess in name only. And they call themselves Christians . . . and there are some of them called Marcionites and others Valentinians and others Basilideans and others Satornilians . . ." (35.5–6). Of these reprobates, only the followers of Marcion are attacked in the *Apologies*.[50] And the *Dialogue* is, of course, always assumed to be later, since it contains a back reference to the *First Apology*—to what Justin, "addressing Caesar in writing," had said about Simon Magus (*Dial.* 120.6).

Now, in the ragbag of the *Second Apology* there are a couple of passages that bear a passing resemblance to ideas that were circulating in Valentinian circles. For example, Justin says that "there is no given name [ὄνομα θετόν] for the Father of all, inasmuch as he is unbegotten. For anyone to whom some name is applied has older than him the one who gave the name" (*2 Apol.* 5[6].1). The *Gospel of Truth* reflects much on the Name and asks, "Who is it who will give a name to him who existed before himself, as if offspring did not receive a name from those who begot [them]?" (*G. Tr.* 39.30–40.1).[51]

Justin then goes on to say that the Father of all has no proper name since titles such as "Father" and "God" and "Creator" and "Lord" "are not names, but labels derived from his benefactions and works" (*2 Apol.* 5[6].2). For the *Gospel of Truth*, the Father is unnamable, except in the sense that "the name of the Father is the Son." That Son can be seen. "The name, however, is invisible because it alone is the mystery of the invisible. . . . For indeed, the Father's name is not spoken, but it is apparent through a Son" (*G. Tr.* 38.7–24).[52]

Justin then moves on to the name "Christ," which is connected with anointing, but "also contains an unknown signification," and the name "Jesus," through which demons are successfully exorcised—no doubt with the application of the sign of the cross, since it is specifically "in the name of Jesus Christ, who was crucified under Pontius Pilate" that they must be adjured (*2 Apol.* 5[6].3–6). According to the *Excerpts from Theodotus*, "those of the right knew the names 'Jesus' and 'Christ' even before his coming, but they did not know the power of the sign"—that is, the sign of the cross (*Exc. Th.* 43.1).

This reflection on names is followed in the *Second Apology* by a difficult (and surely corrupt) passage on "seed." Perhaps the best that can be made of it is something like this: "And hence God refrains from bringing about the dissolution and destruction of the whole universe, which would entail an end to wicked angels and demons and human beings; this he does because of the seed of Christians, which he knows in nature, that it is the cause" (6[7].1).[53]

A part of the thought becomes clear from Clement, who can speak of (choice) Christians as "seed because of which both the visible and invisible things of the world were fashioned . . . and all things are held together as long as the seed remains here, and when it has been gathered together all things will at once be dissolved" (*Quis Dives Salvetur* 36.3). But "seed" is also rich in Valentinian resonance, and there are again parallels in the *Excerpta ex Theodoto*, where Ecclesia is identified with the "superior seeds" (26.1), which were made ready when the world was created (41.1–2). And "when he enters in, the seed too enters in with him into the pleroma" (26.3)—a remark that occurs in the context of the claim that the "invisible" aspect of Jesus is "the Name" (26.1).

The idea that God delays to bring about the end of the world because of those who are yet to believe and be saved occurs in *1 Apol.* 28.2 and 45.1 and *Dial.* 39.2, and in each case with specific reference to God's knowledge or foreknowledge, but with no mention of seed.

Finally, it might be worth remembering that according to Justin, Ptolemy before Urbicus "confessed the school [διδασκαλεῖον] of divine virtue" (*2 Apol.* 2.13). That may be a rather more loaded phrase than it appears to be. According to the *Tripartite Tractate*, "his members . . . needed a place of instruction, which is in the places which are adorned, so that [they] might receive from them resemblance to the images and archetypes, like a mirror, until all the members of the body of the Church are in a single place" (123.11–18).[54] And I might add that in the passage of 2 Apology to which I have just adverted, the name "Christ" is connected with his function of "anointing"—in the active, I believe, not the passive—"and adorning all things."[55]

I am, of course, not trying to suggest that Justin was a Valentinian—crypto- or otherwise. Nor am I trying to suggest that the passages I have adduced—drawn from a group of texts that is itself far from homogeneous—explain what Justin is *really* saying here. What the *Gospel of Truth* has to say on the "Name," for example, is very different from what Justin is saying, despite the fact that they are confronting similar questions and using a similar vocabulary; indeed, the observation that names are given by older to younger, not younger to older, is actually in context a claim put into the mouth of an objector. And in any case, a number of these ideas have good parallels elsewhere in what we might please to regard as materials of less dubious provenance. But the fact remains that there are bits of the *Second Apology* that would have made some of those in a Valentinian milieu feel at home.

What else do we find in the *Second Apology*? There are some passages that might have been deemed to be or ephemeral interest. One of these is the story of *gune tis* and her troubles—as fascinating to us as it fortunately was to Eusebius—and another is the account of Justin's run-in with the Cynic Crescens. Though Eusebius, as we have seen, tries hard to invest the latter with a lasting significance, it might have been thought soon to lose topicality.

There are also the answers to three imaginary objections (at *2 Apol.* 3[4].1, 4[5].1, and 9.1), some of which wander a bit and some of which have close parallels in *1 Apol.*—so close, in fact, that the one can sometimes be used to emend the other. Examples of fairly close parallels are the convoluted argument about moral choice and God's validation of the objective existence of good and evil at *2 Apol.* 6(7).5–9 and *1 Apol.* 28.1–4 and the appeal to Socrates and the charges against him in *2 Apol.* 10.4–6 and *1 Apol.* 5.3–4. It is also instructive to compare the Christians-before-Christ passage in *1 Apol.* with the discussion of Heraclitus, Musonius, and "all those who in any way whatsoever were eager to live in accordance with Logos and to flee vice" in *2 Apol.* 7(8).1–3. The latter, but of course not the former, is couched in terms of "the implanted seed of the Logos" and Justin's seminal idea—if you will forgive the phrase—of *Logos spermatikos*.

Finally, the *Second Apology* contains at least two passages that might have seemed rather to miss the mark. One of these is the appeal at *2 Apology* 4(5).3 to the myth of Genesis 6 about the sons of God having intercourse with the daughters of men. Justin offers that as an answer to the specific objection that if God were the sort of God Justin says he is, Christians would not be left under the power of unjust rulers, but it becomes in effect a general explanation of the existence of evil in the world. To a pagan audience this would scarcely have seemed a philosophically cogent account of the problem. And beyond that, as Oskar Skarsaune has noted, "Justin's polemic against idolatry" is here "dependent on a Jewish tradition—a tradition which was abandoned by the rabbis in the years preceding Justin's days."[56] It is not without significance that when in the *Dialogue* Trypho is "vexed" at the claim that there are wicked and apostate angels, Justin replies with a battery of texts that does *not* include Genesis 6.

The other passage I have in mind is the version of the fable of Heracles, who at a fork in the road encounters two women, Virtue and Vice, which Justin enthusiastically recounts in *2 Apol.* 11.2–5. It is indeed derived from Xenophon,[57] as Justin says it is, but by Justin's day the fable had been told and retold, modified and adapted so often that it had been reduced to the level of a hackneyed commonplace in handbooks of rhetoric for schoolboys. Just how common coin it was can be seen from Lucian's parody in *Somnium* 6–17, when he claims to have had as a lad a dream in which he was being fought over by two women, the beautiful Paideia and the beefy Sculpture. And yet Justin can tell the story with a straight face. It is as if you were addressing the Scottish Parliament and told the assembled worthies that you had this fascinating tale of the Bruce and a spider, which you were sure they would be edified to hear.

V. A Proposal

What I am suggesting, then—to try to draw all of this together—is that the *Second Apology* is essentially clippings from the cutting-room floor. On this theory the first stage would have been a petition, a *biblidion*, a *libellus*, composed by Justin around the year 153 or so.[58] It cannot be reconstructed but would presumably have contained much of our *First Apology* and at least most of our *Second*. It may actually have been handed in to the office of the *a libellis*, and Justin may well have actually hoped for a response.

The second stage, on this theory, would have involved a reworking—perhaps repeated reworking—of this document. New material might have been added, some material will have been replaced with new versions, and some will have been excised. In the last category fall the deletion of sections thought to be dated, the omission (or replacement) of things that could be construed as grist to a Valentinian mill, and the cutting of some of Justin's more infelicitous sallies. This reworking—or its final and definitive form—will correspond to the *First Apology* as we have it.

The gap between stage one and stage two could be anything up to a decade or so, and in the interim there were squabbles within the Roman Church. At some point between stage one and the writing of the *Dialogue*, Justin will have decided that the followers of Valentinus were Christians in name only.

What happened to the material that was dropped at stage two? Presumably it survived as scattered fragments or in working notebooks of some sort. That could explain why so much of the *Second Apology* is structured around the answers to hypothetical objections—it might have been used as a resource for street-corner debate. And it could explain why—as every editor of Justin must have discovered—the text of *2 Apol.* is on the whole so much more corrupt than the text of *1*. At some point this material was gathered up and attached, without much coherence of order, at the end of our *First Apology*. The evidence of Eusebius ("other *logoi*") and John of Damascus ("the second part of the apology") suggests that it followed on after some sort of break, but without a new title of its own.

When might that have happened, and why? It is hard to imagine that Justin himself could have been responsible, so it must have happened at some point in the 130

years or so between Justin's death and the first edition of the *Ecclesisastical History*, and
at some point within the same period the word "apology" was added to the title. The
words "philosopher and martyr" were also added to Justin's name, and the evidence of
Tertullian suggests that *that* may have happened by the end of the second century.

The most economical assumption would be that these changes were made at the
same time. One possibility is that this happened in the immediate aftermath of Justin's
death. As an act of *pietas*, perhaps, the scattered fragments were gathered up.

We can, I think, reinforce that suggestion by a final look at the use of the word
apologia. We have seen that whatever Justin called his own work, it was not "apology."
Apologia, of course, is at home in the courtroom.[59] It means, specifically and originally,
a defense *against*—against charges in court or, more loosely, against accusations, and
as such it is not a genre, but a function.[60] But in Christian usage the meaning shifted.
For Eusebius, the word has largely lost its courtroom connection and can mean not
only defense *against*, but also defense *of* or *on behalf of*. Hence his references to "apology on behalf of Christians" (II.2.4), "for our doctrine" (II.13.2, IV.13.8), "for our cultus" (IV.3.1), "for our faith" (IV.3.3, IV.11.11, IV.18.2), "for the teaching which he
championed" (IX.6.3), and the like. This is a natural shift, but it is a definite one.

Now the bridge between these two senses—defense against (in court) and defense
of (in general)—may be provided by martyr *acta*. Thus, in the *Ecclesiastical History*,
Eusebius says that the "writing" (γραφῆς) about Pionius contained, among other
things, his "apologies for [ὑπέρ] the faith before the people and the rulers" (IV.15.47).

In V.21.2–5, Eusebius reports that one Apollonius[61] was begged by the judge to
deliver a speech before the Senate in Rome and so "presented before all a most literate
apologia for the faith to which he was bearing witness." Anyone who reads his own
collection of *Martrys of Old*, Eusebius adds, would discover "his words before the judge
and the answers which he gave to Perennis' interrogation and the whole apology to
the Senate."

Lucian of Antioch, "having presented before the ruler his *apologia* for the teaching he championed," was executed. The same story can be told in slightly different
terms: Lucian "proclaimed the heavenly kingdom of Christ first by word through apology and then also by deed" (VIII.13.2).

The extant *Martyrdom of Pionius* actually contains a speech of defense (introduced by the verb ἀπολογέομαι) that goes on for some six hundred words,[62] and it
would be easy to imagine a supposed "apology" of Apollonius to the Senate floating free
of its matrix.

So if, in the aftermath of Justin's death, disciples gathered up the scattered fragments of his work and issued a new, enlarged version, it would be a fairly gentle step
to call it an "apology." It was not the courtroom speech of a martyr, but it was a set-piece
defense of Christianity by a martyr who had in fact had his day in court.

On this theory, then, how many apologies are there—two, one, or one and a half?
In one sense or another, all are right, and all shall have prizes. There are two apologies
in the sense that our *Second* is a distinct compilation, put together at a different time
for a slightly different purpose. There is only one in the rather stronger sense that we
are dealing with the remains of two states of the same basic document. And there are

one and a half in the sense that *2 Apol.* turns out to be, after all, an appendix—albeit one composed earlier rather than later.

But if the question is specifically how many apologies Justin wrote, then the answer is none at all. He wrote an "address and petition," προσφώνησις καὶ ἔντευξις, in more than one version, but no apologies.

That means that the invention of the *Second Apology* was a consequence of Justin's martyrdom. He "invented" it—as he perhaps invented "apology"—not by writing, but by dying—when, precisely, Justin the petitioner, "son of Priscus, son of Baccheios, from Flavia Neapolis in Syria Palaestina," became "Saint Justin, philosopher and martyr."[63]

CHAPTER THREE

The *Rescript* of Hadrian

Denis Minns

I

To THE LONGER OF THE *APOLOGIES* of Justin Martyr preserved for us by *Parisinus graecus* 450 there is appended what is claimed to be a rescript written by the emperor Hadrian to Minucius Fundanus, governor of Asia, in answer to a query submitted by Minucius's predecessor, Serenius Granianus. Eusebius reproduces this rescript (*H.E.* IV.9.1–3), which he claims to have translated from the original Latin, which he found in his exemplar of Justin's *Apologies*. Melito of Sardis, in his *Address to the Emperor*, advised Marcus Aurelius that his "grandfather Hadrian clearly wrote to (besides many others) Fundanus the proconsul, who was also governor of Asia."[1] This is the only evidence that Fundanus and Granianus were proconsuls of Asia. Q. Licinius Silvanus Granianus is otherwise known to have been suffect-consul in 106,[2] and C. Minicius Fundanus suffect consul in 107.[3] It is plausible, then, that they succeeded one another as governors of Asia between 123 and 125.[4] It is impossible to determine at what point the corruption of Granianus's name entered the tradition.

There has long been divided opinion about the authenticity of this document, about whether it ever formed part of Justin's apologetic writings, about its position in those writings if it was original, and about whether the Latin version provided by Rufinus in his translation of Eusebius's *Ecclesiastical History* is original or a retroversion of Eusebius's translation. In this chapter I shall examine some of the arguments bearing on these disputed questions and propose that the rescript is authentic, that it belongs where it is found in the manuscript, and that Rufinus's text is a retroversion of Eusebius's Greek. Much of this work has been done in collaboration with Dr. Paul Parvis, with whom I have been preparing an edition and translation of the *Apologies*. I leave out of account the other two documents subjoined to the *First Apology* in the manuscript, a letter of Antoninus to the Commune of Asia and a letter of Marcus

Aurelius addressed to the Senate, on the grounds that it cannot plausibly be supposed that either of them featured in the *Apology* as it left Justin's hands.

For convenience, I include a translation of the rescript here. Some of the problems of the text are discussed below.

Hadrian to Minucius Fundanus.

(*1 Apol.* 68.6) I received a letter written to me from the most eminent Serenius Granianus, whom you succeeded. . . . (68.7) For it does not seem good to me to leave the matter unexamined, lest the people be subject to vexation and accusers be provided with an opportunity for slander. (68.8) Clearly, then, with regard to this petition, should your provincials be able to make a case against the Christians, so as even to answer before a tribunal, let them occupy themselves only with this, and not with petitions and with mere outcries. (68.9) For it would be much more fitting, if someone wanted to make an accusation, that you should hear the case in court. (68.10) If, then, someone should make accusation and prove people did something against the laws, make a determination according to the strength of the offence. But if, by Hercules, anyone should attempt this for the sake of slander, decide according to its gravity and consider how it is to be punished.

In an article published in 1955, Wolfgang Schmid accepted the authenticity of the *Rescript* in the main[5] but suggested that Justin had taken advantage of "*ambiguitas sensus*" to reinterpret its meaning to suit his own apologetic ends.[6] Hadrian's own strictures had been directed against those who falsely accused people of being Christian, but Justin supposed that purpose to have been to forbid the accusing of Christians as Christians when there was no evidence of wrongdoing. In their original context, the words "if, then, someone should make accusation and prove people did something against the laws, make a determination according to the strength of the offence" (*1 Apol.* 68.10) meant that if a charge of Christianity was proved against an accused person, then that person should be punished. In essentials, Hadrian's *Rescript* differs from Trajan's only in its vigorous rejection of the turbulent methods of a fanatical multitude when trying to influence the normal procedure of the court, and Schmid cites from *Codex Iustinianus* 9.47.12 Diocletian and Maximian saying that the empty words of the people were not to be heard, nor their voices believed, when they wanted the acquittal of a criminal or the condemnation of an innocent person.[7]

In an article published some twenty-five years later, Schmid argued that Justin's original *Apology* was a single work consisting of what we call the *First* and the *Second Apologies*, in that order, and without the *Rescript*, or the introduction to it that constitutes chapter 68, sections 3–5 of our *First Apology*. Schmid considers that the line of thought flows naturally from *1 Apology* 68.1–2 to *2 Apology* 1.1. Imperial authorities will not escape the coming judgment of God if they act unjustly, and the recent affair under Urbicus has prompted Justin, out of fellow-feeling for those authorities, to write his *Apology* pointing out the injustice and irrationality of the mistreatment of Christians.[8] Although Capelle had argued that the words that introduce the *Rescript* could have been composed entirely by Justin, in terms of vocabulary, syntax, and style,[9] Schmid considers that this bridging paragraph contains evidence of its composition at a time later than that of the *First Apology*. In this bridging passage Hadrian is described as "greatest and most illustrious Caesar" (μεγίστου καὶ ἐπιφανεστάτου Καίσαρος). This description, in Schmid's view, would be surprising if it had been written by Justin, but a later reviser could well be capable of it.[10] The phrase ἐπιφανέστατος Καῖσαρ must be equivalent to *nobilissimus Caesar* or something similar, but reference to the nobility of the emperor is first discernible in connection with Commodus and is bound up with the fact that he was the first of the Roman emperors to be born to the purple, "*porphyrogenitus.*" If the use of ἐπιφανεστάτου Καίσαρος in the *First Apology* is related anachronistically to this later usage, then this passage, and the *Rescript* it introduces, cannot have been contained in the *First Apology*.

Schmid's argument rests on a short article by Hans Ulrich Instinsky, which makes out a plausible case for a relationship between the description *nobilissimus* and Commodus.[11] However, the Greek equivalent for *nobilissimus* in Herodian's summary at the end of his first book is not ἐπιφανέστατος but εὐγενέστατος.[12] Schmid thinks his argument should not be troubled by this, any more than by the association of the word ἐπιφανέστατος, in the sense of "most manifest," with θεός in the titles of emperors.[13] Schmid himself refers to a papyrus from Faijûm dated February 11, 135, containing the words ἐπιφανέστατος θεός, with reference to Hadrian,[14] and to an inscription from Thera that the *Corpus Inscriptionum Graecarum* dates before 116, since *Parthicus* is not listed amongst Trajan's titles, in which is found "the most great and most manifest of gods, the Emperor Nerva Trajan Caesar Augustus Germanicus Dacicus" (τοῦ μεγίστου καὶ θεῶν ἐνφανεστάτου Αὐτοκράτορος Νέρβα Τραινοῦ Καίσαρος Σεβαστοῦ Γερμανικοῦ Δακικοῦ).[15] This seems to me sufficient to make Justin's use of the phrase τοῦ μεγίστου καὶ ἐπιφανεστάτου Καίσαρος entirely plausible. Justin can hardly be thought to have supposed that the two superlatives could not be used without reference to the emperor's divine status. It is interesting to note that this inscription also refers to the "concord of the holy Senate and of the people of Rome" (καὶ ἱεροῦ συνκλήτου καὶ δήμου Ῥωμαίων ὁμονίας). The "holy Senate and the whole people of the Romans" also featured among the addressees of the *First Apology* (ἱερᾷ τε συγκλήτῳ καὶ δήμῳ Ῥωμαίων).

Schmid believed that about the year 180, under the influence of Melito of Sardis, an edition of Justin's *Apology* was put out that had been shortened by the removal of its last sections (our *Second Apology*), since the account of the execution of Ptolemaeus and Lucius and their companion contradicted Melito's thesis that Antoninus Pius did not persecute the Christians, and because they drew unwelcome attention to the embarrassing failure of Justin's request that his petition be subscribed and posted. It was for this edition that an authentic *Rescript* of Hadrian, which was capable of being interpreted as favorable to Christians, was added after 68.2 to meet the need for a suitable ending to the now-truncated *Apology*.[16]

In 1976 Herbert Nesselhauf was able to write that doubts about the authenticity of the *Rescript* were a thing of the past, before himself launching a thoroughgoing assault upon that authenticity.[17] A. Birley accepted Nesselhauf's arguments in 1987 but a decade later seemed to find the thesis of a genuine exchange of letters between Hadrian and Minicius plausible.[18] Scholars who consider that the *Rescript* is no more favorable to the situation of Christians than the letter of Trajan to Pliny see this as a strong argument for its authenticity, since a forger would have made a stronger case for the relief of Christians. This was the view of J. B. Lightfoot, Theodor Mommsen, and C. Callewaert,[19] among others, and we have adopted it for our edition. However, it needs to be acknowledged that those who deny the *Rescript*'s authenticity, and even some of its defenders—most notably Mommsen[20]—think that it is genuinely favorable to the Christians.

Thus Nesselhauf thinks that the forgery was intended to suggest a complete reversal of the policy set out in Trajan's reply to Pliny, dating from scarcely a decade earlier.[21] Trajan provided for no formal trial in the case of Christians who were not accused of criminal offenses, but simply confirmed that if Christians incurred the hostility of the population and were denounced to the governor as Christians, the governor was to determine whether those denounced were Christians, execute them if they refused to renounce Christ, but release them if they said they were not Christians or did not intend to continue as such.[22] The *Rescript* of Hadrian, on the other hand, without reference to Trajan's letter, provided that henceforth Christians should be prosecuted only by means of a private denunciation in a proper trial before the tribunal of the governor, and only for infringement of the law—under which the mere profession of the Christian name was not included.[23] If the effect of Hadrian's *Rescript* was thus, as Mommsen had thought, to grant religious freedom to Christians,[24] it is remarkable that no trace of this is found in the subsequent literature. Moreover, whereas Trajan had allowed—in "a procedure that was fully consistent with the Roman conception of the rule of law"—that denunciations were admissible so long as they were not anonymous, the *Rescript* allowed only formal accusation-trials.[25]

Nesselhauf's case against the authenticity of the *Rescript* rests on a too-exigent interpretation of the evidence. If the *Rescript* could be interpreted in no other way than as requiring that Christians were to be dealt with exclusively by formal *Akkusationsprozeß*—thus, presumably, bypassing the more flexible procedure of *cognitio extra ordinem*[26]—no further proof would be required of its falsehood. For Hadrian would then be requiring that Christians be dealt with exclusively by an expensive and cumbersome procedure—Nesselhauf describes it as quite ponderous ("ziemlich umständliche")—that was giving way to the more widespread use of *cognitio extra ordinem*.[27] Such a provision would accord Christians a unique distinction in law, for it would have made them liable only for those offenses covered by the *ordo iudiciorum publicorum*, effectively exempting them from prosecution for the wide range of offenses not so covered.[28] Mommsen cannot be supposed to have understood the *Rescript* in this way, and even in the second century such an understanding would have been sufficiently risible to have precluded successful deception.

The *Rescript* is plausible in the context of *cognitio extra ordinem*, which is widely regarded as having been the procedure normally employed by governors in dealing with those denounced as Christians,[29] and which Nesselhauf himself, following

Mommsen, describes as a penal process (*Strafverfahren*).[30] There is no need to suppose that a magistrate proceeding *extra ordinem* would be unable to admit an accuser.[31] Hadrian should be understood to have sought to do no more than rule against clamorous and vexatious denunciation. The phrase "something against the laws" need not refer to infringements of particular statutes or enactments, but simply to wrongdoing, understood loosely.[32] When Cicero described the *Lex Clodia* as "written contrary to custom and all the laws" (*contra omnis leges nullo scripta more*), or as "that law against all laws" (*illam legem . . . contra omnis leges*),[33] his meaning cannot have been that it actually infringed every written law, but simply that it was in every respect illegal. A statute law criminalizing something would have stated what penalties would be incurred for infringement. But a governor proceeding in *cognitio extra ordinem* would determine for himself whether something required punishment and what that punishment should be,[34] just as the *Rescript* instructs. If, then, the *Rescript* is genuine, its intended import may simply have been to provide that in the exercise of *coercitio* in *cognitio extra ordinem*, Minicius Fundanus should not act upon denunciatory petitions or allow himself to be swayed by popular outcry, but should identify an accuser and hold him accountable should the governor decide that there was no cause for his intervention against the accused. Hadrian is not specifying that a particular penal procedure is to be followed, but simply indicating an effective and readily comprehensible means of choking off the nuisance caused to the governor by a certain kind of petitioner or delator. As such, the *Rescript* would really be doing no more than giving some precision to Trajan's proscription of anonymous denunciation.[35] Its utility to Justin lay in the looseness of the phrase "something against the laws." For Hadrian or his governors, this might, indeed, include being a Christian, when and if Christians seemed to be the occasion of social unrest. For Justin it meant not necessarily something in breach of statute law, but something really wrong, and thus not, as he has gone to such lengths to explain, the profession of the name of Christ.

II

Eusebius claimed to have before him the text of the *Rescript* in Latin, saying, "But we translated it into Greek to the best of our ability" (*H.E.* IV.8.8). Veil floated the hypothesis that by "we" Eusebius meant "we Christians," implying that Eusebius himself knew the *Rescript* only in Greek and felt obliged to acknowledge in some way that it would originally have been in Latin.[36] The manuscript of the *Apologies* has the same Greek text as Eusebius, and no Latin. Rufinus's translation of the *Ecclesiastical History* contains the text of the *Rescript* in Latin, naturally. There has been considerable discussion as to whether Rufinus gave the original Latin or simply translated Eusebius's Greek. The point has considerable bearing on the force and meaning of the letter, and hence on the question of its authenticity.

Paul Parvis and I propose that part of the letter, reprising the content of the letter of Granianus, has fallen out after 68.6, perhaps even before it came into Justin's hands, and that the particle οὖν ("therefore," "so") has reference to the missing text. In his letters to Pliny, Trajan frequently summarizes the letter to which he is replying, often reflecting the language of that letter. It is impossible to say exactly what the burden of Granianus's letter was. Trajan had told Pliny that anonymous *libelli* denouncing Christians were not to be acted upon. If Granianus knew of this *Rescript* and had received a *libellus* that was *not* anonymous, he might have sought clarification on a new point of administrative procedure. The demonstrative pronoun "this" before "petition" suggests either that it was referred to in the lacuna or, less probably, that it was attached to the emperor's *Rescript*. According to Birley,[37] the letter from Granianus must have arrived "during Hadrian's stay in Germany or Britain." This might partly explain the delayed reply.

I give below (1) the text of the rescript as Paul Parvis and I have edited it;[38] (2) Mommsen's edition of Rufinus's Latin, which is printed in Schwartz's edition of Eusebius's *Ecclesiastical History*; (3) Paul Parvis's translation into English of the Syriac version of the *Ecclesiastical History*; and (4) a retroversion attempted by Paul Parvis and myself. The object of this retroversion is not to approximate what Hadrian might have written, but to show that a vocabulary for it can be supplied from the correspondence between Trajan and Pliny to produce a letter altogether consistent with the chancellery style of Hadrian's predecessor, which says nothing particularly in favor of the Christians but simply tells the governor to get on with his job and not to allow his or the emperor's time to be wasted by petitions seeking action against Christians outside the existing and adequate procedures. Phrases discussed in detail below are underlined in all four versions.

1. Eusebius's Greek Text
Ἀδριανὸς Μινουκίῳ Φουνδανῷ.
Ἐπιστολὴν ἐδεξάμην γραφεῖσάν μοι ἀπὸ Σερηνίου Γρανιανοῦ, λαμπροτάτου ἀνδρός, ὅντινα σὺ διεδέξω. οὐ δοκεῖ οὖν μοι τὸ πρᾶγμα ἀζήτητον καταλιπεῖν, ἵνα μήτε οἱ ἄνθρωποι ταράττωνται καὶ τοῖς συκοφάνταις χώρα κακηγορίας παρασχεθῇ. ἂν οὖν σαφῶς εἰς ταύτην τὴν ἀξίωσιν οἱ ἐπαρχεῶται δύνωνται διϊσχυρίζεσθαι κατὰ τῶν Χριστιανῶν, ὡς καὶ πρὸ βήματος ἀποκρίνεσθαι, ἐπὶ τούτῳ μόνῳ τραπῶσιν, ἀλλ᾽ οὐκ ἀξιώσεσιν οὐδὲ μόναις βοαῖς· πολλῷ γὰρ μᾶλλον προσῆκεν, εἴ τις κατηγορεῖν βούλοιτο, τοῦτό σε διαγινώσκειν. εἴ τις οὖν κατηγορεῖ καὶ δείκνυσί τι παρὰ τοὺς νόμους πράττοντας, οὕτως διόριζε κατὰ τὴν δύναμιν τοῦ ἁμαρτήματος, ὡς μὰ τὸν Ἡρακλέα, εἴ τις συκοφαντίας χάριν τοῦτο προτείνοι, διαλάμβανε ὑπὲρ τῆς δεινότητος καὶ φρόντιζε ὅπως ἂν ἐκδικήσειας.

2. Rufinus's Latin Version[39]
Exemplum epistulae imperatoris Hadriani ad Minucium Fundanum proconsulem Asiae.
Accepi litteras ad me scriptas a decessore tuo Serennio Graniano clarissimo uiro et non placet mihi relationem silentio praeterire, ne et innoxii perturbentur et calumniatoribus latrocinandi tribuatur occasio. itaque si euidenter prouinciales huic petitioni suae adesse ualent aduersum christianos,

ut pro tribunali eos in aliquo arguant, hoc eis exequi non prohibeo. precibus autem in hoc solis et adclamationibus uti eis non permitto. etenim multo aequius est, si quis uolet accusare, te cognoscere de obiectis. si quis igitur accusat et probat aduersum leges quicquam agere memoratos homines, pro merito peccatorum etiam supplicia statues. illud mehercule magnopere curabis, ut si quis calumniae gratia quemquam horum postulauerit reum, in hunc pro sui nequitia suppliciis seuerioribus uindices.

3. The Syriac Version of Eusebius's *Historia Ecclesiastica*

I received a letter written to me from the most eminent Serenius Granianus, whom you succeeded. For it does not seem good to me to leave the matter unacknowledged lest the innocent be subject to vexation and accusers be provided with broad scope for wickedness. Clearly, then, with regard to this petition, should your provincials be able to be so resolute against the Christians, as even to answer before a tribunal, let them occupy themselves only with this, and not with petitions and with mere outcries. For it would be much more fitting, if someone wanted to make an accusation, that you should hear the case in court. If, then, someone should make accusation and prove people did something against the laws, make a determination according to the strength of the offence. But if, by Hercules, anyone should attempt this for the sake of opportunistic accusation, deal with it according to its gravity and take thought how you might punish it.

4. Retroversion

Minucio Fundano Hadrianus.

Litteras accepi scriptas mihi a Silvano Graniano, uiro clarissimo, cui /in quem[40] successisti. . . . non ergo res uidetur mihi inquisita relinquenda, ne homines perturbentur et delatoribus locus calumniae tribuatur. plane, igitur, erga hanc petitionem, prouinciales si aduersus christianos affirmare possunt ut etiam pro tribunali respondeant, in hoc solo uersentur/uertantur, sed non in petitionibus uel clamoribus tantum. multo enim magis oportet, si aliquis uelit deferre, te rem cognoscere. Si igitur aliquis defert et arguit quosdam contra leges fecisse/egisse, ita statue/constitue secundum uim culpae: sicut, mehercule/medius fidius, si quis propter calumniam hoc praetenderit, decerne pro grauitate et aestima/dispice/delibera quomodo puniendum sit.

The following considerations suggest that Rufinus's text is a translation of the Greek he found in the *Ecclesiastical History* rather than the original Latin, which it has been claimed he might have found either in a copy of Justin's *Apologies* or in Ulpian's treatise *De Proconsule*.[41]

i. Where Eusebius's Greek has "lest the people be subject to vexation" (ἵνα μήτε οἱ ἄνθρωποι ταράττωνται), Rufinus has "lest the innocent be subject to vexation" (*ne et innoxii perturbentur*). Lightfoot, believing that Rufinus's text was the original, proposed that Eusebius wrote ἄθῳοι and that this was corrupted to ἄνθρωποι.[42] This is not as paleographically plausible as might appear at first sight, since ἄνθρωποι would have been written as a *nomen sacrum*, ANOI Rufinus might have supposed that ἄθῳοι would give a better sense, but the word does not mean only "not deserving punishment," but also "not receiving punishment." Ἄνθρωποι must have stood in the Greek tradition of Eusebius at least as early as 463, the date of the earliest manuscript of the Syriac version. *Homines* is not infrequent in Trajan's correspondence with Pliny when there is reference to the people of the province, and at Pliny *Ep.* X.82 Trajan says that he had sought to acquire reverence for his name neither "from the fear and terror of the *people* nor from charges of treason" (*ex metu nec terrore hominum aut criminibus maiestatis*).

ii. Where Eusebius has "an abundance of evil doing" (χορηγία κακουργίας), Rufinus has "the opportunity for brigandage" (*latrocinandi . . . occasio*). The Syriac translation of Eusebius supports Rufinus's *occasio*, but this suggests that an original χώρα (*locus*) in Eusebius was corrupted to χορηγία.

Rufinus's *latrocinandi* is inexplicable as a translation of Eusebius's "evil doing." The Syriac has simply "evil." In a fragment of his petition to Marcus Aurelius, preserved by Eusebius at *H.E.* IV.26.5, Melito says, "For the shameless informers [συκοφάνται] and lovers of other men's goods are taking advantage [ἔχοντες ἀφορμήν] of the ordinances to commit open robbery [ληστεύουσι], by night and day plundering those who do no wrong [διαρπάζοντες τοὺς μηδὲν ἀδικοῦντας]."[43] Very shortly after this extract Eusebius quotes Melito referring, in the same work, to the *Rescript* of Hadrian to Minicius Fundanus (*H.E.* IV.26.10). If, as is possible,[44] Melito has been cannibalizing Justin's *Apology*, then Rufinus's *brigandage* must be correct. Eusebius may have accurately translated a reference to brigandage, giving rise to Rufinus's *latrocinandi*, and a later scribe of Eusebius, not understanding the reference, may have substituted the colorless "evil doing." But this would have to have been done between 403, the date of Rufinus's translation, and 463, the date of the earliest Syriac manuscript of Eusebius's *Ecclesiastical History*, which has here "occasion for evil." The coupling of delation with brigandage occurs in Pliny's *Panegyricus*, where, when speaking of Trajan's punishment of Domitian's delators, he says they were led in like a mass of robbers or brigands: "*Uidimus delatorum agmen inductum, quasi grassatorum quasi latronum.*" But the situation and status of delated Christians would hardly, in Hadrian's eyes, be comparable to that of Domitian's victims, and if the property of condemned Christians was forfeited, it would have been forfeited not to the delators, but to the fisc, as the technical term makes plain: "*damnatione bona publicantur.*"[45] Furthermore, when translating *H.E.* IV.26.5, Rufinus does not translate ληστεύω as *latrocinor*, but has "*more praedonum die noctuque grassantur et diripiunt innocentes,*" while at *H.E.* IV.26.6 he translates Melito's ἐν τοιαύτῃ δημώδει λεηλασίᾳ as "*publico latrocinio iugulari.*"

We suspect that Eusebius's text was corrupt even before it was translated into Syriac and that Rufinus made the best sense he could of a garbled text, perhaps looking ahead to the passages Eusebius excerpted from Melito. In our edition of the *Apologies*, Paul Parvis and I have emended κακουργίας ("evildoing") to κακηγορίας ("slander"), on the supposition that Eusebius read *delatoribus locus calumniae* ("opportunity of slander for accusers") and correctly rendered this in Greek, but that a scribe with ΧΟΡΑΚΑΚΗΓΟΡΙΑΣ before him mistakenly separated the words as ΧΟΡΑΚΑ ΚΗΓΟΡΙΑΣ, supposed that the first member should be ΧΟΡΗΓΙΑ, and being unable to make anything of ΚΗΓΟΡΙΑΣ changed it to ΚΑΚΟΥΡΓΙΑΣ. It is also possible that Eusebius's translation was slightly fuller, χώρα κακούργου κατηγορίας ("opportunity of slanderous accusation")—compare this with his introductory summary of the content of the letter at *Historia Ecclesiastica* IV.8.6, εὐλόγου κατηγορίας ("reasonable accusation")—and that a scribe lost his way in the confusing repetition of groups of letters.

iii. Where Eusebius has "with respect to this petition" (εἰς ταύτην τὴν ἀξίωσιν), Rufinus has "to support this petition of theirs" (*huic petitioni suae adesse*). It looks as though Rufinus has not understood how the Greek phrase fits into the sentence. We suspect that there is reference here to a specific petition of the provincials to Licinius Granianus, asking that Christians be punished, and that this petition was the occasion of his orginal letter to Hadrian. According to Eusebius's Greek text, Hadrian wanted nothing to do with petitions in this matter: "Let them occupy themselves with this . . . and not with petitions."

iv. Where Eusebius has "to answer" (ἀποκρίνασθαι), which looks like a translation of a form of *respondere*, Rufinus has "to prove them guilty" (*eos . . . arguant*). The Greek word, when used in a forensic context, normally refers to defending onself against a charge, though the subject of the verb in Eusebius's sentence must be the provincials who are bringing the charge. The Latin, meaning "to answer a summons, to appear, to present oneself (for duty, for example)," would as easily have the accusers as the accused for its subject. Rufinus has correctly translated Eusebius's Greek and supplied an object (*eos*) to make sense of it.

v. Where Eusebius has "let them occupy themselves only with this" (ἐπὶ τοῦτο μόνον τραπῶσιν), Rufinus has "I do not forbid them to pursue this" (*hoc eis exequi non prohibeo*). We suspect that underlying Eusebius's Greek text is an original Latin using the passive of *uerso* or *uerto* in the sense of "to busy oneself with" or "to be occupied with." It is possible that Rufinus felt it necessary to introduce the first person permission and prohibition because his correct translation of Eusebius's ἀποκρίνασθαι has left him perplexed about what the Greek means.

vi. Where Eusebius has "according to the strength of the offence" (κατὰ τὴν δύναμιν τοῦ ἁμαρτήματος), Rufinus has "according to the deserts of the offences" (*pro merito peccatorum*). Under *peccatum*, the *Oxford Latin Dictionary* cites only poets for the sense of "moral offence, misdemeanour, lapse."[46] It is therefore unlikely to have stood in Hadrian's letter, and Rufinus is translating Eusebius's Greek, which might have translated *culpa*. *Vim* might lie behind δύναμιν.

vii. Where Eusebius has "by Hercules" (ὡς μὰ τὸν Ἡρακλέα), Rufinus has "that, by Hercules" (*illud mehercule*). In Pliny *Ep.* X.38, Trajan uses the oath *medius fidius*, which Tertullian says is a form of taking an oath by Hercules (*De Idololatria* 20.5) If, as is possible, this was the oath used here by Hadrian, it would show that Rufinus's text cannot be the original.

viii. Where Eusebius has "should anyone attempt this" (εἴ τις . . . τοῦτο προτείνοι), Rufinus has "if anyone shall have arraigned any of these as guilty" (*si quis . . . quemquam horum postulauerit reum*). The Greek might translate a form of *praetendo*. Rufinus has expanded the Greek to give clearer sense.

ix. Where Eusebius has "according to its gravity" (ὑπὲρ τῆς δεινότητος), Rufinus has "with more severe punishments in accordance with his wickedness" (*pro sui nequitia suppliciis seuerioribus*). The Greek might translate *pro grauitate*. In the Vulgate of Luke 11:53, δεινῶς is represented by *grauiter*. Rufinus appears to have translated the Greek in two different ways.

III

Of our four questions we have now answered two. The *Rescript* is authentic, and Rufinus's text is a translation of Eusebius's Greek.

But the substantial questions remain. Did Justin insert it in his *Apology*, and if so, where? We consider that it was Justin who inserted it into the text of his *Apology*. The quotation of supporting documentation in a petition is well attested in Egyptian papyri,[47] and, so far from the *Rescript* being out of keeping with the tenor of the *Apology*, as Veil, for example, proposed,[48] it is perfectly plausible to see it as the goal toward which Justin had been heading since the beginning. Justin understands the *Rescript* to say that action should not be taken on the basis of public outcry where no wrongdoing can be established. That is what he asks for in his petition. Punish Christians if they can be shown to have done something deserving of punishment, but not when they are shown not only not to be evildoers (*1 Apol.* 7.1–4), but actually to be people of high virtue (*1 Apol.* 12ff.). We could ask for the punishment of those who delate us, as the *Rescript* provides, but we do not in fact ask for this (*1 Apol.* 7.5). What we ask for is no more than what emperors who are renowned for piety and philosophy should be willing to grant, just as it was granted by your very great and very renowned father.

It should be noted that on the occasion of the condemnation of Ptolemy, as recalled by Justin in the *Second Apology*, Lucius addressed the Urban Prefect, Urbicus, in terms that are very reminiscent of the central argument, the petition, and even the address of the *First Apology*, and that seem to take up the terms of the *Rescript* of Hadrian. He asks why Ptolemy should be condemned when he has not done any evil deed, and says that Urbicus's judgment does not befit a pious emperor or a philosophical Caesar, his son, or the Holy Senate. If these words of Lucius are pure invention on Justin's part and if the *Second Apology* did form a single continuous work with the first, then Justin has clumsily exposed his own fraud. For the punning references to the names of the rulers can hardly have been commonplaces among the Christians of Rome, and Justin will have told a tale about someone speaking in a manner reminiscent of what Justin had himself written earlier in the work. But if Justin does record the substance of what Lucius actually said to Urbicus, then we have to consider the possibility either that Justin constructed the *Apology* in dependence on Lucius's words—perhaps even that Lucius was a teacher of Justin—or that Lucius was familiar with Justin's *First Apology* and deployed it in his impromptu address to Urbicus. In the latter event, we may be close to the original genesis of our two *Apologies*. The *First* was provoked by the unjust delation of Christians who had done no wrong—quite possibly the action of the husband of the Christian convert. When, in the event, Ptolemy was prosecuted for Christianity, Lucius, having read the *First Apology*, reprised its argument in his speech to Urbicus. Faced with the widening threat to the Christians in Rome, Justin reissued his *Apology*, this time with an addendum, setting forth the occasion of its writing and, provoked by the recent hostile attentions of Crescens, adding arguments of a more philosophical flavor.

It is possible, then, that our *Second Apology* is indeed a later piece of writing, separate from but in some way dependent on the *First Apology*, so that Justin feels that he may make reference to the earlier work. The time between the composition of the two might have been very short indeed, perhaps as short as a few weeks, since events in Rome might have developed quite rapidly once the husband of the Christian convert brought charges against her.

Which of these two hypotheses is the more likely, in the truncated state of the *Second Apology*, lacking both a beginning and an end, we cannot be sure. But the second of them would seem to provide an economical explanation of all of the data.

Schmid remarked that the *Rescript* is well situated in its present location in the manuscript, that is, after *1 Apology* 68.2, and not well situated at the end of the *Second Apology*, where Veil supposed it had been tacked on at some time later than the second century.[49] Schmid, of course, thought it had been added at *1 Apology* 68.2 to provide a suitable conclusion to the new edition of the *Apology* issued after 180, and without the original ending of the *Apology*, that is, what we call the *Second Apology*.

In our edition of the *Apologies*, Paul Parvis and I will argue that the *Rescript* does belong where it is found in the manuscript, but that it was originally followed there immediately by the final two chapters of the *Second Apology*. We propose that when the scribe of the manuscript that shed the text of *2 Apology* 2.2–16 came to the Latin text of the *Rescript* of Hadrian, he decided to replace it with the Greek translation that he knew to have been provided by Eusebius and left a space for this in his manuscript, resuming the copying of the remainder of the *Apology*, that is, *2 Apology* 14–15, on a fresh leaf. At some point the original ending of the *Second Apology* became badly damaged. This is evident from the detached and clearly misplaced fragment numbered 15.1. We propose that a copyist sought to remedy this damage by transferring the single leaf containing the last two chapters of the *First Apology* to the end of the *Second Apology*. If he thought of what we call the two *Apologies* as a single work, the need for such a rounding off was all the more apparent. If he thought he was dealing with two separate works, he might easily have supposed (as Schmid was to do) that the *Rescript* of Hadrian itself provided a sufficient conclusion to the *First Apology*. The codicological and other arguments behind this cannot be gone into here in detail, but I draw your attention to how well those final chapters fit the context we propose as their original one.

The opening words of *2 Apology* 14.1, καὶ ὑμᾶς οὖν ἀξιοῦμεν ὑπογραψάντας, which do not connect with what precedes them in *2 Apology* 13, follow on very well immediately after the citation of the *Rescript*: "Therefore, we ask *you also* to subscribe. . . ." The posting up of the subscribed petition will help the detractors of Christianity from incurring the penalties of the *Rescript* for false accusation, because the petition rebuts those accusations and sets out the virtuous character of Christians. And, finally, the last sentence of the restored ending forms a neat inclusion with the opening of the *Apology*.

Part Two

JUSTIN AND HIS BIBLE

CHAPTER FOUR

Justin and His Bible

OSKAR SKARSAUNE

IN THIS ESSAY I WILL FOCUS on what light Justin might throw on the Christian Bible of his day. In saying "his" Bible, I mean the concrete Bible that Justin used, the Bible in front of him on his working desk as he was writing. I will focus on three topics: (1) What was the concrete, physical shape of Justin's Bible? Did he have access to the Bible in the shape of complete manuscripts of complete biblical books, or did he mainly have access to biblical texts through intermediary sources, containing shorter or longer excerpts of the biblical texts? (2) What text-type and which canon of biblical books are discernible in Justin? (3) Which hermeneutical guidelines did Justin follow when interpreting biblical texts? I will argue that the last question is intimately related to the first, and therefore the three questions will not be addressed neatly separated from each other.

By "Justin's Bible" I mean his Old Testament and his New Testament. Saying this is grossly anachronistic, of course. Both terms would have been unknown to him, and as far as the New Testament is concerned, he did not know the specific collection of books that later got that name. Or so we used to think.

Was the Later Christian Bible
Already Known to Justin?

David Trobisch has challenged traditional concepts with his fascinating thesis of the "final edition" of the Christian Old and New Testaments being published during the second century, after Marcion and in response to him, but before Irenaeus.[1] This would make the Christian two-testament Bible roughly contemporary with Justin. And the first literary attestation of the term "the books of the Old Covenant" does in fact come already in Melito,[2] only one or two decades after Justin. Melito's concept of the books of the Old Covenant could even be taken to imply the corresponding concept of the "books of the New Covenant,"[3] but this remains uncertain. The first unambiguous attestation of "Old Testament" and "New Testament" as names of the two parts of the Christian Bible occurs almost simultaneously in Clement of Alexandria[4] and Tertullian of Carthage.[5] Wolfram Kinzig has argued that Tertullian's use of the terms, which begins in his *Against Marcion*, was prompted by Marcion's use of these terms and that Marcion may have been their inventor (as titles for the Jewish Bible on the one hand and Marcion's gospel and *Apostolos* on the other).[6]

Trobisch, as far as I am aware, does not commit himself to any definite statement concerning Justin's relation to this "final edition" of the Christian Bible. This is a question to which I shall return in due course. Here I anticipate my conclusion by saying that it probably remains anachronistic to speak about his "New Testament" and also to speak about his "Old Testament," since this latter collection of books was probably not known to him by that name. He rather calls these books Scripture or the Scriptures, and quite often the books of the Prophets. I will return to this below.

What Did Justin's Bible Look Like?

At this preliminary stage I will be content to pick up two points from Trobisch that I think are valid even independently of his grand theory, and that others before him have made.

The first is that Justin very likely had access to the New Testament books not as isolated scrolls containing one book only, but rather in codex format, each codex containing one or several books.[7] Trobisch has shown that in the ancient New Testament codices, four groups of writings clearly stand forth, and each group is often united in one codex, sometimes two or three of the groups, and quite rarely all four. The four groups are (1) the four Gospels, (2) the letters of Paul (with Hebrews), (3) the book of Acts and the general epistles, and (4) Revelation. It is likely, but not absolutely certain, that Justin already had a complete four-Gospel codex at his disposal.[8]

Second, in another study, Trobisch has argued effectively for the view that Paul's letters quite early were collected and published as one codex, with the same internal order as in our present-day New Testaments, but with Hebrews included (though in different positions within the collection).[9] It is clear that Hebrews entered the collection at a later stage than the rest, though whether prior to or later than Justin is hard to tell. The relevant point here is that if Justin had Romans and Galatians on his desk while writing the *Dialogue*, as I am sure he did (see below), he would have had all of the Pauline letters available to him, possibly also Hebrews.

The fact that Justin's "New Testament" writings were available to him in codex format makes one curious with regard to whether Justin also had access to the Old Testament books in codex format or whether he shows clear signs of using single scrolls in this case. I shall return to this question in a moment.

But first I shall address another question that is of great consequence with regard to both testaments: Did Justin get to know the text of the biblical books mainly by reading the continuous text of complete biblical books, or were there also other literary media that served him as sources for biblical texts? I think the latter question is capable of a clear answer. I shall treat Justin's use of the Old Testament first, and since Justin's preferred word for the Old Testament writings is "Scripture"[10] or "the Scriptures,"[11] I shall use this word when referring to the Jewish Bible/Old Testament.[12]

Two Types of Sources for Scriptural Quotations in Justin

Let us begin with a case study, Justin's treatment of Genesis 49:10-11. There are several complete or partial quotations of these verses in Justin, but the two major expositions of this text occur in *1 Apology* 32 and *Dialogue* 52–54.[13]

1 Apol. 32.1: Gen. 49:10-11	*Dial.* 52.2: Gen. 49:8-12
Moses, the first of the Prophets, spoke literally in these words.	It was also foretold by the patriarch Jacob . . .
	[Vv. 8-9: Judah, your brothers have praised you . . .]
10. There shall not lack a ruler from Judah	10. There shall not lack a ruler from Judah
nor a leader from his loins	nor a leader from his loins
until He come for whom it is prepared.	until that come which is prepared for him.
And He shall be the expectation of the Gentiles,	And he shall be the expectation of the Gentiles.
11. tying his foal to the vine,	11. Tying his foal to the vine and the foal of the ass to the tendril of the vine,
washing his robe	He shall wash his robe in wine,
in the blood of the grape.[14]	and his garment in the blood of the grape.[15] [V. 12].

The following observations leap to the eye. In *Dialogue* 52, the quotation is vastly expanded to comprise the whole oracle about Judah, Genesis 49:8-12. This long quotation represents a rather standard Septuagint text, whereas the two verses quoted in *Apology* 32 exhibit several significant deviations from the LXX text. In the *Apology*, the prophecy is quoted as a prophecy by *Moses*, the first of the prophets. In *Dialogue* 52 Justin has the complete biblical text of Genesis before his eyes and correctly names *Jacob* as the speaker. In short, everything indicates that while Justin in the *Apology* quoted this prophecy from a source in which the quote occurred in isolation from its biblical context, this was not so in the *Dialogue*. When writing the *Dialogue*, Justin had a complete Genesis manuscript at his disposal.

In fact, Justin himself is quite explicit in saying that he knows two textual versions of this prophecy. In *Dialogue* 120.3–5 he has a brief discussion of the problem. His main point is that the authentic translation of the Seventy reads "until he come, for whom it is made ready" (the reading of Justin's short quotation in *1 Apology* 32), whereas the Jewish version of the text reads "until those things come that are made ready for him" (the reading of the LXX text quoted in *Dialogue* 52). Justin implies that in his dialogue with Trypho he has quoted the latter text, since in debates with Jews, he follows the principle of only quoting texts recognized as authentic by the Jewish scholars. In fact, Justin has similar remarks concerning textual differences between short non-LXX quotes and longer LXX quotes of the same texts in five other cases, always making the same point.[16] This demonstrates beyond any doubt that both versions of the quotes are authentic in Justin and not due to corrections by later scribes. It also demonstrates that Justin's short, non-LXX quotes are not free quotations from memory.

There is thus no reason to doubt that Justin knew scriptural texts in two versions, stemming from two sources. (1) In the *Apology* he very often takes his quotes from sources that were *not* manuscripts of entire biblical books.[17] They were Christian works containing biblical quotes separated from their biblical context. As I am going to argue below, these Christian works were not mere anthologies of selected prophecies: they also contained brief interpretations of the prophecies. As a technical term for proof-texts from the Scriptures, I shall use the word "testimonies," and as a general term for Justin's sources for such testimonies I shall use the term "testimony sources" (not "testimony collections," since I believe they contained more than mere quotes from Scripture). If asked what they looked like, I would suggest that the *Epistle of Barnabas* might give us an idea, or perhaps the *Kerygma of Peter*, fragments of which are preserved by Clement of Alexandria. I have argued elsewhere that the main testimony source used by Justin in the *First Apology* (chaps. 32–52) was a source similar to the *Kerygma*.[18] It presented the testimonies according to the pattern of the creedlike summary of the christological kerygma contained in *1 Apology* 31.7. The text in the scriptural quotes taken from this source is clearly based on the Septuagint but regularly deviates from it by being shortened and/or by conflating several quotes into one, or by significant interpolations into the text, interpolations of a Targum-like nature (more on this below). In the *Dialogue*, Justin insists that the text of these non-Septuagint quotations represents the true Septuagint as translated by the Seventy.

(2) In the *Dialogue*, written not more than ten years later than the *Apology*, we still see Justin using, on occasion, such short, non-LXX quotations as he normally offers in the *Apology*. But frequently Justin has turned from these short quotations and has located the quotations in biblical manuscripts, from which he quotes long excerpts, sometimes exceeding one whole chapter. Justin insists that this is a text-form tampered with by the Jews.[19] They have changed or deleted words from the text in order to make the texts less fit as messianic prophecies. I believe this claim makes most sense if we make two assumptions.

The first is that Justin only got hold of complete biblical scrolls that were produced by Jewish, not Christian, scribes. This is a likely assumption anyway. We have independent evidence that Christian production of copies of the Septuagint had barely begun around the middle of the second century.[20]

The second assumption is that Justin had some knowledge of Jewish activity in revising the Septuagint translation in his days. This is not at all unlikely. Barthélemy demonstrated in a famous article that Justin's quotations from the Twelve Prophets did in fact derive from a revised Septuagint text, revised by Jewish scribes so as to make it conform better to the Hebrew text—the so-called *kaige* recension.[21] If we assume that Justin had some knowledge of this fact, it makes his remarks on Jewish tampering with the text of the Seventy translators understandable. When discovering discrepancies between the text-type preserved in his Christian sources and the text-type he found in the Jewish scrolls of biblical books, he took the text of the latter to be the result of Jewish revision of the Septuagint.

Justin's Scriptural Manuscripts: Codices or Scrolls?

I have said a couple of times that Justin probably had access to complete manuscripts of biblical books in the form of scrolls, not codices. I have two reasons to believe so. The first is that Justin's biblical manuscripts likely were produced by Jewish scribes, and we know that Jewish scribes ordinarily used the scroll format for biblical books. The second reason is that one can sometimes observe Justin quoting in sequence different chapters from the same part of the biblical book in question.[22] With a codex you can easily look up passages from any part of any book; in a scroll this is quite cumbersome, and the sheer economy of work induces you to quote more from that part of the book at which you have the scroll opened.

Having made these observations, we are also in a position to make a reasonable guess as to which books of the Old Testament Justin had available to him in scrolls. Justin no doubt had a Genesis scroll, and he was well read in it.[23] He also had an Exodus scroll and was quite familiar with the exodus narrative as a whole. But he quotes directly from the LXX Exodus only once, in *Dialogue* 59–60 (with a doublet in *Dialogue* 126). He has one direct quotation from Leviticus (26:40-41 in *Dial.* 16:1); otherwise, this book was largely unknown to him. He also seems to have only one direct quotation from Numbers (11:23 in *Dial.* 126.6); otherwise, his allusions to and quotations from this book appear to be indirect through intermediary sources. There are several direct LXX quotations from Deuteronomy, showing that Justin had some familiarity with this book. But in all cases there are traditional, shorter testimonies behind Justin's long quotations. There is one direct quotation from the LXX book of Joshua, but no direct quotation from the rest of the historical books from Judges through 2 Kings.[24]

Justin's familiarity with the book of Isaiah competes with his knowledge of Genesis. But even here Justin relies heavily on traditional proof-texts. It is only on rare occasions that he ventures outside the traditional testimony dossier and picks up new proof-texts in this prophet, texts quoted by no one before him and no one after him until Origen.[25] He also, but only in four cases, quotes directly from the LXX Jeremiah;[26] otherwise, his quotations and allusions to this book come through intermediary sources. In all cases of allusions or quotations, Justin is safely within the traditional dossier of testimonies from this book. Much the same remark applies to Ezekiel; here only three apparently direct quotations are found, one of them so long it has to come from an Ezekiel scroll.[27] Justin can be shown to quote from the so-called *kaige* recension of the Twelve Prophets in seven cases,[28] and next to Isaiah this is the prophetic book from which he quotes and to which he alludes most often. The third book to compete with Genesis and Isaiah as Justin's greatest favorite among the biblical books is the book of Psalms. In most cases his many long LXX quotations from Psalms embody traditional proof-texts, but on one occasion Justin thrusts into previously unexploited textual territory. This happens in his continuous commentary on Psalm 22:1-23 in *Dialogue* 98–107 (on which more below). Of all the remaining biblical books, Justin only has long LXX quotations of Proverbs 8:21-36 (in *Dial.* 61.3–5 and the parallel in 129.3) and Daniel 7:9-28 (in *Dial.* 31.2–7, perhaps in a *kaige* version).

To conclude, Justin seems to have had permanent or occasional access to complete scrolls of the following biblical books: the historical books from Genesis through Joshua;[29] Isaiah, Jeremiah, Ezekiel, and the Twelve Prophets; and Psalms, Proverbs, and Daniel. But it is only the three books of Genesis, Isaiah, and Psalms that he uses frequently and from which he quotes extensively.

For the history of the LXX text in the second century, these long quotations in Justin are of considerable interest. One cannot exclude the possibility, of course, that one or more of the scribes transmitting the text (between Justin's autograph c. 160 C.E. and the single preserved manuscript of the *Dialogue* from 1363 C.E.)[30] consciously or unconsciously introduced later readings current in their own time into Justin's quotations. But this line of reasoning only serves to underline the great significance of archaic, prehexaplaric, and non-Byzantine readings in Justin's quotes. The systematic investigation of all Justin's LXX quotations from this point of view is still incomplete.[31]

Justin's Christian Testimony Sources

I have indicated already that Justin's Christian testimony sources were not mere anthologies of scriptural quotations—as has often been assumed, especially in different varieties of the "testimony book" or "testimony collection" hypothesis.[32] Wilhelm Bousset[33] and Helmut Koester[34] have shown convincingly that Justin's Christian sources for his short, non-LXX quotations contained more than the Scripture quotes. They also contained material of an interpretative nature, and these interpretations were accorded a very high authority by Justin. In fact, the text-form of these quotes, and the appended interpretations, shaped Justin's hermeneutics with regard to Scripture to a remarkable degree.[35] Let us take a closer look.

We turn once more to Justin's treatment of the prophecy in Genesis 49:10-11, but this time focusing on his interpretation. When comparing the two parallels in *1 Apology* 32 and *Dialogue* 52–54, one discovers that there is a common basic structure to these two interpretations and that this common groundwork includes short stories of what Jesus did to fulfill the prophecy in great detail. These stories contain a few non-Synoptic elements, and I believe Koester is right in concluding that Justin is following the same source in both cases, a source that contained not only the short quotation in *1 Apology* 32, but also the common elements in the *interpretations* given in the *Apology* and the *Dialogue*.[36]

It deserves notice how finely tuned the exegesis and the deviant readings in Justin's text are. Concerning the promise to Judah in the Hebrew text, "until comes *shilo*," the Septuagint presupposes the reading "until comes *shælo*," *shælo* being a contraction of *asher lo*, "that which belongs to him" or "that which is made ready for him," that is, made ready for Judah. On this reading, the verse is not overtly messianic. Justin's text, however, takes *shælo* in a different sense: "*he* to whom it belongs," *he* being the Messiah and *it* being the messianic kingdom. It is hardly by accident that this reading and interpretation of the text agrees fully with the one found in *Targum Onqelos*: "until the Messiah comes, whose is the kingdom."[37] The other finely tuned detail in Justin's exegesis is that Christ washes his *robe* (*ten stolen*) in *the blood of the grape*. But this is said only in Justin's deviant text, not in the Septuagint, where the *stole* is washed in wine, whereas it is the *garment* (*ten peribolen*) that is washed in the blood of the grape (a clear case of synonym parallelism, eliminated by contraction in Justin's deviant text).

The case studied here is typical of Justin's procedure in the *Dialogue* whenever he brings long quotations from the Septuagint. In the great majority of cases, he has no comment at all concerning those parts of these quotes that exceed the shorter quotations contained in the *Apology* and elsewhere in the *Dialogue*.[38] In other words, the transition from short quotes unrelated to their biblical context to long quotes taken directly from complete biblical manuscripts has not led to a change in hermeneutical approach. Justin is still out to demonstrate the correspondence between specific phrases of prophecy and their realization in the career of Jesus.

If we take a closer look at the text-form of the biblical quotes in Justin's Christian sources, the following observations are in place. The way many of Justin's short quotations handle the biblical text may perhaps best be described as Greek "targumizing" of the standard Septuagint text.[39] As a rule, the biblical text is subject to three types of modifications.

1. The text may be *condensed*. Two sayings referring to the same fact in poetic synonym parallelism may be condensed into one saying.[40] The intention behind these changes seems to be to make the prophecy more precise, so to speak—in order to facilitate a simple one-to-one correspondence between the supposed prophecy and its fulfillment. We find basically the same tendency in the Synoptic fulfillment reports that were also present in Justin's Christian sources. The Synoptic accounts are simplified and cut down to those essentials that have a direct function in the demonstration of the close correspondence between prophecy and fulfillment. Justin's own hermeneutical approach was heavily influenced by this tendency of his sources.
2. The text may be *expanded* by interpretative interpolations and additions, as is often the case in the rabbinic Targumim. The most well-known case is verse 10a

in Psalm 96. In the complete scroll of the Psalms at Justin's disposal, the verse read like this:

> Say among the Gentiles, "The Lord has reigned."
> For he has established the world, which shall not be moved;
> he will judge the people with justice.[41]

In the *Apology*, however, Justin quotes an excerpt of the same text according to a completely different version. It is not really Psalm 96 at all, but is based on the inner-biblical parallel in 1 Chronicles 16:23-31. In this text the corresponding phrases read, "Let them rejoice among the Gentiles, saying, 'The Lord has reigned *from the tree*'" (*1 Apol.* 41.4). Here the verse is made to speak of the message of the cross being received with greater joy among the Gentiles than among the Jews—a favorite theme in Justin's source.

It is interesting to observe that this Christian interpolation did not find its way into the text of Psalm 96 as found in the LXX codices written by Christian scribes.[42] This holds true for other variant readings in Justin as well. In spite of his insistence that these variant readings represented the true LXX, later Christian scribes did not bow to such judgments but copied the "Jewish" text of their manuscripts quite faithfully.

3. Phrases from different verses may be *combined* into one single quote, mostly based on the principle of common themes or catchwords. Once more we may use Justin's quote of Genesis 49:10-11 as an example. In the *Targum Onqelos*, this was one of two texts in the Torah that was given a messianic interpretation, the other being Numbers 24:17. The latter text immediately follows Genesis 49:10-11 in *1 Apology* 32, but in a modified version in which phrases from Isaiah have been added so as to assimilate the structure of the two main messianic prophecies of the Torah:

Genesis 49:10	
(a) There shall not lack a ruler from Judah	A Star shall rise out of Jacob (Num. 24:17)
nor a leader from his loins	and a flower shall spring from the root of Jesse (Isa. 11:1)
until He come for whom it is prepared.	
(b) And He shall be the expectation of the Gentiles.	and in his arm shall the Gentiles trust (Isa. 51:5).[43]

A similar catenation of phrases from different scriptural verses into one text is contained in Romans and in the Dead Sea Scrolls[44] and is a typically Jewish way of handling the text of Scripture.

Through these observations concerning Justin's sources, we get glimpses of an early Christian work with the Scriptures, interpreting them as messianic prophecy and using very Jewish techniques in doing so. The great familiarity with Scripture and the consequent freedom in handling its text are presuppositions for this procedure that are no longer present in Justin. For him, the discrepancies between these free, targumizing quotes on the one hand[45] and the full Septuagint text of the biblical manuscripts on the other represent a hermeneutical problem, not a hermeneutical resource. In this way Justin's works throw light not only on his own procedure in working with the text of Scripture, but also on the approach of other Christian writers before him and at variance with his own.

Original Exegesis in Justin

I have said that Justin rarely went outside the traditional dossier of testimonies in his interpretations of scriptural texts. There are two notable exceptions to this, and they call for further comment. The two exceptions are (1) Justin's commentary on Psalm 22:1-23 in *Dialogue* 97–107 and (2) his treatment of the scriptural theophanies in *Dialogue* 56–60.

1. For Justin, Psalm 22 contained three important scriptural prophecies, all related to the passion story, verses 1, 7-8, and 16-18. It was these three traditional testimonies that provided Justin with his hermeneutical approach to the whole psalm. Concerning those verses of the psalm where tradition gave him no guidance, Justin tried to find correspondences between sayings in the psalm and events in the passion stories of the Gospels, in analogy with the three traditional testimonies:

1b-2:	Prayer in Gethsemane (*Dial.* 99.2–3);
6:	Jesus despised at his passion (*Dial.* 101.2);
11-13:	Jesus surrounded and without help at his arrest (*Dial.* 103.1–4);
15:	Jesus silent before Pilate (*Dial.* 102.5, repeated in 103.9);
15b-16a:	Death of Jesus (*Dial.* 104.1–2);
20:	Death on a cross (*Dial.* 105.2, with excursus on the fate of souls after death, *Dial.* 105.4–6);
20-21:	Jesus' prayer in death (*Dial.* 105.3);
22:	Jesus resurrected (*Dial.* 106.1–2).

    But Justin was not able to apply each and every phrase of the psalm to the story of the passion. Accordingly, he had to go to other parts of the Jesus story, and he does so on several occasions:

4-5:	Jesus recognized the fathers of the people of Israel as his fathers and set his hope on God alone (*Dial.* 101.1–2);
9b:	Jesus was saved from Herod's murder of the children of Bethlehem (*Dial.* 102.1–2, with excursus on free will in 102.3–4);
10b-11a:	Jesus put his hope on God alone, not on his own wisdom or the like (*Dial.* 102.6).

The total impression left by this commentary is that Justin has tried to extend the hermeneutics implied in the traditional technique of isolating prophetical oracles so as to interpret a whole text according to this model. One can hardly avoid noticing that Justin's pioneering attempt clearly shows the limitations of this hermeneutical model. Justin would have few if any successors in this art until Origen began writing complete commentaries to biblical and New Testament books, but from a completely different hermeneutical perspective.

2. In *Dialogue* 56–57 Justin brings an extensive quote of Genesis 18:1—19:28. In the present text, it is actually not brought *in extenso*: only the first three verses are quoted, followed by "and so on, down to," after which the two last verses are quoted. This way of shortening a very long quotation is unlike Justin and probably due to a later scribe who found it unnecessary to bring the whole quote.[46] The reason Justin brings this long text into play at all is a single verse, hidden within the large omission in the present text, namely, Genesis 19:24, "The Lord rained upon Sodom brimstone and fire from the Lord out of heaven." This verse is important to Justin because he regards it as incontrovertible proof that Scripture knows two Lords, in this case one Lord on earth speaking with Abraham, and one other Lord in heaven raining fire and brimstone on Sodom. These two Lords are the Son and the Father, and Justin can sometimes combine this verse with other verses of Scripture in which similar doublets occur, as for example in Psalm 45:7-8 and Psalm 110:1 (*Dial.* 56.12–15; 127.5). In the tractate *Sanhedrin* of the Babylonian Talmud there is an interesting passage concerned with scriptural verses describing acts of God with the verb in the plural. These verses are said to have been exploited by certain *minim* as arguments for a plurality in the Godhead. The climax of the passage is the following discussion:

> A *min* once said to Rabbi Ishmael ben Jose [c. 180 C.E.]: "It is written, 'Then the Lord caused to rain upon Sodom and Gomorrah brimstone and fire from the Lord' [Gen. 19:24]; but 'from him' should have been written!" A certain fuller said, "Leave him to me, I will answer him: It is written, 'And Lamech said to his wives, Ada and Zillah, hear my voice, ye wives of Lamech' [Gen. 4:23]; but he should have said 'my wives'! But such is the scriptural idiom—so here too, it is the scriptural idiom." "Whence do you know that?" asked he [Rabbi Ishmael].—"I heard it in a public discourse of Rabbi Meir." (*b. Sanh.* 38b)[47]

Here the phrase from Genesis 19:24 is discussed in the same isolation from its context as is the case with Psalms 45:7-8 and 110:1 in Justin. And if one looks more closely at Justin's extensive argument in *Dialogue* 56–57, it seems almost tailor-made to refute the interpretation advocated by Rabbi Meir in the Talmudic passage. Justin establishes, starting from the beginning of Genesis 18, that one of the three men visiting Abraham was called both Lord and God, and that this Lord and God was identical with the Lord with whom Abraham negotiated about the fate of Sodom, but not identical with the Lord in heaven from whom fire and brimstone came down. The whole extensive discussion of details in two consecutive chapters of the Genesis text has the one and only purpose of bolstering a christological interpretation of one phrase in Genesis 19:24. But there is no doubt that this need to support a traditional argument with new underpinnings from the context led Justin to one of his most innovative exegetical exercises. In fact, it made him go beyond the traditional proof-text altogether and develop an entirely new hermeneutical concept, namely, that the biblical theophanies should be understood to be appearances not of the Father, but of the *Logos*, his Son. Here the traditional proof-text approach was insufficient; Justin has to relate to larger blocks of narrative material in Genesis and Exodus. There is a noticeable anti-Marcion twist to this section of the *Dialogue*, and it may well be that Justin has here inserted ready-made material from his lost *Syntagma* against Marcion.[48] In any case, it is clear, also from the Wisdom texts quoted in *Dialogue* 61–62, that Justin is here developing points made in a testimony source that had another character than the "kerygma source" he followed in *1 Apology* 32–52. The source that Justin employed in *Dialogue* 56–62[49] was not primarily interested in the fulfillment of messianic prophecies during the career of Jesus, but focused instead on his divine nature and pretemporal birth from the Father. I have elsewhere suggested that this could be the *Controversy between Jason and Papiscus* written by Aristo of Pella.[50]

Justin's Canon of Scripture

As Justin himself makes plain, his Christian sources could quote as Scripture passages that Justin could not find in the biblical books to which he had access. Justin concludes that Jewish scribes must have cut these passages out when they copied the relevant biblical books. The most instructive passages concerning this are found in *Dialogue* 71–73 and 120.5. Here Justin accuses the Jewish scribes of having deleted one passage from the book of Ezra, two from Jeremiah, one from David (i.e., the Psalms), and one from Isaiah. He quotes or paraphrases the allegedly deleted passages, which have in common that they appear as prophecies of Christ's passion, one of which comes from a well-known apocryphon, the *Martyrdom of Isaiah*. This makes it likely that also the other quoted passages come from scriptural pseudepigrapha, now lost. In other words, Justin's Christian sources could sometimes quote and use scriptural material that was not directly quoted from Scripture, but rather came from midrashic embellishments of the scriptural stories, as exemplified by some of the pseudepigraphic works of the centuries around the beginning of our era. In the *Testimonia* of the Dead Sea Scrolls, a reference to the *Songs of Joshua* is treated as Scripture on a par with a quote from canonical Joshua,[51] and the same could well be the case in Justin's sources. But Justin's own concept of canon and Scripture is much stricter. He therefore cannot imagine anything else than that these passages must have been part of the authentic text of the biblical books of Ezra, Jeremiah, David (the Psalms), and Isaiah. It is in these books and none other that he has searched for these passages and not found them. He is completely unaware of the possibility that these passages could derive from other books than those represented in the scrolls of canonical Ezra, Jeremiah, Psalms, and Isaiah. Again we observe a characteristic difference between Justin and his Christian predecessors whose work is visible in his sources. In his debates with Jews, he was leaning more than he liked on the Jewish texts and much more than he knew on the Jewish canon. Since he would only base his argument on texts and complete books recognized as canonical and authentic by the Jews, he really had no choice.

This fact concerning Justin's text and canon of Scripture is an early instance of a phenomenon to be observed all through the patristic period: when it comes to questions of text and canon, the ongoing dialogue with Judaism was perhaps the one most important factor in making the church not finally abandon the Jewish canon and text of the Bible.[52]

Justin and the New Testament Writings[53]

I will begin this part of my essay by asking the same question I raised with regard to Justin's access to the Scriptures: Did he know the New Testament texts only in their later canonical shape, or did he also have access to other types of literary transmission of the same material? This question is of relevance first and foremost with regard to material of the Gospel type: words of Jesus and stories about him.

I will argue that Justin's access to the Gospels was direct and indirect. He sometimes quoted directly from manuscripts of the Gospels or made allusions to one of the Gospels in such a way that it is possible to say which Gospel he was alluding to. In other cases he seems to quote Gospel material from Christian sources other than the Gospels.

Generally speaking, he does the latter most often in the *Apology*, while direct recourse to the full text of specific Gospels is more frequent in the *Dialogue*. In this way, Justin's use of New Testament material in the *Apology* and *Dialogue* is seen to be strikingly parallel to his use of the Jewish Bible in the two works. In both cases there is a move from intermediary sources in the *Apology* toward more direct use of the primary sources themselves in the *Dialogue*. Let me illustrate this with a few case studies.

1. In *1 Apology* 15–17, Justin offers his Roman readers a catechism-like compendium of the ethical teaching of Jesus, his *didachē*. Arthur J. Bellinzoni[54] has studied this catechism in great detail and makes a good case for the view that it was not composed ad hoc by Justin himself when writing the *Apology*.[55] It rather seems as if Justin is using a written source, composed by himself earlier or, perhaps even more likely, by someone else, and still available to and used by later fathers such as Clement of Alexandria, Origen, the author of the Pseudo-Clementine *Homilies*, and others as well. This catechism is clearly based on the Matthean Sermon on the Mount but abbreviates the Matthean text and har-

monizes its sayings with parallels elsewhere in Matthew or with the Synoptic parallels in Mark and Luke.[56]

On more than one occasion one observes that when Justin in the *Dialogue* quotes the same sayings of Jesus as were contained in the harmonistic source used in *1 Apology* 15–17, he turns directly to the canonical versions of those same sayings, as found in Matthew (or Luke). In the *Dialogue* he also adds other sayings of Jesus, obviously taken directly from Matthew. In these cases Justin is an early witness to the text of Matthew, and it is interesting to observe that his text of Matthew already exhibits some of the harmonistic features that later were to become typical of the "Western" text.[57]

It is also interesting to observe that Justin nowhere exhibits the same pedantic concern with different readings in this case that he does concerning important biblical proof-texts. I will return to a consideration of the reasons for this below.

2. Another type of Gospel material is contained in some of the fulfillment reports attached to the biblical prophecies in *1 Apology* 31–52. Since the latter were contained in Christian sources, there is every reason to think the fulfillment reports were also contained in the same sources.[58]

This may be demonstrated in the case study of Genesis 49:10-11 that we made above. In the *Apology*, Genesis 49:11 and Zechariah 9:9 both occur in condensed versions, eliminating the synthetic parallelism between the ass and its foal, present in both texts.[59] There is thus only one animal in both of the prophetic texts, and this is true also in Justin's fulfillment reports in *1 Apology* 32.5 and 35.10:

> For *a foal of an ass* stood *tied to a vine* at the entrance to a village,
> and he ordered his disciples to lead it to him,
> and when this was done, he mounted and sat upon it, and entered
> Jerusalem. . . .

> [I]t was foretold that he was to enter Jerusalem sitting upon *the foal of an ass.*

These fulfillment reports are tailor-made so as to match the respective prophecies perfectly: one animal, a foal of an ass, and this one animal was *tied to a vine*, a non-Synoptic feature taken from Genesis 49:11, "tying his foal to the vine." The fulfillment report is obviously based on the story of Jesus' entry according to the Synoptic Gospels, but the story is condensed and modified and focused upon providing a detailed correspondence with the two prophecies of Genesis 49:11 and Zechariah 9:9, these latter also condensed and modified.

We have seen already that when we turn to the treatment of the same two prophecies in the *Dialogue*, Justin has substituted for his condensed non-LXX biblical quotes good LXX texts taken directly from the primary sources, complete biblical manuscripts of the respective books. But this requires him to do some adjustments to the fulfillment reports as well, because in both texts there is a synonym parallelism mentioning two animals, an ass and its foal. One would expect that Justin would feel a need to turn from his one-animal-only fulfillment reports and go directly to canonical Matthew, which has a story of two animals. And this is, in fact, exactly what Justin seems to have done. After quoting the full LXX version of Genesis 49:11 in *Dialogue* 53.1, mentioning "the foal" and "the foal of an ass," Justin goes on to report the fulfilment of the prophecy as follows:

> [O]ur Lord Jesus Christ, when he was about to enter Jerusalem,
> ordered his disciples to get him *an ass with its foal,*
> being tied at the entrance of the village of *Beth[s]phage,*
> and he rode upon [it/them] as he entered Jerusalem. (*Dial.* 53.2)

As noted by Koester, Justin is obviously dependent here, once more, on the modified version of the Synoptic story he used in the *Apology.*[60] But he has modified it according to canonical Matthew:

> When they had come near Jerusalem and had reached *Bethphage* . . .
> Jesus sent two disciples, saying to them:
> "Go into the village ahead of you,
> and immediately you will find *an ass tied, and a foal with her,*
> untie them and bring them to me." . . .
> They brought *the ass and the foal* . . . and he sat on them. (Matt. 21:1-7)

The phenomenon observed here, Justin having direct recourse to the canonical Gospels in the *Dialogue* in cases where he only used the noncanonical fulfillment reports in the *Apology,* is most clearly and most extensively to be observed in his commentary on Psalm 22 in *Dialogue* 97–107. The reason for this is obvious. In this commentary Justin ventured outside the traditional dossiers of prophetical proof-texts, since the majority of verses in the psalm had never been part of this dossier. And for these verses Justin himself had to provide the appropriate fulfillment stories *directly from the canonical Gospels.* It is therefore hardly by accident that in the entire *Dialogue,* it is only in this section, the commentary on Psalm 22, that he repeatedly refers explicitly to the Gospels under the title *Memoirs of the Apostles.* In other words, he is not only working directly with the full LXX text of Psalm 22 here; he is also working directly with the canonical Gospels, a fact that he emphasizes by, in all, thirteen explicit references to them in this part of the *Dialogue,* and in this part only.[61]

Having established this point, I will comment only briefly on the character of the noncanonical sources for Gospel material in Justin. As we have seen, they come in basically two varieties.

First, we have collections of *logia* of Jesus, apparently composed for catechetical purposes. They look like compendia of the *didachē* of Jesus, that which Jesus told his disciples to teach all the nations according to Matthew 28:20. The text of these compendia was to a large extent based on the Matthean Sermon on the Mount but also exhibits distinct features of a harmonization process, toward a kind of average Synoptic text. Nowhere is direct recourse to any precanonical material evident—for example, direct use of Q material. What we have is postcanonical harmonization, not use of precanonical sources. Nothing indicates that we have to do with anything like a full-fledged Gospel harmony like Tatian's *Diatessaron*. At best, Justin's compendium or compendia are small beginnings of that ambitious project.

Second, we have the fulfillment reports, showing how prophecies were fulfilled to the letter in different episodes of the Gospel story. In this case also we can observe a harmonistic tendency, only this time the harmonization takes place between the wording of biblical prophecies and Gospel story. The report of the fulfillment gets words from the prophecy inserted into it. In these cases, too, it seems we are facing postcanonical modifications of Gospel material, but with possible influence in some cases from noncanonical Gospels of the second century (*Gospel of Peter?*[62] *Gospel of the Ebionites?*[63]). Among the canonical Gospels, Matthew is most frequently recognized as the main source but is often harmonized with Luke.

Since it is almost an established dogma of scholarship that John does not make an appearance in Justin,[64] I would like to point out that echoes of John are in fact to be seen in some of Justin's fulfillment reports. Let me substantiate this by two case studies.

1. In *1 Apology* 35.5–8 Justin quotes Psalm 22:16b/18b in a condensed version: "They have pierced my hands and my feet, and have cast lots for my garment." He then goes on to explain that the first phrase "refers to the nails which transfixed his hands and feet on the cross." This detail about the *nails* in Jesus' *hands* (but not feet) is only mentioned in John 20:25. Next, Justin explains how the second phrase came true: "After he was crucified, they cast lots for his garment (*himatismon*, singular), and [in this way?] his crucifiers divided it among themselves." The interesting thing here is that none of the Synoptic Gospels explicitly quotes Psalm 22:18b as a prophecy. They merely weave its wording into their own account: "When they had crucified him, they divided his clothes (*ta himatia*, plural) among themselves by casting lots (about the clothes, what each should have)" (Matt. 27:35/Mark 15:24, parenthesis only in Mark). John is the only Gospel to quote the whole verse of Psalm 22:18 as a prophecy fulfilled, to the letter, by what the soldiers actually did. The full text of the psalm has two phrases in synonym parallelism: "They divided my clothes among themselves, and for my garment they cast lots" (John 19:24b). Both phrases were realized according to John 19:23, 24a. (a) The soldiers divided *ta himatia* (plural) into four parts, thus fulfilling the first phrase. (b) But the *himatismon* (singular) for which they cast lots is taken to be the tunic of Jesus, which they would not tear apart. Accordingly, the casting of lots became necessary for this one piece of clothing. This focus on the second phrase of the psalm verse, the casting of lots with regard to the singular *himatismon*, is preserved in Justin's shortened Psalms quote as well as in his fulfillment report. Justin's source is at this point closer to John than to any of the Synoptics.

2. In *1 Apology* 52.10–12 Justin brings an expanded, non-LXX version of Zechariah 12:10-12. Within this long quotation he pays especial attention to the phrase "they shall look upon the one *whom they pierced*" (*exekentēsan*, a non-LXX reading), as is shown by his repeated allusions to this particular phrase in *Dialogue* 14.8, 32.2, 64.7, 118.1. This prophecy does not appear in any of the Synoptics but is given a prominent position in the passion story of John as one of three explicit fulfillment quotations. The soldier pierced Jesus' side so that the prophecy should come true: "They will look on the one whom they have pierced (*exekentēsan*)" (John 19:34-37).

I find it fair to conclude that in Justin's sources for the proof-from-prophecy argument, material from John's passion story was used as a source for important prophecies as well as for fulfillment reports—less frequently than Matthew, but comparably to the use of Luke and Mark in the same sources.

In the first part of this essay, I argued that Justin's exegetical and hermeneutical approach to the complete text of biblical books or passages was decisively influenced by his nonbiblical Christian sources and the biblical quotations contained in them. By way of analogy, I will argue that his approach to the complete Gospels, and even to the other main component of the New Testament collection, Paul's epistles, was also decisively influenced by the intermediary, postcanonical sources we have seen used by him. I shall develop this point somewhat by focusing on Justin's concept of what an apostle is and what an apostle does. Briefly stated, I think his concept of an apostle was decisively shaped by the two kinds of Gospel material contained in his postcanonical sources.

Justin's Concept of an Apostle

According to Justin, an apostle does two things: (1) he transmits and puts into writing what he *remembers* about Jesus—what he said and did; and (2) he reveals how the whole story about Jesus was predicted in the prophecies of Scripture. This apostolic proof from prophecy also goes back to Jesus himself. After his resurrection, Jesus himself opened the Scriptures to his disciples. In their writings they transmit this opening of the Scriptures.

> After his crucifixion, all his close followers deserted his cause and even denied him. Afterwards, when he arose from the dead, and appeared to them, and taught them to read the prophecies in which all the above happenings were predicted as about to take place, and after they had seen him ascending into heaven, and had believed, and had received the power he thence sent them, they went forth to every nation to teach these things, and they were called Apostles. (*1 Apol.* 50.12)

> Now, if the prophets foretold cryptically that Christ would suffer first and then be Lord of all, it was still practically impossible for anyone to grasp the

full meaning of such prophecies, until Christ himself convinced his Apostles
that such things were explicitly proclaimed in the Scriptures. (*Dial.* 76.6)

There are more passages like these in Justin, and they all contain a remarkably
fixed and stable picture of the commission of the apostles. They were "twelve illiterate
men, unskilled in the art of speaking" (*1 Apol.* 39.3). Having had the prophecies
explained to them by the risen Christ (*1 Apol.* 50.12, 67.7; *Dial.* 76.6, 106.1), the twelve
apostles went *out from Jerusalem* proclaiming God's *word* (*1 Apol.* 39.3, 45.5, 53.3), in
fulfillment of Isaiah 2:3b (= Mic. 4:2b: "For out of Zion the law shall go forth, and *out
of Jerusalem* the *word* of the Lord," *1 Apol.* 39.3; *Dial.* 109.1, 110.2). The twelve apostles went to every nation under heaven (*1 Apol.* 39.3, 42.4, 45.5, 50.12, 53.3; *Dial.* 42.1);
they "(1) preached about Christ and (2) gave the Gentiles the prophecies" (*1 Apol.*
49.5). On hearing the message of the apostles, the Gentiles were freed from the power
of demons and were filled with joy (*1 Apol.* 42.4, 49.5, 53.3; *Dial.* 41.1, 109–10, 114.4,
119.6). Through the powerful message of his apostles, the enthroned Christ reigns
(*1 Apol.* 42.4, 45.5; *Dial.* 42.1, 109–10). I need hardly point out that this portrait of the
apostles and their mission looks very much like a synthesis of Luke 24, Acts 1–2, and
Matthew 28.

It is worthwhile pointing out, however, that this picture of the apostles is also very
close to that portrayed in the *Kerygma of Peter* (c. 125 C.E.), fragments of which are preserved in Clement of Alexandria.[65] In the *Kerygma* we find the following relevant
elements:

1. Christ is identified with the *Law* and *Word* (going out from Jerusalem according to Isa. 2:3b) (frag. 1).
2. Christ chose twelve apostles and sent them, after his resurrection, "into the
   world to proclaim to men in all the world the joyous message that they may
   know that there is one God, and to reveal what future happenings there would
   be through belief in [Christ]" (frag. 4). He enjoined the apostles first to preach
   to Israel for twelve years (presumably in Jerusalem), then go out to the Gentiles
   (frag. 3).
3. The apostles "opened the books of the prophets . . . which partly in parables,
   partly in enigmas, partly with certainty and in clear words name Christ Jesus,
   and found his coming, his death, his crucifixion and all the rest of the tortures
   which the Jews inflicted on him, his resurrection and his assumption to heaven
   . . . how all was written that he had to suffer and what would be after him." Recognizing this, the apostles "believed God in consequence of what is written of
   [Christ]." The apostles therefore "say nothing apart from Scripture" (frag. 6).

The *Kerygma of Peter* demonstrates that in portraying the apostles the way he
does, Justin was not alone and not the first. If we use the terminology of Robinson and
Koester,[66] we could perhaps say that what we face here is a Lukan trajectory in early
Christianity, at least as far as the concept of the apostles is concerned.

This concept of the apostles is also of great significance to Justin's understanding
of himself as an exegete and a teacher. Basically, he is doing the same as the apostles,

but only as their disciple and successor. Because all later Christians have been taught the meaning of the Scriptures by the apostles, Justin can claim that Christians have their understanding of the Scriptures directly from Christ. The Christian proof from prophecy derives from Christ's own expositions of the Scriptures to the apostles after his resurrection. "[Christ] revealed, then, to us by his grace all that we have understood from the Scriptures" (*Dial.* 100.2). "[Christ] appeared to the Apostles and taught them to read the prophecies . . . and they went forth to every nation to teach these things" (*1 Apol.* 50.12). When summing up what he has presented in his *Apology*, Justin says that on Sunday Christ "appeared to his Apostles and disciples, and taught them the things *which we have passed on to you also* for your consideration" (*1 Apol.* 67.7). In the *Apology* as well as in the *Dialogue*, Justin presents himself as passing on an exposition of the prophecies of Scripture that is not his own, but something received from Christ himself through the mediation of the apostles.[67]

Having outlined Justin's concept of the apostles, let us see what consequences this would have for his way of reading the New Testament writings. Basically, he would look for two things in these writings, the two things the apostolic authors were supposed to do. He would look for their remembrances of what Jesus taught and did. And he would look for their teaching on how the prophecies of Scripture were fulfilled in the ministry of Jesus. Among the Gospels, Matthew's would be the one that answered Justin's requirements in the most complete way. Matthew had the most comprehensive and continuous catechism-like compositions of the teaching of Jesus. And it had the most explicit references to which prophecies were fulfilled throughout the career of Jesus. As an apostle, Matthew was the most "complete" among the Gospel writers.[68] But even Matthew was rather short on explicit exegesis and exposition of prophecies, and I suspect this is the reason Justin relied heavily on one or more noncanonical sources in which the teaching of the apostles, and especially their exposition of the Scriptures, was presented more broadly. I have argued elsewhere that at least one of Justin's sources for Scripture quotations and interpretations of them was, if not identical with the *Kerygma of Peter*, then at least quite similar to it.[69]

But the other canonical Gospel with explicit fulfillment quotations was John, and this once again raises the question whether Justin himself had direct access to John and used it as a source for apostolic exposition of Scripture. I have argued above that such was the case in the fulfillment reports in Justin's postcanonical sources, but what about Justin himself?

As I have said already, Justin is more independent of the exegetical tradition in his commentary on Psalm 22 in *Dialogue* 97–107 than he is anywhere else. Here he goes directly to the Gospels, called *Memoirs of the Apostles*, to find how Christ fulfilled different sayings in the psalm. Does Justin ever go to John for such material? I believe he does.

In *Dialogue* 105.1 Justin has the following summary of what the *Memoirs* say about Christ:

He is the Only-begotten [*monogenēs*, John 1:14, 18; 3:16, 18] of the Father of the universe, having been properly begotten from him [*ex autou gegennē-*

menos, patristic reading of John 1:13] as his Word [*logos*, John 1:1, 14] and Power, and afterwards becoming man [*anthrōpos genomenos*; John 1:14, *sarx egeneto*] through the Virgin [Matthew and Luke], as we have learned from the *Memoirs* of the Apostles.[70]

But Justin's concept of an apostle would also predetermine how he approached the Pauline epistles. In them little was to be found concerning Jesus' words, and only summary reports on the Jesus story, except for Paul's extensive rendering of the eucharistic words of Jesus. On the other hand, Paul could compete with Matthew in the fullness of his scriptural quotes and his exposition of them. And this is how Justin reads and uses Paul: therefore his use of Romans and Galatians is far more extensive than his use of any other Pauline letter. I shall look a little more closely into Justin's use of the Gospels and Paul from this perspective.

Justin and the Gospels

Justin has two names for the Gospels, and both occur in one passage in the *Apology*:

> The Apostles in the *Memoirs* produced by them, which are called *Gospels*,[71] have handed down what Jesus ordered them to do; that he took bread and, after giving thanks, said: "Do this in remembrance of me; this is my body." In like manner, he took also the chalice, gave thanks, and said: "This is my blood"; and to them only did he give it. (*1 Apol.* 66.3)

Apart from this passage, the name "Gospel" occurs in two other passages:

> *Dial.* 10.2 (Trypho): But the precepts in your so-called *Gospel*[72] are so marvellous and great that I don't think anyone could possibly keep them. For I took the trouble to consult them.

> *Dial.* 100.1: Not only in the blessing of Joseph and Judah have things been predicted in a mysterious manner of him, but also in the *Gospel* it is written that he said, "All things have been delivered to me by my Father; and no one knows the Father except the Son; nor does anyone know the Son except the Father, and those to whom the Son will reveal him" (Matt 11:27).[73]

Obviously, "Gospel" is the Christian name for these documents. In *1 Apology* 66.3 Justin implies that they are called Gospels among Christians; in *Dialogue* 10.2 Trypho uses the Christian name when he refers to them as the "so-called Gospels," that is, as they are called among Christians.

The other name is probably Justin's own, and one has reason to think that he chose it with great circumspection. *Apomnēmoneumata*, "Remembrances" or "Memoirs," was a genre of its own, and by association connected with one man in particular, Socrates. Xenophon's *Memoirs* of Socrates were known to Justin; he renders a passage from the book in *2 Apology* 11.3–5 (*Mem.* 2.1.21–33) and has two more allusions to it.[74] In both of the *Apologies* Justin compares Christ with Socrates.[75] Socrates was wise through his partial participation in the *Logos*; Jesus was the whole *Logos* incarnate. The wisdom of Socrates was not written down by himself, but by faithful disciples who, like Xenophon, faithfully *remembered* the teaching of their master. Jesus did not write anything, but his faithful disciples, the apostles, faithfully *remembered* and *wrote down* what he said, what he did, and what happened to him. In the *Apology* Justin has prepared his readers for the name *Memoirs* by what he says in *1 Apology* 33.5. Having quoted freely from Luke 1:31-32 and Matthew 1:21, Justin continues, "This was taught by *those who remembered* [*hoi apomnēmoneusantes*] everything concerning our savior Jesus Christ, and we have believed them, because the Prophetic Spirit, through Isaiah whom I mentioned earlier, foretold that these events would happen." In the *Dialogue* he also prepares his readers for the name *Memoirs of the Apostles* by saying that when Jesus emerged from the waters of the Jordan, "the Apostles of this our Christ *wrote* that the Holy Spirit alighted upon him in the form of a dove" (*Dial.* 88.3—this and the former quote my own translations).[76]

In addition to this genre model of *Memoirs* provided by Xenophon's well-known work, there are good reasons to assume that Justin was also prompted into calling the Gospels *Memoirs* by one Christian predecessor, namely, Papias. As Richard Heard pointed out in a well-known article,[77] Justin's word-field in talking about the *Memoirs* has full coverage in Papias. According to the latter, *Mark* had *followed* Peter and had *written* what he *remembered* Peter to have *taught* about the *words* and the *deeds* of Christ. Matthew, on the other hand, being an apostle himself, had *put together* (*synetaxato*) the *words* of the Lord.[78] Justin says the apostles themselves[79] or *their followers* (*hoi ekeinois parakolouthēsantes*, *Dial.* 103.8) *put together*[80] or *wrote* what they *remembered* (*apomnēmoneusantes*)[81] the Lord to have *said*[82] or *taught*[83] or *done*.[84] Quite specifically, Justin seems to echo Papias quite closely in the way he introduces his only specific reference to Mark in *Dialogue* 106.3: "We learn from his [Peter's] *Memoirs* that he [Christ] changed the name of one of the Apostles to Peter, besides having changed the names of the two brothers, the sons of Zebedee, to that of Boanerges, which means 'sons of thunder.'" Calling Mark *Peter's Memoirs* is a clear echo of Papias on Mark: *Mark*, Peter's *follower*, *wrote* what Peter [or Mark, listening to Peter][85] *remembered*. And the quote following his meticulous phrase "the Apostles or their followers" in *Dialogue* 103.8 is from Luke (22:44), which indicates that for Justin, Luke was Paul's follower, an idea very likely contained in Papias.[86] In short, Justin's different sayings about the *Memoirs* are most easily explained on the assumption that he already knew the concept of four Gospels, two of which had direct apostolic authorship (Matthew and John) and two of which were written by followers of the apostles: Mark by Peter's follower and Luke by Paul's.[87]

If so, why is Justin not more forthcoming in spelling out these ideas in order to underpin the authority of the documents from which he is quoting? In the *Apology* as well as in the *Dialogue*, Justin is arguing with people for whom the Gospels were in no way authoritative, nor could they be made authoritative by explicit reference to their authors, since these would also not be authorities in their capacity as apostles. Neither Gentiles nor Jews would recognize the Gospels as any more authoritative by the fact that they were written by so-called apostles.[88] Justin counters this by implying that the Gospel accounts are historically reliable in the ordinary way of such accounts. The Gospels were written by Jesus' disciples or their successors, who faithfully and reliably *remembered* what Jesus had said and done. There is nothing more to it, and nothing more is needed. Justin evidently sees considerable argumentative value in the fact that these *Memoirs* were *put into writing* at an early stage, by Jesus' closest disciples, the apostles, or by their immediate followers. We therefore do not have to rely on oral tradition only, transmitted through a large number of intermediary transmitters.[89]

This, I think, explains how Justin relates to the Gospels and how he uses them. They contain the *teaching* of Jesus, and their reliability in this case is guaranteed by the faithful *remembering* of Jesus' words by his disciples. The exact *wording* of their different renderings of his words is not the issue; the wordings may—and do in fact— vary. What matters is the content of Jesus' words, for "they have in themselves such tremendous majesty that they can instill fear into those who have wandered from the path of righteousness, whereas they ever remain a great solace to those who heed them" (*Dial.* 8.2).

The Gospels also contain *stories* about what Jesus did and what was done to him. As with the *logia* of Jesus, the exact wording of these stories is of minor concern to Justin. He is not handling sacrosanct texts here, in which even details in the wording are important, as is the case with exact biblical prophecies. In the case of the *Memoirs*, it is the event itself that matters. It is the *event* that fulfills the text of the prophecy, not a new text.[90] Variations in wording among the Synoptics have not bothered Justin at all. In his many quotations and allusions to the Synoptic Gospels, one can observe the beginning of the harmonization process that was later continued in the Gospel man- uscript tradition itself, although to a lesser degree here than in the widespread trans- mission of Gospel material outside the complete manuscripts.

This also explains why there is never in Justin a detailed interpretation of any New Testament text. There is nothing similar in this case to the detailed exposition he offers of scriptural quotes. The prophecies need exposition; with the stories of fulfillment it is enough simply to recount what happened.

Within Justin's economy of argument, two entities mutually legitimize each other. *The biblical prophecies* are shown to be divinely inspired by the fact that what they pre- dicted in advance actually happened. *The events in the career of Jesus* are shown to hap- pen according to a divine purpose by the very fact that they were predicted several hundred years in advance. Again I call to mind what Justin said in *1 Apology* 33.5: "This was taught by those who remembered everything concerning our savior Jesus Christ, and we have believed them, *because* the Prophetic Spirit, through Isaiah whom I mentioned earlier, foretold that these events would happen."

Having said all this, I would like to add, though, that in Justin's quite emphatic references to the *Memoirs*, especially in the *Dialogue*, there is an incipient recognition of these written records as having a special authority, simply by being written by the disciples closest to Jesus, his apostles and their followers. Writing to an audience of fellow Christians, and without any constraints of fictional settings, Justin might well have emphasized this point quite clearly.

Justin and Paul

I think Justin's concept of an apostle explains not only his approach to the Gospels. I think it also explains his use of Paul. There is no reason to doubt that Justin made extensive use of Paul's letters, especially Romans and Galatians.[91] The reason he preferred these two letters is obvious: it was here more than anywhere else he found Paul engaged in extensive and detailed interpretation of scriptural texts. In these letters Paul has many quotations and many expositions of the texts he quotes, and Justin can be shown to have borrowed many of Paul's quotations directly from him, as well as some of Paul's expositions.[92]

In Romans and Galatians, Paul is at work on one of the prominent apostolic tasks: he presents and interprets the prophecies. It is interesting to see how Justin's approach to Paul radically differs from that of modern exegetes. Many modern exegetes are fascinated by Paul the theologian, Paul the thinker, but only moderately interested in Paul the interpreter of the Scriptures. With Justin it is quite the opposite. What he looks for, and finds, in Paul are important scriptural quotations and guidance as to the meaning of these texts.

Would Justin have considered Paul an apostle? It is hard to tell. He sometimes speaks about the apostles being *twelve* with such emphasis that there appears no room for an apostle number thirteen.[93] And Paul did not pass on the teaching of Jesus, nor tell stories about him, in the same way the apostles supposedly did in their *Memoirs*. But Paul was a gifted interpreter of the Old Testament, and Justin must certainly have noticed that Paul presented himself as the apostle to the Gentiles, and with much emphasis, in his letters. I suspect that Justin, had he pronounced anything on the question, would have evinced much the same ambiguity as Luke does in Acts and as many second-century authors do after Luke. The twelve-apostles model soon became very dominant, and it tended to exclude Paul, especially when it also was developed in the direction of making the twelve apostles evangelize the entire world of the Gentiles.[94] At the same time, Paul held the position he had claimed for himself as an apostle, even in some of the same writings that extolled the Twelve. Apparently, this was a tension that many early Christian authors found they could live with, and very likely Justin was among them.

One final point concerning this issue. When Justin seems to have Mark and Luke in mind when he speaks of *Memoirs* written by the followers of the apostles, he would probably have thought of Luke as Paul's follower, thus indirectly characterizing Paul as an apostle.

One question concerning Justin and the Pauline corpus of letters[95] is hard to decide: Did his corpus of Paul's letters contain Hebrews? It is reasonably certain that

Justin knew Hebrews, and there are some allusions to it in his works, bordering on unrecognized quotes.[96] But this does not decide the question. One could perhaps see an indication in the fact that Justin's use of Hebrews often occurs near quotes from Romans and other Pauline material, but this can also be explained from the themes treated in those passages. So I am inclined to leave the question open.

Justin's Use of the Other New Testament Writings

As far as the rest of the New Testament writings are concerned, the only thing we can state with certainty is that Justin knew John's Revelation (*Dial.* 81.4): "[A] man among us named John, one of Christ's apostles, received a revelation and foretold that the followers of Christ would dwell in Jerusalem for a thousand years, and that afterwards the universal and . . . everlasting resurrection and judgement would take place." But this is the only certain reference to Revelation in Justin.[97] In his chiliastic doctrine Justin is quite independent of Revelation.[98]

Justin also seems to be strikingly independent of the scriptural proof in Acts, although some of the main ideas of Acts are familiar to him, and there is hardly any reason to doubt that he knew Acts.[99] As for the remaining writings, James may be echoed once in Justin,[100] 1 Peter possibly on three occasions, none of them certain.[101] To 1 John there is only one possible allusion in Justin, far from certain.[102]

Concluding Remarks

In conclusion, picking up where I began, it seems to me that Justin is to be placed before, not after, the grand edition of the Christian Bible postulated by Trobisch. His Jewish Scriptures lay assembled before him not as one or several codices, but as separate scrolls, written by Jewish, not Christian scribes. In his reading of these books, Justin was heavily indebted to a prior encounter with the Jewish Scriptures through selected testimonies quoted and interpreted in Christian books: the Gospels, Paul, one or more tracts similar to the *Kerygma of Peter*, perhaps Aristo of Pella's *Controversy between Jason and Papiscus*. With regard to the Jewish Scriptures, the exact wording of the prophecies is important to Justin, and different readings in the scrolls and in the Christian sources represent a major problem for him.

Among the books that were later assembled as the New Testament, it is first the Gospels and second the Pauline letters that Justin quotes from and makes extensive use of. Very likely he had these books before him in codex format. We have seen that his use of these documents is consonant with his concept of what it means to be an apostle and that this concept was apparently presented to him in one or more of his postcanonical sources for Gospel material, and in addition by Luke, in the Gospel and in Acts. The text of these books is not sacrosanct and invariable in the same way as with the prophetic books, but it carries the authority of the Lord and his apostles.

A prophet's words have authority because he is *inspired*, by the Holy Spirit of prophecy, to predict events hundreds of years before they happen. The apostles have authority because their reports on the fulfillment of these prophecies are *reliable*. They tell truthfully what happened and what Jesus taught. They faithfully passed on to the church how Jesus himself interpreted the prophecies and applied them to himself.

In Justin there is not yet a canonical text of the New Testament books, not even the Gospels. And there is not yet any clear delimitation of exactly which documents should be considered authoritative above others, once we are outside the category of *Memoirs* or Gospels. On the other hand, Justin has an incipient canon in the way he refers to the Gospels, exactly as *Memoirs*, and he has a kind of implicit canon in the decisive role he accords to the apostles. In many ways Justin is a threshold figure. He writes after Marcion and before Irenaeus, and the more I ponder Justin's works, the more it strikes me to what extent he anticipated and prepared what came to full fruition in his successor Irenaeus.

CHAPTER FIVE

Justin and Israelite Prophecy

Bruce Chilton

Introduction

Justin's account in his *Dialogue with Trypho* (3–8) of how he converted to Christianity sets out a model of conversion whose pivot is the prophetic literature of Israel. What Justin goes on to say in the *Dialogue*, together with his earlier treatment of the prophets in his *Apology*,[1] permits the reader to see how Justin understands this model to function. This approach takes Justin's narrative in its context as exemplary, rather than raising historical issues in regard to the circumstances of Justin's personal conversion.

Considerable attention has been accorded the identity of the *palaios tis presbutes* (3.1) who spoke with Justin during a conversation that occasioned his conversion. Typically, he is called "the Old Man" in English translation, although Justin's language at this point emphasizes the antiquity and the traditional wisdom of his interlocutor more than the English phrase does. Oskar Skarsaune has described him as a "Christian Socrates," a designation that will serve well, provided the limits of the statement are observed, as well as its positive comparison.

Skarsaune specifies the limits of comparison with Socrates:[2]

> On one point Justin the Platonist and the Old Man agree: true knowledge of God only comes through direct encounter with God. As we have seen already, Justin in the *Apologies* hints that Socrates himself had only a partial and incomplete knowledge of God or His Logos, and he therefore was content with exhorting others to *seek* the Unknown God. At this point the Old Man, the Christian Socrates of the *Dialogue*, goes one significant step further: The Old Testament prophets really had such a direct and complete knowledge of God that they could impart it to others without any inhibition.

The sage convinced Justin that the highest good that Platonism can attain, the human soul, should not be confused with God himself, since the soul depends upon God for life (*Dial.* 6). Knowledge of God depends rather upon the revelation of God's Spirit (*Dial.* 7). Here is a self-conscious Christianity, which proclaims itself the true and only adequate philosophy. Justin's account of the truth of the *Logos* depends upon two sources of revelation, resonant with one another: the prophetic Scriptures that attest the Spirit and the wise reader who has been inspired by the Spirit.[3]

To this extent, it would complement Skarsaune's approach to balance the characterization of a Christian Socrates with that of a Platonic Moses or Isaiah. After all, what merits faith in the prophets according to Justin's interlocutor is not only their words, but also their "powers" (*dunameis*; *Dial.* 7), a consequence of their direct apprehension of divine truth. In any case, the identity of the *presbutes*—the "Old Man"—within Justin's presentation appears less important than what the *presbutes* points to: the prophetic Scriptures of Israel that speak to all who believe in them "much knowledge of the beginning and end of things, and all else a philosopher ought to know."

Skarsaune has devoted a monograph to this issue, assessing the text-type as well as the usage of Scripture in Justin.[4] Following Dominic Barthélemy,[5] he characterizes Justin's text as a rendering that corresponds to its Hebrew antecedent more formally than the Septuagint, in this regard appearing closer to the *kaige* translation (named after the combination of terms representing *gam* in Hebrew) unearthed at Nachal Chever, Murabba'at, and Qumran Cave 4. This leads Skarsaune to suggest that Justin used a source of "testimonies"—that is, proof-texts—used for purposes of evangelism with a "Jewish Christian" environment that exerted a powerful influence on "the 'mainstream' theology of the second century."[6] Skarsaune then goes on to suggest that Justin's account of the origin of his translation in the *Apology* is the introduction of this testimony source.[7]

Justin's description of this translation departs from the description of the Septuagint's origins in the *Letter of Aristeas*, insisting that precise copies of the Hebrew Bible, going back to originals five thousand years earlier in some cases, were sent to Alexandria and translated under the aegis of Herod (*1 Apol.* 31.1–8). This account corresponds to a degree with Barthélemy's suggestion, but two cautions are in order, both of which are consonant with Skarsaune's contribution. First, establishing text-types of the Septuagint has proven parlous. In the case of Justin, he agrees sometimes with the *kaige* recension, sometimes with the Septuagint (in its wide diversity of witnesses), sometimes with the way Paul cites the Scriptures of Israel in Greek, and in fact varies from one citation to the next. These observations militate against the finding of a single text-type, as Judith Lieu has commented.[8]

Similar considerations suggest that the model of a fixed source of "testimonies" for apologetic purposes can become too restrictive. Influenced by the identification of catena fragments, especially from the Byzantine period, Rendell Harris attempted to explain the origins of the Gospels in those terms,[9] but subsequent discussion has not confirmed the existence of a first-century source of testimonies as he suggested. The second century has proven no more productive for the hypothesis. It appears, rather, that Justin spoke within the terms of reference of a *tradition*, a way of conceiving of the significance of the prophets of Israel in respect of a stable of favorite passages as expressed in preferred recensions, rather than a fixed set of scriptural proof-texts. Justin, arguing on the basis of this tradition, insists that the prophets, beginning with Moses and including David, (1) attested Christ, (2) inspired the best of Greek philosophy, (3) forecast the transfer of the prophetic Spirit from Israel to Christians, and (4) agreed that the divine *Logos* lies at the core of human cognition of God.

Each of these four assertions might be instanced in many citations from the *Apology* and the *Dialogue*. In aggregate they have been well established in previous studies, to which references will be made as we proceed. The purpose here is less to argue that these themes are Justin's—which has already been demonstrated—than to assess them, and then to observe that at each of these points, Justin puts himself into a philosophical argument with the Judaism *of his time*, that is, as reflected in the Mishnah and some Targumim rather than later rabbinic literature, on the basis of patterns of thought for the most part already traditional within Christianity.

1. That the Prophets, Beginning with Moses and Including David, Attested Christ

Justin sets his *Dialogue with Trypho, A Jew* in the period after the revolt under Simon called Bar Kokhba (*Dial.* 1.3), which lasted between 132 and 135. Thematically, Justin disputes Trypho's conception of the permanent obligation of the law (chaps. 1–47) and sees the purpose of the Scriptures in their witness to Christ's divinity (chaps. 48–108), which justifies and indeed requires the extension of the divine covenant to Gentiles (chaps. 109–36). Trypho, that is, is portrayed as arguing in agreement with the axiom of the Mishnah that the systemic meaning of the Scriptures is the law, while Justin argues that their systemic meaning is Christ.

Justin spells out the structure of the prophetic tradition beginning with Moses more precisely in his *Apology* (32.1), insisting that "all we affirm to have learned from Christ and the prophets who preceded him is only truth" (23.1). He invokes Moses as the "first prophet," citing Genesis 49:10-11, Jacob's prophecy that the scepter would not depart from Judah (*1 Apol.* 32.1). By treating Moses in this way, as the author of *Jacob's* blessing and the agent of the prophetic Spirit (cf. *1 Apol.* 44), Justin can proceed through the prophets (Isaiah, above all) to speak of their reference to Christ and then culminate in the testimony of David—as both prophet and king—within the Psalms (*1 Apol.* 40.1).

These extensive citations over a long run of chapters systematize the claim of the risen Jesus among the disciples in Luke 24:44 (cf. v. 27) that "everything written about me in the law of Moses, the prophets, and the psalms must be fulfilled." A setting of communal instruction and worship, akin to the meetings of Christian worship as Justin briefly describes them (*1 Apol.* 67.3), at which the apostles' memoirs or the writings of the prophets were read and studied is the likely point of origin of Justin's christological tradition of reading the Scriptures.

In concluding her penetrating reading of the *Dialogue*, Tessa Rajak suggests "It is perhaps not wholly far-fetched to suggest that the *Dialogue with Trypho*, though presented as an apologetic dialogue, is less a discussion than a Christian *pesher* on Isaiah and the other prophets."[10] Rajak is appropriately tentative in making this suggestion, because the *Dialogue* does not comport with the genre of *pesher* ("interpretation") in providing a continuous commentary on Isaiah or any other prophet. But a similar technique is instanced in episodic exegeses of Scripture also discovered at Qumran.

In a recent study of the usage of Scripture attributed to James in Acts 15, namely, Amos 9:11, it has been pointed out that an analogy to the episodic usage of that passage by James is offered by the texts of Qumran designated florilegia by the editors. In one citation (in 4Q174 3:10-13), the image of the restoration of the encampment of David is associated with the promise to David in 2 Samuel 7:13-14 and with the Davidic "branch" (cf. Isa. 11:1-10), all taken in a messianic sense.

Given the expectation of a son of David as messianic king within early Judaism (see *Psalms of Solomon* 17:21-43), the messianic application of the passage in Amos, whether in 4Q174 3:10-13 or by James in Acts 15, is hardly strange. On the other hand, it is striking that the passage in Amos—particularly the "fallen hut of David"—is applied in the *Damascus Document* (CD 7:15-17), not to a messianic figure, but to the law that is restored. Clearly, neither Trypho nor the rabbis innovated the insistence that the prophets attested the Mosaic law.

Indeed, the book of Amos itself makes Judah's contempt for the Torah a pivotal issue (Amos 2:4) and calls for a program of seeking the Lord and his ways (Amos 5:6-15), so it is perhaps not surprising that "the seeker of the law" is predicted to restore it in the *Damascus Document*. Still, CD 7:15-20 directly refers to the "books of the Torah" as the "huts of the king," interpreted by means of the "fallen hut of David." Evidently, there is a precise correspondence between the strength of the Messiah and the establishment of the Torah, as is further suggested by the association with the seeker of the law *not only* in the *Damascus Document*, but also in the Florilegium. This kind of interpretation, although pursued to different ends, by means of briefer citations, and without a framing argument such as Justin's, offers a useful analogy to the treatment of Scripture in the *Dialogue* as well as in the *Apology*.

The Essene interpretation and Justin evidently go their separate ways when it concerns the Torah. By insisting upon Moses' role as a prophet, indeed the first prophet, Justin contends with the portrait of Moses that animated rabbinic literature from the second century onward, where Moses appears preeminently as the giver of the Torah, both in writing and in the oral tradition of the sages. Justin does not engage rabbinic literature in any detail (even as interpreted in the *Mekilta*, the only second-century midrash) and sometimes makes apparent errors in what he takes to be the practice of Judaism in his time. Yet he does know that he is confronting a Jewish *paradosis*—tradition—unlike his own, and he warns Trypho away from it (*Dial.* 38.2, 120.5) while maintaining his own ground within a setting of traditional learning (*2 Apol.* 10.1–2).[11] The particular passage that Justin uses to make his case is quite striking, because rabbinic interpretation in its most popular form during the second century—as represented in the Targumim, designed for usage within synagogues—also understood Genesis 49:10-11 as a messianic prophecy.[12]

2. That the Prophets Inspired the Best of Greek Philosophy

In taking Moses as a prophetic figure, of course, Justin aligns himself with the portrait of Philo, and that alignment bears fruit. Like Philo (*De aeternitate mundi* 17-19), Justin believes that Plato imitated Genesis in the *Timaeus* (*1 Apol.* 59–60).[13] His statement of the analysis is actually more aggressive than Philo's (44.9): "Whatever both the philosophers and poets said concerning the immortality of the soul or punishments after death or about perception of things heavenly or similar doctrines they were able to understand and explain because they borrowed the essential features from the Prophets." This perspective is by no means limited to cosmological issues but specifically includes ethics (44.8): "So when Plato said, 'The responsibility of choice is for him who makes it, God is not responsible,' he took it from the prophet Moses." The paucity of explicit reference to Philo in Justin has troubled some commentators,[14] but it should be kept in mind that Justin is sometimes least explicit when he is most influenced by other literary sources. He paraphrases the satire against those who make idols (*1 Apol.* 9), for example, without citing its source in Isaiah 44 or its repetition in Acts 17. Justin explicitly writes as a philosopher[15] and for that reason absorbs literary influences more than he cites them. Citation is not routine; Scripture is specified when there is a matter of doubt or Justin believes the scriptural meaning is deeper than a literary motif.

Justin famously portrays Socrates as executed for his opposition to idols (*1 Apol.* 5.3–4), so close is the fit between the prophets and Greek sages. To Justin's mind, a rejection of *eidolothuta*—food sacrificed to idols—remains a constitutive feature of faith in Jesus (*Dial.* 35), as was the case of James's teaching according to Acts 15:19-21.[16] That agreement with the Apostolic Decree is striking, because Justin goes very much his own way as compared to James when it comes to circumcision.

The comparison between Philo and Justin shows the extent to which Judaism in the first century and Christianity in the second century relied upon the revival of Platonism to provide them with a way of expressing how their respective religions were philosophically the most appropriate. The Platonic picture of perfect intellectual models was their common axiom, invoked in Philo's rhythmic, elegant Greek and in Justin's controversial, rhetorical Greek. One can easily imagine a debate between Philo and Justin. Had it occurred, that would have been an encounter between Judaism and Christianity in antiquity on philosophical terrain that they both claimed and with which both were comfortable. Had they met and disputed, Judaism and Christianity would have been represented as approximate equals, and on a level playing field.

But that meeting never happened. What divided what were by then two different religions[17] was not only one hundred years, but watershed events. The temple in Jerusalem had been burned under Titus in 70 C.E. and taken apart by Hadrian's order in 135. Judaism was still tolerated in a way Christianity was not, but it was now under suspicion, the remnant of a destroyed nation that had rebelled, and it needed to reconstitute itself as a postnational and postcultic religion in the wake of the failed revolts against Rome that resulted in the double destruction of the temple. The rabbis who invented a new form of Judaism during the second century did so not on the basis of Platonism, but on the grounds of a fresh intellectual contention. They held that the categories of purity established in their oral teaching, as well as in Scripture, were the very structures according to which God created and conducted the world. Mishnah, the principal work of the rabbis, is less a book of law (which it is commonly mistaken for) than a science of the purity[18] that God's humanity—that is, Israel—is to observe.

So complete was the rabbinic commitment to systematic purity at the expense of Platonism that Philo's own work was not preserved within Judaism but only became known as a result of the work of Christian copyists. And the very philosophical idiom that the rabbis turned from as a matter of survival, apologetic argument, was what Justin turned to, also as a matter of survival.

3. That the Prophets Forecast the Transfer of the Prophetic Spirit from Israel to Christians

In his recent study of the *'Aqedat Yitschaq*, Edward Kessler has characterized Justin as illustrating "a pervasive patristic supersessionist teaching, which is known as the doctrine of replacement theology."[19] The basis of this teaching, however, as Kessler clearly indicates, is not a claim about the standing of one community in relation to another, but an analysis of prophecy. As Justin says (*Dial.* 29.2; see also 32.2):

> For these words have neither been prepared by me, nor ornamented by human art; but David sang them, Isaiah evangelized them, Zechariah proclaimed them, and Moses wrote them. Are you acquainted with them, Trypho? They are contained in your scriptures, or rather not yours, but ours. For we are persuaded by them; but you, though you read them, do not recognize the mind that is in them.

At its theological foundation, Justin's "supercessionism" is no greater than Paul's, who offered an analysis of the obscured reading of Scripture among Jews (2 Cor. 3:12-18)[20] that has clearly influenced Justin here as much as Paul's teaching of the "mind" of Christ (1 Cor. 2:16).

In his *Dialogue*, Justin portrays Trypho as being limited to the immediate reference of Scripture, enslaved by its specification of laws. Justin, on the other hand, is committed to a typological reading of Scripture, the Christian norm during the second century. He understood the prophets to have presented "types" of Christ, impressions on their minds of the heavenly reality, God's own Son, in their writings. Trypho, by contrast, is portrayed as becoming lost in the immediate minutiae of the prophetic text. So prevalent was this understanding of Judaism that by the end of the century, Christians such as Clement of Alexandria and Tertullian called any limitation to the immediate reference of Scripture (its "literal meaning") the "Jewish sense."

Justin presents the shift in the possession of the Spirit that animates the Scripture, moreover, in a way Paul does not. While Paul famously still hopes that "all Israel will be saved" (Rom. 11:26), Justin is categorical—by means of Isaiah 51:4 and Jeremiah 31:31—that "there is to be an ultimate Law and Covenant superior to all, which now must be kept by all people who claim God's inheritance" (*Dial.* 11.2–3). This eternal covenant (Isa. 55:3-4) establishes who is a true, spiritual Israelite *and* Judaite, and who is not (*Dial.* 11.5), taking the place of all other aspirants to those names. As Philippe Bobichon has said, "the logic is no longer one of fulfillment (as in the New Testament), but of substitution."[21] Bobichon makes plain that supersession and replacement are not one and the same. The way in which Justin makes the transition from one to the other is instructive and prepares the way for yet another move.

The periodization of prophecy is the key to Justin's position in this regard. In taking this position, I take a different view from those who attempt to explain Justin on the basis of a periodization of Scripture. Philippe Bobichon attempts such a reading, arguing that "For Justin the relationship between 'eternal' precepts (intended for all humanity) and precepts of the Law (restricted to Israel) is inclusive. They stem from the same God and serve the same salvific purpose."[22] That "inclusive" reading is accurate, it seems to me, but its generative term of reference is "the prophetic Spirit" in Justin, rather than being determined by the nature of particular texts or a specific view of salvation history.

Bobichon's reading represents a simplification of the argument of Theodore Stylianopoulos, who argues that Justin divides Scripture into "(1) ethics, (2) prophecy, and (3) historical dispensation."[23] Treating Scripture as conditional indeed permits Justin to get out of the force of Trypho's observation that Jesus kept the law (*Dial.* 67.5–6), but that is because the whole of Scripture is prophetic: any part of it might prove to be binding or to be conditional in the light of what attests to Christ. For that reason, a "ritual" requirement—such as avoiding *eidolothuta*—might remain crucial, while an "ethical" requirement—such as leaving part of a field unharvested for the benefit of the poor (which receives treatment in an entire tractate of the Mishnah)—might receive no emphasis.

Basic to Justin's view of prophecy are the Gospels' portrayal of John the Baptist as the successor of the prophets and Justin's claim that prophecy came to an end after Jesus' death (*Dial.* 51.1—52.4). The former theme, of course, is taken directly from the Gospels (Luke 16:16; Matt. 11:13), but the latter idea is also attested—and in surprising sources. From the time of 1 Maccabees (4:43), Jewish teachers had held that the era of prophecy had come to an end, so that the time had come to await a prophet, and this notion is specifically endorsed by rabbinic literature during the second century and later as part of the explanation for the destruction of the temple.[24] Although no connection is made to Jesus, the Talmud also dates portents of the temple's demise to the period "forty years before the destruction of the Temple" (Bavli, Yoma 39b; cf. Yerushalmi, Sota 6:13). As in the case of his messianic exegesis and his recourse to arguments reminiscent of Philo's, Justin appears to adapt motifs of Judaism available to him.

His purpose, however, goes beyond the supersession or even the replacement of Judaism. Justin appears clearly to believe that with the defeat of Bar Kokhba, Judaism is coming to an end. Referring again to Genesis 49 (this time, v. 8), Justin declares that there will be two comings of Christ, "that in the first he would be suffering, and that after his coming there would be neither prophet nor king in your race, and—I added— that the Gentiles who believe in the suffering Christ will expect his coming again" (*Dial.* 52.1). Once these sufferings of Christ had been accomplished,[25] Israel no longer had a place, which is why Isaiah predicts the devastation of Judea (*1 Apol.* 47) as well as the conversion of the Gentiles (49), and why—finally—even the seal of the covenant in Genesis 17 itself is, as Rodney Werline has explained, completely reinterpreted (citing *Dial.* 16): "For Justin, then, circumcision is the sign for the recent historical national disaster for the Jews."[26] To this extent, Justin stands not simply for supersession or replacement, but for the elimination of Israel as commonly understood on the basis of the prophetic Spirit. Now "those who justify themselves and say they are children of Abraham will desire to inherit along with us even a little place, as the Holy Spirit cries aloud by Isaiah [a citation of 63:15 follows]" (*Dial.* 25.1; cf. 55.3).

The "Spirit of prophecy" is precisely what Targum Jonathan to the Prophets, largely extant during the second century, said would return to Israel in the mouths of the prophets at the end of time.[27] Justin's reply—echoing targumic language—is that the "prophetic Spirit" has already made its move. He produces a hermeneutic of Christian experience out of Jesus' prophecy in Matthew that "the kingdom of God shall be taken from you and given to a nation producing its fruit" (Matt. 21:43) as well as the declaration of Paul and Barnabas that, having attempted to speak to the Jews in Pisidian Antioch, "we turn to the Gentiles" (Acts 13:46). The speech of Paul in Pisidian Antioch bears comparison with Justin's approach to Scripture and the range of texts cited. At the same time, when Paul and Barnabas make their claim, they do so as envoys of the Holy Spirit (13:2).

Prophecy as a contemporary phenomenon is an emphatic theme of Luke-Acts, and it is a major aspect of Justin's argument (*Dial.* 88). Indeed, Justin becomes so enthusiastic in his argument that he makes false prophecy among Christians into an argument that the Spirit is among them (*Dial.* 82). Christian failings, on this reading, become stronger than Jewish virtues. In an attempt to save Justin from his own trenchancy, Sylvain Sanchez has argued that there were, after all, other forms of Judaism in the second century that Justin does not mention.[28] Given what he says about any form of Judaism he can think of, that was their good fortune.

4. That the Prophets Agreed That the Divine *Logos* Lies at the Core of Human Cognition of God

Justin believes that the apostles preach the *Logos* of God (*Dial.* 109), and that is also what Paul and Barnabas say they articulate (Acts 13:46) after the synagogue leaders invite them to speak of *logos parakleseos*[29] (13:15). God's *Logos* is so closely tied to prophecy for Justin that Balaam's oracle—the scriptural justification for the Bar Kokhba revolt—is attributed to Moses (*Dial.* 106.4, 126.1). Eric Osborn has observed the role of the *Logos* in prophecy of all types in Justin: "Prophecy is the word of the logos and

not merely a part of the logos."[30] The fit is so tight, Osborn claims, that Justin sometimes does not distinguish the *Logos* from the prophetic Spirit. In discussing the
appearance at Mamre, Justin invokes what the "Word" says, or the "holy prophetic
Spirit" (*Dial.* 56). The connection of the *Logos* with inspiration become explicit when
Justin says in *1 Apology* 36:1, "When you hear the utterances [*lexeis*] of the prophets
spoken as by a player, don't think that they were spoken by those inspired, but think
rather, by the divine Logos who moved them." His picture of the *Logos* is indeed
dynamic, and the distinction between the *Logos* and the Spirit needs sorting out.
Appreciating Justin's context, both Judaic and Hellenistic, permits a resolution of the
question.

Philo's *Logos*, together with its Stoic and Platonic resonances and its relationship
to Justin, has long been a part of discussion, and generally this ground has been better covered than most aspects of the study of Justin.[31] The closer the association with
Socrates (*1 Apol.* 46.3), and the more universal the claim of the reach of the *Logos* "in
which the whole human race partakes" (*1 Apol.* 46.2), the more natural this seems.
Philo's case, argued in his brilliant continuous commentary on the Pentateuch in Greek,
identified the creative *Logos* behind our world and in our minds as the Torah that God
revealed perfectly to Moses. Justin, in a less voluminous way, more the essayist than the
systematician, insisted that our knowledge of the *Logos* implies that it is eternally
human (cf. *Dial.* 62). More specifically, he calibrated his case to address the reason
(*Logos*) that should animate imperial policy in *1 Apology* 2: "Reason (*Logos*) enjoins
those who are truly reverent and philosophers to honor and desire only the true. . . ."[32]
Yet it is striking that Justin says that both Jews *and* Christians agree that "those who
prophesy are God-born by nothing other than divine *Logos*" (*1 Apol.* 33.9). He even has
Trypho say the *Logos* speaks in Scripture (*Dial.* 68.5). Something of the qualities of
Justin's conception should, therefore, be discernible in Judaic sources apart from Philo.

Skarsaune has suggested that biblical works such as Proverbs (to which Justin
refers in *Dial.* 61) and pseudepigraphal references such as 4 Maccabees 5:22-25 should
be taken into account.[33] If we pursue this line of inquiry, the fit between prophecy and
"Word" in the Judaism of Justin's period, we are brought to Targum Jonathan to the
Prophets and its usage of the term *Memra*. This term has in the past been explored in
relation to John's Gospel,[34] but it may be investigated even more fruitfully in relation
to second-century literature. The *Memra* is portrayed in the Targumim as active at the
beginning of creation, as being directed in the mouths of the prophets by the Holy
Spirit, and as being subject to rejection as well as acceptance by the people of God,
among other usages. As a result, like the *Logos* in *Dialogue* 141, the *Memra* may speak
of punishment as well as blessing.

This range of usage is only to be expected, because the noun *Memra* is closely
related to the verb of speaking, *'amar*; only an emphasis distinguishes the noun *memra*
from the infinitive *memar*. So in the Targumim as in Justin, the *Memra/Logos* is the act
of speaking, while the Spirit of prophecy/prophetic Spirit is the power of speech. Justin
can be bold in his application of the possibilities these usages offer precisely because
they are so widely agreed as to be axiomatic. Even the *presbutes*—the "Old Man"—like
the Prophets, speaks the "divine word" (*theion logon*; *Dial.* 23.3).[35]

Conclusion

After the *presbutes* left Justin, a fire suddenly kindled in his soul, and he found the one sure and useful philosophy (*Dial.* 8.1). Bobichon observes the Platonic connection with fire,[36] but that is another case of a very widely appearing image, specifically connected in Luke 24:32 to the moment when the risen Jesus "opened" the Scriptures to two of his disciples. Justin also compares fire to how, when we say something, "we engender a word," but without any diminution or loss to ourselves (*Dial.* 61.2).

With knowing innovation, Justin appropriates the prophetic Spirit and *Logos* to Christianity. And he uses this appropriation to articulate a consistent eucharistic theology (*1 Apol.* 66.2).

> Because we do not take as ordinary bread or ordinary drink, but in the same way as through God's *Logos* Jesus Christ our incarnate savior had flesh and blood for our salvation, so also the food given thanks for through an oath of a Logos from him, from which our blood and flesh are nourished by assimilation, is—we have learned—the flesh and blood of that incarnate Jesus.

In this case Justin builds upon the Johannine understanding of Eucharist, as consumption of Jesus, which can only have offended Jewish readers and hearers.[37] To a dramatic extent, Justin locates himself within this conscious separation from Judaism at the same time that he perfects his synthetic understanding of the *Logos*.

How specifically aware Justin was of Jewish teaching, specifically in its rabbinic form, remains unclear. Yet anyone who is familiar with the development of Judaism from the second century onward will appreciate the irony of his understanding of Judaic interpretation. The second century was just the period when Scripture was being interpreted within Judaism in terms of its eternal meaning, when any limitation to its immediate reference came to be overridden by an appeal to the significance of the eternal Torah.

Interpretation of Genesis 22 is a case in point: from the second century, it came to be asserted that Isaac was slain on Moriah, that he accepted his fate as a fully grown adult, and that God raised him from the dead. In other words, Isaac was a type in Judaism, as well as in Christianity, but of a different truth: an emblem of a martyr's obedience to the Torah rather than of a prophet's vision of Christ. Justin manages not to refer to any of the innovative developments of the Judaism of his time in respect of the sacrifice of Isaac, the '*Aqedat Yitschaq*. Justin may be aware of Judaic ritual as a practical matter, and even of specific Mishnaic requirements in regard to the Day of Atonement,[38] but his dialogue with Judaism does not involve direct, exegetical engagement.

So what is presented by Justin as a meeting of minds is in the event a missing of minds. Both Judaism and Christianity made the immediate reference of Scripture ancillary to its systemic significance. But because Christianity was committed to the *Logos* as its systemic center, and Judaism to the Torah as its systemic center, the two could not understand one another. Any objection from one side to the other seems silly: it misses the systemic point. In the absence of a language to discuss systemic relationship, the two sides fell to disputing which made better sense of the immediate reference (the "literal meaning," as would be said today) of the texts concerned. What is billed as a dialogue is really a shadow play: learned leaders reinforcing their own positions by arguing over what neither side believes really matters.

Nonetheless, the ground Justin chooses to fight on is redolent of his social location. His argument regarding circumcision, for example, is not likely to have convinced anyone like Trypho and represents a reversal of the privilege afforded circumcision (without the requirement that Gentiles should circumcise) within the position of James. Yet perhaps the true target of Justin's argument is not "Trypho" at all, but—as Graham Stanton has suggested[39]—his friends. Those styled "believing Pharisees" in Acts insisted upon the covenant of circumcision in any assertion of faith in Christ, and there is good evidence that position thrived through and beyond the second century.[40] If that is the case, it would be one example of how Justin's arguments might be related to the evolving social history of the second century.

Looking back, from a distance of several centuries, at a position that Justin articulated, Tanchuma (Y. Titissa 34) observed: "Moses wanted to write Mishnah, as well [as the Torah]. But the Holy One, Blessed be He, foresaw that ultimately the nations of the world would translate the Torah into Greek and would claim, 'We are Israel.'" At the moment, we cannot prove that the rabbis read Justin, any more than that Justin read the rabbis. But the rabbis interpreted him correctly, with or without direct knowledge of his works, because they understood that Christians claimed that they were Israel and that the instrument of their claim was the prophetic corpus. Their insight is also our lead into a critical reading of Justin.

CHAPTER SIX

Was John's Gospel among Justin's *Apostolic Memoirs*?

C. E. HILL

JUSTIN REPORTS THAT CERTAIN GOSPELS, which he calls *Memoirs of the Apostles*, were the subjects of homiletic exposition in Sunday gatherings of Christians in his day (*1 Apol.* 67.3). It is generally agreed that these *Memoirs* included the Gospels of Matthew, Mark, and Luke. But while a fair number of scholars believe Justin knew and sometimes used the Fourth Gospel, John Pryor would speak for the vast majority when he judges that "the evidence for including the 4G in Justin's term 'memoirs of the apostles' is quite lacking."[1] Graham Stanton, on the other hand, thinks that the possibility cannot be ruled out and prefers to leave it an open question. This chapter shall propose that we may now affirm that when Justin designated a number of Gospels as *Memoirs of the Apostles*, one of those he had in mind was indeed John's.[2]

Justin's only quote, or near quote, of the Fourth Gospel is of Jesus' saying from John 3:5, 7 about being reborn and seeing the kingdom of heaven (of God, in John) (*1 Apol.* 61.4).[3] While this, combined with other less substantial allusions, could be sufficient evidence to conclude that Justin knew John, these borrowings do not necessarily point to its inclusion among the *Memoirs*. One might say something similar about the influence of John's prologue on Justin's *Logos* Christology.[4] I have argued elsewhere that certain of John's statements in the Prologue were foundational to Justin's Christology.[5] But while this might mean he considered John a highly significant source and possibly one of the apostolic *Memoirs*, it is still true that most of these christological passages are not in the context of his references to the *Memoirs*.

Dialogue 105.1

There is, however, one exception in the *Dialogue*, where Justin's reference to the Word's incarnation *seems* to give his source for the teaching. "For I have proved that he was *monogenes* to the Father of all things, begotten of him in a peculiar manner as Word and Power, and later having become man through the virgin, as we have learned from the memoirs"[6] (*Dial.* 105.1; cf. 100.2, 4).

Pryor has argued that what Justin here attributes to the *Memoirs* should be restricted to the virgin birth[7] and should not include that Jesus is *monogenes* to the Father, because Justin claims he has already "proved" his case, and Pryor finds no evidence of direct dependence on John 1 in the immediately preceding chapters.[8] But Justin does not say here that he has "proved" anything "from the *Memoirs*"—as though he were saying that he had laid out all his alleged evidence explicitly from them—only that he and other Christians have learned these things from the *Memoirs*. For the plural "we" in "as we have learned from the *Memoirs*" evidently refers not to Justin and Trypho, but to Justin and other Christians.[9] Moreover, even if we should restrict the information derived from the *Memoirs* to the virgin birth, we must recognize that Justin does not simply speak here of a "virgin birth"—a miraculous birth of a human being—he speaks of a divine figure (the *monogenes* of the Father, begotten of him in a peculiar manner as Word and Power) "becoming man" through the virgin. Both the description of this divine personage and the description of his "becoming man"[10] are given in language that here and elsewhere in his writings arguably shows the imprint of John's prologue.

For instance, Christ's "becoming man" (ἄνθρωπος γέγονεν) is elsewhere specified as his "having been made flesh" (σαρκοποιηθείς), reflecting the conception and wording of John 1:14 (σάρξ ἐγένετο) in *1 Apology* 32.10. And his "becoming man according to his [God's] will" (καὶ τῇ βουλῇ αὐτοῦ γενόμενος ἄνθρωπος, *1 Apol.* 23.2; cf. *Dial.* 63.2) elsewhere reflects the christological application of John 1:13, "born not of blood, nor of the will of the flesh, nor of the will of man, but of God" (see also *1 Apol.* 21.1; 22.2; 23.2; 32.9–10; 63.2).[11] That Justin says he learned from the *Memoirs* about the *Logos*, the only-begotten of the Father, begotten by him after a peculiar manner, "having become man through the virgin," is as much as saying that John's gospel was one of the *Memoirs*.

"The Acts That Took Place under Pontius Pilate"

In *1 Apology* 28.1 Justin tells the emperor and the Senate they can learn something about the Christian tradition "by looking at our writings." This begins a string of probably seven references throughout the rest of the apology to specifically Christian writings, the last two of which are his references to the *Memoirs of the Apostles* (see 28.1, 33.5,[12] 35.9, 38.7, 48.3, 66.3, 67.3).[13] Three of these seven are to an obscure and variously rendered title, which I'll translate "The Acts That Took Place under Pontius Pilate" (35.9, 38.7, 48.3).[14] In these three places he asserts that his illustrious readers "can ascertain from the Acts which occurred under Pontius Pilate" (ἐκ τῶν ἐπὶ Ποντίου Πιλάτου γενομένων ἄκτων) that certain events concerning the Christ that were prophesied of old have indeed come to pass.

All seem to agree today that whatever source Justin has in mind, it has nothing to do with the later apocryphal "Pilate literature," such as the *Acts of Pilate* that are now contained in the *Gospel of Nicodemus.*[15] His word "acts" (ἄκτων), a Latin loanword given in Greek characters, seems to lend to this source an official character.[16] What Justin attributes to these "acts," however, makes it impossible to conceive of them as any official Roman document chronicling the events of the procuratorship of Pilate. For they allegedly narrate Jesus' birth and growth to manhood; his healing of those afflicted with various physical handicaps and diseases and his raising of the dead (*1 Apol.* 48.3); the gainsaying, denial, and torture of him by his persecutors; their setting him on a judgment seat; his crucifixion; the soldiers' using nails to affix his hands and feet to the cross; and their casting of lots for his vesture.

Instead, Helmut Koester appears to be correct in saying that Justin is in fact referring to "gospel materials."[17] By "gospel materials" Koester seems to mean not any of the four canonical Gospels, but materials that were part of their prehistory, which may have been used in the composition of these and other Gospels. Yet this solution, too, is quite problematic. No materials that fit this description have ever been found. And Justin refers to these "acts" as something not only current in his day, but publicly accessible, and to which the emperor could easily have had access.[18] This makes it hardly likely that he is referring to such obscure, nonliterary, and, to the present day, unidentifiable sources. If they are "gospel materials," they would most likely be the Gospels at that time in wide use among Christians in Rome and therefore at least somewhat readily obtainable.

Justin had certain precedents for this terminology. The elder known to Papias in Eusebius, *Ecclesiastical History* 3.39.15 (almost certainly the Elder John), used to speak of the evangelist Mark writing down accurately "the things either said or done [τὰ ἢ λεχθέντα ἢ πραχθέντα] by the Lord." In what I believe is another portion of this same elder's recorded tradition, summarized and paraphrased by Eusebius in *Ecclesiastical History* 3.24,[19] Eusebius uses the term "the acts of Jesus" (τῶν τοῦ Ἰησοῦ πράξεων) three times to refer to the contents of one or another of the Gospels.[20] The companion volume of one of these Gospels had probably acquired by this time, if it did not originally possess,[21] the title "The Acts [πράξεις] of the Apostles," which title itself could imply that Luke's former volume might be viewed as the Acts of Jesus.[22]

Ignatius of Antioch, when speaking of the key events of Jesus' life, stressed, as does Justin, the historical nature of these occurrences by referring to deeds done by Jesus "under Pontius Pilate": "Be convinced of the birth and passion and resurrection which took place [γενομένης] at the time of the procuratorship of Pontius Pilate; for these things were truly and certainly done [πραχθέντα] by Jesus Christ" [Ign. *Magn.* 11.1; cf. Ign. *Trall.* 9.1; Ign. *Smyrn.* 1.2). Justin follows the same practice, referring several times in the *Apologies* and the *Dialogue* to Pontius Pilate—to Jesus' crucifixion "under Pontius Pilate" (*1 Apol.* 13.3; 61.13; *2 Apol.* 6(5).6; *Dial.* 30.3; 76.6; 85.2) and (once) to his teaching "under Pontius Pilate" (*1 Apol.* 46.1). By referring his readers to the Acts, Justin only makes clear that these things that took place "under Pontius Pilate" are recorded in written sources.

And there are two instructive parallels in the *Dialogue* that confirm this identification of the "Acts" with the *Memoirs*. In *1 Apology* 35 and 38 Justin's christological exposition of Psalm 22 figures prominently. There he claims that the emperor may read of the fulfillment of Psalm 22:16, 18 ("They pierced my hands and feet" and "They parted my garments among them, and cast lots upon my vesture") in "the Acts which occurred under Pontius Pilate." But in *Dialogue* 104 he attests to Trypho that the fulfillment of Psalm 22.15c-18 "is written to have taken place in the memoirs of his apostles" (ἐν τοῖς Ἀπομνημονεύμασι τῶν ἀποστόλων αὐτοῦ γέγραπται γενόμενον). It is the same with Psalm 22:7, "They spake with their lips, they wagged the head, saying, 'Let Him deliver Himself,'" for the fulfillment of which Justin refers in *1 Apology* 38 to the "Acts," but which in *Dialogue* 101.1–4 he refers to the *Memoirs of the Apostles*. This, I believe, seals the fact that what Justin refers to as "the Acts which occurred under Pontius Pilate" are the acts of Jesus recorded in the Gospels, and are in fact another way Justin has of referring to "memoirs" of the apostles.

Seeing, then, that the "Acts" is another name for the *Memoirs*, it remains to observe that certain of the points mentioned by Justin as contained in these "Acts" rely on information related in John's unique account of Jesus' life and death.

The Judgment Seat

The first comes in his claim that Isaiah 58:2, "They now ask of me judgement, and dare to draw near to God" (*1 Apol.* 35:4), was fulfilled at the time of the crucifixion of Christ. Justin says, "As the prophet spoke, they tormented him, and set him on the judgment-seat [αὐτὸν ἐκάθισαν ἐπὶ βήματος] and said, 'Judge us.'" This goes back to a reading of John 19:13, the only Gospel that could be read as indicating that Jesus sat on a judgment seat (βῆμα) at his trial:[23] "When Pilate heard these words, he brought Jesus out and sat down on the judgment seat [ἐκάθισαν ἐπὶ βήματος]" (John 19:13). But instead of Pilate sitting on the βῆμα, Justin has understood ἐκάθισαν, "he sat down," as transitive, *he*, meaning Pilate, "sat him [Jesus] down."[24] Some modern commentators have done the same.[25] This is in fact what allows Isaiah 58:2, "They now ask of me judgment," to be related to the events of the passion of Jesus. The same exegetical tradition, related again to the ἐκάθισαν of John 19:13, is known to the author of the *Gospel of Peter*, but as Koester says, "the *Gospel of Peter* cannot have been Justin's source, because he [Justin] uses the word βῆμα for 'judgment seat,' like John 19:13,"[26] whereas the *Gospel of Peter* has changed βῆμα to καθέδραν κρίσεως, seat of judgment.[27] Instead, both use the same exegetical tradition of interpreting what is evidently the report of John 19:13 as the fulfillment of Isaiah 58:2. Thus when Justin alleges that the emperor and Senate can learn of the fulfillment of Isaiah 58:2 from "the Acts which occurred under Pontius Pilate" (*1 Apol.* 35.9), he is certainly not referring to Matthew, Mark, or Luke, but could well be referring to John.

The Nails

In the same chapter Justin cites the words of Psalm 22:16, "They pierced my hands and my feet," and says this expression "was used in reference to the nails (ἧλοι) of the cross which were fixed in his hands and feet" (*1 Apol.* 35.7). Psalm 22, of course, does not refer to any nails. Neither Matthew nor Mark nor Luke mentions nails in its account of the crucifixion; neither is there in any of their accounts any special reference to Jesus' hands or feet being pierced. From these three accounts one would not know if Jesus had been nailed to the cross or perhaps strapped with leather or tied with ropes, as we know happened to at least some crucifixion victims.[28] John, however, mentions the marks of the nails (τὸν τύπον τῶν ἥλων) in Jesus' hands (it does not mention feet) in its account of the appearance of Jesus to the disciples and Thomas in 20:25, 27.[29] Justin, like other Christians,[30] knew that Jesus had been nailed to the cross. And while such a detail might have been very generally known, Justin in *1 Apology* 38.7 tells his readers specifically that they "can learn" about this fulfillment of Psalm 22:16, "They pierced my hands and my feet," from a written source, alluding again to the source he had mentioned three chapters earlier, "the Acts which occurred under Pontius Pilate." We recall that Justin tells Trypho in *Dialogue* 104 that this piercing in fulfillment of Psalm 22:16 "is written to have taken place in the memoirs of his apostles" (ἐν τοῖς Ἀπομνημονεύμασι τῶν ἀποστόλων αὐτοῦ γέγραπται γενόμενον). Again, this cannot be a reference to any of the Synoptics (as we now have them) but could well be a reference to John's account.

Casting Lots for Jesus' Garment

Justin goes on in *1 Apology* 35 to mention the dividing of Jesus' garments and the casting of lots, according to Psalm 22:18, something all four of the canonical Gospels record. Though all of these Gospels clearly allude to this psalm text in their description of the events, John's is the only one to cite it formally, as does Justin. In one of his references to the casting of lots for Jesus' garments (*Dial.* 97.3), Justin substitutes another word for lot, λαχμός, for the word κλῆρος, which is used in the LXX and in all four of the Gospels. (This change is also found in *Gospel of Peter* 4.12.) John's account, however, is the only one of the four to use a cognate of λαχμός. It uses the verb λαγχάνω, when the author, just before citing Psalm 22:18, quotes the soldiers conversing about Jesus' seamless tunic, "Let us not tear it, but cast lots [λάχωμεν] for it to see whose it shall be" (19:24).

Another detail may be mentioned here. In his *First Apology* when Justin cites the fulfillment of Psalm 22:18, he cites only the second half of the verse, "and for my vesture they cast lots," which refers to the singular ἱματισμόν (*1 Apol.* 35.5, 8; 38.4).[31] This is in contradistinction to each of the Synoptic accounts, which allude only to the plural garments of Psalm 22:18a, "They divided my garments among them" (διεμερίσαντο τὰ ἱμάτιά μου ἑαυτοῖς).[32] It is John's account alone that has the story of the soldiers casting lots for Jesus' singular tunic (ὁ χιτών), thereby showing that the second half of Psalm 22:18 was fulfilled, the casting of lots for a single garment (ἱματισμόν).

Thus, though Justin does not mention the tunic itself, his citation of only Psalm 22:18b and his reference to Jesus' singular "garment" in the *First Apology*, combined with his use of the word λαχμός, certainly seem to demonstrate his awareness and use of John's unique account of the crucifixion. And significantly, he alleges that his readers "can learn" that all these things happened to Jesus in "the Acts which occurred under Pontius Pilate" (35.9).

Healing of Those Afflicted "from Birth"

In *Dialogue* 69 Justin cites from Isaiah 35:1-7, including the words, "Then the eyes of the blind shall be opened, and the ears of the deaf shall hear. Then the lame shall leap as an hart, and the tongue of the stammerers shall be distinct." Justin understands the fulfillment of this prophecy to be in Christ, who "healed those who were maimed, and deaf, and lame in body from their birth, causing them to leap, to hear, and to see, by His word" (69.6). The detail that Christ healed those afflicted "from their birth" (ἐκ γενετῆς) has its only apparent source in John 9:1, 19, 20, 32, which repeatedly point out that the man healed by Jesus in that chapter had been blind "from birth" (ἐκ γενετῆς). Evidently the account of Jesus' healing of the man born blind in John 9 is one text that, in Justin's mind, showed the fulfillment of Isaiah 35:1-7. In *1 Apology* 48.2–3 Justin cites the same verses from Isaiah 35 and goes on to say, "And that he did those things, you can learn from the Acts which occurred under Pontius Pilate." This, too, seems to show that John's account of the healing of the man born blind was among the Acts referred to.

This, I believe, makes it morally certain that the several details in this section that correspond only to the Fourth Gospel and not to the Synoptics are indeed signs of Justin's dependence upon that Gospel. That the Fourth Gospel was an important authority for Justin's views of Jesus' deity, incarnation, and baptism (*Dial.* 88.3, 7),[33] and for his understanding of the meaning of Christian baptism (*1 Apol.* 61.34),[34] could already have been affirmed. His words about "the Acts which occurred under Pontius Pilate" appear to demonstrate that John's account was also useful for Justin's understanding of the healings Jesus performed, perhaps the raising of the dead Lazarus, and the sufferings of Jesus—all in fulfillment of Old Testament prophecy. But most significantly, his words about the "Acts" demonstrate independently that the Fourth Gospel was indeed among the collection of writings Justin calls the *Memoirs of the Apostles*, thus confirming and amplifying our conclusion already drawn from *Dialogue* 105.1 (see above). This naturally means John's Gospel was among those read and expounded upon along with the prophets in Roman churches in the mid-second century (*1 Apol.* 67.3).

The only alternative I can see to this conclusion would require the supposition that there once existed another Gospel (for Justin says that the *Memoirs* are called Gospels, *1 Apol.* 66.3) that contained all of these details that occur in John but not in the Synoptics. We would have to assume not only that such a Gospel once existed, but that it remained in circulation until past the midpoint of the second century, and not only that it remained in circulation, but that it was as accessible as the Gospels of Matthew, Mark, and Luke and held a place alongside them in the Roman Church as worthy of exposition in Christian worship on Sundays, and all of this while at the same time the Gospel of John was not known, or perhaps was known but studiously avoided. This, I think, is quite beyond belief.

As some recent monographs have shown,[35] there is ample evidence from which the historian may gather that the Fourth Gospel was in fairly wide use within the mainstream of the Christian tradition in the first half of the second century, and even in Rome at about the time Justin wrote. If John was among the *Memoirs*, this would help explain how it would soon figure prominently alongside the Synoptics in Tatian's *Diatessaron*, how Celsus, probably in Rome, could associate it with the writings of the "Great Church,"[36] how Irenaeus in his correspondence with Rome could assume its validity and use there, how Tertullian could do the same, and how paintings based on its contents could be found among the earliest Christian catacomb art at the dawn of the third century.

It is true that Justin in his surviving writings uses the Synoptics much more than he uses John. Whatever the reasons for this (and I think there are several), it may at least be observed that Justin's indebtedness to John may be seen to be far more profound than his dependence on Mark can be demonstrated to be (for he seldom relies on distinctively Markan material), though we know that Mark was one of the *Memoirs* (being the memoirs of Peter, to be exact). This begs the question, if the Fourth Gospel was among the apostolic *Memoirs*, whose memoirs was it thought to contain? But this is a question for another essay.

CHAPTER SEVEN

Interpreting the Descent of the Spirit

A *Comparison of Justin's* Dialogue with Trypho *and Luke-Acts*

SUSAN WENDEL

IN HIS *DIALOGUE WITH TRYPHO*, Justin attempts to claim Israel's identity and inheritance for Gentile Christ-believers. The corollary of this assertion appears to be a denunciation of the Jewish nation.[1] According to Justin, ethnic Israel rightfully incurred punishment in the destruction of the temple in 70 C.E. and after the Bar Kokhba revolt (*Dial.* 16.1–4, 25.5, 108.3; *1 Apol.* 47–49); their culpability, especially in killing Christ, led to their ultimate disinheritance.[2] He maintains that Christians had displaced the Jews as the true people of God, the spiritual Israel (*Dial.* 11.5, 123.9), and would become the rightful priests and heirs of Jerusalem in the age to come (82.1, 116.3). These elements of the *Dialogue* lead some scholars to conclude that it preserves a transitional stage between earlier Christian texts that argue for the inclusion of Gentiles as a part of God's people and later "proto-orthodox"/"orthodox" texts that presume the Gentile church is the God-ordained replacement of ethnic Israel (for example, Tertullian, *Adversus Iudaeos*; Chrysostom, *Kata tôn Ioudaiôn*).[3]

Nevertheless, the writings of Justin appear to stand in continuity with New Testament traditions. For example, a number of scholars of Christian origins interpret Luke-Acts as an account of the church's replacement of Israel,[4] an agenda that is explicit in the *Dialogue* (c. 160 C.E.). Moreover, Helmut Koester, Graham Stanton, and others have noted the continuity between some aspects of Justin's thought and the writings of Luke.[5] Oskar Skarsaune has further suggested that Lukan theology is embedded in the writings of Justin; in his view, a trajectory of thought can be traced from Luke to Justin. In particular, Skarsaune points out the marked correspondence between the postresurrection instructions found in the two texts, the similarity between the setting of the missionary activity in each, and the authors' common purpose in citing the LXX.[6]

Both Luke and Justin seek to display the ways in which scriptural promises have come to fruition in the life, death, and resurrection of Jesus. A number of studies have examined Justin's reinterpretation of the Jewish Scriptures for the Gentile Christian church.[7] Likewise, scholars of Luke-Acts frequently note and discuss Luke's use of the LXX as a means of presenting the events that he narrates as the fulfillment of ancient prophecy.[8] Just as Justin takes on the role of an inspired exegete of the LXX (*Dial.* 92.1, 119.1), so Luke seeks to extend biblical history by recounting the story of Jesus and the early church as the consummation of God's plan.[9]

Although numerous features of the *Dialogue* stand in continuity with Luke-Acts, I will suggest that in his discussion of the activity of the Spirit in *Dialogue* 87, Justin departs from Luke's account of how God acted to fulfill his promises to Israel. At first sight, Justin's assertion that the Gentile church had become the beneficiary of God's promised blessings for Israel may seem like an extension of a supposed theme of supersession in Luke-Acts. Closer analysis, however, exposes a telling difference. Luke often uses Scripture to reaffirm Israel's place in God's plan (for example, Luke 1:46-55, 68-79; 2:29-32; Acts 15:16-18) and portrays the descent of the Spirit upon believers as an initial phase of a long-awaited, Jewish restoration (Acts 2:17-42).[10] Justin, however, inverts this aspect of Luke-Acts by arguing that God had removed the Spirit from Israel and given it to Jesus and Christ-believers, the new people of God (*Dial.* 87).

In order to explore these similarities and differences, this study will compare Luke's account of the descent of the Spirit on Jesus and the disciples (that is, Luke 3–4 and 24; Acts 1–2) with a parallel portrait of the activity of the Spirit in the *Dialogue* (87–88). In Luke-Acts, the action of the Spirit on the day of Pentecost is a focal point for the depiction of a Jewish restoration, whereas in the *Dialogue* the descent of the Spirit upon believers is pivotal for the assertion that the church supersedes Israel. A study of their respective representations of the Spirit thus highlights some significant differences between the two texts, both in their exegesis of the LXX and in their sentiments about the Jewish people.

I will begin my study with a comparison of Luke 3–4 and *Dialogue* 87–88, both of which recount the descent of the Spirit upon Jesus. I will then turn to a discussion of the differences between the description of the Spirit-baptism of the disciples in Acts 1–2 (cf. Luke 24:44-48) and the representation of the Spirit's activity among believers in *Dialogue* 87. Key here will be a comparison between the two authors' use of LXX Joel 3 to portray the Spirit's descent as the fulfillment of ancient prophecy (Acts 2:17-21 and *Dial.* 87.6). In conclusion, I will consider the significance of this departure from Luke-Acts for our understanding of early Christian representations of Judaism.

The Spirit and Jesus

The depictions of the descent of the Spirit upon Jesus in the Gospel of Luke and the *Dialogue* contain a number of common features.[11] In the two accounts, the Spirit-baptism takes place immediately after water-baptism, the Holy Spirit descends upon Jesus in the form of a dove (εἴδει ὡς περιστερὰν in Luke 3:22; εἴδει ὡς περιστερᾶς in

Dial. 88.8), and a voice from heaven pronounces the words, "You are my Son" (σὺ εἶ ὁ υἱός μου ὁ ἀγαπητός, ἐν σοὶ εὐδόκησα in Luke 3:22; υἱός μου εἶ σύ, ἐγὼ σήμερον γεγέννηκά σε in *Dial.* 88.8).[12] Additionally, Justin and Luke both associate John with the baptism of Jesus but avoid mentioning explicitly that he was the baptizer of Jesus (Luke 3:18-22; *Dial.* 88.3–8).[13] Moreover, the prominence that Justin gives to the "powers" (δυνάμεις) of the Spirit (87.2, 3, 4; 88.1, 2) resembles this same emphasis in Luke 3–4.[14] Although Justin appears to rely on more than one source, he tells the same basic story as Luke and even emphasizes some features of the Spirit-baptism of Jesus that are unique to the Lukan narrative.

Emerging from these parallels, however, is Justin's claim that the Spirit departed from Israel's prophets when it descended upon Jesus. In *Dialogue* 87.1–2, Justin initiates his discourse about the descent of the Spirit upon Jesus by placing a citation from LXX Isaiah 11 on the lips of Trypho. This passage indicates that the promised Davidic leader would be empowered by the Holy Spirit to perform his role as messianic deliverer, but Trypho wonders why Jesus would need the powers of the Spirit to fulfill this messianic mission if he was in fact preexistent:[15]

Εἰπὲ οὖν μοι, διὰ τοῦ Ἡσαΐου εἰπόντος τοῦ Λόγου· Ἐξελεύσεται ῥάβδος ἐκ τῆς ῥίζης Ἰεσσαί, καὶ ἄνθος ἀναβήσεται ἐκ τῆς ῥίζης Ἰεσσαί, καὶ ἀναπαύσεται ἐπ᾽ αὐτὸν πνεῦμα θεοῦ, πνεῦμα σοφίας καὶ συνέσεως, πνεῦμα βουλῆς καὶ ἰσχύος, πνεῦμα γνώσεως καὶ εὐσεβείας, καὶ ἐμπλήσει αὐτὸν πνεῦμα φόβου θεοῦ. . . . πῶς δύναται ἀποδειχθῆναι προϋπάρχων, ὅστις διὰ τῶν δυνάμεων τοῦ πνεύματος τοῦ ἁγίου, ἃς καταριθμεῖ ὁ Λόγος διὰ Ἡσαΐου, πληροῦται ὡς ἐνδεὴς τούτων ὑπάρχων;[16]

Tell me, therefore, the word that was spoken through Isaiah: "There shall come forth a rod from the root of Jesse and a flower shall be raised up from the root of Jesse and the Spirit of God shall rest upon him, a spirit of wisdom and understanding, a spirit of counsel and strength, a spirit of knowledge and piety, and the Spirit of the fear of God will fill him." . . . How can he be demonstrated [as] pre-existent, who was filled with the powers of the Holy Spirit, which the scripture enumerates through Isaiah, as if he was deficient of these things that existed? (*Dial.* 87.2)

In other words, Trypho uses this description of the anticipated coming of the Spirit upon the Messiah to call Justin's claims about Jesus' preexistence into question.

The narrative strategy of the two-way conversation gives Justin the opportunity to affirm Christ's preexistence and to explain that Jesus in no way needed the Spirit (*Dial.* 87.3a), a feature of his argument that he reasserts again in *Dial.* 88.3–8. In this immediate context, however, Justin's answer to Trypho's question takes up a surprisingly different theme. Since the preexistence of Jesus precluded any need for the power of the Spirit, according to *Dial.* 87.3b, it must have been bestowed upon him for some other reason, namely, that the prophets and the powers of the Spirit would no longer exist among Jews:[17]

Ταύτας τὰς κατηριθμημένας τοῦ πνεύματος δυνάμεις οὐχ ὡς ἐνδεοῦς αὐτοῦ τούτων ὄντος φησὶν ὁ Λόγος ἐπεληλυθέναι ἐπ᾽ αὐτόν, ἀλλ᾽ ὡς ἐπ᾽ ἐκεῖνον ἀνάπαυσιν μελλουσῶν¹⁸ ποιεῖσθαι, τουτέστιν ἐπ᾽ αὐτοῦ πέρας ποιεῖσθαι, τοῦ μηκέτι ἐν τῷ γένει ὑμῶν κατὰ τὸ παλαιὸν ἔθος προφήτας γενήσεσθαι,¹⁹ ὅπερ καὶ ὄψει ὑμῖν ἰδεῖν ἔστι· μετ᾽ ἐκεῖνον γὰρ οὐδεὶς ὅλως προφήτης παρ᾽ ὑμῖν γεγένηται.

The scripture states [that] these powers which were enumerated by the Spirit have come upon him, not because he was in need of them, but because they were destined to make their rest upon him—that is, to make themselves complete upon him, in order that prophets would no longer be among your race according to the ancient custom even as it is plain for you to see, for after him, no prophet has actually come from among you. (*Dial.* 87.3b; cf. 88.1)

In view of Trypho's earlier assertion that the true Messiah would be anointed by Elijah (for example, *Dial.* 8.4, 49.1), we might have expected Justin to argue here that Jesus did receive the messianic anointing of Elijah when he was baptized by John (John = Elijah; *Dial.* 49.3–5). Such a rejoinder would serve two purposes. It would explain why Jesus was anointed with the Spirit, even though he was preexistent, and would counter Trypho's earlier challenge that Jesus could not be the Messiah since he had not been anointed by Elijah (*Dial.* 8.4, 49.1). In *Dialogue* 87.3—88.2, however, Justin resists this avenue of reasoning.[20] In fact, his answer employs a logic that is quite the opposite. Rather than presenting the descent of the Spirit upon Jesus as a messianic anointing by John, a Jewish prophet and type of Elijah, Justin asserts that the Spirit-baptism of Jesus had the effect of removing the Spirit from Jews and their prophets. In this way, the Spirit-baptism of Jesus represents a transfer of the very presence and powers of God from the Jewish people to Jesus.[21]

This transfer of the Spirit is nowhere described in the Lukan record of the Spirit-baptism of Jesus. On the contrary, Luke interprets the descent of the Spirit upon Jesus at his water-baptism as an event that initiates his prophetic and messianic ministry to and among the Jewish people.[22] For example, in the inaugural Nazareth sermon that follows his water-baptism, Jesus announces that he will effect deliverance for the Jews through the anointing of the Spirit (Luke 4:18-19; cf. 4:14). Throughout the narrative, moreover, Luke presents Jesus as a prophet of old (7:16-17; 9:8) who is "mighty in word and deed" (24:19). These examples illustrate the way in which Luke presents Jesus as a traditional Jewish prophet who directs his Spirit-empowered ministry toward, rather than away from, the Jewish people.[23]

The Spirit and Israel

Neither Justin nor Luke confines his discussion of the activity of the Spirit to its descent upon Jesus. Each author also describes the Spirit-baptism of those who believe in him. Here, too, their accounts seem similar yet not wholly congruent. A difference, again, lies in their view of the status of the Jews.

As we shall see, Luke portrays the descent of the Spirit upon the disciples as an initial phase in God's restoration of the Jewish people. In contrast to Luke, Justin introduces his account of the activity of the Spirit upon believers by expanding his discussion of the Spirit's removal from Israel. After presenting his version of how the Spirit came to rest upon Jesus instead of the prophets of Israel, Justin states that Jesus then transferred the Spirit to Christ-believers (see *Dial.* 87.3–6a). According to Justin, the powers that once resided with the Jews now rest instead upon those who believe in Jesus as Christ:

Ἀνεπαύσατο οὖν, τουτέστιν ἐπαύσατο, ἐλθόντος ἐκείνου, μεθ᾽ ὅν, τῆς οἰκονομίας ταύτης τῆς ἐν ἀνθρώποις αὐτοῦ γενομένης χρόνοις, παύσασθαι ἔδει αὐτὰ ἀφ᾽ ὑμῶν, καὶ ἐν τούτῳ ἀνάπαυσιν λαβόντα πάλιν, ὡς ἐπεπροφήτευτο γενήσεσθαι *δόματα,* ἃ ἀπὸ τῆς χάριτος τῆς δυνάμεως τοῦ πνεύματος ἐκείνου τοῖς ἐπ᾽ αὐτὸν πιστεύουσι *δίδωσιν,* ὡς ἄξιον ἕκαστον ἐπίσταται.

Therefore, it rested, that is, it stopped, when *he* came, after whom, in the times which were of his arranged plan among men, it was necessary for these things to cease from you [that is, the Jews]—and when they received rest again in this one, as it was prophesied would happen to the gifts, which, by the grace of the power of his spirit, he gives to those who believe in him, even as he decides each one is worthy. (*Dial.* 87.5)

In Justin's thought, then, the Spirit-baptism of Jesus led to the cessation of the Spirit's activity among the Jewish people and to the subsequent initiation of its descent upon Christ-believers. In this sense, the new locus of the Spirit's activity serves to distinguish Jews, the former people of God, from Christ-believers, the new people of God.[24]

Following Justin's explanation of the transfer of the Spirit from the Jewish people to Christ-believers, he appears to marshal a Luke-like explanation for this event. Justin states that it was prophesied that the Spirit would descend upon believers after the departure of Jesus to heaven:

Ὅτι ἐπεπροφήτευτο τοῦτο μέλλειν γίνεσθαι[25] ὑπ᾽ αὐτοῦ μετὰ τὴν εἰς οὐρανὸν ἀνέλευσιν αὐτοῦ, εἶπον μὲν ἤδη καὶ πάλιν λέγω.

I said already and again I say that it was prophesied that this was destined to take place through him after his departure to heaven. (*Dial.* 87.6a)

Justin specifies that the descent of the Spirit occurred through the agency of Jesus (ὑπ᾽ αὐτοῦ) and according to God's foreknowledge and plan (ἐπεπροφήτευτο). This parallels Luke's portrait of the coming of the Spirit, especially Peter's speech in Acts 2, where we read that according to the predetermined plan of God and in fulfillment of prophecy, Jesus ascended to the right hand of the Father and poured out the promised Holy Spirit (Acts 2:17-36). To what extent, however, does Justin's version of the activity of the Spirit in *Dialogue* 87 parallel the Lukan account?

Contrary to Justin's interpretation of the Spirit's withdrawal from the Jewish people, in *Dialogue* 87, Luke links the coming of the Spirit with a Jewish restoration in statements of Jesus that presage the event in numerous ways, three of which I will mention here. First, Jesus refers to the imminent descent of the Spirit as "the promise of my Father" (ἐπαγγελίαν τοῦ πατρός μου; Luke 24:49; cf. Acts 1:4), thereby presenting it as the realization of God's promise to his people Israel.[26] Second, Luke depicts this activity of the Spirit as the fulfillment of God's promises to the Jewish people by alluding to LXX Isaiah 32:15 in Luke 24:49b; in this passage, Jesus instructed the disciples to wait until they were "clothed with power from on high" (ἐνδύσησθε ἐξ ὕψους δύναμιν), a phrase that recalls the anticipated role of the Spirit in the restoration of Israel (ἕως ἂν ἐπέλθῃ ἐφ᾽ ὑμᾶς πνεῦμα ἀφ᾽ ὑψηλοῦ; LXX Isa. 32:15). By alluding to Isaiah 32:15, Luke presents the arrival of the Spirit as the actualization of God's promises to restore the Jewish people.[27]

Third, Jesus' predictions of the descent of the Spirit in Luke 24:44-48 and Acts 1:1-8 portray the event as an aspect of restoration for the Jewish people by alluding to the servant poems of Isaiah. In Acts 1:8 (cf. Luke 24:47-48), for example, Jesus affirms that the disciples will be Spirit-empowered "witnesses" (μάρτυρες) "to the end of the earth" (ἕως ἐσχάτου τῆς γῆς) and "to all the nations" (εἰς πάντα τὰ ἔθνη). The phrases "you shall be my witnesses" (ἔσεσθέ μου μάρτυρες) and "to the end of the earth" (ἕως ἐσχάτου τῆς γῆς) recall LXX Isaiah 43:10-12 (γένεσθέ μοι μάρτυρες . . . ὑμεῖς ἐμοὶ μάρτυρες) and LXX Isaiah 49:6 (ἕως ἐσχάτου τῆς γῆς)[28]—biblical passages that depict the role of restored Israel/Jacob as a witness of the Lord and as a messenger of justice, hope, and light to the nations.[29] Significantly, LXX Isaiah 42:1 also links the Spirit's presence with the servant's ability to bring justice to the nations (ἔδωκα τὸ πνεῦμά μου ἐπ᾽ αὐτόν, κρίσιν τοῖς ἔθνεσιν ἐξοίσει). By alluding to the Isaiah servant poems in Acts 1:8 and Luke 24:48, Luke invites the reader to interpret the first descent of the Spirit as a restoration of the Jewish people's vocation as servant of the Lord.[30]

Although it is true that Justin elsewhere links the commissioning of the apostles with the fulfillment of Scripture in a manner similar to Luke (for example, *1 Apol.* 39.1–3, 49.5, 50.12; *Dial.* 83.3–4, 109.1–3, 110.2), he depicts the sending of the Twelve as God's law going forth from Zion (for example, *1 Apol.* 39.2; cf. Isa. 2:3) and as the rod of his power proceeding from Jerusalem (for example, *1 Apol.* 45.5; *Dial.* 83.2; cf. LXX Ps. 109:2) without making explicit mention of the Spirit.[31] Moreover, Justin repeatedly presents the mission of the apostles as the fulfillment of God's promises for the nations, rather than for Jews, arguing that the majority of the Jews had rejected their message (*1 Apol.* 49.5, 53.3-12). According to Justin, some Jews performed the antithesis of the apostolic mission; they chose and sent out men from Jerusalem who spoke lies against Christ-believers and the gospel with the result that the name of God was blasphemed among the nations (*Dial.* 17.1–2).

In sum, Justin and Luke both affirm that Jesus brought about the outpouring of the Spirit after his ascension and in fulfillment of prophecy. Yet Jesus' farewell speeches in Luke-Acts present the event as an actualization of God's promises to the Jewish people. *Dialogue* 87, by contrast, paints the activity of the Spirit among Christ-believers as a manifestation of God's withdrawal from Jews. In this passage Justin sees Jesus, in essence, as taking the Spirit away from the Jewish people and giving it to Christ-believers instead.[32]

LXX Joel 3 and the Spirit

Perhaps the most striking link between Luke's version of the descent of the Spirit upon the disciples and Justin's description of the same event in *Dialogue* 87 is their mutual use of LXX Joel 3 (Acts 2:17-21; *Dial.* 87.6). Both authors cite LXX Joel 3 to prove that the descent of the Spirit upon believers was the fulfillment of ancient prophecy. Justin uses an excerpt from LXX Joel 3:1-2 in conjunction with Ephesians 4:8 (see LXX Ps. 67:19)[33] to explain how Jesus came to bestow the gifts of the Spirit upon believers:

Εἶπεν οὖν· Ἀνέβη εἰς ὕψος, ᾐχμαλώτευσεν αἰχμαλωσίαν, ἔδωκε δόματα τοῖς υἱοῖς τῶν ἀνθρώπων. Καὶ πάλιν ἐν ἑτέρᾳ προφητείᾳ εἴρηται· Καὶ ἔσται μετὰ ταῦτα, ἐκχέω τὸ πνεῦμά μου ἐπὶ πᾶσαν σάρκα καὶ ἐπὶ τοὺς δούλους μου καὶ ἐπὶ τὰς δούλας μου, καὶ προφητεύσουσι.

Therefore it is said: "When he ascended on high, he took captivity captive and he gave gifts to the sons of men." And again, in another prophecy it says: "And after these things it shall be [that] I will pour out my Spirit upon all flesh and upon my manservants and my maidservants and they shall prophesy." (*Dial.* 87.6b)

Luke also cites LXX Joel 3:1-2, describing the event as the fulfillment of God's promises to Israel and applying it to those who had experienced the first outpouring of the Spirit:

Καὶ ἔσται ἐν ταῖς ἐσχάταις ἡμέραις, λέγει ὁ θεός, ἐκχεῶ ἀπὸ τοῦ πνεύματός μου ἐπὶ πᾶσαν σάρκα, καὶ προφητεύσουσιν οἱ υἱοὶ ὑμῶν καὶ αἱ θυγατέρες ὑμῶν, καὶ οἱ νεανίσκοι ὑμῶν ὁράσεις ὄψονται, καὶ οἱ πρεσβύτεροι ὑμῶν ἐνυπνίοις ἐνυπνιασθήσονται καί γε ἐπὶ τοὺς δούλους μου καὶ ἐπὶ τὰς δούλας μου ἐν ταῖς ἡμέραις ἐκείναις ἐκχεῶ ἀπὸ τοῦ πνεύματός μου, καὶ προφητεύσουσιν.

And it shall be in the last days, God says, I will pour out my Spirit upon all flesh and your sons and your daughters shall prophesy and your young men shall see visions and your elders shall dream dreams. Indeed, I will pour out my Spirit upon my male and female servants in those days and they shall prophesy. (Acts 2:17-18)

In their common dependence upon LXX Joel 3:1-2,[34] both authors forge a link between the activity of the Spirit and prophecy such that the Spirit's action can be summed up as a prophetic empowerment. Elsewhere in the *Dialogue*, Justin makes marked connections between the Spirit and prophecy and uses "the prophetic Spirit" as a phrase that refers to the activity of the Spirit and prophecy (for example, *Dial.* 32.3; 38.2; 43.3, 4; 49.6; 53.4; 55.1; 56.5; 77.3; 84.2; 91.4; 139.1).[35] Likewise, Luke connects the descent of the Spirit with the gift of prophecy by repeating the phrase "and they will prophesy" (προφητεύσουσιν) at the end of his citation of LXX Joel 3:1-2 (Acts 2:18). In short, both authors present the descent of the spirit as the fulfillment of LXX Joel 3 and place emphasis upon the prophetic aspect of the activity of the Spirit.

Justin and Luke both use LXX Joel 3:1-2 to describe the activity of the Spirit, but their respective representations of the fulfillment of this prophecy still diverge. In addition to applying LXX Joel 3:1-2 to the group of disciples who first received the Spirit, Peter's speech in Acts 2 indicates that the eschatological gift of the Spirit was intended for the Jewish nation. This application of LXX Joel 3:1-2 is evident in Peter's appeal, in addressing the crowd that is gathered for the feast, to the "whole house of Israel" (2:36). He presents these "Israelites" (2:22) as a repentant group who want the blessing of the Spirit (2:37-38). Furthermore, Peter tells this Jewish group that God's promise of restoration, which he provides by giving the Spirit, is for them and for their children:

ὑμῖν γάρ ἐστιν ἡ ἐπαγγελία καὶ τοῖς τέκνοις ὑμῶν καὶ πᾶσιν τοῖς εἰς μακράν, ὅσους ἂν προσκαλέσηται κύριος ὁ θεὸς ἡμῶν.

For the promise is for you and for your children and for all those who are far off, as many as the Lord our God shall summon. (Acts 2:39)

Peter's speech in Acts 2 thus presents the descent of the Spirit as the fulfillment of God's promise to pour out his end-time blessing upon Jews. Moreover, Luke depicts the crowd as responding to this offer of restoration in the affirmative (Acts 2:38, 40-41). By contrast, Justin cites LXX Joel 3:1-2 to sum up his argument that it was necessary for the gifts of the Spirit to cease from operating among the Jewish people (*Dial.* 87.5). For him, LXX Joel 3:1-2 confirms his conclusion that the Spirit was taken from the Jews and given to Jesus and Christ-believers instead.

In view of this difference, the manner in which Luke and Justin cite LXX Joel 3 is striking. Luke follows the text of LXX Joel 3 closely and affirms that the Jewish people are recipients of the end-time blessing of the Spirit by stating explicitly that "your sons and your daughters" (οἱ υἱοὶ ὑμῶν καὶ αἱ θυγατέρες ὑμῶν), "your young men" (οἱ νεανίσκοι ὑμῶν), and "your elders" (οἱ πρεσβύτερου ὑμῶν) are the recipients of the Spirit.[36] This element of the citation is conspicuously missing from the citation of the passage provided by Justin. He makes no reference to the phrase from LXX Joel 3:1 that includes second-person plural pronouns; it is completely absent from his quotation of this passage. The omission is significant, insofar as the inclusion of such a phrase would run contrary to his thesis that the Spirit no longer resides with Israel. Indeed, his argument is clearly not compatible with Peter's declaration that God had fulfilled his promise to Jews by sending the Spirit upon their sons and daughters, their elders and youths. Although it is possible that Justin relied on an unusual or condensed version of the citation,[37] it seems telling that he (or the tradition upon which he relied) neglected the specific segment of the passage that explicitly refers to the restoration of the Jewish people. It betrays an agenda that contradicts both the promise of LXX Joel 3:1-2 and the Lukan tradition of its interpretation.

Conclusion

Although in many ways, Justin's account of how the Spirit came upon Jesus and Christ-believers parallels that of Luke, his interpretation of these events represents a significant departure from the Lukan tradition. For Luke, the outpouring of the Spirit signals the eschatological restoration of the Jewish people. For Justin, the descent of the Spirit upon Jesus and the disciples is but another indication of God's denunciation and rejection of the Jews.

Helmut Koester has argued that Justin seeks to heighten the connection between the LXX and Lukan traditions. He suggests that "Justin did not hesitate to revise the texts of Matthew and Luke on several occasions in order to establish an even closer verbal agreement between the prophecies of the Greek Bible and the record of their fulfillment in the text of the gospels."[38] If Justin was also working with a Lukan tradition when he cited LXX Joel 3 in *Dialogue* 87, then the distance between the two accounts of the Spirit's activity is particularly remarkable. Justin's departure from Luke's presentation of the Spirit—and especially his unusual citation of LXX Joel 3—would seem to represent an irregularity in his typical pattern of exegesis.

In my view, this irregularity can be explained by taking note of the dominance of apologetic concerns in Justin's treatment of the Spirit. His interpretation of the work of the Spirit in *Dialogue* 87 was primarily geared toward his desire to validate the church's legacy as the rightful heir to Israel's traditions. Although Justin could have made the connection between the descent of the Spirit and the fulfillment of God's promise to restore the Jewish people, as Luke does, such an affirmation would weaken his thesis that the church was the replacement of Israel. Consequently, in his depiction of the activity of the Spirit in *Dialogue* 87, Justin redirects the promises of LXX Joel 3 and, in so doing, reaffirms his own view that the Jews were no longer God's chosen people.

CHAPTER EIGHT

The Relationship between the Writings of Justin Martyr and the So-Called *Gospel of Peter*

PAUL FOSTER

The Methodology of Establishing Literary Dependence

AS YET THERE IS NO AGREED METHOD, in relation to early Christian writings, for deter-mining whether one text is citing or alluding to another. Neither is there consensus regarding what authors expected their audiences to make of any quotations they rec-ognized in the derivative text. Such questions have arisen largely in the context of the discussion of the use of the Old Testament by the authors of texts that later formed the New Testament. For Richard Hays the common scriptural knowledge of an author such as Paul and his readers,[1] who were drawn predominantly from synagogue con-verts, implies that the audience brought a preknowledge of the context of the original citation. Consequently, Hays argues, the resonance the quotation evoked for the orig-inal target audience arose from the wider meaning of the Old Testament passage from which the brief citation was drawn.[2] Such claims have been effectively dismantled by Christopher Tuckett, who has demonstrated, with a range of counterexamples, not only that it is unlikely that audiences apprehended the wider context of the cited pas-sage,[3] but more fundamentally, that even when Paul employs citations on certain occa-sions when he quotes adjacent Old Testament verses, this often results in contradictory interpretations that reveal no sensitivity to contextual nuances.[4] Such issues sur-rounding wider context may be less relevant in the case of writings from outside the corpus of Old or New Testament, since there was potentially less at stake in terms of the authority of such texts.[5] Thus perhaps the question of authorial intention in citing texts can be left a little more to one side when canonical writings are not under dis-

cussion. Instead, the central and prior question that is of concern in the present discussion is how a quotation can be identified, even before one asks what it means for
either the author or the audience.

There appear to be at least three ways that a citation can be identified. First, the
author making the citation can utilize a direct reference to the previous author or
employ some type of formula. Such techniques are used by both New Testament writers and other early Christian authors. Famously, Matthew uses a set of citation formulae in his birth narrative and also at other points in the gospel to demonstrate the
fulfillment of the Jewish Scriptures.[6] Justin similarly refers to the source of material he
cites, but not altogether unambiguously. For instance, when recalling the words of
institution of the Eucharist, he introduces the citation with the reference, Οἱ γὰρ
ἀπόστολοι ἐν τοῖς γενομένοις ὑπ' αὐτῶν Ἀπομνημονεύμασιν ἃ καλεῖται Εὐαγγέλια
("For the apostles, in the memoirs composed by them, which are called Gospels . . .";
1 Apol. 66.3). The use of such formulae shows that an author believed he was citing
from an existing tradition or, if his motives were somewhat more disingenuous, that
he at least wanted his readers to believe he was citing some authority. If there is no
explicit reference to the prior source, however, as in the vast majority of cases of citations, then dependence can still be established.

The second test requires an extended piece of shared text. It is debatable as to what
constitutes sufficient shared text to allow such an identification to be made, and how
many deviations between the two portions of text should be allowed before excluding
the possibility of dependence. Even in such cases large blocks of parallel text do not
necessarily establish direct borrowing. There may be a common literary ancestor upon
which both surviving texts have drawn independently. This set of circumstances has
necessitated the Q hypothesis in New Testament studies. This is because, notwithstanding the striking parallels between Matthew and Luke in certain passages that they
uniquely share in the Gospel tradition,[7] there are other so-called double-tradition passages that they share in which the deviations are so great that the case for direct borrowing of Matthew from Luke or Luke from Matthew becomes implausible. Instead,
the most likely explanation is that of independent reworking of an underlying, but no
longer extant, source.[8]

The third criterion is actually a factor that modifies the second. The rarity of the
terminology needs to be taken into account. Thus if particularly unusual terms or
phrases are employed, then less overlapping text is required to establish the case of literary dependence. Again, this criterion perhaps is impossible to represent in a strictly
quantifiable way; instead, it can only be used with a somewhat subjective sensitivity
regarding what constitutes a plausible case of an example of citation, as opposed to a
random coincidence of similar words or parallel concepts.

Finally, it needs to be noted that when a later author is citing a passage from the
Gospel tradition, an added layer of complexity is involved. If the material being quoted
occurs in one or more of the Gospels, then it may be impossible to accurately identify
the source. This is especially the case with a number of the "triple-tradition" passages
common to the Synoptic Gospels. In such cases the difficulty of determining a later
writer's dependence specifically on one of the Gospel writers (as opposed to one of the

other evangelists who has a parallel account) is usually resolved by looking for evidence of redactional material in the later document.[9] This is the principle that guided Helmut Koester in his work. He states, "So the question of usage depends upon whether in the cited portion the redactional work of an evangelist is found."[10] This more rigorous approach does unfortunately exclude a number of potential parallels, but to include them would only lead to a lack of precision and results that would be indeterminate. Fortunately, in considering the relationship between the writings of Justin and the *Gospel of Peter*, this problem does not greatly impinge on the analysis of potential parallels as examples of direct literary dependence.

Possible Contacts between the *Gospel of Peter* and Justin Martyr

Alongside the debate concerning the relationship with the canonical texts (in particular the four Gospels of the New Testament), investigations into the *Gospel of Peter* have also considered whether there are any demonstrable relationships with other early Christian texts. Although interest in these questions of literary dependence has not been as intense as interest in those relating to the canonical Gospels, nonetheless such issues were raised at the time of the initial discovery of the text and have since been revisited, albeit sporadically. One of the most important collections of texts to come under discussion as potentially standing in a literary relationship with the *Gospel of Peter* is the writings of Justin Martyr. In particular the discussion relates to parallels between passages in Justin's *First Apology* and *Dialogue* alongside texts drawn from the first apocryphal text discovered in a codex interred at Akhmîm, which contained the partial remains of a total of four extracanonical writings.

Apart from a strict analysis of potential literary parallels, the relationship with the works of Justin has fascinated certain scholars because of the temporal proximity between Justin's writings and the date of Serapion's reported visit to Rhossus, when the *Gospel of Peter* is first attested in the extant sources.[11] Thus for Peter Pilhofer, who advocates the literary dependence of Justin upon the *Gospel of Peter*, it is accordingly possible to push back the date of composition of the noncanonical Gospels prior to the writings of Justin. He argues for a *terminus ad quem* of no later than 150–160 C.E. However, he feels that one must allow time for the *Gospel of Peter* to circulate prior to its use by Justin. Consequently, he suggests a date of composition no later than 130 C.E. He states, "The *terminus ad quem* for the Gospel of Peter lies in the writings of Justin (c. 150/160). Therefore the nascence of the Gospel of Peter is at the latest found around 130."[12] Not all scholars have come to the same conclusions concerning the direction of literary dependence. Discussing the question of Justin's use of the *Gospel of Peter*, H. B. Swete makes the following assessment: "There is at present no satisfactory proof that our fragment was used by any writer before the end of the second century."[13] Such conflicting views require reexamination of the relevant texts; as is often the case, however, the difference of opinion arises not through considering an alternative set of texts, but rather because there are varying understandings of what constitutes textual dependence and how the direction of that dependence is demonstrated.

In the case of the writings of Justin, there is not only a shared tradition to consider containing literary parallels. Also of significance is the fact that Justin alludes to the process of the transmission of traditions concerning the apostle Peter. He writes:

καὶ τὸ εἰπεῖν μετωνομακέναι αὐτὸν Πέτρον ἕνα τῶν ἀποστολῶν, καὶ γεγράφθαι ἐν τοῖς ἀπομνημονεύμασιν αὐτοῦ γεγενημένον καὶ τοῦτο, μετὰ καὶ ἄλλους δύο ἀδελφούς, υἱοῦς Ζεβεδαίου ὄντας, ἐπωνομακέναι ὀνόματι Βοανεργές, ὅ ἐστιν υἱοῖ βροντῆς . . .

And when it is said that he changed the name of one of the apostles to Peter; and when it is written in the memoirs of him that this so happened, as well as that he changed the names of other two brothers, the sons of Zebedee, to Boanerges, which means sons of thunder . . . (*Dial.* 106.3)[14]

Debate has arisen concerning the referent of the third-person singular genitive pronoun that follows the term ἀπομνημονεύμασιν ("memoirs").[15] It has been variously suggested that the phrase ἀπομνημονεύμασιν αὐτοῦ refers to the memoirs either of Jesus or of Peter. Traditionally the former option has been preferred, with the most widely used English-language translation indicating this by capitalizing the pronoun, that is, "the memoirs of Him." In opposition to this interpretation, Pilhofer argues strongly for understanding the pronoun as referring to Peter. Directly in relation to *Dialogue* 106.3, he argues that "Justin here in point of fact is speaking of the Gospel of Peter, since, if one takes Justin's citation method into account, one would regard it as quite possible that he is bringing together a story from the Gospel of Peter with another which possibly did not come from the Gospel of Peter, without characterizing that any further."[16]

Primarily, Pilhofer bases his argument on the other uses of ἀπομνημονεύματα found in Justin's writings. The term occurs fifteen times in total,[17] and apart from this occurrence it usually occurs in close connection to a reference to the apostles in the plural (for example, ἀπομνημονεύμασιν τῶν ἀποστολῶν; *Dial.* 100) or in the absolute form τῶν ''ἀπομνημονευμάτων (*Dial.* 105). As is apparent from the absolute form, this has become an abbreviation of the fuller title "memoirs of the apostles," conveniently designated as "the memoirs." However, Pilhofer takes the replacement of a collective reference to the apostles in *Dialogue* 106 by the singular pronoun αὐτοῦ as showing that one member of the group is being described, namely, Peter, who was mentioned in the previous clause. Graham Stanton, likewise, after a careful and qualified discussion, leans slightly in favor of taking the pronoun as referring to Peter. He, however, does not draw the conclusion Pilhofer advances that this constitutes a reference to the *Gospel of Peter*; instead, he suggests that "Justin is here referring to Peter's memoirs, i.e. Mark's Gospel."[18] Thus Stanton marries Justin's comment with the early tradition known through the writings of Papias and other church fathers that Mark was the amanuensis of Peter. What Pilhofer does not entertain is the possibility that the genitive αὐτοῦ does not depict a possessive relationship but is functioning as an objective genitive. In this sense Justin could be referring to "the memoirs [of the apostles] about Jesus (or Peter)," where the bracketed reference to the apostles is implied, as is elsewhere the case with the shorter form that Justin only uses in *Dialogue* 105–7. Furthermore, on grammatical grounds the pronoun αὐτοῦ is far more likely to refer to the same person who changes the names of the sons of Zebedee, since the infinitive ἐπωνομακέναι assumes Jesus as its subject without signaling any change from the previous subject designated by the pronoun αὐτοῦ. Thus the case Pilhofer advances is not compelling since it depends upon a grammatically unlikely reading of the text and also creates a reading that stands in tension with other uses of the phrase ἀπομνημον-εύμασιν τῶν ἀποστολῶν/τῶν ἀπομνημονευμάτων as it occurs in Justin's writings.

This leaves consideration of similar literary traditions in order to determine the nature of the relationship between the *Gospel of Peter* and Justin. Swete considered only three parallels between the two authors, but he dismissed the first of these (*G.Pet.* 1.1 and *1 Apol.* 40) as being of little consequence.[19] Adolf Harnack produced a longer list of potential parallels, consisting of six items, but conceded that a number of these are not conclusive.[20] Theodor Zahn also drew up a similar list.[21] Pilhofer appears to have rearranged the potential parallels suggested by previous authors into two categories. First he looks at general narrative features such as heightened guilt being placed upon the Jews and more interest in the role of Herod Antipas or the people in the trial and crucifixion.[22] While such features may indeed be shared by the respective texts, they are not unique elements and in fact reflect part of a general tendency evidenced from the second century onward to shift blame for the death of Jesus from Roman authorities to the Jews and their leaders. In fact, Pilhofer considers only two direct textual parallels (coincidentally the same two that Swete examined as being potentially interesting). The first of these describes the mob violence in dragging Jesus away for execution and placing him on the judgment seat.

1 Apol. 35.6	*G.Pet.* 3.6-7
Καὶ γὰρ, ὡς εἶπεν ὁ προφήτης, διασύροντες αὐτὸν ἐκάθισαν ἐπὶ βήματος καὶ εἶπον κρῖνον ἡμῖν.	Οἱ δὲ λαβόντες τὸν Κν ὤθουν αὐτὸν τρέχοντες καὶ ἔλεγον Σύρωμεν τὸν υἱὸν τοῦ θυ, ἐξουσίαν αὐτοῦ ἐσχηκότες. 7. καὶ πορφύραν αὐτὸν περιέβαλλον, καὶ ἐκάθισαν αὐτὸν ἐπὶ καθέδραν κρίσεως, λέγοντες Δικαίως κρῖνε, βασιλεῦ τοῦ Ἰσραήλ.

There are a number of significant points of contact here. First, both texts refer to the "dragging" of Jesus, although Justin uses the compound form διασύροντες, where the *Gospel of Peter* has the simplex form σύρωμεν. The two accounts agree in the use of the verb ἐκάθισαν and the act of sitting Jesus on a seat associated with the judicial process. Finally, in both texts, Jesus is called upon to provide judgment. For Harnack this parallel offered incontrovertible proof that Justin had drawn upon the *Gospel of Peter*. He concludes, "With it Justin's source appears incontestably to be revealed."[23] Yet no supporting reasons are given for this assertion. Obviously Harnack feels the common elements demand direct literary dependence, but he fails to explain how the direction of dependence is determined. By contrast, Swete is far more detailed in his treatment of this passage and outlines three reasons for rejecting direct literary dependence:

> (1) The incident seems to rest on a misinterpretation of John xix. 13 which might have occurred to both writers independently; their way of stating it is certainly independent. (2) The words put in the mouth of the mockers differ, and seem to be based on passages of the Old Testament; Justin expressly refers to Isaiah lviii. 2, Peter seems to have in view similar words in Psalms and Proverbs. (3) Peter's σύρωμεν may certainly have suggested Justin's διασύρ- οντες, yet the resemblance is in sound rather than meaning, and it is more likely that διασύροντες was supplied by the Old Testament.[24]

The second of these points appears to be the strongest of Swete's arguments, since the verbal dissimilarity speaks against literary dependence. The perceived "misinterpretation" of John 19:13 described in the first point may well be an intentional ambiguity introduced by the author of the Fourth Gospel. Thus the Fourth Gospel creates an uncertainty concerning whether Pilate or Jesus sat on the judgment seat, the βῆμα, allowing the audience to understand that in fact it is Jesus judging Pilate, contrary to surface appearances. The plurality of meaning in the Fourth Gospel is disambiguated by both Justin and the *Gospel of Peter* by making the more subversive reading of the Gospel text the single interpretation of this passage. However, the differing ways in which this alternative reading of the Fourth Gospel is exploited by both authors suggests that they have independently chosen to promote the more radical perspective of the Johannine narrative. With the third point, Swete is correct that the compound form διασύρω, "to torment"[25] and the simplex form σύρω, "to drag," differ significantly in meaning, yet it is striking that morphologically related verbal forms have been chosen.

Perhaps of even greater weight are the observations Swete makes in relation to the direction of dependence in what he considers to be the hypothetical case that literary dependence was to exist between these two passages.

> If . . . it is thought that one of the two writers had the other in view, the evidence seems to point to a use of Justin by Peter; in Justin the words of St John are given exactly, in Peter they are varied; Justin's account of the incident is brief, Peter's is more diffuse, after the manner of a writer who is working upon the lines of an earlier authority.[26]

While we must remain remain fully cognizant of E. P. Sanders's demonstration that such perceived tendencies of a later writer can often be shown not to hold,[27] Swete's generalized hypothetical assessment of the direction of dependence is helpful. For, as he outlines, if one were to suggest the most probable direction of literary relationship based on the text alone, then it would be more likely that the *Gospel of Peter* was drawing on Justin than the reverse.[28] The resemblance between these two passages is extremely slight, however, and thus no firm evidence of literary dependence can be found here.

The second example that has been discussed by previous scholars as potentially showing dependence in fact reveals far less shared terminology. Comparison of the parallel reveals that it is based upon the shared use of a single word. Admittedly, this is an example where Justin and the *Gospel of Peter* agree in their choice of a rare term, against the word choice of the canonical Gospels. It is questionable, however, whether this single term is sufficient to exclude the possibility either of coincidental agreement between the two authors or of their independently having drawn upon a no longer extant form of the LXX text of the Psalms that employed this term.

Dial. 97	*G.Pet.* 4.12
Δαβὶδ . . . εἶπον ἐν εἰκοστῷ ψαλμῷ . . . Διεμερίσαντο τὰ ἱμάτιά μου ἑαυτοῖς καὶ ἐπὶ τὸν ἱματισμόν μου ἔβαλον κλῆρον . . . οἱ σταυρώσαντες αὐτὸν ἐμέρισαν τὰ ἱμάτια αὐτοῦ ἑαυτοῖς λαχμὸν βάλλοντες ἕκαστος κατὰ τὴν τοῦ κλήρου ἐπιβολὴν ὃ ἐκλέξασθαι ἐβεβούλητο.	καὶ τεθεικότες τὰ ἐνδύματα ἔμπροσθεν αὐτοῦ διεμερίσαντο καὶ λαχμὸν ἔβαλον ἐπ᾽ αὐτοῖς.

Harnack does not draw any direct conclusion from this example; he simply outlines the correspondence: "In *Dialogue* 97 Justin offers the expression λαχμὸν βάλλοντες at the dividing of the clothing of the Lord. No canonical Gospel offers this, but in the Gospel of Peter we read in v. 12 λαχμὸν ἔβαλον ἐπ᾽ αὐτοῖς."[29] Pilhofer, however, sees this as decisive evidence for the dependence of Justin on the *Gospel of Peter*. Hence in relation to the rare term for "lot," λαχμός, he argues, "This finding is in my judgment the strongest argument for a literary dependence of Justin on the Gospel of Peter."[30] Not only does this appear to overburden the significance of one shared term, but more fundamentally, Pilhofer does not demonstrate why the direction of dependence is self-evidently that of Justin utilizing traditions from the *Gospel of Peter*. By contrast, Swete sees this shared term as stemming from an earlier rendering in one of the revisions of the LXX. He helpfully notes that although the nominal form λαχμός is not evidenced, there is support for the related verbal form. "Now St John with this verse in view uses λάχωμεν, and Symmachus in the Psalm itself rendered יַפִּילוּ גוֹרָל by ἐλάγχανον. Is it overbold to conjecture that in another version which followed the Hebrew more closely, the reading was βάλλοντες or ἔβαλον λαχμόν?"[31] Although

Swete's suggestion is impossible to verify without further textual discoveries, as a hypothesis it is perhaps more plausible than the notion of direct dependence. This is not only because the independent use of source material would account for the infrequently used shared term λαχμὸς, but because recourse to a common source would also explain the striking discrepancies between the two texts.

For the sake of completeness and to illustrate fully the tentative nature of the case for literary dependence, it is worth looking briefly at the other examples that have been put forward in support of a literary relationship between the writings of Justin and the *Gospel of Peter*. First, the role of Herod Antipas in the trial of Jesus has been noted as a shared feature of both authors.[32] For Cassels, the agreement of Justin and the *Gospel of Peter* in describing Antipas as "King of the Jews" is highly significant.[33] The title is used in Justin (*Dial.* 103) but does not in fact occur in the *Gospel of Peter*, where the appellation is "Herod the king" (1.2). While it is interesting that these two texts apply the title "king," which strictly speaking is historically inaccurate, this title was not uncommonly applied to Antipas (cf. Mark 6:14; but for the correct title "tetrarch," see Matt 14.1; Josephus, *Ant.* 18.5.2). This designation of Antipas as "king" and his role in the trial, which is dependent on Luke 23:6-12, provide no basis for establishing a direct literary relationship between Justin and the *Gospel of Peter*.

Similarly, Harnack and Cassels see the report of the two texts of the desertion and dispersal of the disciples after the crucifixion as another point of significant contact.[34] In relation to the note of this given by Justin (*1 Apol.* 50), Cassels states, "This representation is found in the first Synoptic only, but agrees still better with *vv.* 26, 27 and 59 of our fragment."[35] In fact, the "representation" is found in John 20:10 and not in "the first Synoptic," and while both Justin and the *Gospel of Peter* recount this incident in greater detail, there are no significant extended parallels in the actual wording of their accounts. It is better to see both authors independently reflecting upon the Johannine tradition.

The account of the rumor that the disciples stole the body from the tomb is transmitted by both Justin (*1 Apol.* 108) and, at length, the *Gospel of Peter* in 8.30ff. For Harnack this is another possible example of dependence between the two written accounts.[36] Once again, there is little (if any) significant shared terminology, and it is far more plausible that both writers drew independently on the account in Matthew's gospel (Matt. 27:64ff.) or some pre-Matthean source.[37]

These additional examples might be beneficial for establishing a cumulative case if, and only if, the two strongest pieces of evidence were found to be compelling in demonstrating a direct literary relationship between the writings of Justin and the *Gospel of Peter*. Since this is not the case, the additional very loose thematic parallels offer in themselves nothing that makes the case of direct dependence plausible. In fact, the failure of these cases to reveal any unique terminological overlap actually points in the opposite direction and strengthens the case for the independence of the two authors. With these further examples it is interesting to note that the *Gospel of Peter* has the more detailed and expansive narrative, which possibly would be a sign of later composition, if literary dependence was felt to be compelling.

Conclusions

Although the case for Justin's use of the *Gospel of Peter* has been supported by a number of scholars, the evidential base for assessing this claim is remarkably narrow and usually based on only two potential parallels. While there exist a couple of interesting shared elements, there is no extended verbatim agreement between the two authors that would be most convincingly explained through the theory of direct literary dependence. It is also interesting to note that since Pilhofer takes the statement about the "memoirs," ἐν τοῖς ἀπομνημονεύμασιν αὐτοῦ, as a reference to the *Gospel of Peter*,[38] he makes no further attempt to establish the direction of dependence based purely on an analysis of the parallels. Had he done so, it might have become apparent in the two examples considered that perhaps a stronger claim could be made for the primitive character of the version contained in the writings of Justin. Therefore, if direct literary dependence were held to explain the textual relationship, it could be concluded that the *Gospel of Peter* was drawing upon traditions contained in Justin, rather than the opposite case that is usually asserted. As A. J. Bellinzoni noted, however, "Not only are there no parallels between Justin's text and the *Gospel of Peter*, but there is a definite difference in their versions of Jesus' words from the cross."[39] Thus, since the hypothesis of direct literary dependence cannot be supported, it is perhaps more plausible to suggest that shared traditions circulating in the early church offer a better explanation for these two slight points of agreement that exist. Perhaps the most appropriate conclusion to draw is that the two parallels do not provide enough evidence on which to base any firm conclusions concerning either a literary or an oral relationship between Justin's writings and the *Gospel of Peter*.[40]

Part Three

JUSTIN AND HIS TRADITION

CHAPTER NINE

Justin Martyr and the Apologetic Tradition

SARA PARVIS

THE APOLOGETIC TRADITION IS ONE OF THOSE many categories of early Christian literature that has recently begun to make scholars feel a little uneasy. It is acknowledged to be very useful from a teaching perspective, giving lecturers a handy means of designating the next period in Christian literature after the New Testament and the Apostolic Fathers (itself another problematic category). But Bernard Pouderon, writing recently on the second-century Greek apologists, is not the first person to note how difficult the category is to pin down.

> One of them writes a discourse, another a dialogue, another a letter or a treatise. . . . The addressees are not the same either: sometimes the imperial authorities, sometimes the pagan public, even threatened communities. And even their enemies are various: certainly paganism, for most of the writings, but also Judaism, or even heterodox currents like Gnosticism or Marcionism.[1]

Pouderon comforts himself, nonetheless, with the view that the association of these works with one another goes back a very long way. Like so much else in second-, third-, and fourth-century church history, the category of apology as we know it today was initially foisted on us by Eusebius of Caesarea, further shaped by Byzantine librarians, contributed to by a French professor of the late Renaissance, and refined into its modern form by nineteenth-century German scholarship. As with many such categories, it is worth asking whether it should not now be deconstructed again.

I am not here proposing to do away with the category of Christian apology, at least not entirely. Nonetheless, I am proposing that we should think of the apologetic tradition differently: not as a vague group of writings offering some kind of defense of Christianity that could be expanded indefinitely, but as a phenomenon invented in its classic form by Justin Martyr in very specific circumstances, developed by the next generation, and perfected and retired by Tertullian, though its influence on Christian literature continued long afterward in a variety of different forms.

The Construction of the Category of Christian Apology

Eusebius first uses the term *apologia* in passing, in referring (*H.E.* II.2.4) to a work of Tertullian's, the *Apology for the Christians*. (He refers to this work, which he knows in a Greek translation, four more times in the *Ecclesiastical History*, on the last occasion describing it as addressed to the Senate [V.5.5]). Thereafter, he uses the word to describe the products of another six writers, all from the second century: those of Quadratus and Aristides, which he describes as addressed to the emperor Hadrian (IV.3.1–3); those of Justin, addressed to Antoninus Pius and the Senate and to Marcus Aurelius and Lucius Verus (IV.18.2); those of Melito of Sardis and Apolinarius of Hierapolis, both addressed to Marcus Aurelius (IV.26.1–2); and a work of the anti-Montanist writer Miltiades, whom he places in the reign of Commodus, described as addressed to οἱ κοσμικοὶ ἄρχοντες, the earthly rulers (V.17.5).

Of these seven Eusebian apologists, the works of only three have survived more or less complete. Tertullian's brilliant work, at the fountainhead of Latin Christian literature, has a very rich manuscript tradition. Justin's works made the perilous journey past antiquity only thanks to *Parisinus graecus* 450. Aristides', meanwhile, was rescued from an eighth-century Greek novel, *Barlaam and Josaphat*, with the help of manuscripts and fragments in Syriac and Armenian. These three surviving Eusebian apologies were all transmitted independently of one another; the others only survive in fragments, mostly from the *Ecclesiastical History* itself.

Other works, meanwhile, which are either not described as apologies by Eusebius or not mentioned by him at all, were gathered together in Byzantine times to form what is now generally thought of as the first apologetic corpus: the Arethas codex of 914, *Parisinus graecus* 451, named after the bibliophile bishop of Palestinian Caesarea who had the collection made. The codex includes (or in the case of Tatian, once included) Athenagoras's *Embassy*, Tatian's *Against the Greeks*, various pseudo-Justinian works, Clement's *Exhortation* and *Tutor*, Eusebius's own *Preparation for the Gospel*, and his *Against Hierocles*. Eusebius had mentioned Tatian, but without using the word *apologia* to describe a work he nonetheless praised highly; he makes no mention of Athenagoras at all.

The French scholar Fédéric Morel brought together in 1615 most of the collection of texts that still controls the genre as we think of it today, though without using the term "apologist." This included—besides Justin's *Apologies*, the *Dialogue with Trypho*, and the pseudo-Justinian works—Athenagoras and Tatian, the three-book work of Theophilus of Antioch known as *To Autolycus*, and the *Irrisio* of Hermias, an odd work that is generally now considered satire rather than apology. (Theophilus, which Eusebius knows, though not as an *apologia*, was transmitted separately from the two Paris manuscripts that housed most of the other works, in the Venetian manuscript

Marcianus graecus 496, which also contains the only independent copy of Eusebius's two works *Contra Marcellum* and *De Ecclesiastica Theologia*, and hence most of what survives of the work of Marcellus of Ancyra). J. C. Th. von Otto used this collection as the basis of his *Corpus apologetarum christianorum saeculi secundi* of 1851, thus tying the texts definitively to Eusebius's term "apology," an association he gave firmer ground by including the fragments of the Eusebian apologists Quadratus, Aristides, Miltiades, Melito, and Apolinarius of Hierapolis, adding also the *Dialogue of Jason and Papiscus*. Most of the pseudo-Justinian works (with the exception of the so-called *Letter to Diognetus*) have since been tacitly excised from the corpus of apologetic works, but otherwise Otto's collection gives us the category of "apology" (or at least "the Greek apologists of the second century") more or less as we still study it today.[2]

The authors of the recent collaborative volume *Apologetics in the Roman Empire* attempted to set the genre in a wider context by looking at literary expressions of "defence of a religion against actual or perceived opponents" among pagans, Jews, and Christians in the empire's first three centuries.[3] They drew on the expertise of scholars in theology, Jewish studies, Greek philosophy, and Roman history and looked beyond the second-century Greek apologists to the Acts of the Apostles, Tertullian, Minucius Felix, Cyprian, Origen, Eusebius, Lactantius, and Arnobius, and even Constantine's *Oration to the Saints*, as well as Josephus and Philostratus. But their work showed above all that, diverse though the texts normally grouped in the category of early Christian apology are, there is little in the empire of the time to compare with them, at least until the third century. Martin Goodman, in particular, examining the supposed genre of Jewish apology, argues that it comes down to one author, if not one text: Josephus's *Against Apion*. "It will not do to treat it simply as a specimen of a whole genre of pre-existing, but now lost, Jewish literature," he argues: it was "a response by one author to particular pressures at a particular time."[4]

The same is true, I want to argue, of Justin Martyr's apologies. They were not, as they are generally held to be, examples of a preexisting genre, already populated by the analogous writings of Quadratus and Aristides and soon to be joined spontaneously by other works in the same mold. Rather, it was Justin himself who forged the genre of Christian apologetic, in response once again to particular pressures at a particular time, and those who came after him were self-consciously his imitators. If he had a model, it was Josephus; but the genre he created was entirely his own. This should leave us with a much sharper category of Christian apology, which takes better account of the ancient evidence and above all pays sufficient tribute to Justin's achievement.

The Hadrianic Eusebian *Apologiai*

Let us return to Eusebius of Caesarea and his very specific use of the word *apologia*. For Eusebius, what distinguishes the category is clear: it is entirely composed of works that address those with the power to decide policy concerning the execution of Christians, at either an empire-wide or a local level. Eusebius presents five of the seven as addressing emperors, as we have seen, and the other two as addressing the Senate (thanks to the Greek translation of Tertullian's *Apologeticus*, which Eusebius is using), and in the case of Miltiades the "earthly rulers."[5] He knows the works we often call the apologies of Tatian and Theophilus, but calls them a λόγος ("discourse") and a σύγγραμμα ("treatise") respectively, referring to Tatian's work twice by the term λόγος.[6]

The implication of this consistent distinction is that an apology as Eusebius understands it always presents itself as *apologia* in the normal classical sense of the trial speech for the defense. The form of an apology might in fact be a letter or a treatise merely modeled on forensic oratory, as Frances Young notes, but an *apologia* addressed as though to a court is nonetheless always its content.[7] A polemical attack on Greek culture in general such as Tatian's, or a general defense of the reasonableness of Christian belief and practice such as Theophilus's, is something different. Eusebius is very clear about the distinction, in a way in which modern scholars generally are not.[8] On this reckoning, Eusebius, at least when he wrote the *Ecclesiastical History*, would clearly have accepted Athenagoras's *Embassy* as an *apologia* alongside his other seven, and probably also Tertullian's *To Scapula*, but no other work in the apologetic corpus as currently accepted or proposed: neither Justin's *Dialogue with Trypho*, nor Origen's *Against Celsus*, nor indeed his own defensive or polemical works.

The question next arises, however, as to the usefulness of defining the category so tightly: "It is not clear how much is gained by making such a notion [as apology] very precise," objects Michael Frede, "especially if there is no sign that such a precision reflects the way the ancient authors and their readers thought about these writings."[9] Eusebius's very consistent usage, at least in the *Ecclesiastical History*, must reflect the way he, and therefore presumably other readers, thought about the writings he describes as *apologiai*, possibly even the way they were described in manuscripts he had or had heard of, but the question is a fair one nonetheless. After all, such precision would leave us only four or five complete apologies extant, the first of which, Aristides', has very little in common with the others. Indeed, it has much more in common with some of our nonapologies (in particular the *Letter to Diognetus*). It makes no reference to a court of law or to the legal powers of the emperor to whom it is supposedly addressed, and it makes no petition for Christians to be treated better.[10] Instead, it merely argues the foolishness of different forms of paganism, briefly dismisses the claims of the Jews, and praises Christians for having discovered the truth, exhorting listeners in general terms to embrace it and escape the coming judgment of the human race.[11]

The apology of Aristides, indeed, barely fits the Eusebian definition of apology established above: there is nothing forensic about it at all. This is less of a problem than it seems, however, because Eusebius had no copy of Aristides' apology, and perhaps had no idea what was in it, other than that it was supposedly addressed to the emperor Hadrian. He mentions the apology of Quadratus a few lines earlier (IV.3.1), noting that it is extant among many of the brothers and that "we have a copy," which he goes on to quote a little of, commenting in passing on Quadratus's orthodoxy. In the case of Aristides, he merely says, "And Aristides, too, a faithful man committed to our piety, like Quadratus left behind an apology for our faith, having addressed it to Hadrian. And his writing, too, is still preserved among many."

Aristides' work, in these circumstances, need not invalidate our Eusebian category of *apologia*: we have merely to assume Eusebius knew too little about the work to realize it did not fit, not a difficult assumption. We have still to consider its relation to Justin's apologies, however, because (along with Quadratus) it currently rather stands in the way of any claim on Justin's behalf that he invented the genre.

First of all, we should note that the view that it predates Justin is far from secure. Two datings are offered by the textual tradition of Aristides: the reign of Hadrian (the Armenian text, corroborated by Eusebius, who in the *Chronicon* dates it more precisely to the ninth year of Hadrian), and that of Antoninus Pius (according to the address of the Syriac text).[12] Eusebius's account in the *Chronicon*, in which Aristides is an Athenian philosopher and he and Quadratus address their apologies to Hadrian while the latter is visiting Athens, seems circumstantial enough, but a close look at the text shows that there is actually no intrinsic connection in Eusebius's narrative between the account of Hadrian's visit and the two apologies, and it is to the former that the date is attached.[13] Eusebius has dropped the precise date by the time of the *Ecclesiastical History*, showing that he no longer thinks he has any reliable information on the point. The juxtaposition of the two events appears to be based simply on the intelligence that Aristides is an Athenian (it is possible that Eusebius was confusing Aristides with Athenagoras at this point), but even this information has been quietly dropped by the time of the *Ecclesiastical History*, where Eusebius fails to cite any evidence linking either writer to the reign of Hadrian. The link with Hadrian may, in effect, merely be a deduction, by Eusebius or by an earlier source, from the rescript of Hadrian attached to Justin's *Apology*: it seemed to make sense to assume that this had been prompted by some earlier Christian petition along the same lines as Justin's.[14]

The text of Aristides' *Apology* itself is of little help with dating: references to the adorers of the gods, the Jews, and the Christians are all too general to supply an immediate context. There is no reference to the Bar Kokhba revolt of 132–135 in the Jewish section, which was to loom so large in Justin's *Dialogue with Trypho*, but nor is there a reference to the destruction of the temple under Vespasian and Titus, which would have seemed apposite in the earlier period. The Christian theology seems self-confident and timeless, with its emphasis on the lordship of Christ and his judgment in the age to come, plausible at any point in the second century or even into the third; likewise, the polemic against idols could spring from before or after Justin. The one thing that seems clear is that this discourse was not pronounced in the presence of either Hadrian or Antoninus Pius: it makes no real attempt to engage with the non-Christian world at all, let alone to present itself as a plausible address to an emperor. The address to the supposed kingly interlocutor is entirely ungrounded in any reality of protocol or identity, and even in the syntax itself: every single use of the vocative "O king" (ὦ βασιλεῦ) could be removed from the text without affecting either the grammar or the argument. They could be replaced by an individual's name, as in the *Letter to Diognetus* (which shows far more interest in the opinions of its interlocutor, fictional or real), or left out entirely, leaving merely the occasional rhetorical second-person singular of the conventional Greek discourse. The ease with which this can be done leaves us with the definite impression that we are dealing with an apology manufactured from a general treatise, ascribed to Aristides (wherever the name came from) and given a location in the reign of Hadrian in order to match Hadrian's rescript, all after the pattern of Justin.

The claim that Aristides is a philosopher, deducible from the text insofar as it deals in passing with some of the stock philosophical questions, also follows the model of Justin suspiciously closely. It looks as though, whether he wrote before or after him, Aristides became an apologist only in the wake of Justin.

We should turn now to the other candidate for the invention of apology, Quadratus, whose claims cannot be dismissed so easily, because Eusebius actually has a copy of and had definitely read his work, and still thought it worthy of the technical term he denied Tatian and Theophilus. We ourselves, meanwhile, are at a disadvantage, because almost none of Quadratus's apology survives. Nonetheless, there are some odd features about what we do know that bear further scrutiny.

First, there is the way Eusebius sees Quadratus and Aristides as a pair, both in the *Chronicon* and in the *Ecclesiastical History*. In Jerome's translation of the *Chronicon*: "Quadratus, a disciple of the apostles, and Aristides, a philosopher from among us, dedicated to Hadrian works composed in favor of the Christian religion." In the *Ecclesiastical History*, though Quadratus comes first and a short discussion of him ensues, together with one fragment, he is still joined with Aristides by a μέν and δέ construction: τοιοῦντος μὲν οὗτος. καὶ Ἀριστείδης δέ . . . τῷ Κοδράτῳ παραπλησίως ὑπὲρ τῆς πίστεως ἀπολογίαν ἐπιφωνήσας Ἀδριανῷ καταλέλοιπεν ("And Aristides, too, . . . like Quadratus . . ."; IV.3.3, translated in full above).

As Eusebius tells the story in the *Chronicon*, the two seem to catch Hadrian together when he is in Athens in 124–125 being initiated into the Eleusinian mysteries. In the Armenian version, as noted above (as well as the Syriac text of Aristides), Aristides is an Athenian philosopher. In Jerome's own account, in *De Viris Illustribus* 19, Quadratus is bishop of Athens: in other words, he is identified with the bishop Quadratus of Athens to whom Dionysius of Corinth refers in one of his letters (*H.E.* IV.23.3). If some tradition Eusebius had access to termed Aristides and Quadratus as a philosopher and bishop of Athens, and claimed that they both addressed Hadrian, the idea that they did so together the year he came to Athens would have been more or less inescapable.

Eusebius seems, nonetheless, to have rejected the idea that Quadratus was the bishop of Athens to whom Dionysius refers, despite the fact that this notion seems the only plausible origin of his initial setting of Quadratus's apology in Athens. It is likely that he did so precisely for reasons of chronology. He knows that Dionysius of Corinth wrote to Soter, who became bishop of Rome in the seventh year of Marcus Aurelius (168), and that Dionysius also refers to Quadratus as bishop of Athens (*H.E.* IV.23.3). But one thing he definitely knows from Quadratus's writing is that Quadratus is much earlier than that: it is the one thing he is keen above all to tell us about Quadratus in the *Ecclesiastical History*.

> Trajan having held rule for a whole twenty years less six months, Aelius Hadrianus succeeds to power. Quadratus, having addressed a discourse to him, delivers it, having put together an apology concerning our Godly piety, because some wicked men were trying to cause trouble for our people. It is still in circulation among very many of the brothers, but we also have the treatise (σύγγραμμα). From which can be seen shining proofs of the intelligence of the man and of his apostolic alignment. And he shows his own antiq-

uity (ὁ δ' αὐτὸς τὴν καθ' ἑαυτὸν ἀρχαιότητα παραφαίνει) through the things he tells thus in his own words:

> "But the works of our Savior remained always present, for they were real: those who had been healed, those who had risen from the dead, who did not only appear when they were healed and raised, but were also always present, not only when the Saviour was sojourning, but for a good length of time after he departed, so that some of them even reached to our times." (*H.E.* IV.3.1–2)

By the time of the *Ecclesiastical History*, in other words, Eusebius has lost his nerve altogether about the link with Athens, in the cases of both Quadratus and Aristides. He has also lost his nerve about making Hadrian's rescript in part a response to their apologies. He continues to link the two men together, and to link both with Hadrian, but what he has to say about both is now far more guarded. Even his description of the address to Hadrian, given above, does not say in so many words that the text Eusebius has is Quadratus's apology, or that it was the apology that Quadratus addressed to Hadrian. He has come to see since writing the *Chronicon* that something is wrong with the account he has inherited of Aristides and Quadratus. Perhaps the problem is that he actually read the works in the intervening period.

He may have read something else also: the anonymous anti-Montanist writing addressed to Abercius Marcellus (passages from it are given in *H.E.* V.16.3—17.4), which mentions another Quadratus as part of a succession of prophets of the province of Asia (V.17.4).[15] This gave Eusebius another powerful reason to push the apologist Quadratus as early as possible. It is clear from the anti-Montanist source that this Quadratus was claimed by the Montanists in their line of prophetic succession, though the anonymous writer sees Quadratus as a very different kind of prophet from the Montanists. Scholars of Montanism have argued on the basis of the twelfth-century chronicle of Michael the Syrian that Quadratus may even have been buried in the tomb of the prophets Priscilla, Maximilla, and Montanus at Pepuza, a suggestion made the more likely because Quadratus is significantly omitted from the list of great Christians who lie asleep in the various cities of Asia awaiting the resurrection given by Polycrates and the Asian synod in their letter to Victor about the date of Easter of the early 190s (*H.E.* V.24.2–5).[16]

Eusebius, interestingly, leaves it ambiguous whether the prophet Quadratus and the apologist Quadratus are the same person.[17] He discusses the prophet Quadratus first, in the reign of Trajan, after his discussion of Ignatius of Antioch and Polycarp, stressing their early date and the fact that they "take the first rank in the apostolic succession" (which is why they become known as the Apostolic Fathers). But he says curiously little about Quadratus at this point: "And among those who were renowned in these times was Quadratus, who, it is said, together with the daughters of Philip, was distinguished because of his prophetic gift" (III.37.1). He then briefly discusses 1 and 2 Clement, and the remainder of book III is given over to a discussion of Papias. When he introduces Quadratus in the following book (after a short discussion of the Jewish rebellions of 115–117), as given above, he neither says of him, as he usually does when reintroducing someone, "whom we have already spoken of," or some such formula, nor does he give his usual little epithet on introducing someone for the first time (as he does with Aristides, "a faithful man devoted to our piety").[18] On the other hand, his placing the prophet Quadratus in the company of the first postapostolic generation only really makes sense on the basis of the extract he quotes from the apologist Quadratus. In addition, his insistence on the intelligence and orthodoxy of the apologist Quadratus seems to answer anxieties that belong with the prophet Quadratus. Perhaps he is merely hedging his bets, but he seems to believe it is at least possible that the two are the same person.

In fact, the arguments for the identity of the two are strong, because all of the apology's connections are with that same Asian milieu. There are close parallels between the fragment Eusebius cites and passages in both Papias (bishop of Hierapolis) and Irenaeus (originally from the same region).[19] In addition, three of the other apologists mentioned by Eusebius—Melito of Sardis, Apolinarius of Hierapolis, and Miltiades—are also theologians of the province of Asia, and all are involved in the lively disputes of the 170s and 180s about prophecy in general and Montanism in particular. Melito is probably largely pro-Montanist (like Irenaeus, without having himself become a Montanist, an anachronism in the 170s anyway), because he writes a treatise on prophecy (IV.26.2), and is described by Polycrates as having "lived entirely in the Holy Spirit," while both Apolinarius and Miltiades are described by Eusebius as having written treatises against the Montanists (though there was also a Montanist Miltiades, about whom equally little is known, to whom the apology could also easily be ascribed).[20] When we consider that Tertullian was also drawn to Montanism, the origins of Eusebius's collection of apologies, assuming they were all available in a single volume, begin to look very interesting indeed.

What seems clear is that neither Aristides nor Quadratus can any longer be securely dated to the reign of Hadrian. Their dating there looks to have come from a manufactured attempt to make Hadrian's rescript the response to apologies like Justin's, by doctoring Aristides' treatise to make it look like an apology addressed to an emperor, presumably doing something similar with Quadratus's, turning them into a bishop and philosopher of Athens and connecting their works with Hadrian's visit there of 124–125. Eusebius had largely seen through this fiction by the time of the *Ecclesiastical History*, having now read at least one of the works involved, but was unsure what else to do with them and so left them in the reign of Hadrian as addressed to him, thinking that Quadratus must in any case be early, having no warrant to think there had been any apologies addressed to Trajan, and being keen to keep Quadratus safely away from any proximity to the rise of Montanism. But if Papias could argue that some of those healed by Christ were still alive in the time of Hadrian, Quadratus could have been born as late as the same reign and still have spoken of their "reaching to our times." There is no difficulty, from the manuscript evidence, in assigning Aristides to the reign of Antoninus Pius, and since the tradition Eusebius inherited clearly presents him and Quadratus as a pair, there is not too much difficulty in moving Quadratus to that reign also, particularly since Antoninus Pius began his full title with the names Aelius Hadrianus in any case. The influence of Justin's achievement on the Aristides tradition, at least, is clear. Aristides was turned into an apologist in the wake of Justin, and it is likely that the same was true of Quadratus. We are therefore at liberty to consider Justin as the first Christian apologist.

Justin and His Successors

Let us now turn to Justin himself, for there is much positive evidence to support his candidacy as the inventor of apologetic, if not yet of its name. He is the first writer who has a clear reason for addressing the emperor and his sons: the fact that γυνή τις, the woman whose case seems to have sparked his decision to address the emperors, has herself petitioned the emperor and had her request, to disentangle her financial affairs from those of her estranged husband, granted (*2 Apol.* 2.1–8).[21] Unlike Quadratus, Justin is not described by Eusebius as having a particularly notable understanding, for obvious reasons. But he does have a desire to engage with the outside world, which can only strike us, I think, as new, compared with the thought-world inhabited by Clement of Rome, Ignatius, or indeed the probably contemporary Polycarp, who is shown as turning down the opportunity to offer an apology before a Roman governor and a stadium crowd of pagans and Jews (*Mart. Pol.* 10.1). Polycarp is not prepared to engage with the crowd that wants him dead. Justin does want to engage and, despite the manifest inadequacies of his education, begins a tradition of addressing the concerns and prejudices and assumptions of the dominant culture that will in the end be startlingly successful, albeit in other hands.

The best indication of the newness of Justin's work is that it attracted the greatest of all scholarly compliments—to start a debate so stimulating and vigorous and well received that it soon moves far beyond the position established by the person who began it, with all its idiosyncrasies. This, as far as I understand, is what had happened to Mark's gospel: writing a continuous narrative of Jesus' life, shot through with theological interpretation, was so good an idea that it quickly stimulated other attempts better adapted to an audience with an increasingly refined literary and theological palate, and left Mark itself undervalued for a considerable length of time. This, I would argue, is also what happened to Justin.[22] His idea of attempting to explain Christianity to the emperors in their own philosophical terms, and take issue with their treatment of Christians according to their own legal norms, was so appealing that a number of people sought to do exactly the same thing over the next fifty years, and many more did something similar by addressing treatises to Greeks, Romans, or Jews in general, even if they were often in practice addressed rather more to an internal audience than an external one. As far as we can tell, every one of these people understood pagan culture better than Justin did, and most of them could write rather better, too. But no one could better his initial insight that if Christianity was true, it ought to be able to give an intelligible account of itself to a culture that also claimed to value truth, however little that culture valued Christianity.

We can see Justin's influence most clearly on Athenagoras, for Athenagoras's *Embassy* (or *Supplication*) is essentially a rewriting of Justin's (first) *Apology* in more intellectually respectable terms. Athenagoras deliberately employs, in the *presbeia*, a petitionary form farther up the social scale than Justin's humble private petition, the *libellus*, to signify the huge change in Christian confidence that had occurred between the mid-150s and late 170s.[23] His work is presented as an embassy as though from a city—the first use of the idea of the City of God, perhaps. But a petition, like Justin's work, it still is.

Turning to the text itself, the parallels are clear.[24] Athenagoras begins by complaining of the injustice of Christians' being persecuted for the mere name of Christianity, just as Justin does, although since Athenagoras is presenting himself as a gentleman talking to gentlemen, he dwells on the persecutions of the crowd, the lower classes, rather than directly on the actions of the magistrates, and simply complains that the magistrates take the crowds seriously and listen to their denunciations, when they ought to ignore them as the mischievous lies they are (*Supp.* 1–2).

Athenagoras goes on, just like Justin, to deal with charges of atheism, disloyalty to the empire, and immorality. In the case of the refutation of atheism, his argument is a great deal more involved than Justin's. He considers at length the fact that various cities of Greece and Asia Minor worship incompatible gods, since Menelaus is a god to the Spartans, while he is a bitter enemy to the Trojans, and the Carthagians honor Hamilcar as a god, who was a bitter enemy of the Romans (14.1). He also discusses the nature of God in much more plausible philosophical language than Justin's, while making the same points as Justin, that God should be immaterial, beautiful, perfect, and without need of anything (15.1, 16.3), whereas idols and traditional gods are not. He never makes the assumption, as Justin does, however, that the emperors themselves believe these inappropriate things about God—they are always ascribed to the Egyptians or the lower classes, or some such body slightly removed from the educated Greco-Roman world that Athenagoras implicitly claims he and the emperors both inhabit. The emperors are expected to accept immediately that gods should be immaterial and all-powerful—a much more realistic view of their likely beliefs than Justin's. Athenagoras's radical step is to go on to argue that these views are incompatible with the notion that there is nothing wrong with honoring the gods through statues.[25] Athenagoras has found a chink in the Greco-Roman religious armor here, using traditional syllogistic logic rather than Justin's more straightforward hectoring—a chink Tertullian, in particular, will seek to widen into a splitting apart of the whole rationale of Greco-Roman worship.

Athenagoras, like Justin, explains evil and disorder in the world by the presence of both the devil, the "ruler of matter and the forms that are in it" (24.5), and the demons, who are the souls of giants who were born from the women lusted after by fallen angels (24.6—25.1), in the interpretation of Genesis 6 that was current at the time.[26] Like Justin, Athenagoras argues that the demons are the ones who want the blood that the pagans sacrifice to idols (26.1), and we can imagine that at this point Athenagoras, too, would have lost any pagan audience he still had, as Justin would presumably have done much earlier in his narrative. But even here, Athenagoras is better informed than Justin and uses arguments better calculated to appeal to educated Greco-Romans, by mentioning quackery associated with statues of men (26.3–5) and by considering some alternative philosophical treatments of the presence of evil in the world, such as Aristotelianism (25.2), and arguing that the Christian worldview is rather more moral.

Athenagoras then turns to the charges of cannibalism and incest to which Justin had also referred, and here he is quite interesting in the polemical moves he makes. Like Justin, he points out how stringent Christian morality is. But he is rather more hard hitting than Justin in his criticism of pagan morality in return. "It is of great importance to us," writes Athenagoras, "that the bodies of those whom we regard as brothers and sisters and every sort of kin remain free of abuse and corruption" (32.5; we shall see the implications of this in a moment). And he gives us a charming little detail—Christians are not allowed to kiss one another twice at the kiss of peace, just because it is enjoyable, since "we are excluded from eternal life if our intention in the act is even a little bit muddy" (32.5).

But it is at this point that Athenagoras becomes as rude about Greco-Roman society as he ever does, in talking about their sexual mores. "But these people—what can I say about what shouldn't be spoken of? It's like the proverb about the prostitute and the chaste woman," he says in exasperation (34.1), citing the prevalence of prostitution of both men and women. "Adulterers and pederasts reproach those who are (spiritual) eunuchs and those who have but one partner, while they live like fish, since these people too swallow up whoever runs into them, the stronger driving into (ἐλαύνοντες) the weaker. And this is what it means to taste human flesh" (34.3). It looks as though this had been a particular problem for the Athenian community, perhaps as part of the febrile culture of Athens as a center for elite education. Justin's argument that it is the pagans who are the real cannibals has been taken one rhetorical step further. Athenagoras then takes up Justin's own arguments: Christians will not even be present at the slaughter of justly convicted criminals (Justin describes this as human sacrifice to idols; *2 Apol.* 12.5), or expose their children, so how could they possibly be practitioners of cannibalism (*Supp.* 35)? He adds one further argument of his own: How could those who believe in the resurrection make their bodies the tombs of the bodies of others who will also rise again (36)?

This is where Athenagoras's argument concludes; he leaves out all of the lengthy prophecies and liturgical explanations that Justin includes, perhaps considering that they would make little sense to pagan hearers, or that he did not want his treatise to be unfeasibly long. He also leaves out any attempt to explain how pagan philosophers were able to have access to the truth, the question that Justin addresses with his doctrine of the *Logos spermatikos*. Athenagoras does not have Justin's naïve endorsement of Socrates, and he seems to take it as read that philosophers should sometimes arrive at the truth unaided. Nonetheless, he is still trying to do essentially what Justin was: to engage with the philosophical and legal norms of the dominant culture and force those in power to face up to the ways in which their treatment of Christians breaches these.

Athenagoras, it is clear from all of this, did not spring from a general apologetic tradition of which Justin furnished him one example. Instead, he modeled his work specifically on Justin's and may have known of no other such works at all. His innovation was to take Justin's arguments and make them intellectually respectable to educated Greeks and Romans in a way Justin's were not. But even while Athenagoras's modifications to those arguments silently rebuke Justin's naïveté and his educational deficiencies, the fact that he sought to update Justin's work twenty years after it was written tells its own story. The idea Justin had had of producing a written case for the defense of Christianity against the customary charges it faced, addressed to those with the power to dismiss those charges, remained an inspiring and attractive one, whose recommendations were patent.

It may be that the apologies of Melito, Apolinarius, and Miltiades, written in the reigns of Marcus Aurelius and Commodus, followed closely the same pattern set forth by Justin's of address to the rulers, complaint about the anomaly of punishment for the mere name of Christian, and refutation of the charges of atheism, incest, and cannibalism. At the very least, they followed Justin's idea of addressing the emperor or the earthly rulers. But Tertullian's apology, the only other apology mentioned by Eusebius that survives in its entirety, is still using the same basic structure in 197.

Tertullian[27] once again begins his appeal (which is here acknowledged to be specifically that of a literary treatise; 1.1) by discussing the unfairness of punishing Christians for the mere name of Christianity (1.4—3.8). He has a great deal of fun, for example, with the picture of Christians' being tortured to make them deny, when everyone else is tortured to make them confess (2.10-17). He proceeds then to the charges of atheism, cannibalism, and incest, but deals with these last two first (7.1—9.20). Again, he makes great rhetorical play by asking his readers to imagine how a scene of baby-eating would actually work in practice: how someone could stand by and watch the child dying and then dip his bread in the blood and eat it (8.1–2). He mocks next the notion of the diners looking around to check where their mothers and sisters are so they can be sure they really do commit incest when the lights go out (8.3). He then goes on to point out that it is the pagans who really do these things, having indulged in human sacrifice in the past in Africa and Gaul, and continuing to do so at the games in honor of Jupiter, even if those who die are condemned criminals (9.5), and practicing the exposure and abortion of their children (all arguments Justin had used). He finishes the cannibalism section with a new (and very effective) charge of his own: those who eat the flesh and even the offal of animals killed in the hunt, which have themselves just killed and eaten human beings, are not very far from cannibalism of a very literal kind (9.11-12). People who sleep around across the whole empire, meanwhile, may have many children of whom they know nothing, and have no guarantee of not ending up committing incest with them (9.18). Tertullian also uses the argument Justin used (*1 Apol.* 27.1-3), that exposing one's children and leaving them to be picked up by prostitution rackets risks the promiscuous committing incest (9.17).

Most of the rest of the long work then deals with the charge of atheism, once again employing arguments very similar to those of Justin, though adding many more to them. The pagan gods are not gods, so there is no duty to worship them (10.1-2). Gods were all originally men: men continue to be declared gods after their deaths, even now (10.10). A greater God cannot have made them gods as reward for merit, because according to the stories they are all extremely immoral (11.10-13). Their images should not be worshiped, because they are merely made out of various materials: Christians are condemned to the mines; the pagan gods come from the mines (12.2-7). Pagans dishonor their own gods anyway in the theaters and in their sacrifices (15.1-8).

Tertullian turns to describing the Christian God, just as Athenagoras had (17.1—18.3), and then to discussing the Scriptures and their prophecies, as Justin had (21.1-16); the life and death of Christ (21.14-31); and Satan, the angels, and the demons, children of the fallen angels (22.1—23.19), who are the ones who lap up the sacrifices offered to the images. He carries on, following Athenagoras, to point out that some of the Roman gods are incompatible, and some belong to their traditional enemies (25.1—27.7). He then looks at the treason charges (28.1—38.5) and goes on, like both

One of the challenges posed by Justin Martyr—both to his contemporaries, Christian, Jewish, and pagan, and to us who read him today—is that he is a man who learned to move between cultures. He is a figure who tried heroically to span the chasm between at least three competing worlds—the Greco-Roman paganism in which he grew up; the Greek-speaking diaspora Judaism, whose methods he so enthusiastically adopted and whose conclusions he so vigorously rejected; and the emerging, nascent Christianity, whose theology he so helped to shape.

These plates are meant to illustrate those worlds.

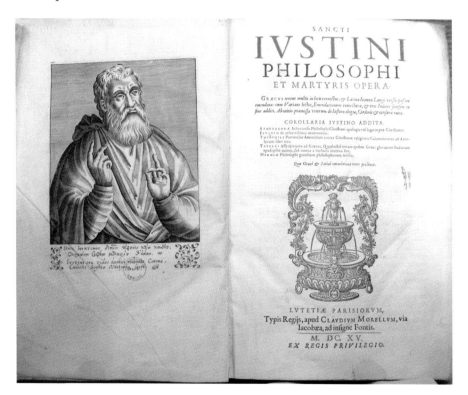

The first edition of the works of "Saint Justin, Philosopher and Martyr" was published at Paris by the great scholar printer Robert Stephanus in 1551. That edition, improved and amended in various ways, was included in what was really the first collected edition of the Greek Apologists—indeed, the work which largely created the category of "Apologist"—also published at Paris, by Fédéric Morel in 1615. **Plate 1** shows the title page of that edition, facing a piously imaginative engraving of a pensive Justin. Photo courtesy of the Library of Blackfriars, Oxford. Used by permission.

At the beginning of his *First Apology*, he introduces himself as "Justin, son of Priscus, son of Baccheios, from Flavia Neapolis in Syria Palestina." The Neapolis in question was a new Roman foundation—a Greek-speaking pagan city—built almost on the site of the biblical Shechem in Samaria. From the city, as he was growing up, he would have had a view of Mount Gerizim, on which the Samaritans held (as they still do) their traditional Passover sacrifice. On one of its twin peaks the emperor Hadrian had built—within Justin's lifetime—a pagan temple dedicated to Zeus the Highest. **Plate 2**, the reverse of a coin of the emperor Trebonianus Gallus, shows Gerizim, as Justin would have seen it, with its Greek-style temple. Photo courtesy of Ray Wilk. Used by permission.

Justin's thought was shaped by contact with an academic, text-based Judaism and its methods of exegesis. But that Judaism was—like the interlocutor and opponent in his *Dialogue with Trypho*—Greek-speaking. Justin by preference uses the standard Greek translation of our Old Testament, the Septuagint. But when Trypho objects to it, he can argue from another version to which he had access and which Trypho can also accept. In 1952 a manuscript of the Minor Prophets in Greek was uncovered at Nahal Hever in the Judaean desert. It turned out to be a manuscript of the type Justin used, a version previously unknown to scholars and now commonly known as the *kaige* version. **Plate 3** shows two columns of that manuscript. Photo courtesy of Israel Antiquities Authority. Used by permission.

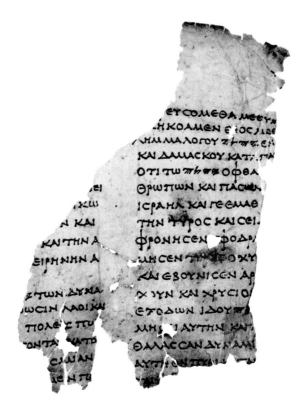

Justin presents himself as a man immersed in and prepared to take on the Greek philosophical tradition. At the beginning of the *Dialog*, Trypho recognizes Justin as a philosopher by the rough and heavy philosopher's cloak he is wearing and hails him as such. That initiates the whole long discussion, which takes place in the *xystus*—a covered walkway or track—of a gymnasium. It was an impeccably Hellenic setting, for the gymnasium was one of the major civic institutions of the Greek world, where not only athletic contests took place, but also lectures, academic debate—and philosophical disputation. The city (Eusebius of Caesarea says) is Ephesus, and the *Dialog* ends abruptly since Justin has a ship to catch. The largest gymnasium complex in Justin's Ephesus was the so-called Harbor Gymnasium. It had a huge *xystus* and lay about three hundred yards from the main quay of the port. **Plate 4** shows the street leading down to the ancient shoreline with remains of the so-called Theater Gymnasium on the right and, just beyond, the site of the *xystus*. Photo by Richard A. Wright, 2006. Courtesy of the Pitts Theology Library, Candler School of Theology, Emory University. Used by permission.

Most of Justin's teaching career was spent in Rome, and it was of course there that he met his death and so became "Justin, philosopher and martyr," as he is regularly called in the tradition. One place in Rome that we know for a certainty that he knew is the Isola Tiburina in the middle of the Tiber. He says that he there saw a statue dedicated to Simon Magus, the father of all heresies, who was, like Justin himself, from Samaria. The statue base he saw was uncovered in 1574 and is now in the Vatican Museum. It is in fact a dedication to the ancient Latin god Semo Sancus. But the island, now so peaceful, was in Justin's time entirely devoted to pagan cult. The whole island had been carved out into the shape of a ship to commemorate the arrival of the healing snake god Asclepius in 293 B.C. We can only imagine the shiver up the spine Justin must have felt as he stared at what he took to be a statue of Simon in this—for him—totally demonic realm. **Plate 5** shows a model of the island as it would have appeared when Justin was there. Photo courtesy of André Caron, maquettes-historiques.net. Used by permission.

Pagan Rome was the heart of a pagan empire that shaped the political, social, and economic side of the world in which Justin lived. When he was writing his *Apologies*, the very northernmost frontier of that whole vast empire lay along the Antonine Wall in Scotland, running between the Forth and the Clyde. It had been built by Q. Lollius Urbicus when he was governor of Britain—the same Lollius Urbicus whose persecution of Christians in Rome a few years later, when he was Urban Prefect, triggered the writing of the *Apologies*. **Plate 6** shows the military bathhouse of a fort on the Wall, at Bearsden in Glasgow. **Plate 7** shows a stretch of the base of the wall, in New Kilpatrick Cemetary, Bearsden, Glasgow, running west toward the Clyde estuary and the Atlantic. The great Roman road ("Dere Street") that connected the south with the eastern end of the wall must have passed within a few hundred yards of the present site of New College, Edinburgh, where the conference on which this book is based was held. Photos courtesy of Sara and Paul Parvis. Used by permission.

ICONS OF JUSTIN MARTYR

Image courtesy of Holy Transfiguration
Monastery, Brookline, Mass.
Used by permission.

Image courtesy of the Orthodox
Church in America.
Used by permission.

Justin and Athenagoras, to discuss why Christians are virtuous and model citizens (39.1–21).

Tertullian then turns to some newer themes—the disasters said to be caused by Christians,[28] the fact that they are bad for business (40.1—55.7), and comparison of pagan virtue with Christian (46.1—47.11). Finally, he returns to two more themes of both Justin and Athenagoras—the notion that God will judge all people and assign them to hell or to paradise, and the resurrection from the dead (47.12—59.4). He ends his apology with a return to the spectacle of martyrdom—the Christians are the ones with the real power, which they give to those who execute them. They show the sort of endurance that the Romans admire enormously in anyone else. And executing them merely attracts more Christians. For execution is its own vindication—condemnation by the Romans is acquittal by God (49.5—50.16).

With this, Tertullian has argued Christian apologetic proper to a standstill. He has talked himself into a position where it does not matter whether the magistrates listen to him or not: in his mind, he wins either way. He has also talked the formula out of its petition mode and into a fully literary mode, because he has shown that that is now the most effective means of changing the minds of Roman legislators: the "*occulta via tacitarum litterarum*" (1.1).

With Tertullian, therefore, the apology proper merges with the other forms that had been developing in the wake of Justin's work: the polemical discourse "to the Greeks," such as that of Tatian, defending Christianity by attacking the dominant culture, and the explanatory work to some assumed neutral friend, such as the *Letter to Diognetus* or Theophilus's *To Autolycus*. They would shortly be joined by the treatise in defense of Christianity against a literary attack, such as Origen's *Against Celsus*. All of these could be considered apology in an attenuated sense, particularly the last, but apology proper, I would argue, dies with Tertullian.

It may also, paradoxically, have started with Tertullian. The manuscript tradition of the *Apologeticus* makes it fairly clear that that was the work's original title,[29] whereas neither Justin nor Athenagoras seems originally to have been designated in this way. I would hypothesize an early collection, known to Eusebius at least by library catalog title, which contained all of the Eusebian apologies, including a Greek translation of Tertullian, with the title Ὑπὲρ Χριστιανῶν Ἀπολογίαι (cf. *H.E.* II.2.4; IV.11.11; IV.13.8; IV.18.2).

But it was Justin who invented what Eusebius called the *Apology*, on this showing. It was he who had the brilliant idea of attempting to bring before the emperor himself the legal anomaly under which Christians were suffering, for nothing more than the name of Christian. It was he who believed that it must be worth attempting to persuade people who called themselves Pius and philosophers that Christianity was neither impious nor philosophically bankrupt. It was he who first risked his life, lifted his head above the parapet, to try to do so. It is no accident that Christianity comes out of the shadows with Justin, and into a period of theologians whose names and histories we know, at least to some extent. Because it was he who worked out that if you try hard enough to understand them, it must be at least theoretically possible to persuade other human beings to understand you—and that if you could do that, maybe you could even make the killing stop.

CHAPTER TEN

"Jesus" as God's Name, and Jesus as God's Embodied Name in Justin Martyr

LARRY W. HURTADO

JUSTIN IS WELL KNOWN AMONG STUDENTS of early Christianity as the key figure reflecting the early effort to articulate Christian faith in categories meaningful to the wider intellectual environment of his time.[1] But he is also important for his preservation of earlier, and what soon thereafter became more antiquated, expressions of Christian faith and piety, at least some of which probably originated in early circles of Jewish Christians, or at least in Christian circles whose faith was influenced by, and expressed more typically in, categories deriving from Jewish/biblical tradition. Among these very early expressions of Christian faith are the ways in which the name "Jesus" is seen as itself a divine name, and the figure of Jesus is affirmed as the embodiment of God's own "name." For whatever reasons, these expressions of Christian faith/piety did not endure much beyond Justin, which makes them all the more interesting historically as very "primitive" features of earliest devotion to Jesus.

The emphasis on Jesus' name and the articulation of his significance with reference to the divine name have been noted as strong features of Jewish Christianity previously, and amply surveyed, especially by Daniélou.[2] Neither Daniélou nor the other main studies with which I am acquainted, however, devote sufficient attention to Justin. This is unfortunate, as Justin's writings preserve some of the best evidence on these matters. Actually, the origins of these themes go back much earlier than Justin, earlier than any of the extant sources in which they are more presumed than explained. As Daniélou judged, in the New Testament references we are encountering "a continuation of an archaic Jewish Christian theology earlier than Paul or John."[3] To cite one of our earliest texts (and one that I regard as likely very influential on some subsequent Christian speculation), in Philippians 2:9-11, Jesus' superlative exaltation involves being given "the name above every name," which must mean that the glorified Jesus now shares the divine name itself. Moreover, the universal acclamation "Lord Jesus

Christ" projected here is also reflected in the hints of actual worship practices of Christian circles in other Pauline texts (Rom. 10:9-13; 1 Cor. 12:1-3). For instance, the liturgical practice "to call upon the name of the Lord," alluded to in several New Testament texts (for example, Rom. 10:9-13; 1 Cor. 1:2; Acts 2:21-36), represents a highly significant early Christian adaptation of an Old Testament formula originally referring to cultus directed to YHWH, but in Christian circles it referred to the corporate invocation of Jesus by name.[4]

We also know that the name "Jesus" itself was deemed to have surpassing power when invoked in baptism (the most characteristic setting), and also exorcism and other such occasions, as reflected in numerous passages in the New Testament (for example, Mark 6:13; Acts 3:6, 16), and also affirmed by Justin in his own day (*Dial.* 30.3, 76.6–7; 85.1–3).[5] In short, the articulation of Jesus' significance with reference to the divine name represents what Daniélou described as "one of the essential aspects of Jewish Christian theology."[6] This theological development obviously drew upon Old Testament traditions about God's name, which include the idea that the name can be conferred to give special authority to a deputy (especially Exod. 23:20) and can even function as a way of referring to God himself, especially in God's self-revelation and immanent relations with humans (for example, Deut. 12:11; 14:23).[7] But what we have in earliest Christian faith and piety is also a genuine, novel, and highly significant *development*, both in thought and in devotional practice. Through the direct linkage of the real figure of Jesus with the divine name, there results what I have termed a genuinely novel "binitarian" form of monotheistic faith and devotional practice, with Jesus being revered *along with God* in remarkable ways as a distinguishable and closely associated figure.[8]

This, however, is not the occasion to develop further this line of thought. Our more precise task here is to note Justin's own deployment of particular emphases on Jesus' name and Jesus as God's embodied name, and to this we now turn.

"Jesus" as God's Name

In the Matthean nativity narrative (1:21) we find our earliest direct evidence of an interest in and awareness of the etymological meaning of the name Ιησους.[9] Justin shows an acquaintance with the matter also in *1 Apology* 66.3, quite likely through the reading of Matthew.[10] But I want to focus first here on another, more striking claim made by Justin that the name Ιησους is itself actually a divine name. The claim involves some interesting exegetical moves that may be regarded today more as curiosities than persuasive but that are nevertheless intriguing and also, I submit, historically significant.[11]

The first of several passages where Justin registers these moves is in *Dialogue* 76. But before we look at this passage, we should note the immediately preceding discussion in *Dialogue* 73–74 (material to which we will return later for closer attention), in which Justin presents a thorough christological reading of Psalm 96 (LXX 95), insisting that Jesus is the regnant Lord referred to in verse 10, who, in the closing words of the psalm, will come to judge the earth and who is acclaimed in the psalm by the Holy

Spirit as worthy of worship along with the Father. Then *Dialogue* 75 commences with Justin making the further point that "the name of God Himself, which, He says, was not revealed to Abraham or to Jacob, was Jesus."[12] In support, Justin cites Exodus 23:20-21, where God promises the Israelites to send "a messenger [ἄγγελον] before you to guard you on the way and to bring you into the land which I have prepared for you.[13] Attend to him and listen to him, do not disobey him, for he will not pardon you, for my name is in him." In his ensuing exegesis, Justin asserts that this promised figure has to be the biblical Joshua, who led the people of Israel into Canaan, and Justin supports his claim by reminding Trypho of another text (Num. 13:16), where Moses changes the name of Hoshea to Joshua/Ἰησοῦς. In short, Justin's exegetical logic is as follows: (1) God promised a figure who would lead Israel into Canaan and who would bear God's name; (2) in the biblical record the figure who led Israel into Canaan is Joshua; and (3) this figure had been given this name by Moses; therefore, (4) "Joshua/Ἰησοῦς" must be God's name, given to Hoshea to prefigure his greater namesake, Jesus.[14]

Thereafter, at several points, this exegetical claim is echoed, which suggests that Justin regarded it as important. In *Dialogue* 89.1 Trypho is pictured as acknowledging the force of Justin's exegesis as inclining him toward adopting Justin's christological claims. Also, in *Dialogue* 90.4 and 91.3, Justin alludes to this prior argument about Jesus' name in making further typlogical claims from the account where Moses defeats Amalek with the help of "Joshua/Jesus" and by making the sign of the cross in his outstretched hands. Then in a very lengthy exposition of Psalm 22 (LXX 21), Justin takes the statement "I will declare your name to my brethren" (Ps. 22:22) as a basis for reiterating the claim that "it was he by whom Jacob was called Israel, and Hoshea called Jesus [Joshua], under whose name the people . . . were conducted in the land promised to the patriarchs" (*Dial.* 106.2–3).

In *Dialogue* 111–13, the theme reappears and is given extended treatment, Justin here expounding "the type of the cross [in the scapegoat ritual] and the type of the name [Joshua/Jesus]" (*Dial.* 111.1). In this same body of material, Justin refers again to the typological significance of Moses' outstretched hands and the support of "him who was named Jesus (Joshua)" (112.2). In *Dialogue* 113 Justin presses Trypho once more to face Justin's assertions about Moses' renaming of Hoshea as Joshua/Jesus, complaining that although Jews probe the possible meaning of the biblical references to the modifications of the names of Abraham and Sarah, they ignore the much larger significance of the changing of Hoshea's name to Joshua/Jesus and of this figure's elevation as Moses' successor and leader of Israel (113.1–3). Then Justin makes an extended typological comparison and contrast between the Old Testament Joshua and Jesus (113.4–7). In comparison with the temporal inheritance of land given by Joshua, Jesus provides an eternal inheritance of resurrection. In comparison with Joshua's second circumcision of Israel with knives of stone (Josh. 5:2-3), Jesus "has circumcised us from the idols made of stone and other materials" with the gospel (*Dial.* 113.6).

There are still further references to Joshua's typological significance as closely connected with his name in subsequent passages of the *Dialogue*. In 115 Justin notes the reference to a certain "Joshua/Jesus the high priest" in the prophetic vision of Zechariah

(Zech. 3:1-10), underscoring the significance of this name and reiterating the point about the name being given to Hoshea, whose miraculous deeds were intended to fore-shadow the miracles of Jesus. In short, Justin claims that the name borne by both the adjutant of Moses and the priest in Zechariah's vision itself shows their typological significance. There is also a passing reference to Justin's earlier exegesis of the renaming of Hoshea again in *Dialogue* 128.1, and yet another summary-assertion of the claim in 131.4–5, where Justin again urges the typological meaning of the account of the defeat of Amalek.

Finally, in *Dialogue* 132, Justin first cites the account where Joshua orders the sun to stand still as another typological incident prefiguring Jesus' mighty power. Then he immediately moves to the Old Testament story about the capture and return of the ark of the covenant (1 Samuel 5–6), pointing out that the cows who pulled the cart on which the ark was returned, "led by no man, went not to the place whence the ark had been taken, but to the fields of a certain man whose name was Oshea, the same as his whose name was altered to Jesus (Joshua)" (132.3).[15] Obviously, the link with this passage is purely the appearance of the name "Oshea" (Hoshea). Justin's point here seems to be that this incident is likewise typological and predictive of Jesus' redemptive significance. Basically, Justin is saying that the return of the ark (the emblem of Israel's relationship to God and of God's presence with Israel) to a field owned by a man of the same name as the figure of Moses' time who had been given the name of the future Messiah/Redeemer shows symbolically that in Jesus is to be found God's presence and true redemption for Israel.

In these several passages from the *Dialogue*, Justin combines claims about the typological meaning of Old Testament figures and incidents with the particular christological assertion that is of interest here: that Ιησους is itself the name of God. This is both remarkable and also, I contend, not likely original with Justin. The exegetical moves that he makes to support the claim, visible most explicitly in *Dialogue* 75, look very much like the sort of techniques otherwise well known in Jewish circles (for example, catchword connections of passages in various Old Testament writings), although, of course, Justin's specific exegesis is distinctively Christian.[16]

Moreover, we have noted already other indications that from earliest years the name of Jesus was regarded as bearing special significance and even a potent efficacy (at least when used in a genuine faith-stance), and that invoking Jesus by name was a characteristic feature of gathered worship in first-century Christian circles.[17] In other early Christian sources we also have indications that Jesus' name was itself the subject of numerological speculation, which continued on into putatively "gnostic" texts and circles but likely originated from Jewish-Christian traditions.[18] To cite one early phenomenon, as I have argued in an earlier publication, the curious scribal convention referred to as *nomina sacra* (in which certain sacred words or names were regularly written in contracted or suspended form) may have originated in a special scribal treatment of the name Ιησους, written as IH and intended to be read both as the abbreviated form of the name and also by gematria as the numerical equivalent of the Hebrew word for life, *chay* (חי = 18).[19] In short, I contend that there is ample reason to see Justin's claims about the divine significance of the name "Jesus" as part of a wider body of devotional beliefs and practices in earliest Christianity in which the name of Jesus featured prominently.[20]

I also submit that Justin's repeated references to the Old Testament character Joshua and the significance of his renaming may help us to understand better a curious feature of some early Christian Old Testament Greek manuscripts in which Joshua's name (Ιησους) is written in *nomina sacra* form.[21] This phenomenon does not represent a careless or confused scribe, and in its own time was not nearly so bizarre as it may seem today. Instead, it reflects the view for which Justin is our clearest extant witness, that the Old Testament figure in question, Joshua, was given the divine name that was to be borne by the Son of God. That is, the *nomina sacra* treatment of the name "Joshua" in early Christian Old Testament manuscripts reflects the profoundly Christian reading of the Old Testament figure as a type of Jesus and reflects a view of the name given to the Old Testament figure as bearing a divine significance.

Jesus as God's Embodied Name

I now turn to another striking feature of Justin's christological views: the conviction that Jesus, the Son of God, is also the personal/embodied manifestation of God's name. For this as well, a passage in the *Dialogue* is crucial, in this case *Dialogue* 65.

Before we deal with this passage, however, once again it will be helpful first to take note of the immediately preceding material in *Dialogue* 64. Here Trypho is pictured as granting in principle that Justin has given a certain cogent rationale for why Gentile Christians reverence Jesus, but Trypho then insists that as a Jew he could never consent to confessing or worshiping him (64.1), for this would violate Trypho's monotheistic scruple. To this objection Justin replies by invoking further Old Testament passages that he interprets in support of recognizing Jesus as rightfully to be given worship.

I note that one of the things that links the Old Testament passages Justin cites here involves references to God's name. In 64.4, the citation from Psalm 99:1-7 includes the exhortation to confess God's "great name" (Ps. 99:3), and in *Dialogue* 64.6 Justin culminates his citation from Psalm 72 (LXX 71) with the words of verses 17-19:

> *His name* endures before the sun, and all the tribes of the earth shall be blessed *in him*. All nations shall call him blessed. Blessed be the Lord, the God of Israel, who alone does wondrous things; and *blessed be his glorious name* for ever and ever, and the whole earth shall be filled with his glory. Amen, Amen. (Trans. modified from ANF; emphasis added)

It appears that Justin interpreted "His name" and "his glorious name" in these verses as references to the person of Jesus, and so a second and distinguishable divine figure, and Justin understood "him" as referring back to God's "name" = Jesus. Justin then urges Trypho to recognize that the Scriptures indeed teach the descent from heaven of the divine Son and his return in exaltation to heavenly glory, and Justin concludes his exhortation with a quotation from Psalm 19, in which the opening statement about the heavens declaring the *glory of God* is taken as another reference to Jesus. Justin here reflects another early christological category in which Jesus' divine status is expressed in terms of his sharing in, and manifesting, God's glory.[22]

In short, in *Dialogue* 64, Justin lodges Old Testament citations in support of the view that *Jesus himself* is the manifest name and glory of God. That is, the effect of Justin's exposition in *Dialogue* 64 is to urge what we may term a strongly "binitarian" view, in which Jesus is to be given divine honor and properly joined with God in confessional and devotional practice as a second, distinguishable, but closely linked figure.

In the face of Justin's claims, quite credibly, Trypho's immediate response, which opens *Dialogue* 65.1, is to express bewilderment, invoking the solemn declaration from Isaiah 42:8, "I am the LORD; this is my name; my glory will I not give to another, nor my virtues." This may seem to be a fairly effective rebuttal, but Justin proceeds to argue that, properly understood, the biblical statement quoted by Trypho actually supports his own binitarian outlook and shows that actually "God gives glory to his Christ alone" (*Dial.* 65.3). In doing so, Justin unpacks still further his view of Jesus as the name (and glory) of God.

Here, as in a number of other places in the *Dialogue*, Justin's tactic is to cite a goodly portion of the wider context of the text under dispute, in this case the whole of Isaiah 42:5-13. I suggest that for Justin the crucial material in this wider passage is the series of statements in verses 6-8, where God addresses another figure as divinely called and fitted and given as a covenant to "the people" (γένους, which Justin likely took to be Israel) and as a "light of the nations" (ἐθνῶν, that is, Gentiles). In fact, references to this figure commence in Isaiah 42:1, where he is designated (by God) as "my servant [ὁ παῖς μου], whom I uphold, my chosen, in whom my soul delights" and who is endowed with the divine Spirit to "bring forth justice to the nations."

But in the material as quoted by Justin, it appears that he takes the statement in verse 8, "I am the LORD; this is my name," to be God's reference to this same figure, God's "servant" and "chosen one," further designated here as "my name." Although Justin does not quote the opening verses of Isaiah 42, I suspect strongly that at verse 4 his text had the LXX wording, "and the nations shall hope *in/on his name*," and that Justin took "his name" here also as a designation for Jesus.[23]

That is, once again, it appears that we have here a striking "binitarian" exegesis of a biblical passage. Over against Trypho's view of Isaiah 42:8 as an emphatic affirmation that it is inappropriate to imagine that God shares his glory with any other, Justin confidently sees the same statement as declaring that God obviously does share his glory with this one other figure, this "servant" who is also here designated as God's own "name." To capture more clearly Justin's view, we might paraphrase Isaiah 42:8 as follows: "I am the LORD; this [one] [τοῦτο; that is, the figure referred to in the preceding statements as the covenant and light to the nations] is my name; my glory I give to no *other* [than he]." In my view, it is also likely that Justin took the following reference to the "new things" to be declared (Isa. 42:9), the exhortation to "sing to God [τῷ θεῷ] a new song" of praise, and the future universal scope of the celebration of God's glory as all predictive of, and fulfilled now in, Jesus and the spread of the gospel.[24]

A bit later, in *Dialogue* 73–74, Justin points to Psalm 96 (LXX 95), from which he also quotes at some length, urging that here as well Jesus' divine significance is declared. The opening words of the psalm echo the first line of Isaiah 42:10, "Sing to the LORD a new song" (another instance of catchword association), and this is followed in verse 2 with the exhortations, "Sing to the LORD; bless his name."[25] Now Justin's main point here also is to assert an essentially "binitarian" view in which Jesus is entitled to divine honor along with the Lord God, and I contend that Justin took these exhortations in Psalm 96:1 (LXX 95:1) as referring to the praise of God *and Jesus*, the latter here referred to as God's *name*.

This is confirmed, I contend, in *Dialogue* 74.1, where Trypho is portrayed as recognizing that Justin and he differ over whether the psalm refers to God alone or includes any other. Justin responds first by repeating the words of Psalm 96:1-3 (LXX 95:1-3), and then he explicitly claims that this scriptural text urges all the inhabitants of the earth to "sing and give praises continually *to God the Father* of all things, and to recognize also that he is to be praised and feared who made the heaven and the earth, and who wrought this salvation for the human race, *and also the one who was also crucified, and died, and deemed worthy by God* [ὑπ' αὐτοῦ] *to reign over all the earth.*"[26] I submit that Justin's claim presupposes the view that "sing to the LORD" and "bless his name" are related exhortations to engage in binitarian devotion to *two* figures, God *and Jesus*.

To sum up at this point, we have now examined several passages in the *Dialogue* where Justin reflects and asserts the view that Jesus in his person is the manifest "name" of God. Moreover, I want to emphasize that Justin is not unique in this view. It has been noted by other scholars previously that this view of Jesus as God's name is reflected in other texts that seem to preserve remnants of a very early period of Christian faith and piety and that likely reflect a Jewish-Christian heritage/influence.[27] It will suffice here to consider only a few key texts.

In *1 Clement* 58.1, Clement urges fellow believers to obey God's "most holy and glorious name" and to trust "in his most holy and majestic name," and toward the end of the long prayer that occupies nearly all of 59.3—61.3, we have similar phrasing, where Clement appeals to God for harmony and peace, "while we render obedience to your almighty and most excellent name." In 59.2 we have the introduction to, and the opening words of, this lengthy prayer, which is commonly recognized as reflecting still earlier liturgical phrasing. Clement here refers to God as the creator of the universe and to Jesus as God's "beloved servant" (τοῦ ἠγαπημένου παιδὸς αὐτοῦ), through whom God "called us from darkness to light, from ignorance to the knowledge of the glory of his name." Then in 59.3, somewhat abruptly, Clement commences direct petition to God, asking "to hope on your name, which is the primal source of all creation [τὸ ἀρχέγονον πάσης κτίσεως]; and open the eyes of our hearts, that we may know you, who alone are 'Highest among the high, and who remain Holy among the holy.'" As Daniélou judged, "The prayer is addressed to the Father, and the Name designates the Son."[28] The reference to God's name as "the primal source of all creation" certainly seems to reflect the very early and well-attested notion that Jesus was the divine agent through whom the world was created, which is reflected in 1 Corinthians 8:5-6 and Colossians 1:15-16 and, most famously, in John 1:1-3.

In *Didache* 10:2, we have another text commonly seen as preserving very early liturgical expressions and practice, and here also we have an interesting reference to God's name, which I propose designates Jesus:

> We give you thanks, Holy Father,
> for your holy name, which you have caused to dwell in our hearts,
> and for the knowledge and faith and immortality which you have made known
> to us through Jesus your servant [τοῦ παιδός σου].

As Kurt Niederwimmer noted, God's "name" here designates "God's epiphany, God in person," and, we may add, the reference to God's name as made to "dwell [κατεσκήνωσας] in our hearts" clearly draws upon Old Testament phrasing to refer to Christ.[29] In further support of this, we should note the psalm-like nature of the prayer, which is structured in synonymous parallelism, the second part of the thanksgiving expressing in alternate wording the same thought as the first part. That is, the thanksgiving for "Jesus your servant" corresponds to, and is synonymous with, thanksgiving for the indwelling of "your holy name."

We could also look at still other texts that preserve this early Jewish Christian way of referring to Jesus' divine status. But Justin is our focus here, and these will adequately show that Justin's references to Jesus as God's name are neither peculiar nor radically innovative. Instead, they are fascinating vestiges of a christological category that was obviously very meaningful among early Jewish Christians and other Christian circles shaped by biblical/Jewish traditions about the name of God. In his analysis of these traditions, Daniélou judged that God's name could designate his "ineffable reality, and is therefore a Semitic equivalent of what the divine οὐσία [substance] was to be for the Greeks."[30] This seems to me also a fair judgment.

In short, the ancient references to Jesus as God's name (and glory) should probably be taken as functionally equivalent to the sort of claims about Jesus' full divine status that were expressed later in what became more familiar categories in such classical statements as the Nicene Creed. I mean that the direct identification of Jesus with God's glory and name amounts to ascribing to Jesus the most exalted categories available in Jewish/biblical tradition. At the same time, defining Jesus' divine status and significance with reference to God ("the Father") was intended (as was the case characteristically with later, classical christological affirmations) to avoid ditheism. The affirmation that Jesus shares God's glory or name was intended to express a profound unity of God and Jesus in divinity and in the devotional practice of Christians, while also clearly identifying two divine figures.

Conclusion

In this limited exploration of one of Justin's writings, I have concentrated on two noteworthy features of how he advocates Jesus' divine significance in the context of a representation of an evangelistic dialogue with Jews. References to Jesus in connection with God's name do not feature in Justin's *Apology*, likely because the category was not so useful or even meaningful to readers unappreciative of Jewish/biblical religious tradition. Likewise, perhaps because of the growing cultural distance from Jewish traditions in emergent Christianity in the second century and thereafter, the category largely disappeared also from Christian theological discourse. All the more reason, therefore, to be grateful that Justin's *Dialogue* survives, confirming Justin's notable status as perhaps the key hinge-figure between the more Semitic-flavored christological rhetoric of the earliest period of Christianity and the subsequent rhetorical and conceptual developments that characterized the period that followed Justin.

CHAPTER ELEVEN

Altercatio Jasonis et Papisci as a Testimony Source for Justin's "Second God" Argument?

WILL RUTHERFORD

IN HIS DESCRIPTION OF OLD TESTAMENT THEOPHANIES[1] as narratives portraying preincarnate appearances of a "second God" (ἕτερος θεός)[2] who preexisted alongside the Father of the Universe, Justin Martyr offers a key witness to one second-century solution to the issue of divine unity raised by devotion to Jesus,[3] and he provides us with one of the more creative theological and exegetical moments in the story of emergent Christianity. Scholars have long been fascinated by the question of Justin's source material in the "second God" passages, but their analyses have generally focused upon locating traditional *interpretive* patterns that Justin may have used. The early *Christian* witnesses for a christological interpretation of Old Testament theophany are few and far between and certainly not of the character of Justin's treatment of this material.[4] Seeming parallels between Justin's account of theophanies and that offered by the Alexandrian Jew Philo have suggested to some a strong dependence of Justin upon this key representative of Hellenistic Judaism.[5] Philonic influence upon Justin's exegetical development of a "second God" cannot be altogether excluded given the similarities. Yet in light of recent rebuttals to this thesis, it now seems doubtful at best to suppose Philo as the key conceptual source for Justin's "second God" proof,[6] and there has been a general move away from this position.[7]

With respect to his christological exegesis of theophany, Justin may well have been at his most creative, but with respect to his use of proof-texts, he stands on more traditional footing. In his landmark study of Justin's exegesis, Oskar Skarsaune demonstrated that in addition to biblical manuscripts, Justin relied upon two written *testimonia* anthologies that carried great authority for him—a "kerygma" and a "recapitulation" source. He regarded *Dialogue* 61.1–62.4 as "obviously traditional" and linked it to the "recapitulation" source. The argument on the theophanies of chapters 56–60, however, he claimed "was not met with prior to Justin" and is "quite singular in the whole *Dialogue*."[8] What interests me here is Skarsaune's tantalizing proposal that the "recapitulation" source behind *Dialogue* 61–62 "might be identical with" the lost *Disputation between Jason and Papiscus* (hereafter *JP*).[9] In this paper I explore the possibility that Justin was aided by *JP* not only for proof-texts in chapters 61–62, but perhaps for the entirety of his "second God" demonstration. In light of recent research on the Christian-Jewish dialogues, it may now be possible to investigate this issue from a different direction than previously pursued.

Locating Justin's Proof-Texts

The first task is to set Justin's key proof-texts within the scope of his "second God" argument and to provide some frame of reference for their traditional status within the early Christian proof-text tradition.[10] I focus upon *Dialogue* 56–62, the most extended and involved of Justin's "second God" discussions. It can be divided into two segments, chapters 56–60 (cf. 126—128.1) and 61–62 (cf. 128.2—129).[11]

In the first section Justin expounds the theophanies associated with Abraham at Mamre and again at Sodom (*Dialogue* 56–57; cf. Genesis 18–19); to Jacob at Bethel, Peniel, Luz, and Haran (*Dialogue* 58; cf. Genesis 31–32, 35, 28); and to Moses at the burning bush (*Dialogue* 59–60; cf. Exodus 3) to prove the existence of "another God" who preexisted alongside the supreme Father of the universe and manifested himself in human form to the patriarchs. To accomplish this Justin uses three key "two powers" proof-texts: Genesis 19:24 and LXX Psalms 109:1 and 44:7-8. Justin begins by refuting what he regards as the traditional Jewish interpretation (cf. 56.10) of the theophany at Mamre, namely, that God appeared first to Abraham under the oak tree and was later followed by three angels.[12] Trypho concedes the impossibility of this interpretation, but he is unwilling to grant that the Scripture refers to "another God" (56.9). Nevertheless, he shows a fresh willingness to follow Justin in the remainder of his demonstration (cf. 56.12: ἵνα καὶ τούτῳ συνθώμεθα ["that we might agree with this also"]), which Justin picks up with great force in *Dialogue* 56.11–15, *the* central passage of the entire demonstration from chapters 56–60.

He quotes a foundational proof-text, Genesis 19:24, to show that there exists "another God" numerically distinct from the Father of the universe. The argument from Genesis 18–19 pivots around the presence of the double occurrence of the word "Lord" in this single verse, where it is related that one "Lord" rained down fiery judgment upon Sodom from another "Lord" who remained in the heavens. Justin complements this proof for the existence of "two powers" by quoting additional texts, Psalms 109:1 and 44:7-8. The identification of this second figure, whom Scripture calls "God" and "Lord," with one of the three men who spoke with Abraham under the oak at Mamre, the next link in Justin's argument, begins immediately after these verses and carries on to the end of the chapter (56.15–23). The two psalmic proof-texts appear somewhat abstracted from the overall argument from theophany, being primarily adduced to demonstrate a point previously confirmed by the more directly theophanic text of Genesis 19:24.[13] The one substantive element they add is the presence of not only a "two Lords" passage (Gen. 19:24), but also a "two Gods" passage (Ps. 44:7-8),[14] thereby strengthening the scriptural claim to "two powers" by reference to that teaching "not only by Moses but also by David" (56.14). They bear the imprint of traditional, forensic *testimonia* collected around the theme of demonstrating the existence of "two powers" in heaven, whether designated "God" or "Lord."[15]

Three "two powers" texts are then identifiable from *Dialogue* 56 and are foundational to Justin's entire argument from theophany (cf. 55.1; 56.4, 11). A reading of the theophanies to Jacob and Moses and of the relevant parallels in *Dialogue* 126—128.1 establishes no new proof-texts.[16] Rather, the conclusions already gained from the discussion of the Abraham episode recur repeatedly in the following sections, where the argument is designed to demonstrate that the "same" figure[17] who appeared to Abraham and was called "God" also appeared to other patriarchs and was called by various names, "Angel," "Lord," "God," and "man."

As early as the final decades of the first century, Christians were aware of such "two powers" proof-texts and utilized them in debates with Jews.[18] The most common of these was Psalm 109:1.[19] It is present in parallel in all three Synoptic Gospels (Matt. 22:43-44//Mark 12:35-37//Luke 20:42-43), preserving the memory of some early Christian communities' debates with Jewish leaders toward the last decades of the first century. It reappears as a key messianic testimony in Peter's speech on Pentecost (Acts 2:32-36) and in the epistle to the Hebrews (1:13), where it follows additional "two powers" texts, Psalm 44:7-8 and an ingenious reading of LXX Psalm 101:26-28,[20] alongside other royal, messianic psalms (Psalm 2:7) to combat an angel Christology.[21] It further receives the force of a christological proof-text in an anti-Jewish setting somewhere on the border of the first and second centuries in the *Epistle of Barnabas* (12:10-11), where it is joined to a Christianized form of Isaiah 45:1,[22] apparently from a tradition independent of the Synoptics.[23] None of these sources demonstrates direct literary dependence upon another, helping substantiate the claim that already in the first century Christians gathered certain "two powers" texts into various *testimonia* collections—whether written or oral—for the purpose of messianic debate with Jews and fellow Jewish Christians.[24] Connections between these traditional "two powers" texts and Justin's use of Psalms 109:1 and 44:7-8 within his extensive exegesis of Christophany are too weak to posit direct literary dependence upon any one of them (though the contact with Hebrews 1 arouses interest).

Genesis 19:24 is enigmatic. It is *the* primary text for Justin's "second God" argument, inasmuch as it represents the *single* "two powers" proof-text native to the theophanic material of Genesis and Exodus.[25] Skarsaune posited the possible existence of an earlier Christian testimony-tradition for Genesis 19:24 rooted in Judeo-Christianity,[26] yet to my knowledge no such reference to this passage exists in any extant "two powers" text before Justin. The passage is so smoothly integrated into Justin's argument as to demonstrate his full command of it within the larger scriptural context. This suggests it may not have been part of his received *testimonia* tradition but was "discovered" by Justin himself. In this case he supplemented his thorough reading of the Genesis-Exodus theophanies with two already traditional "two powers" *testimonia*, Psalms 44:7-8 and 109:1. On the other hand, its proximity to the "two powers" texts ascribed to David might indicate that it was part of an inherited tradition that already cataloged these three texts under nominal rubrics ("Moses says," "David says"). One cannot be dogmatic from an analysis of the *Dialogue* as to whether Justin received Genesis 19:24 from a traditional store.

The second part of Justin's argument, *Dialogue* 61.1—62.4, is concerned more closely with demonstrating the emission, preexistence, and creative activity of the second God. Justin sets out to demonstrate by means of "another witness" that God begat from himself "a certain rational power" before all creatures. To this end he offers an explanation by means of analogy to the acts of speech and of kindling fire (61.2). Scriptural demonstration is adduced from Proverbs 8:21-36 applied christologically. His argument from Proverbs focuses more explicitly upon the emission (8:22-25) and preexistence (8:26-31) of the "second God" than did the theophany proofs.[27] Three times in Proverbs 8:22-25, the passage mentions that "the Lord created/established/begot [ἔκτισε/ἐθεμελίωσε/γεννᾷ] me [Wisdom]." Twice in Proverbs 8:26-31, the text affirms that Wisdom was "with him [God]" (παρ᾽ αὐτῷ; συμπαρήμην αὐτῷ) during the act of creation, and once it refers to Wisdom's assistance in that event. In Proverbs 8:21-36 we thus possess a "two powers" text of a different sort from those discussed above, linked not with theophany, but with the figure of Wisdom. Once Justin identifies Christ with Wisdom,[28] it is clear that in the figure of Wisdom we have not a divine hypostasization as in certain Jewish speculation, but a fully substantial, preincarnate "second God." Justin further derives another of his titles for the "second God" via Proverbs 8:22: "The LORD created me as 'the Beginning' [ἀρχὴν] of his ways for his works." Quite possibly it is this very identification that allows him thematically to link Proverbs 8 with Genesis 1 by association with the "in the beginning" of verse 1, though this connection is never made explicit in the *Dialogue*.[29]

Justin supplements the Solomonic text with two additional "two powers" passages from Moses in the first and third chapters of Genesis (62.1), which emphasize not only the presence of the "second God" at creation but his very *involvement* in the event. The creation of the universe happened *by means* of the "second God." Justin supports the argument by reference to the plural "let us make" (ποιήσωμεν) and "our [ἡμετέραν] image and likeness" of Genesis 1:26-28 (esp. v. 26). To obviate any potential Jewish objection that God spoke merely to himself or to the material elements (cf. 62.2), Justin places great weight upon Genesis 3:22a: "Adam has become like one of us [ὡς εἷς ἐξ ἡμῶν], knowing good and evil." From this it is indisputably (ἀναμφιλέκτως) clear that God conversed "with someone numerically distinct and a rational being" and further that there are "a number of persons associated with one another, and they are at least two" (62.2–3).

JP as Source Material?

We have seen it is possible to isolate several central traditional proof-texts critical for the entirety of Justin's "second God" argument: Genesis 19:24 *may* have been traditional, but certainly Psalms 109:1 and 44:7-8 in *Dialogue* 56–60 were such.[30] The same may be asserted of the Wisdom speculation involving Proverbs 8:22 and Genesis 1:26 and 3:22 in *Dialogue* 61–62. Since *JP* constitutes the first of the Christian-Jewish dialogues about which we have some direct knowledge, it seems reasonable to inquire

whether Justin may have borrowed his "second God" *testimonia* from *JP*. Any suggestion of dependence, however, would seem to stand on shaky ground since only a few
ancient citations and brief descriptions of *JP* survive.[31] Nevertheless, we may yet retain
remnants of *JP* in several later Christian-Jewish dialogues:[32] the Greek dialogues of
Athanasius and Zacchaeus (hereafter *AZ*; late fourth to early fifth century) and of *Timothy and Aquila* (hereafter *TA,* preserved in a Long Recension [LR] and a Short Recension [SR]; fifth to sixth century), as well as the Latin *Simon and Theophilus* (hereafter
STh; early fifth century).[33] Frederick Conybeare speaks of these three as "independent
recensions" of some older dialogue, which he supposes to be *JP*.[34] He is followed by others[35] amid some dissenting voices.[36] The question of dependence on *JP* therefore remains
debated, and William Varner is right to warn against "dogmatism about the conclusions
of source-critical study."[37] Nevertheless, I find the initial arguments of Lawrence Lahey
presented in his Cambridge doctoral thesis intriguing if not entirely convincing. Lahey
takes up Conybeare's proposal and prepares a series of three tables comparing shared
material within these later dialogues. He obviates any suggestion that this shared material was derived from Tertullian's *Adversus Judaeos* or Cyprian's *Testimonia* by omitting
elements that might have come from these two stores. He comments:

> This material extends beyond shared Bible testimonies; it includes incidents,
> arguments, order, and small remarks. *AZ* and *STh* share some different and
> some of the same material as *TA* and *AZ*, showing that *AZ* and *STh* share the
> same *contra Iudaeos* dialogue source. Because of the great amount of material
> shared between *TA* and *AZ*, perhaps it could be argued that *TA* is dependent
> upon *AZ*. But *TA* has strong resemblances with *STh*, which show that they
> shared a dialogue source independently of *AZ*. This probably indicates that
> *TA* independently obtained the material shared with *AZ* from the same source
> *AZ* and *STh* share.[38]

He believes these "close resemblances" offer sufficient evidence to demonstrate
that the shared source "almost certainly is *Jason and Papiscus* since the source is a *contra Iudaeos* dialogue, probably quite early, and *Jason and Papiscus* existed in a Latin
translation."[39] It does not appear to have been Justin's *Dialogue*.[40] The presence of the
Jewish disputant requesting baptism at the end of all three post-Constantinian dialogues is particularly conspicuous[41] and indicates that they derive from a precursor
within the dialogue tradition. It further suggests *JP* as that source since this nicely fits
Celsus Africanus's description in the preface to his Latin translation of *JP*, which he
claims recorded Papiscus's coming to the belief that "Jesus Christ is the Son of God"
(*Iesum Christum filium dei*) and promptly requesting "the seal" (*signaculum*, that is, of
baptism) from Jason.[42]

    If Lahey's identification of the shared source of these dialogues as *JP* is correct—
and I grant it here for the sake of argument—then we have some substantive basis upon
which to make claims regarding material in *JP*. Specifically, material contained in all
three later dialogues stands a chance of being original to the source behind them, presumably *JP*. Lahey conveniently cataloged eleven examples of triple tradition material,
the first five of which are particularly interesting. I quote him here:

1. Quite near its beginning, *Jason and Papiscus* prominently featured the Jewish objection that Christians violate the unity of God by worshipping Christ, and thus two Gods. Isa 44:6 and some other scriptures treating the unity of God are given as proof. Minor Christian denials. (LR 1.5-6 [SR II.4-6], 1.8; *AZ* 1, 2b; *STh* 2a-4a, 6a-b.)
2. The Jewish objection is countered with Christian proofs from Genesis ch. 1, especially 1:1, showing the Son is the Beginning by whom God created heaven and earth, and 1:26 where "Let us make" shows God addressing the Son. . . . (LR 4.10-14 [SR VII.1-3]; *AZ* 3c, 4d-5b; *STh* 8b.)
3. Jewish objection that Gen 1:26 was spoken to the angels, and sarcasm noting that the Son is not mentioned alongside the Father in Genesis. (LR 4.19-20 [SR VII.8-9]; *AZ* 6a, 12c; *STh* 8a, 9a.)
4. Further Christian proof of the Son with the Father during creation based on Prov ch. 8. (LR 5.5 [SR VIII.3; X.4-5]; *AZ* 13a; *STh* 11b.)
5. Jewish objection that Prov 8 speaks of God's Wisdom. (LR 5.21; *AZ* 13b, d; *STh* 12a.)[43]

This standardized form in all three independent dialogues renders it likely that *JP* contained something approximating this basic pattern. Lahey's reconstruction and Justin's "second God" argument seem to overlap in the "two powers" *testimonia* from Wisdom Christology.

As can be seen from table 1, despite variations in order, the "two powers" Wisdom texts (highlighted in bold) are closely clustered within their respective arguments; they occur no more than several chapters apart from one another and always within a demonstration of a second divine being. These texts have the "feel" of having been inherited as part of an already well-established argument for "two powers" from Wisdom traditions, and it is plausible that this kind of argument was contained in *JP*.

Table 1. Dialogue Proof-Texts

Justin's *Dial.*	*AZ*	*STh*	*TA* LR [SR]
Gen. 19:24	15-16		6.9, 28.25-44
Ps. 109:1	81-87	25	6.9, 10.56 [XI.35]
Ps. 44:7-8	58-59: Ps. 44:8	6	
Prov. 8:22-31	13: Prov. 8:27, 30	11: Prov. 8:22-31	5.5: Prov. 8:27-30 [X.4-5: Prov. 8:27, 30] [VIII.3: Prov. 8:25, 30]
Gen. 1:1 (implicit?)		8b	4.6 [VII.1, VIII.9, IX.42]
Gen 1:26	3-8, 11, 12	8c	4.12-14, 20; cf. 6.7, 19.14 [VII.2-3; IX.40]
Gen. 3:22	12		

What we know of *JP* comes from only a few fragments and descriptions, among which Jerome tells us that it contained a reading (*scriptum est*) of Genesis 1:1 in which the Son is regarded as the "Beginning": "In the Son God made heaven and earth" (*In filio fecit Deus caelum et terram*).[44] Jerome is mistaken in assigning this same textual reading to both Tertullian and Hilary,[45] and it is not at all certain he "remembered" the precise wording of *JP* correctly.[46] However, if Maximus of Turin's *Contra Judaeos* is dependent on *JP*, as Conybeare suggested,[47] the argument for this reading in *JP* is bolstered.[48] The argument appears in *STh* (dependent upon the Latin *JP*?), and "neither the interpretation of Christ as beginning nor the use of Gen ch. 1 for even a related purpose occur in the two works of Tertullian and Cyprian."[49] It is reasonable then that *JP* contained either a text of Genesis 1:1 reading "*In filio* God created the heavens and the earth" or a christological interpretation of Genesis 1:1 according to the formula *in principio = in Christo*.[50] As noted above, the same argument (Christ = Beginning [ἀρχή]) might be presupposed in *Dialogue* 61–62.

There are, however, matters in which Justin's argument does not follow that of a (hypothetically) reconstructed *JP*. In every one of the late dialogues, Proverbs 8 follows on the heels of Genesis 1, which usually proceeds from Genesis 1:1 to 1:26. This order may be due to the rhetorical constraints of each dialogue. *AZ* and the long recension of *TA* begin their scriptural demonstration from Genesis expressly as a matter of principle,[51] and though no explicit parallel program is found in *STh* or the short recension of *TA* (cf. VI.6–7), the practice of beginning from "in the beginning" remains. Alternatively, perhaps *JP*'s original order is here faithfully preserved. At any rate, this is not the order in Justin's *Dialogue*. Further, several variations in the extent of Proverbs 8 are manifested in our late dialogues. We cannot therefore be certain what part of Proverbs 8 was present in *JP*, though it appears to have contained at a minimum 8:27, 30. We might further surmise that if Justin used *JP*, he must have added reference to Genesis 3:22 unless *AZ* singly preserves *JP*'s use of the passage. Perhaps it is best to speak of Justin having inherited a "two powers" Wisdom tradition similar to that contained in *JP*. If he did inherit some such tradition from *JP*, he was certainly no slave to it.

What, then, of the remaining "two powers" texts? The presence of Psalm 109:1 in triple tradition suggests it was contained in *JP*. However, its contextual function within all three later dialogues is so inconsistent as to render its appearance as a "two powers" proof-text in *JP* doubtful at best. In *STh* Psalm 109:1 comes as the sole witness to the third component of a resurrection–ascension–installment–return pattern, focusing on the priestly inauguration of Messiah's reign at God's right hand. Any "two Lords" element is entirely subordinated to the heavenly inauguration. In *AZ* Psalm 109:1-4 proves that Christ was "Lord and God and Priest"; the author joins a messianically focused "anointing" context to a divine "two powers" context. Only *TA* presents Psalm 109:1 in a full-blown "two powers" debate without reference to a priestly component; it is conjoined with Genesis 19:24 and Psalm 2:7. The same conclusion appertains with regard to Psalm 44:7-8. *AZ* utilizes verse 8 as a key for the anointing of the Messiah; one needs both verses 7 *and* 8 for the passage to be applied as a "two powers" text at all! As a "two powers" text, Psalm 44:7-8 only appears, then, in the Latin *STh*. There is no consistent pattern of usage for the texts within the later dialogues and no clustering of them as in

Justin's *Dialogue*. It is very difficult to conceive of them as having been drawn from a single coherent *testimonia* argument present already in *JP*.

Nor do we achieve the desired certainty with respect to Genesis 19:24. The passage, which occurs once in *AZ* and twice in the long recension of *TA*, appears consistently as a "two powers" proof-text. In critical sections of the "two powers" debate within each of these dialogues (*AZ* 14–16; *TA* 27.5—28.48), Genesis 19:24 is quoted not in isolation, but in reference to the larger context of the Mamre theophany (cf. *STh* 6). *AZ* cites Genesis 18:1, 17-26; *TA*, Genesis 18:1—19:24. These appear to me to be later reflections upon earlier traditions involving christophanic exegesis. Are we seeing here evidence of the reception of Justin's *Dialogue* (doubtful) or a reflection of earlier theophanic speculation in *JP* (doubtful) or some other mediating tradition? Here we hit a methodological stumbling block and recognize the limitations of this kind of speculation. The remaining occurrence in *TA* contains a brief clustering of Genesis 19:24 with Psalm 109:1 in an isolated *testimonia* format; again, hardly sufficient to claim dependence on *JP*. All in all, it is highly dubious to conclude from the later dialogues that "two powers" theophanic speculation was present in *JP*.

Conclusions

In this presentation I brought together Skarsaune's suggestion that *JP* may lie behind *Dialogue* 61.1—62.4 with Lahey's proposal that *JP* may have influenced three later dialogues, *AZ*, *STh*, and *TA*. I granted Lahey's proposition and compared key *testimonia* in Justin's "second God" argument with the same texts in these later dialogues. It appears that at least some of Justin's traditional material was present in *JP*, particularly a "two powers" argument from Wisdom speculation involving Proverbs 8 and Genesis 1, but was he directly dependent on *JP* for this tradition? Probably not, and it seems preferable to speak of Justin as having inherited a broader exegetical "tradition" of "two powers" Wisdom Christology. In the first half of his argument from theophany, Justin relied upon traditional stores of "two powers" texts—Psalms 109:1; 44:7-8; and possibly Genesis 19:24—which the analysis above also indicates likely came from somewhere other than *JP*. Had these texts been present in *JP* in a "two powers" argument and had the later dialogues been dependent upon *JP*, it is difficult to explain why the later dialogues employ them so inconsistently. In *Dialogue* 56–60 Justin is probably at his most creative exegetically. Having inherited certain traditional material, he expands it into a programmatic exegesis of OT theophanies as Christophanies. Without more detailed form- and source-critical analysis of the later Christian-Jewish dialogues, a firmer basis for the conclusions above cannot be established.

CHAPTER TWELVE

Justin and the Pontic Wolf

Sebastian Moll

Introduction

When it comes to the task of portraying Marcion, we certainly cannot complain about a lack of witnesses. There is hardly a church father who does not mention him in his works, whether in the form of a small note or of five entire volumes. Therefore, Justin's few remarks on Marcion in his *First Apology*[1] have not been of much interest to scholars, especially as he—compared to the other Fathers—does not provide any additional information. Ironically, it is the other way around. For it is not Justin who does not provide any additional information on Marcion: if anything, it is the other Fathers who do not provide any additional information compared to Justin. He is our very first witness of Marcion's activity and also the only contemporary witness we have. But not only was he a contemporary; Justin also lived in Rome at the same time as Marcion did, which makes it quite probable that he actually knew him in person. Therefore, it seems hard to understand why so little attention has been paid to Justin's report, and it should thus be most promising to paint a portrait of Marcion exclusively based on the only "eyewitness."

Simply filtering out all the information Justin provides about Marcion, however, will be only one small, though essential, part of this essay. The really intriguing questions I am trying to answer are these: What does he *not* mention and *why*? Why has he chosen to present to his addressees specifically this description of the arch-heretic? And why does he mention him at all?

In order to examine these issues, the very first step must be to consider the addressees of the *Apology*. This topic would, of course, be quite enough for an article of its own. Yet, as it is of the utmost importance for the actual question of this essay, we cannot avoid at least touching upon it. So I will need to digress a little from the topic of Marcion for a moment—although digressions are only to be expected when dealing with Justin!

The Addressees of the Apology

The question of the addressees of Justin's *First Apology* seems rather superfluous at first glance. After all, unlike most other writers of early Christianity, Justin plainly names his addressees at the very beginning of his work:

> To the Emperor Titus Aelius Hadrianus Antoninus Pius Augustus Caesar; to Verissimus, his son, the philosopher; to Lucius, the philosopher, by nature son of Caesar and by adoption son of Pius, lover of learning; to the sacred Senate and to the whole Roman people.[2]

Nevertheless, there has been a long line of scholars denying that Justin actually intended his *Apology* to be read by the imperial court, considering it rather to be a literary fiction.[3] Before looking into this matter further, we should remember one important methodological principle first: the burden of proof lies with whoever wants to show that Justin did *not* address his *Apology* to the emperors, the Senate, and the Roman people. Therefore, I shall begin by taking a look at the arguments put forward by those scholars who deny the authenticity of Justin's address. An article by Lorraine Buck[4] not only is the most recent one on this matter, but also provides some of the most recurrent arguments for this point of view. It is thus a good example for my analysis.

All in all, Buck puts forward four reasons why Justin's *Apology* could not have been an actual official imperial petition, a so-called *libellus*. First, she detects several "careless and inexcusable errors"[5] in Justin's address to the emperor. In her opinion, Justin would have had to place the title *Caesar* directly following *Emperor*, to exclude Antoninus's two adopted sons from the address, and to salute Marcus Aurelius as Caesar also. Even if these things may have been errors on Justin's part, they can hardly be considered an argument against the authenticity of his address. It is perfectly possible that Justin was simply ignorant of these official formalities. He may have been an educated man, but that does not mean he was familiar with all the rules and regulations of a correct imperial address.[6] Peter Lampe, for example, feels that the form of the *Apology* rather attests a certain amount of juridical knowledge on Justin's part: "Not everyone is knowledgeable in the ways of administrative authority and official procedure."[7] Moreover, even if we consider Justin to be aware of all these formalities, even if we assume that he wanted to create a literary fiction, why would he deliberately make a mistake? Buck's answer to that question is that Justin, "in his address, is laying the foundation for the sarcasm and insults which immediately follow," that he "has set a literary trap for the emperors and exploits it to the fullest," and that he challenges "the emperors' right to their noble titles."[8] I must say that to derive such an amount of insidious ingenuity from a few minor mistakes is somewhat far-fetched, to say nothing about the fact that even if Justin really intended all of this, it still would in no way be an argument against his intention actually to present his work to the imperial court. Buck, in general, seems to mix up two completely different questions in her article. To investigate whether Justin intended his *Apology* to be read by the emperors has nothing to do with the question of whether his *Apology* is an accurate, appropriate, and correct *libellus* or whether the emperors would actually have taken notice of the *Apology*.

This mistake then makes her continue in the same sort of argument, stating her second point that the content of the *Apology* is "equally unacceptable,"[9] which she tries to prove by referring to Justin's frequent digressions and repetitions. As before, Buck might even be right about the fact that his works "would never have been admitted as official imperial petitions," but again this is hardly the point. Justin's style does not contradict his intention, especially as he himself never makes a secret of the fact that he is not the most talented writer[10] and also admits that he repeats himself quite regularly.[11]

Buck's third point is the inappropriate tone of Justin toward his imperial audience. What has been said so far about the difference between an appropriate style on the one hand and Justin's actual intentions on the other obviously applies to this case, too. However, we need not even concede that Justin's tone is actually inapposite. Certainly, to threaten the emperors with "the eternal punishment of fire,"[12] for example, may not be all that nice, but Justin really has no time and no reason for pleasantries. He is trying to save his fellow Christians from being unjustly put to death by the very authorities to whom he is writing. Thus he says himself, "We have not come before you to flatter you by this writing nor to gain your favor, but to demand that you form a judgement according to a thorough and reasonable investigation."[13]

This brings us to the last and surely most questionable argument Buck puts forward. She denies the legal possibility of a second-century Christian addressing the imperial authorities.[14] What are we supposed to make of this argument? That Justin (who does not go by the name "Martyr" for nothing) could not have intended to address that petition to the emperor because he was not allowed to? Christians are being persecuted simply for being Christians; are they supposed to wait for the legitimization of their cause before they plead for it?

All in all I think it is fair to say that there is simply not enough evidence to give rise to any reasonable doubt that Justin did indeed expect his work to be read by the imperial court.[15] Whether he actually had in mind *all* the personages mentioned in his address (the address to SPQR—the Senate and people of Rome—for example, may have been just a phrase) is of little relevance to us. The important thing is that Justin addressed his *Apology* to an educated pagan audience in an attempt "to directly influence the religious politics of the Antonini."[16]

Marcion

The Information Justin Provides

> And there is a certain Marcion of Pontus, who is even now still teaching his obedient followers to believe that there is some other god who is greater than the Demiurge. By the assistance of the demons he has made many people in the whole world speak blasphemies, to deny that God is the Creator of all, and to confess that there exists a greater god, who has done greater things than He.[17]

And, as we have said earlier, the evil demons have put forward Marcion of Pontus, who is even now teaching to deny that God is the Creator of all heavenly and earthly things and that the Christ predicted through the prophets is his Son, and proclaims some other god than the Demiurge of all things and, correspondingly, another son. There are many who have become followers of his as of the only one who knows the truth, and they make fun of us, although they have no proof of what they are saying, but are snatched away irrationally as lambs by a wolf, and become the prey of godless teachings and of demons.[18]

These are the only two passages in Justin's *Apology* (and in his entire work known to us) in which he mentions the arch-heretic.[19] Although Justin offers no more than these quite short and very similar reports, it is possible to retrieve a concise portrait of Marcion from them:

1. He has many followers all around the world;
2. his followers revere him;
3. he believes in a god who did not create the universe and who is superior to the Demiurge;
4. he believes in a son of this superior god, who is not the Christ predicted by the prophets; and
5. his teaching is ἄλογος—irrational—and without ἀπόδειξις—proof.[20]

Why Mention Marcion at All?

Adolf von Harnack commented that "in his apologetic naivety, Justin believes that his addressees would take an interest in his pieces of information on the evil heresies."[21] To Harnack, of course, everyone who did not acknowledge the genius of Marcion must have seemed naïve. Still, the question remains why Justin would consider it important to inform the emperors about heretics. Apart from Marcion, he only mentions Simon, his "companion" Helena, and his "disciple" Menander in his *Apology*.[22] Again, Harnack cannot help but notice that "the juxtaposition of Marcion with the founders of sects who posed as gods is completely inappropriate and particularly spiteful, but it does show how dangerous Marcion appeared to Justin . . . and in what great esteem Marcion was held in his church."[23] We can leave it open as to whether his grouping of these people is indeed malicious and unfounded; in Justin's view it certainly was not. Nevertheless, it seems confusing at first that he would mention his contemporary Marcion, with his apparently large number of followers, in connection with other heretics who must have been dead for decades and who—at least as Justin seems to think[24]—did not have many followers in Rome anymore. Therefore, Harnack's statement gives us a good hint at the reasons for Justin's choice. He is not after a particular heretical system or movement; he is after the "big names" in heresy,[25] after those men who are worshiped by their followers[26] and who claim that they alone know the truth.[27]

In order to understand this, we have to consider that one of Justin's main aims in his *Apology* is to show that Christianity is not some novel innovation, but in continuity with the Jewish Scriptures, which also formed the source for the teachings of the Greek philosophers.[28] He is also trying to demonstrate that Christianity is by no means irrational or "beneath the notice of intelligent men,"[29] but is in fact not in conflict with philosophy—although of course "superior to all human philosophy."[30] The teachings of Christ, according to Justin, certainly surpass those of Plato, but they are not completely different from them:[31] "Christ is . . . the Reason every human being has a part in. And those who lived according to Reason are Christians"[32] (even before the appearance of Christ). Having this in mind, it becomes obvious that Justin is strictly opposed to any claim of radical exclusiveness, as this was the major reproach of his pagan addressees.[33] His mission is to clear the Christian name, and so he has to prevent himself and his fellow Christians at all cost from being lumped together with people who are considered to have special and exclusive knowledge, especially as these people are—as Justin keeps mentioning with disapproval[34]—also called Christians. Therefore, he has to make Marcion look as bad in the eyes of his addressees as possible.

This explains the pieces of information Justin reports about Marcion. The fact that there is a god superior to the Demiurge might not have been all that irritating to an audience familiar with contemporary philosophy,[35] but to completely separate the Supreme God from the creation of the universe would have been unthinkable[36] and is thus perfectly suitable for discrediting Marcion. His defiance of the prophecies has to be pointed out most clearly as it "supported the objection of the philosophers that Christianity was completely new."[37] Furthermore, Justin is most anxious to make his audience see that Christians—unlike poets or philosophers[38]—are able to offer proof (ἀπόδειξις) for what they are saying, so he has to deprive Marcion's followers of this privilege. And finally, a doctrine that is contrary to Reason—is there a greater horror for a Stoic emperor?

The Rest Is Silence

It can be considered certain that these five pieces of information mentioned above, although profound, were not all that Justin knew about Marcion. As Justin states himself, he had, at the time he was writing the *Apology*, already written a "treatise against all the sects which have come into being" (σύνταγμα κατὰ πασῶν τῶν γεγενημένων αἱρέσεων),[39] which he is kindly willing to offer to the emperor in case he would like to read it. Surely this treatise did contain more information on his heretical adversary; otherwise it would have made no sense to present it to his readers in addition to the *Apology*. Moreover, Irenaeus reports that Justin wrote a work especially directed against Marcion,[40] which is further proof that Justin's knowledge of Marcion's heresy went far beyond his testimony in the *Apology*.

As I indicated in the introduction, the reports on Marcion's doctrine are anything but rare, so a list of potential supplements to Justin's information would be nearly endless. I have therefore decided to name five of the most essential (and best attested) features of Marcion's theology[41] that are not mentioned by Justin, but constitute the main points of criticism by later writers:

1. He believes in Jesus Christ (as the son of the superior god);
2. he rejects the Mosaic law (as the law of the Demiurge);
3. he has written two works—the *Antitheses* (in which he juxtaposed statements from the "Old Testament" and the "New" in order to demonstrate their irreconcilability) and his "Bible" (the Gospel according to Luke and ten letters of Paul, all of these texts "cleansed from judaistic interpolations");
4. he does not believe in resurrection of the flesh; and
5. he was a strict ascetic (no drinking, sexual intercourse, or the like).

Silence does not equal ignorance.[42] Unless these elements belong to a later development of Marcionite doctrine—and we have no reason to believe that this is the case—it is most likely that Justin was aware of (at least most of) these features of Marcion's theology, without mentioning them, however. The big remaining question thus is why?

The Reasons for Justin's Silence

I have tried to show above that Justin mentions certain elements of Marcion's theology in order to "knock" him in front of his audience. In the same way, he seems to have withheld some other parts, being afraid that they might elevate Marcion in their opinion.

Justin does mention that Marcion does not believe in the Christ predicted by the prophets, but he manages to express it in a way that does not reveal the fact that Marcion does indeed believe in the very same Christ he worships. Justin has to withhold that information as it would hinder his attempt to distinguish himself and other Christians from the Marcionite community, to whom he does not grant the right to go by the name of Christians.[43]

Marcion's rejection of the prophets came in handy for Justin in order to discredit him, but he does not report that Marcion also disapproved of the Mosaic law. As a matter of fact, the Mosaic law is not mentioned in the *Apology* at all![44] Moses does appear several times, but only as "the first of the prophets."[45] Here again, Justin seems deliberately to keep quiet about this feature of Marcion's theology, since it would have been possible that his pagan readers, to whom the Mosaic law was strange, might have had some sympathy with Marcion's position. In this context, however, it must also be noted that Justin himself—although of course not completely rejecting the "Old Testament" as Marcion did—believed that the law has "ceased to be valid, and has been supplanted by the New Law, Christ."[46] Did Justin in the end perhaps not mention this characteristic of Marcion's heresy because it appealed to him in some way?

As to Marcion's works, the existence of the *Antitheses* in particular would have been risky to reveal. Marcion's approach might be questionable, yet inconsistencies between the "Old" and the "New Testament" are undeniable. Thus a philosophically educated reader, trained in the art of logic, might in fact have found Marcion's arguments conclusive rather than irrational (ἄλογος).

Justin's silence about Marcion's denial of the resurrection of the flesh is probably the easiest one to understand. "For the soul He might be able to provide an everlasting life; but as Heraclitus says, 'corpses ought to be thrown away as worse than dung.'"[47] Celsus's statement—though of course written some time after the *Apology*—serves as a good example of the "Hellenistic horror of the flesh."[48] It can be considered almost certain that a pagan audience would have sided with Marcion on that point.

Finally, as to Marcion's lifestyle, Justin probably would have agreed with Origen: "The most dangerous heretics are those whose lives are good."[49] That is why he had to be careful not to speak of Marcion's asceticism. This might easily have made quite an impression on a virtuous Roman statesman.

Conclusion

Justin is a man of considerable cleverness. Whatever one may think of his frequent digression, repetitions, and his own admission that he is not a good writer, he does have his audience in mind and knows exactly what they want to hear and what not. Apart from the case of presenting Marcion to the Roman emperors, this becomes most obvious in the differences between his *Apologies* and the *Dialogue with Trypho*. Justin's admiration of the pagan philosophers, for example, which is recognizable throughout the entire *Apology* (a writing for philosophically educated pagans), turned into "sharp words of criticism for all philosophical schools and derogatory remarks for all philosophers"[50] when he was writing his *Dialogue* (for a completely different audience).

As we have seen, in the case of Marcion, Justin skillfully manages to give his imperial addressees the worst possible image of his heretical adversary—without lying, however. Justin is a man of truth. Yet in his *Apology* he must act like a lawyer for his cause. As such he is aware of one most important rule: silence is golden.

CHAPTER THIRTEEN

Questions Liturgists Would Like to Ask Justin Martyr

C{o}lin B{u}chanan

L{iturgists} {tend} {to} {approach} {a} {second}-{century} Christian author with a different agenda from those of other scholars. This is not only because of their natural tempta- tion to concentrate on a few select passages (though that is there and has to be care- fully corrected by an awareness of context, both in the author's work on the one hand and in the historical circumstances on the other). The starkly distinguishing factor is that many latter-day scholars in the liturgical world have been trawling the evidence of the early centuries for models to be used in today's worship. This produces a schol- arly discipline that is different in kind from research into second-century apologetics or early Christologies; for in these other fields no one expects the results of research to impinge on present-day equivalent formulations, and history remains firmly history. For the liturgist, Justin has an inevitable fascination: Is he indeed a signpost in an oth- erwise largely trackless area, and a signpost toward the worship of today?

I am perhaps particularly conscious of this factor as an Anglican liturgist, for Anglicans have a varied, but never indifferent, attitude concerning the degree of authority to be accorded to patristic evidence. I quote the classic "mission statement" (as it would be called today) of one major school of thought that is to be found in the report of the section on liturgical revision of the Lambeth Conference of 1958: "It was Cranmer's aim to lift worship in England out of the liturgical decadence of the late medieval Church in western Christendom, and to recover as much as possible of the character of the worship of what he called the 'Primitive Church.'"[1] Now I do not myself believe this was Cranmer's aim, and certainly not his central one. Furthermore, the statement of it has often (as it was at that Lambeth Conference) been backed by the assertion that he didn't have enough information at his disposal—but that now we do. Curiously, there have been those who thought Cranmer did not know Justin, on the grounds that the first printed edition of Justin was published in 1551, late on in the development of his thought. There is, however, at least one place where he was clearly quoting Justin before that date, and there is some evidence that the passage about the Eucharist from which he quotes did circulate in a detached form and could well have come under his nose in manuscript.[2]

However, the conviction of Anglican liturgists in the mid-twentieth century that we do now have sufficient information to recover "the worship of the early church" would, if credible, certainly have to give a key place to Justin, though it has often looked as though he were being elbowed out by Hippolytus (one of the authors not available in the sixteenth century). But in truth, we have nothing like the requisite information to reconstruct with any certainty either general principles or specific models. To inspect the liturgical evidence of the first and second centuries is like flying from Cairo to the Cape in order to get a picture of Africa, only to find that there is thick cloud cover all the way, with but half a dozen gaps in it. If through those gaps in the clouds we get a hasty glimpse of water on two occasions, and later of a snowcapped mountain, a desert, a city, and an extensive ostrich farm on other occasions, what have we learned about Africa? Is it one continent or more than one? If it *is* one, is there any geophysical, climatic, zoological, anthropological, or economic relation between the parts? The flight and its six camera snaps simply will not tell us. Our equivalent in the world of liturgy is to look at Clement of Rome in the late first century (with one or two hints about worship), at Ignatius of Antioch with a few more, at Pliny's letter with a two-liner, at the *Didache* (which might be the wild card, like my snowcapped mountain in Africa), and then at Justin himself midcentury, before we come to further little hints in Irenaeus and Tertullian (though the latter at the end of the second century at last *does* have more than a little hint—indeed, an actual sustained treatment—in relation to baptism [a somewhat larger gap in the clouds as we come in to land?]). Throw in Hippolytus for the moment, though recent scholarship has called into question much of the supposed solid ground on which he was thought to stand thirty or forty years ago. Then we must remember that we are talking about a period of, say, 120 years, and we are talking of practice in a Roman Empire that stretched from the Antonine Wall to the Near East (and the tiny shreds of evidence I have cited come from different parts of that empire and in different languages).[3] Furthermore, this was a religion that was strictly *illicita* and lived and worshiped out of the public gaze much of the time. I submit that if we are seeking universally accepted norms of Christian worship, the evidence from these two centuries does not add up to a row of beans. We merely glimpse vastly disconnected scenes briefly through gaps in the cloud cover.

If Justin apparently gives a slightly fuller glimpse than some other authors, that does not affect the limitations of the whole exercise. And if, to revert to the earlier point, we discern today a few more gaps in the clouds than Thomas Cranmer enjoyed, we deceive ourselves if we think we have thereby either encountered a universal pattern or hit upon an authoritative model. None of this need inhibit our questioning of Justin's information, but it stands as a caution against giving to any answers that we elicit too much weight for the present day.

Of course precedents do have some weight, and at times it is an advantage for today's liturgists to draw imitatively upon second-century evidence. Thus, for instance, the use of the words "president" and "presider" for the leader of worship events must have come by direct jump from Justin to our liturgy—I was myself involved in putting it, in exactly that way, into the rubrics of our Series 3 Eucharist in England in 1971. It was no doubt helped by a desire to say that the whole congregation "celebrates" the Eucharist (and thus the officiant can no longer be called the "celebrant"), but the precedent supplied by Justin was, I think, determinative. Similarly, the position in the rite of the kiss of peace, in its congregational role that has revived in the last forty years, is (except in Roman Catholic circles) an exact lifting of a usage from Justin. The position we use for the intercessions at the Eucharist also imitates Justin. Quite possibly the latter-day return to the very naming of the great prayer over the elements in the eucharistic rite "the great thanksgiving" or indeed the "eucharistic prayer" owes much also to him. Certainly the rite was called the "Eucharist" before his time, and the *Didache* has a haunting but muddling reference to the itinerant prophets "giving thanks as much as they will" (10.7), but Justin's clear statement that this prayer is central and is the offering of thanksgivings has, I suggest, been determinative. However, none of these piecemeal imitations is more than contingent—they take the form of "Oh, here is a good idea," rather than of "Here is an authoritative norm."

My warning is against believing we can discern the topography of a nation from a gap in the clouds. Yet the temptation to think we know something is strong, and as an illustrative caution, I cite a one-liner I discovered in Leslie Barnard. It goes as follows: "The catechumenate did not receive definite form until c. 200 C.E."[4] That is worth unpacking. It is saying that for the years prior to 200, we *know* there was no definite catechumenate—perhaps, to follow his mind, we should add the word "anywhere." Proving a negative is always difficult, but this is simply asserting one without attempting proof. For it is like saying about the flight over Africa not only that we saw no sign of trees anywhere, but that, *tout simple*, there are no trees in Africa. How can anyone know such a negative? And that is before we question the positive part of our quotation. For then we ask: What could it mean to say that *the* catechumenate—a single, defined, universal form—*did* assume some definite form around 200 C.E., and how do we know it, and what was that definite form? Note, too, that Justin himself says, "Whoever have been persuaded and believe that those things which we have taught and asserted to be true are true, and undertake that they can live accordingly— these people are taught both to pray and to ask of God while fasting the forgiveness of their former sins. We pray and fast together with them."[5] This surely implies a known pattern that included a program of teaching and finally of praying and fasting together. It could even be dubbed a catechumenate with a "definite form." If there are strong implications here that the church in Rome in the 150s *did* know what it was doing in preparation when it scheduled someone for baptism, how can any commentator, when writing on Justin, say as a kind of universalized truth that the catechumenate had not reached a "definite form" at that period of history? We simply do not know.

The upshot of the above is that we dare not construct a single grand liturgical scene of the first two centuries. In terms of our metaphor, we cannot tell from the small gaps in the cloud whether Africa is a single continent or not, nor, if it is one continent, how the topography of one part relates to that of another. Not only does Paul

Bradshaw's school of "splitters" hold the field, but it is unimaginable that a serious challenge to it can arise.[6] This in turn means that the liturgists should take Justin simply as they find him. He can only be said to show what he does show. We may ask whether his account is true to the Scriptures. We may ask whether anybody coming after him may be imitating him (though it appears few if any are). We may perhaps ask if there are any common features of all the glimpses we have (as, for instance, in the universal use of baptism in water), but we cannot "discover" something in the third century and read it back into Justin at a point where he is himself silent. He can only say what he does say, and he himself did not have the benefit of later Christian history and its authors from the end of the second century or anywhere in the third. We cannot even say (as, for instance, some authors have obviously wanted to say about a postbaptismal anointing or laying on of hands), "Well, he does not mention this or that, which *must* have been happening, but he obviously concealed it as inappropriate to put under the emperor's nose." I mention this, not only because it has been raised by reputable authors, but also because the very invoking of such a supposed instinct of Justin's for secrecy betrays the interest such modern authors have had in making Justin conform to some preconceived grand liturgical plan, a plan that is constructed in order ultimately to be implemented in Christian worship today.

Have we access to anything crucial to being Christian that Justin knows but vetoes and omits as being unsuitable to tell the emperor? The more I reflect on his readiness in *1 Apology* 66 to tell the emperor that ordinary food becomes the flesh and blood of the incarnate Jesus, the more certain I become that, far from his observing some supposed *disciplina arcani*, Justin has taken the view that nothing is off-limits if it will assist the transparency of his presentation to the emperor. One would have expected, if he wanted to be discreet, an account more like the woebegone tale told by the people Pliny had interrogated nearly half a century before in Bithynia, who first had to tell Pliny they had given up the faith as much as twenty-five years before that, but then, even at that great distance of time, still had to insist that the food they had at that time eaten together was harmless and everyday. Justin is telling the emperor quite a contrasting tale, one that in the wrong hands (and one assumes there were plenty of wrong hands around) could easily be represented as magic or as some form of cannibalism or as both. Yet Justin, far from hurrying past such an embarrassing feature of his account of the Eucharist, deliberately pauses in chapter 66 and discusses it in a totally unguarded way. So if he does not defend that flank with any reticence at all, what reason would we have for asserting he is being economical with the Christian truth elsewhere? We are not to want him to be other than he is. He stands out for us as a uniquely expansive Christian witness from the mid-second century, a voice from Rome itself at the heart of the empire. He has to be valued very highly indeed for his transparency.

Nevertheless, even surrounded by scholarly cautions, the liturgist would still like to penetrate further into Justin's liturgical world. I start with the baptismal questions.

1. Did Justin know infant baptism? The account of baptism in *1 Apology* 61 has apparently adult candidates. But Jeremias, in *Infant Baptism in the First Four Centuries*, drew on a reference in *1 Apology* 15.6 to those "who were made

disciples of Christ from childhood [*ek paidon ematheteuthesan*]."[7] As *matheteuein* in the passive is virtually interchangeable with "being baptized" in *Dialogue* 39.2, Jeremias urged that Christians who were in their sixties and seventies in the middle of the second century, and had been disciples from their youngest days, had in all probability been baptized *as infants within the first century* C.E. Aland had to attack this in his controversy with Jeremias. He provided evidence that *ek paidon* may well mean "from youth" (and, he submits, *cannot* mean "from infancy" in *1 Clement* 63, as that would have had those disciples baptized before the Christian church began!).[8] Jeremias in his further reply responded with a trenchant confrontation, appealing to the Justin context—where "Justin contrasts those born as Christians with those who became Christians" (and the *ek paidon* group are the former).[9] The infant baptism question is not going to be solved in and through Justin's possibly glancing reference alone, but the answer we reach will be contributory, and I know of no further attempt to refute Jeremias.[10] If on other grounds we think infant baptism was *practiced* in midcentury Rome, then we also have to read the baptismal account in *1 Apology* 61 as including infants and young children with their parents. *Mutatis mutandis*, that is not too difficult.

2. Did Justin have an "Easter" or other fixed occasion? In the New Testament, baptism occurs as adults receive the gospel—so there is no catechumenate. In Tertullian, there is a half-mention of forty days' preparation; in Hippolytus, there are three years. In part the length of preparation is related to whether or not there is a fixed point in the year for baptisms. Tertullian prefers the fifty days of "Pentecost." But did Justin have a fixed point in the year? And what preparation was actually given?

3. Did the rite itself have a fixed baptismal profession? There is reference to repenting of sin; there is reference to the candidate's "assent" (*1 Apol.* 65.1); there is not quite an overt creedal adherence—but was it there? Furthermore, did the rite have a fixed baptismal formula? There appears to be a "naming" of Father, Son, and Spirit—but how was this done, and how fixed was the usage?

4. Did Justin know (and suppress from his account) something like "confirmation"? Purveyors of the "Mason-Dix Line" had to believe that something like confirmation (either by anointing or by laying on of hands) followed immediately upon baptism, and Edward Ratcliff in particular wrote an essay to demonstrate the likelihood of this in Justin.[11] But we know that he was striving to make the author fit his theory; and in the Mason-Dix era it became conventional to say that the early "integrated" rite included both water baptism and this subsequent ceremony, and it was this "integrated" rite that later "disintegrated." But if the early evidence does not reveal such an "integrated" rite, do we then take such evidence at face value, or challenge it in the interests of a theory? In the question of what we call "confirmation," quite a lot hangs on Justin, at least as far as the West is concerned. If we think he had no postbaptismal ceremony, then any attempt to assert the universality (and therefore the normative character) of a two-stage initiation ceremony from the apostolic

days onward collapses. That which is being asserted to be the "primitive" and "integrated" rite, as it cannot be traced as a regular feature of initiation earlier than Tertullian in the West and rather later in the East, can hardly be fathered upon the apostles or deemed to be vital to the present day.[12]

5. Do the prayers and the kiss have incorporating significance?
6. What kinds of ministers are involved? Was there a "minister of baptism"? There is a paucity of active transitive verbs—though in *1 Apology* 65.1 it is said that "we washed him."

We go on then to eucharistic questions: the first two questions here are about what we would call consecration—the first about what consecration effects (and it looks strong and "realist"); and the second about what effects consecration.[13] These may in turn pull in the fifth question and the role of the narrative of institution.

1. What is Justin's understanding of the "flesh and blood" of Christ? Is the use of "flesh," rather than "body," as Bradshaw muses, of significance?
2. What is meant by "eucharisticizing"? Has Justin any doctrine of "consecration" (as later authors would call it)? Or of change in or to the elements?
3. What does Justin teach about the "shape" of the liturgy? Is he the first fixed point in the development of Gregory Dix's "shape" of the liturgy, or are the features he describes all in fact contingent?
4. What are we to make of the bringing in of water and wine already mixed (65.3)? Is it possible (as scholars from Harnack to Bradshaw have speculated) that there is something wrong with the text and that the reference to the *mixture* of water and wine is some sort of scribal addition?[14] More to the point, if water and wine were mixed, what was the reason—does it include the "apologetic" purpose of underlining the relatively temperate stance of the congregation in relation to strong drink? And if it is brought in mixed, how would that bear upon present-day liturgical practice?
5. Is there a given content to his eucharistic prayer? Indeed, is it one prayer or two—for Paul Bradshaw has suggested seriously that the plural indicates, or may indicate, separate thanksgivings over each of the two elements?[15] Whichever is the answer to the latter question, how do we handle the former one? There appears to be an allusively trinitarian structure to the prayer, but was it variable, was it extemporary, or was it at least a script in the presider's back pocket or at the back of his mind? Furthermore, did it include the institution narrative that is reproduced in chapter 66 but is not actually associated with the description of the presidential thanksgiving? Or was the institution narrative catechetical rather than liturgical?[16]
6. How significant is Justin's use of Old Testament typology and prophecy when speaking to Trypho about the Eucharist? How can (or should) the offering of the cleansed leper (in *Dial.* 41) or the prophecy of the offering of a pure sacrifice among the Gentiles (Mal. 1:11, cited in Dial. 28.5, 29.1, 41.2, 116.3, and 117.4) be expounded? Are they actual, tightly theological expositions of the

Eucharist, or are they more like handy implements for showing a Jew how his religion looked forward to Gentile Christianity? If the passages are teaching that the Eucharist is in some substantial and distinctive sense a "sacrifice," what does that mean? And granted that the references are all in the *Dialogue,* is there here some central aspect of the Eucharist about which Justin is deliberately— even disingenuously—silent when describing the Eucharist at length to the emperor in the *First Apology*? A further large question also lurks in the citation of Malachi 1:11—for here even a splitter cannot but see a repeated invoking of the Old Testament text in a variety of second-century authors, to show that the beliefs of the Gentiles fulfill the Old Testament (a main theme in the *Dialogue*); and in this process the authors at least suggest an entrenched notion of a "pure sacrifice."[17] While in *Dialogue* 117 this is at one point clearly identified with the bread and cup of the Eucharist, elsewhere in the same chapter Justin insists that pure hearts and lives, along with praise and thanksgiving, are the only sac- rifices we can offer. It leaves us with a question as to whether it is at all appro- priate to offer the bread and cup to God, and whether Justin's presidential prayers of thanksgiving included such an offering. The *puram hostiam,* the "pure sacrifice," passed of course into the anamnesis of the Roman rite and was in time expounded as the offering of Christ himself. But was Justin's use of Malachi 1:11 simply within a stream of conventional pro-Gentile exposition of the Old Testament, and perhaps not intended to fasten particular ideas onto the Eucharist?

Finally, there are some questions that touch on the eucharistic descriptions in the *First Apology* but that are not quite eucharistic themselves.

1. What time of day did they meet? If Justin is using the Roman division of the day when addressing the emperor, it looks as though the gathering "on the day of the sun" was in the early morning. Was this an innovation?

2. How did they run "the prayers of the people"? Justin uses the first-person plural, in contrast to the third-person singular used about the eucharistic prayer (or its equivalent). Does that mean that several voices articulated the prayers (an extemporary prayer meeting?) or simply that the involvement of the congregation in these prayers was somehow viewed differently from their part in the eucharistic prayer?

3. Then there is the question of the "presider." One of the baffling (even infuriating) features of communications to and from Rome in the period from 50 to 150 (I include Paul's letter to the Romans, Luke's account of Paul's arrival in Rome, the letter of Clement to the Corinthians,[18] the letter of Ignatius to the Romans, and Justin's *Apology* here) is that we learn nothing about that line of bishops of Rome that historians in the next generations start to tell us existed since Peter. Indeed, we learn little about any structure of leadership at all. The participle "the presiding (person)" has indeed been imitated in recent years, and it is arguable that to identify him by his function rather than his "order" is

dynamic and helpful—but it leaves us with unanswered questions. Here we are entitled to ask whether Justin is being "reserved" because he is addressing the emperor, or whether perhaps in a local congregation (within a larger network around the city) the presider was not a bishop but was his delegate.[19] What is clear is that the "pure offering" of Malachi 1:11 was offered by the Christian priesthood of the whole company, and this seems to preclude any sacrificing role for a ministerial "priest" to fulfill.

If these questions could be authoritatively answered, Justin's role in the development of Christian liturgy would be far more clearly discerned. Until such a day of final answers, this heuristic approach and a dealing with degrees of probability may represent the most rigorous scholarship to which we can currently aspire. But answers of any sort, even the interim, provisional, and conjectural, are well worth eliciting, evaluating, and incorporating according to their merits. As an intended outcome of the 2006 Conference, I have given time in the subsequent twelve months to pushing further towards those elusive answers. The upshot is my monograph, Alcuin/GROW Joint Liturgical Study no. 64, *Justin Martyr on Baptism and Eucharist: A Text for Students with Introduction and Commentary* (Norwich: SCM-Canterbury Press, December 2007). But my use of "pushing further towards" is itself a recognition of how our glimpsing through a brief gap in the clouds leaves intriguingly unfinished our picture of Justin's liturgical world.

CHAPTER FOURTEEN

Justin and Hellenism

Some Postcolonial Perspectives

Rebecca Lyman

WHILE PREPARING FOR THIS ESSAY, I did an Internet search on "Hellenism." I heartily recommend this research diversion since "original sin" or "perichoresis" can point you to some very interesting Web sites not usually explored or considered by the professional historian. One of the first links to appear on my screen was an irresistible entry: "Hands-on Hellenism." This led to a site by a "reconstructionist" from Mississippi with instructions on to how to practice libations, prayers, and sacrifices to the deities of the Mediterranean basin. The essential ingredients for "Hands-on Hellenism" were explained as wine, incense, a chicken, and a hibachi. As I read the blog of a solitary Southern evening of grilling and offering libations to Zeus, I couldn't help but think of other far-flung and perhaps unlikely sites of Mediterranean devotion, such as Lullingstone villa in forested Kent or the half-obscured foundations of a Roman villa on an inland plain in Madera, Bulgaria.

Comparing twenty-first-century Mississippi with second-century Neapolis as a context for understanding Hellenism perhaps gives Justin an unfair advantage. One can only imagine the reaction of Celsus to "Hands-on Hellenism" with a hibachi! Although the relation of Justin to Hellenism is a well-worn topic, recent methodological shifts in the study of ancient history and religion encourage us to look at this aspect of Justin's work yet again. In contrast to our inherited nineteenth-century view of conflicting, and to a degree even incompatible, systems of thought and culture, contemporary theories on religion and culture have encouraged us to look at practices or overlapping identities especially in eras of intense communication and interchange. As Judith Lieu recently pointed out about religion in late antiquity, they may not be the "same sort of thing," but then, "none of them is only one sort of thing."[1] If we understand culture itself to be multifaceted and containing a series of different positions rather than being a closed or consistent system, then we will begin to see relations between different groups not as either accommodation or opposition, but more commonly as negotiation; identity and difference are therefore produced as much as defended through controversy.[2]

In matters of historical interpretation and new methodologies, those of us with gray hair may say, "Cast out one demon and let in seven," but the tools of cultural criticism can offer much to historians of theology. Postcolonialism can be particularly helpful, I believe, for several reasons. First, as with other contemporary theories concerning society and language, its critics have offered insights into the strategies of definition and domination in analytical discourse as outlined, for example, most famously, if also controversially, by Edward Said in *Orientalism*. Second, these critics have worked on the problem of the human agency of those being defined, that is, the recovery of occasions of resistance and complicity between dominant and dominated cultures. Many scholars within this field are in some sense subjects of study "talking back"; those whose cultures have been investigated and defined by Western analysis are engaged in recovering voices that were either erased or obscured under the weight of colonial epistemologies. These postcolonial critics then share with historians an attention to the difficult retrieval of particular human histories through limited and usually ideologically weighted sources. In part a reaction against abstractions in Said's work, their focus on the concrete "subaltern" has allowed them to further the critique of transhistorical categories such as "colonial" or "patriarchal" or even "orientalism" itself. In her article "Can the Subaltern Speak?" Gayati Spivak cautioned that neither imperial discourse nor the political interests of contemporary scholars may allow the voice of the "subaltern" to emerge, especially in moments of "difficult history." For example, any actual historical agency of the individual self-offering of a widow was effectively erased by both British and feminist analysis. Such a practice as voluntary was "impossible" in both worldviews, providing a "double colonization" of the historical subject or agency one wished to recover.[3] Homi Bhabha has also challenged Said's focus on the totalizing power of discourse by attempting to find places where disruption reveals the resistance of the "colonized"; resistance and complicity are often simultaneous.[4] Dipesh Chakrabarty recently highlighted the importance of caution with regard to usual historical trajectories of identity or the illuminating power of intellectual explanation. By preferring at this point fragmentary and episodic studies of the past, we may continue to critique both traditional categories and our own in order to have "the capacity to hear that which one does not already understand . . . to allow the subaltern to challenge our own conceptions of totalities."[5] These tools of analysis, which acknowledge both the power of definition and the often opaque reality of individual historical agency, offer an important critique of the traditional patterns of anthropological or dogmatic investigation that have long characterized the study of religions in the past. Historical transparency based on assumptions of development or system is often a mirage, so that acknowledging the persistent puzzle or discomfort of "difficult history" may in fact offer the better course in our present investigations.

Our own "burned-over district" of the second century with the entrenched definitions of "Hellenism," "Judaism," and "Christianity" has, of course, had its own layers of intellectual colonizations, including the Enlightenment apologetics of Gibbon concerning superstitious Christianity or the theological teleologies of the development of dogma or Christian supersessionism regarding Judaism. Over the past decade studies by G. Bowersock, Simon Swain, and Tim Whitmarsh have focused on the creative diversity and the often problematic status of Greek culture in the imperial Roman era to redefine "Hellenism."[6] Shaye Cohen, Erich Gruen, and Daniel Boyarin have explored the construction of Judaism as a "religion" within as well as against the imperial context of Roman Hellenism.[7] What is increasingly clear is that Roman imperial power or Greek *paideia* did not in fact create a stable cultural synthesis or a tolerant syncretism as usually outlined in Christian theological histories, but in fact stimulated authors to define themselves in various relations to Roman political universality, Greek intellectual traditions, and local practices or beliefs. In the second century "Greekness" was a "culture" to be purchased and mastered through education, that is, *paideia*, but its cultural value and power in the writings of Eastern intellectuals or Romans had a range of meaning whose creation as well as contestation are evident in our literary remains.[8] Equally important, this "new" Hellenism was increasing not based on the traditional binary opposition of Greek and barbarian, but within Roman realities it became "the pluralist, multicultural, Roman-inspired web that embraced the entire civilized world."[9]

It is precisely in this multivalent and dynamic imperial context that the familiar variety of pre-Nicene Christian writings and authors emerged. Our historical or theological questions, especially for a text like Justin, which is rich in liturgical, exegetical, and philosophical material, often have a centrifugal effect, so that the author is fragmented, if not erased, by our analytical categories. Ancient Christian authors not only are sources to be mined or marginalized in narratives of emerging orthodoxies, but also reveal particular strategies of self-presentation within the culture of their time. As in subaltern studies, a continuing, if theoretically nuanced, attention to human agency should be one of our goals as historians, especially in the ideologically laden and textually dominated "difficult history" of pre-Nicene Christianity.[10] Conventional doctrinal structures or issues should not be privileged over their contemporary intellectual questions. Equally important, attention to individual agency may help balance our current and often abstract emphasis on power in theological history. "Contestation" has become a replacement for the older binary histories of orthodoxy and heresy since it conveys the dynamism of competing elites as well as an equality of all thought, yet this analysis is often limited since it ironically reinstates the binary categories it is seeking to replace by its narrow focus on opposition. Aesthetics, epistemology, and spirituality, for example, were fruitfully explored in ancient philosophy, so theological topics may also have cultural dimensions beyond dominance or apologetics.[11] Undoubtedly, because I am a Midwesterner and a woman, often feeling like Jude the Obscure in my Oxford days, I am interested in issues of cultural dominance, but also in the varied and creative results of resistance and complicity. Rather than presupposing attributes of essential categories to be extracted from our authors or determining their work, we need to explore their literary self-presentation as a whole to understand the form of Christianity they are writing into existence in their texts of the second century.[12]

As I have discussed elsewhere, from a postcolonial perspective Justin's provincial origins as well as his conversion to Christianity through philosophy provide a rich source for any discussion of second-century religion and identity.[13] As Fergus Millar pointed out, every element in Justin's self-identification in the *First Apology* is a product of the rapidly changing circumstances under the Roman Empire: his descent from Greek parentage in a Roman colony established in a city built by Vespasian in Samaria after the destruction of the Jerusalem temple.[14] His subsequent search for truth through varied philosophies from this origin also sums up the social and cultural life of many educated men of the second century: colonization, educational mobility, religious interchange.[15] Although uncircumcised and therefore probably raised in traditional Greco-Roman religious practices, he is aware of Samaritan customs as well as some patterns of rabbinic exegesis. He identifies himself as a Samaritan, even if he did not practice the religion of the area. His presentation of the interchange of geographies, religions, and cultures is a description of his "Hellenism" just as much as his philosophical dress or knowledge, and we should also say that these are also then a description of his "Christianity." If we consider these elements as interactive and overlapping constitutive aspects of his identity and culture, then we may resist a tendency to privilege one over another, and accept their deliberate presence and even authority in his writings.

Therefore, the persistent ambivalence in the history of theology concerning Justin as a Christian philosopher reveals as much about our analytical assumptions as about the complexity of religious identity in the second century. First, if we assume that Hellenism and Christianity are mutually exclusive religious systems or cultures, then Justin is often characterized as either idiotic or duplicitous. The first characterization (idiocy) is often offered because of an obvious incompatibility of philosophy and Christianity. Justin's attempt to portray Christianity as a universal philosophy is as simplistic as Jude the Obscure's attempt to learn Latin or Greek. As Simon Swain commented, "The more Christianity fancied itself a philosophy, the more Greek philosophy had to respond"; or take the comment of Richard Lim, "Justin knew well his own arguments were unsatisfactory from a philosophical perspective."[16] From a theological perspective William Frend described Justin as "a Platonist before he became a Christian, and he never grasped the essential incompatibilities between Platonism and Christianity. He assimilated Jesus to the Logos of an eclectic Platonic and Stoic philosophy arbitrarily."[17] Christopher Stead's comment is characteristically astute: "His attachment to Christianity was in many ways an advantage as setting him new problems outside the traditional agenda of the Platonic schools."[18] Frances Young commented on his false hope that anyone would read his work as philosophy: he was self-deceived.[19]

Or his use of philosophy is a deceptive attempt by an outsider to argue in fact the dominance of his own Christian truth. Like his gown, his literary genre is an evangelical tool and therefore a cover-up for exporting Christian revelation and asserting Christian power. Tessa Rajak comments, "Platonism is given the most space in Justin's account of his personal quest, but that is partly because its pretensions were greatest at this period. . . . Justin continues to seduce by means of his philosophical posture."[20] Or consider Frances Young's view:

> What we are observing, I suggest, is the adoption of a contemporary preoc-
> cupation with the history of culture for the purposes of relativizing that cul-
> ture. . . . This is scandalous on both counts, namely, the appropriation of an
> alien canon of literature to which these upstarts might be regarded as having
> no claim and the attempt to subvert the established basis of Hellenistic
> culture.[21]

His philosophical persona is therefore only a pretense for the purpose of a religious and cultural coup.

Echoing what is seen as the essential incompatibility of his intellectual and spiritual commitments, Justin is then often described as having a "double nature." According to Tessa Rajak, he "continued through life to wear two hats, though given a character of such extremism and intensity . . . it is dubious whether the balance was perfectly maintained."[22] Or Mark Edwards notes that he carried his theology in "two wallets."[23] His devotion to Socrates as martyr as well as his gown give him a "double loyalty"; his conversion has a "*beide Motive*."[24] The historical reference to his gown seems particularly problematic to many commentators, making him some sort of illicit intellectual crossdresser. This sign of philosophical status should have perhaps been discarded at baptism. On the idiocy side, Leslie Barnard sympathetically describes it as a sort of security blanket, so that as a result of his long quest, "it is therefore natural that he should wear the philosopher's cloak, even after his conversion";[25] Richard Lim sees a naïve self-deception—"still wearing his philosopher's gown."[26] On the duplicitous side, Rajak comments, "Like Justin this tract walks in philosopher's garb. And in spite of its unsophisticated and unappealing use of the Greek language, it has walked effectively."[27]

Several insights from postcolonial interpretation are helpful at this point, whatever we may think of Justin's intellectual abilities or choice of dress. Bhabha has worked on how "disruptive" figures are described by dominant discourse. He notes that figures of "doubling" disrupt normative structures of authority by their simultaneous resemblance and disavowal: "The ambivalence of colonial authority repeatedly turns from *mimicry*—the difference which is almost nothing, but not quite—to *menace*—a difference that is almost total but not quite."[28] For Adolf Harnack, Justin's description of Christianity as "philosophy" was simply a strategy that was appropriate for a teacher on the margins of the church; this fits neatly into Harnack's developmental view of primitive Christianity obscured historically by Greek culture and thereafter declining into dogmatic Roman Catholicism. As a Protestant, he confidently contrasted the essence of Christianity with its Hellenistic husk, reflecting the transcendent cultural and racial dualisms of his era.[29] Hellenism for Harnack allowed Christianity to become the universal philosophy in contrast to the localized, and therefore inferior, religious cult of Judaism.[30] Within Harnack's larger model, Justin's mimicry of philosophy was simply an example of creeping Hellenization through an evangelistic intention. Evaluated within the canon of liberal Protestant theology, therefore, Justin's imitative work meant he was neither a true Christian nor a worthy philosopher.

Curiously, such Christian theological disdain for a tainting of the gospel echoes the classicist's tone of Swain or Lim in which the pretensions of Christians to "philosophy" may be easily exposed. As J. C. M. van Winden commented, if theologians find Justin inadequate, then classicists equally find him second-rate.[31] This traditional opposition of essential Christianity or philosophical Hellenism therefore finds Justin easily dismissed in his project of "mimicry," a pale imitation of a foreign discourse that violates the essence of both. In Justin's case, to be so poorly Hellenized was ironically not to be Greek or Christian at all; he is here interpreted in a "double colonization."[32]

Menace, however, is also a part of that association of philosophy and theology that is Justin's legacy. We begin again with Harnack's comment on Justin's assertion from the *Second Apology* that "whatever truth is uttered anywhere came from us": "Did it never dawn on him, or did he really suspect, that his entire standpoint was upset by such an extension of its range and that what was specifically 'Christian' was transformed into what was common to all men?"[33] In this representation, the consequences of syncretism emerge so that the utility of Hellenism is overwhelmed by the peril of its parasitic relationship and there is an eventual dilution of Christian identity itself. Postcolonial theorists have noted the "terror" and "instability" that the appearance of hybridity creates in the midst of traditional authoritative dichotomies. Hybridity undermines the purity of difference, and therefore its authority. "Hybridity intervenes in the exercise of authority not merely to indicate the impossibility of its identity, but to represent the unpredictability of its presence."[34] The very cultural and intellectual impossibility of a Christian in philosophical drag is no longer a joke, but becomes a subversive danger to both Christian orthodoxy and pure Hellenism. However, if Greekness was itself in a process of negotiation in writers such as Lucian and Plutarch through broader cultural trends of the second century, then the concerns of a writer such as Celsus reflect not static conservativism, but unease in the culture. A Christian such as Justin is therefore subversive to both Harnack and Celsus for transgressing the boundaries maintained by the essential definitions of Christianity and Hellenism: "What is irremediably estranging is the presence of the hybrid. . . . The differences in cultures can no longer be identified or evaluated as objects of epistemological or moral contemplation: cultural differences are not simply there to be seen or appropriated."[35]

Hybridity as imagined by Bhabha within the realities of twentieth-century colonialism is not a balanced *tertium quid*, but an unstable and problematic transgressing of imagined boundaries that robs them of their purity and hence their power. As a response to cultural conflicts, Bhabha imagines a third space of intentional hybridity for the purpose of challenge and resistance. This allows the creative work of imagination; here an author may deprive the original categories of their power by resisting their discursive purity and asserting claims of authenticity in the "in-between space."[36] Spivak has warned that "hybridity" as a category may in fact legitimate the very categories we wish to challenge historically, rather like the limits of contestation discussed above; however, Bhabha's emphasis has been on the creativity and the new that emerges in the place of complicity and resistance.[37] Chakrabarty has argued recently that historians need both skepticism and imagination to allow the unknown possibilities to appear, especially in moments of "the undesirable past" whose presence is difficult or erased through conventional narratives. This past cannot be achieved by simply "historicizing" given the strength of the presuppositions of our categories, but rather by emphasizing the human values of negotiation. He contrasted "identity," in which the relation to difference is fixed, with "proximity," in which "difference is neither reified nor erased, but negotiated."[38] Rooted in the ethical problems of writing a history in which difference prompted violence (the partition of India), Chakrabarty notes that the current modern interest in diversity rather than development often does not address how human lives have been shaped by or may live within the politics of difference. To begin with "proximity" in analysis is to restore a common humanity that may have disappeared in actions and discourses of "identity" and "difference."[39]

Given the discursive and political religious violence of the second century, this model of attempting to understand difference through negotiation rather than opposition stimulates our imagination to see Justin's "disruptive history" as a Christian philosopher in a new way. As has been extensively studied, Justin's presentation of Christianity as the original ancient truth built on familiar arguments and terminology concerning universality and antiquity within Judaism and Roman Hellenism, but scholars continue to argue as to the authority or reason for these in his writings.[40] Yet these ambiguities are precisely the points where the "subaltern" may speak to enlarge our imaginations and challenge our hermeneutical totalities. As described by Bhabha and Chakrabarty, we are encountering in this "apologist" an authentic "doubling" in which the differences between Christianity and Greek philosophy are not denied, yet the value of both is necessary to the working of his history of truth or his *Logos* theology. In his *Dialogue with Trypho* and the *Apologies*, we find a sophisticated argument for a truth whose antiquity, explanation for evil, and universal practice offer an original blend of complicity and resistance to traditional *paideia*. Justin as an "apologist" did not translate an existing religion—that is, Christianity—into an external culture for explanation or defense, but reflects an attempt within Roman Hellenism by an educated provincial to address contemporary problems of religious authenticity and multiple authorities. What we may see as doubling, Justin presents as "one" within the third space of his own *Logos* theology.

As in other contemporary authors, Justin uses "Greekness" as a means of resistance to the legitimacy of Roman authority: "Why do you persecute us when we say the same things as the Greeks?" (*1 Apol.* 2.1).[41] By appealing to common philosophical values, Justin claims common ground with his Roman rulers as well as portraying himself and other Christians as legitimate religious subversives who should be judged, but also acquitted, if not emulated, because of their consistent philosophical practices. In this era of philosophical revitalization in part patronized by emperors, the comparison of Christianity with philosophy is not only a shrewd strategy, but, given Justin's consistent presentation in his extant writings, an analogy or ideal he wishes to sustain. For example, his focus on Socrates as martyr and teacher was an important bridge; Socrates not only offered a critique of religion internal to the philosophical tradition, but also exemplified in his martyrdom the *bios* of the one who contains the *Logos*.[42] This, of course, does not put Christianity on the same footing as Greek philosophy, since Christians have the fullness of truth that other philosophers seek. Christians contemplate the whole word, whereas philosophers struggle with only innate rationality.[43] As studied by Arthur Droge, Justin here places Christianity at the origins of the contemporary debates about the history of philosophy and its corruption.[44] Thus Plato is not alien, but he is not the "same" as Christian truth. He is in fact dependent on Moses, and in this way Justin draws in the contemporary arguments and apologetics about barbarian wisdom from Judaism. In contrast to the Greeks, who intellectually represent a single nation, Christians are drawn from every race, including the barbarians, and therefore have true universality as well as consistent practice.[45] Prophecy is thus superior to philosophy, for it is older. He asks Trypho, "Why do you look for philosophy when you have the prophets?" (*Dial.* 1).

His claim that original wisdom is Christian should not distract us from the power of this category philosophically, however distracted we may be by the later historical narrative of Christian exclusivity. In the second century, argument about origins and corrupt genealogies were common in the philosophical schools, perhaps in response to the diversity of interpretation; Atticus, for example, argued that Plato can best be understood by Greeks, and Numenius traced the truth through Plato, Pythagoras, and assorted barbarian peoples.[46] To claim that Christianity is the original philosophy that inspired Plato and Moses is rather the same claim as "Everything is Greece to the wise," or more specifically, "Everything is *Logos* to the wise."[47] Justin's presentation of ancient and universal Christianity thus mirrors current cultural disputes about universality, and multiple traditions in relation to the intellectual primacy of Greek *paideia* and Roman political universality. If Justin is indeed creatively dependent on Neo-Pythagoreans such as Numenius, as argued by Edwards and Droge, then it is difficult to rule such a move as "outside" Hellenism or philosophy.[48] Justin's *Logos*-centered "Christianness" is building on cultural arguments already in place concerning the antiquity of truth, the unity of human culture, the relation of philosophy and religion, and the ethics of society. If we acknowledge that indigenous traditions were not antithetical to second-century authors such as Plutarch and Lucian, then Justin's original blend of philosophical and biblical language is hardly illegitimate, but a common negotiation of cultures.

If we follow Tim Whitmarsh in thinking of "Greekness" as an "aggregation of civilized and intellectual values" so that "in this respect every civilized person had the capacity to be a Hellene," we may see then how the "Christianness" of Justin could be culturally and theologically positioned to be the only "safe" philosophy, while at the same time criticizing the multiplicity of philosophical schools or the errors of Greek religion.[49] Christian truth was not wholly other from cultural truth but rather was the original type from which others drew their usually inferior imitation. The declension of truth for Justin was a product of plagiarism from prophecy, students who innovate, and the deliberate perversion by demons of the images of the true philosophy into idolatrous religion. This cultural history resulted in both deficient practice and the widening chasm between the true and its imitation. In Justin the argument about truth was about completeness or corruption as much as genealogy or succession. The parallels for Justin between Socrates and Jesus or the sons of Jupiter were used to illustrate the connection, but also the disintegration of the seed of the *Logos*. Deceptive likeness or incorrect teaching became diabolical imitation in his understanding of the universality of original truth. For Justin the *daimones* have produced a destructive spiritual mimicry of the authentic themes of ancient truth. Thus the original truth has been distorted in pagan and Jewish teaching, which Christianity only could restore. We find in Justin the danger of poor imitation rather than difference within a world infused with rationality: "I confess that I both pray and with all my strength strive to be found a Christian not because the teachings of Plato are different from those of Christ, but because they are not in every respect equal. . . . For the seed and imitation of something is one thing, and another is the thing itself" (*2 Apol.* 13). Imitation not only is potentially inferior as partial, but also can be manipulated into deception. In Justin's view philosophy is not the explanation of the origin of truth, but is in fact only a mimicry of the true, which is Christianity.

Justin in his philosophical persona therefore must be seen as a representative of second-century Christianity, even if this evokes the terror and unease of hybridity that is neither orthodox Christianity nor religious Hellenism. If Justin's creative appeal to the values of Socrates and Moses is therefore a recognizable Hellenistic project, this does not strip his work of its criticism of Rome or his Christian commitments. The site of his "complicity" is the site of his resistance as he constructed a universal philosophy that is Christianity, albeit mimicry and menace to the later colliding worlds of orthodoxy and Neoplatonic Hellenism. To be understood as a Christian, Justin needs therefore to be placed "inside" Hellenism. In this way he does not represent a settled "third race," but opens our eyes to the dynamic third space where tradition, practice, and culture are innovatively combined in his *Logos* theology. This has been an attempt not to read "through" the works of Justin, but to appreciate the shifting complexities of second-century religious and philosophical thought as expressed in his Christianity.

NOTES

1. Justin Scholarship

1. There are ample bibliographical resources available on Justin, even after the demise of the admirable *Bibliographia Patristica*. Stefan Heid's article in the *Reallexikon für Antike und Christentum* and Oskar Skarsaune's in the *Theologische Realenzyklopädie* contain the wealth of material one would expect from those august reference works. For those who have access to it, there is now André Wartelle, *Bibliographie historique et critique de saint Justin, philosophe et martyre, et des apologistes grecs du IIe siècle, 1494–1994, avec un supplément* (Paris: Lanore, 2001), (1031 pp. !).

2. This manuscript, *Codex Argentoratensis*, is described in great detail in J. C. T. Otto, *S. Iustini Philosophi et Martyris Opera quae feruntur omnia*, T. II, editio altera (Iena: Frider. Mauke, 1869), xiv–xvii. The date for the destruction of this manuscript is taken from Henry G. Meecham, *The Epistle to Diognetus* (Manchester: Manchester University Press, 1949), 68.

3. See now Lorenzo Perrone, "Eine 'verschollende Bibliothek'? Das Schicksalfrüh-christlicher Schriften (2.-3. Jahrhundert) am Beispiel des Irenäus von Lyon," *ZKG* 116 (2005): 1–29.

4. *Iustini Martyris Apologiae pro Christianis*, ed. Miroslav Marcovich (PTS 38; Berlin: Walter de Gruyter, 1994), 7–8; and *Iustini Martyris Dialogus cum Tryphone*, ed. Miroslav Marcovich (PTS 47; Berlin: Walter de Gruyter, 1997), 6–7.

5. These are listed in the "*Editionum abbreviationes*" of Marcovich's editions. Erwin R. Goodenough, *The Theology of Justin Martyr* (Amsterdam: Philo, 1968 [= Jena, 1923]), x–xi, adds to the list, for the *Apologies*, Gallandius (1765), Ch. Fr. Hornemann (1829), B. L. Gildersleeve (1877), C. Gutberlet (1883), and A. Leventopoulos (1900); and, for the *Dialogue*, C. Koch (1700), J. A. Göz (1796).

6. Goodenough, *Theology*, 87, cited by Oskar Skarsaune, *The Proof from Prophecy, A Study in Justin Martyr's Proof-Text Tradition: Text-Type, Provenance, Theological Profile* (NovTSup 66; Leiden: Brill, 1987), 1.

7. Justin, *Apologies*, texte grec, traduction française, introduction et index de Louis Pautigny (Textes et documents pour l'étude historique du christianisme 1; Paris: A. Picard, 1904).

8. Justin, *Dialogue avec Tryphon*, texte grec, traduction française, introduction, notes et index de Georges Archambault (Textes et documents pour l'étude historique du christianisme 8 et 11; Paris: A. Picard, 1909). Daniel Ruiz Bueno, *Padres Apologistas griegos (s. II)* (Madrid: Biblioteca de Autores Cristianos, 1954), 298, informs his readers that he reproduces the Greek text of Archambault; for the *Apologies* he uses Rauschen's 1911 Bonn edition.

9. A. W. F. Blunt, *The Apologies of Justin Martyr* (Cambridge Patristic Texts; Cambridge: Cambridge University Press, 1911).

10. Edgar J. Goodspeed, *Die älteste Apologeten* (Göttingen: Vandenhoeck und Ruprecht, 1914).

11. André Wartelle, *Saint Justin. Apologies*, introduction, texte critique, traduction, commentaire et index (Paris: Études augustiniennes, 1987).

12. Miroslav Marcovich, *Pseudo-Justinus. Cohortatio ad Graecos, De Monarchia, Oratio ad Graecos* (PTS 32; Berlin: Walter de Gruyter, 1990).

13. Charles Munier, *Saint Justin. Apologie pour les chrétiens*, édition et traduction (Paradosis 39; Fribourg: Éditions universitaires, 1995).

14. See his argument in Charles Munier, *L'Apologie de saint Justin, philosophe et martyre* (Paradosis 38; Fribourg: Éditions universitaires, 1994), 152–56 ("Annexe: L'unité de l'Apologie"). Counterarguments have been presented by others, most recently by P. Lorraine Buck, "Justin Martyr's *Apologies*: Their Number, Destination, and Form," *JTS*, n.s., 54 (2003): 45–59.

15. Philippe Bobichon, *Justin Martyr. Dialogue avec Tryphon*, édition critique, traduction, commentaire (Paradosis 47/1–2; Fribourg: Academic Press, 2003).

16. Charles Munier, ed., *Justin, Apologie pour les Chrétiens*, Introduction, texte critique, traduction et notes (Sources chrétiennes 507; Paris: du Cerf, 2006). A companion volume of commentary on the French text was issued at the same time: Charles Munier, *Justin martyr, apologie pour les chrétiens* (Patrimoines, christianisme; Paris: du Cerf, 2006).

17. See their contributions to this volume for an indication of their approach to the text.

18. Goodenough, *Theology*, 295–320. He lists 488 items.

19. Interest in the latter testimony was already reflected in the excerpt from *1 Apology* 65–67 that begins *Codex Ottobonianus graecus* 274, copied in the sixteenth century.

20. Carl Andresen, "Justin und die mittlere Platonismus," *ZNW* 44 (1952–53): 157–95.

21. Carl Andresen, *Logos und Nomos. Die Polemik des Kelsos wider das Christentum* (Arbeiten zur Kirchengeschichte 30; Berlin: Walter de Gruyter, 1955).

22. Ibid., 308–9. Andresen credits Bengt Seeberg, "Die Geschichtstheologie Justins des Märtyrers," *ZKG* 58 (1939): 1–81, and Seeberg's book of the same title (Stuttgart, 1939), with helpful insights into Justin as a theologian of history.

23. Niels Hyldahl, *Philosophie und Christentum. Eine Interpretation der Einleitung zum Dialog Justins* (Acta theologica danica 9; Kopenhagen, 1966).

24. J. C. M. van Winden, *An Early Christian Philosopher: Justin Martyr's Dialogue with Trypho, Chapters One to Nine* (Philosophia Patrum 1; Leiden: Brill, 1971). Van Winden's book also has some strong comments on the faults of Justin editions in current use.

25. Heinz Kraft, "Der mittlere Platonismus und das Christentum," *ThLZ* 83 (1958): 333–40, takes direct issue with Andresen on whether Celsus really took history seriously. Other works at that period that dealt with the relation to philosophy were Ragnar Holte, "*Logos spermatikos*. Christianity and Ancient Philosophy according to St. Justin's Apologies," *StTh* 12 (1958): 109–68; Henry Chadwick, "Justin Martyr's Defence of Christianity," *BJRL* 47 (1964–65): 275–97; Chadwick, *Early Christian Thought and the Classical Tradition* (Oxford: Oxford University Press, 1966), 1–30; and Heinrich Dörrie, "Die platonische Theologie des Kelsos in ihrer Auseinandersetzung mit der christlicher Theologie," *Nachrichten der Akademie der Wissenschaften zu Göttingen*, philologisch-historische Klasse, 1967, 2:19–55.

26. *The Cambridge History of Later Greek and Early Medieval Philosophy*, ed. A. H. Armstrong (Cambridge: Cambridge University Press, 1970). Part 2, "Philo and the Beginnings of Christian Thought" (pp. 137–92), is by Henry Chadwick and includes Justin as well as Philo, the Gnostics, Clement of Alexandria, and Origen.

27. Michel Spanneut, *Le stoïcisme des Pères* (Patristica Sorbonensia; Paris: Seuil, 1957).

28. Ludwig Edelstein, *The Meaning of Stoicism* (Martin Classical Lectures 21; Cambridge: Harvard University Press, 1966).

29. John Rist, *Stoic Philosophy* (Cambridge: Cambridge University Press, 1969).

30. Robert Joly, *Christianisme et philosophie: Études sur Justin et les Apologistes grecs du deuxième siècle* (Bruxelles: Éditions de l'Université Libre de Bruxelles, 1973).

31. C. J. de Vogel, *Greek Philosophy: A Collection of Texts*, vol. 3: *The Hellenistic-Roman Period*, 2nd ed. (Leiden: E. J. Brill, 1964).

32. Pierre Prigent, *Justin et l'Ancien Testament* (ÉtB; Paris: J. Gabalda, 1964).

33. J. Smit Sibinga, *The Old Testament Text of Justin Martyr*, vol. 1, *The Pentateuch* (Leiden: Brill, 1963). W. A. Shotwell's *The Biblical Exegesis of Justin Martyr* (London, 1965) did not go into as much depth.

34. His section "Justin and the Holy Scriptures" (pp. 315–18) lists only one example: A. Hilgenfeld, "Die alttestamentliche Citate Justins in ihrer Bedeutung für die Untersuchung über seine Evangelien," *Theologische Jahrbücher* 9 (1850): 385–439, 567–78. More relevant (but not in this section of Goodenough's bibliography) was Wilhelm Bousset, *Jüdisch-christlicher Schulbetrieb in Alexandria und Rom* (FRLANT, n. F. 6; Göttingen, 1915).

35. Leslie W. Barnard, *Justin Martyr: His Life and Thought* (Cambridge: Cambridge University Press, 1967).

36. Eric Francis Osborn, *Justin Martyr* (BHTh 47; Tübingen: Mohr [Paul Siebeck], 1973).

37. Skarsaune, *Proof from Prophecy*.

38. Ibid., 97. By contrast, Yves-Marie Blanchard, *Aux sources du Canon, le témoignage d'Irénée* (Cogitatio Fidei 175; Paris: du Cerf, 1993), 108, is surprised at the "effacement de Paul" in Justin.

39. Skarsaune, *Proof from Prophecy*, 108, 104.

40. Pseudo-Clement, *Recognitiones*, I.33–71.

41. Skarsaune, *Proof from Prophecy*, 234, 252.

42. Ibid., 371–72.

43. Ibid., 373.

44. Ibid., 250–51.

45. Despite its subtitle, I regard Sylvain Jean Gabriel Sanchez, *Justin Apologiste chrétien: Travaux sur le* Dialogue avec Tryphon *de Justin Martyr* (Cahiers de la Revue Biblique 50; Paris: J. Gabalda, 2000), as belonging to the earlier phase of concentration on the *Apologies* and the prologue to the *Dialogue*. The same observation could be applied to a recent Italian edition, *Apologie. Prima apologia per i cristiani ad Antonio il Pio; Seconda apologia per i cristiani al Senato romano; Prologo al Dialogo con Trifone*, intoduzione, traduzione, note e apparati di Giuseppe Girgenti (Testi a fronte 25; Milano: Rusconi, 1995).

46. Philippe Bobichon, "Justin martyr: étude stylistique du *Dialogue avec Tryphon*, suivie d'une comparaison avec l'*Apologie* et le *De resurrectione*," *Recherches augustiniennes et patristiques* 34 (2005): 1–61. Many of the same arguments about the unity of the *Dialogue* are presented also in the introduction to Bobichon's edition, pp. 23–40.

47. Timothy J. Horner, *"Listening to Trypho": Justin Martyr's* Dialogue *Reconsidered* (Contributions to Biblical Exegesis and Theology 28; Leuven: Peeters, 2001).

48. Ibid., 9.

49. Anette Rudolph, *"Denn wir sind jenes Volk . . .": Die neue Gottesverehrung in Justins Dialog mit dem Juden Trypho in historisch-theologischer Sicht* (Hereditas 15; Bonn: Borengässer, 1999). Her comments on Justin's style and the plan of the *Dialogue* are on pp. 69–82.

50. Ibid., 266–73.

51. James D. G. Dunn, *The Parting of the Ways between Christianity and Judaism and Their Significance for the Character of Christianity* (London: SCM, 1991). See the same author's edited volume, *Jews and Christians: The Parting of the Ways, AD 70 to 135* (Tübingen: Mohr

[Paul Siebeck], 1992); and also Stephen G. Wilson, *Related Strangers: Jews and Christians 70–170 C.E.* (Minneapolis: Fortress Press, 1995).

52. Sanders and others edited three volumes under the title *Jewish and Christian Self-Definition* (Philadelphia: Fortress Press, 1980–82). E. P. Sanders should not be confused with Jack T. Sanders, whose *Schismatics, Sectarians, Dissidents, Deviants: The First One Hundred Years of Jewish Christian Relations* (Valley Forge, Pa.: Trinity Press International, 1993), is also germane to the issues under discussion here.

53. Martin Hengel, *Judentum und Hellenismus. Studien zu ihrer Begegnung unter besonderer Berücksichtigung Palästinas bis zur Mitte des 2. Jh.s vor Christus*, 2nd ed. (Tübingen: Mohr, 1973), trans. into English by John Bowden as *Judaism and Hellenism* (Minneapolis: Fortress Press, 1974), did much to alert scholars to the mixed character of Palestinian culture in the first and second centuries C.E.

54. One example would be the contributions of Christoph Markschies and Daniel P. Bailey to the volume whose English version is entitled *The Suffering Servant: Isaiah 53 in Jewish and Christian Sources*, ed. Bernd Janowski and Peter Stuhlmacher, trans. Daniel P. Bailey (Grand Rapids: Eerdmans, 2004).

55. Judith M. Lieu, *Neither Jew nor Greek? Constructing Early Christianity* (London: T&T Clark, 2002), 233–55. Lieu has done other work in this area; see particularly her *Image and Reality: The Jews in the World of the Christians in the Second Century* (Edinburgh: T&T Clark, 1996), esp. 103–53; *Christian Identity in the Jewish and Graeco-Roman World* (Oxford: Oxford University Press, 2004); and the book she coedited with John A. North and Tessa Rajak, *The Jews among Pagans and Christians in the Roman Empire* (London: Routledge, 1992).

56. For a lengthy discussion of this issue from the Christian side, see William Horbury, "The Benediction of the *Minim* and Jewish-Christian Controversy," *JTS*, n.s., 33 (1982): 19–61.

57. A brief summary of the material in Justin that points to Jewish hostility toward Christians is given by Claudia J. Setzer, *Jewish Responses to Early Christians: History and Polemics, 30–150 A.D.* (Minneapolis: Fortress Press, 1994), 128–49. See also David Rokéah, *Justin Martyr and the Jews* (Leiden: Brill, 2002).

58. Neusner's books are too many to mention. Less controversial (but perhaps in some quarters more influential) have been David Flusser, Louis Feldman, Saul Lieberman, Samuel Sandmel, Martin Goodman, Nicholas de Lange, and others.

59. Alan F. Segal, *Two Powers in Heaven: Early Rabbinic Reports about Christianity and Gnosticism* (Leiden: Brill, 1977). Segal's *Rebecca's Children: Judaism and Christianity in the Roman World* (Cambridge: Harvard University Press, 1986), was an early attempt to provide an ordinary educated audience with an account of Christian and Jewish origins that integrated the new scholarship.

60. Marc Hirshman, *A Rivalry of Genius: Jewish and Christian Biblical Interpretation in Late Antiquity*, trans. Batya Stein (Albany: State University of New York Press, 1996).

61. Daniel Boyarin, *Dying for God: Martyrdom and the Making of Christianity and Judaism* (Stanford: Stanford University Press, 1999); *Border Lines: The Partition of Judaeo-Christianity* (Philadelphia: University of Pennsylvania Press, 2004), esp. chap. 2, "Justin's Dialogue with the Jews: The Beginnings of Orthodoxy," 37–73 (with notes on pp. 238–64).

62. Rodney Stark, *The Rise of Christianity* (Princeton: Princeton University Press, 1996; paper ed., San Francisco: HarperSanFrancisco, 1997). Among the mixed reviews given to Stark's book, one should note Birger A. Pearson, "On Rodney Stark's Foray into Early Christian History," *Religion* 29 (1999): 171–76, and the more hostile review by Harry O. Maier in *JTS*, n.s., 49 (1998): 328–35.

63. Stark, *Rise of Christianity* (1997), 70.

64. See Harold Remus, "Justin Martyr's Argument with Judaism," and Jack Lightstone, "Christian Anti-Judaism in Its Judaic Mirror: The Judaic Context of Early Christianity Revised," in *Anti-Judaism in Early Christianity* (Studies in Christianity and Judaism 2: Separation and Polemic, ed. Stephen G. Wilson; Waterloo: Wilfrid Laurier, 1986), 59–80, 103–32. John J. Collins, *Between Athens and Jerusalem: Jewish Identity in the Hellenistic Diaspora*, 2nd ed. (Grand Rapids: Eerdmans, 2000), is helpful as far as it goes, but it stops with the Bar Kokhba revolt.

65. With a nod to Jonathan Z. Smith's helpful metaphor.

66. Shaye J. D. Cohen, *The Beginnings of Jewishness: Boundaries, Varieties, Uncertainties* (Berkeley: University of California Press, 1999). Cohen makes no mention of Stark here, and I do not know if he commented on Stark's hypothesis elsewhere; it is not my intention to suggest that he would endorse that hypothesis, only that he makes it easier to see how it might be plausible.

67. Ibid., 67. See also John M. G. Barclay, "Who Was Considered an Apostate in the Jewish Diaspora?" in *Tolerance and Intolerance in Early Judaism and Christianity*, ed. Graham N. Stanton and Guy G. Stroumsa (Cambridge: Cambridge University Press, 1998), 80–98.

68. See Graham N. Stanton, "Justin Martyr's *Dialogue with Trypho*: Group Boundaries, 'Proselytes' and 'God-fearers,'" in *Tolerance and Intolerance*, 263–78, esp. 275.

69. F. Stanley Jones, "Jewish Christianity of the *Pseudo-Clementines*," in *A Companion to Second-Century Christian "Heretics,"* ed. Antti Marjanen and Petri Luomanen (VCSup 76; Leiden: Brill, 2005), 331.

2. Justin, Philosopher and Martyr

1. Bernard Pouderon, *Les Apologistes grecs du IIe siècle* (Initiations aux Pères de l'Église; Paris: du Cerf, 2005), 138.

2. *Kompromiss* is Schwartz's word: *Eusebius Werke*, II, *Die Kirchengeschichte*, ed. Eduard Schwartz and Theodor Mommsen (GCS 9, 3 vols.; Berlin: J. C. Hinrichs, 1903–09), 3:cliv n. 2.

3. Adolf Harnack, *Geschichte der altchristlichen Litteratur bis Eusebius*, Zweiter Theil, *Die Chronologie*, i., *Die Chronologie der Litteratur bis Irenäus* (Leipzig: J. C. Hinnrichs, 1897), 274: "Dass die als II. und als I. in der einzigen selbständigen Handschrift überlieferten Apologien Justin's umzustellen und als eine Schrift zu betrachten sind, ist ein so evidentes Ergebniss der Kritik, dass es nach den Nachweisungen von Boll, Zahn, dem Verfasser, und Veil einer erneuten Darlegung nicht mehr bedarf." One need only ask, "Ob der kürzere Theil der von Anfang an beabsichtigte Schluss der Apologie oder ein Anhang ist?"

4. Schwartz, *Kirchengeschichte*, 3:clvi–clvii.

5. F. C. Boll, "Über das Verhältnis der beiden Apologien Justins des Märtyrers zu einander," *Zeitschrift für die historische Theologie* 12.3 (1842): 3–47.

6. Harnack, *Chronologie*, 274: "die sogen. 1 Apologie ein abgeschlossenes Ganze für sich ist."

7. Johannes Quasten, *Patrology*, vol. 1, *The Beginnings of Patristic Literature* (Utrecht: Spectrum, 1966), 199. Frances Young asserted in 1999, "It is now commonly thought that the second was an appendix to the first" ("Greek Apologists of the Second Century," in *Apologetics in the Roman Empire: Pagans, Jews, and Christians*, ed. Mark Edwards, Martin Goodman, and Simon Price (Oxford: Oxford University Press, 1999), 81–104, at 82.

8. Wolfgang Schmid, "Ein Inversionsphänomen und seine Bedeutung im Text der Apologie des Justin," in *Forma Futuri: Studi in onore del Cardinale M. Pellegrino* (Turin: Erasmo, 1975), 253–81, reprinted in Schmid, *Ausgewählte philologische Schriften*, ed. H. Erbse and J. Küppers (Berlin: Walter de Gruyter, 1984), 338–64; I cite from the latter.

9. See, for example, H. H. Holfelder, "Εὐσέβεια καὶ φιλοσοφία. Literarische Einheit und politischer Kontext von Justins Apologie," *ZNW* 68 (1977): 48–66, 231–51. And Munier's edition of 1995 (Saint Justin, *Apologie pour les chrétiens*, ed. and trans. Charles Munier [Paradosis 39; Fribourg: Éditions universitaires, 1995]), actually prints one continuous text of one *Apology* and renumbers the chapters of what is normally regarded as the *Second Apology* accordingly.

10. Justini Martyris, *Apologiae pro Christianis*, ed. Miroslav Marcovich (PTS 38; Berlin: Walter de Gruyter, 1994), 10. This is also the option favored by Pouderon, *Apologistes grecs*, 137–38.

11. Thus, at the very beginning of the work, in setting out his stall, Justin affirms that for those (Christians) unjustly hated, "I have made my address and petition" (τὴν προσφώνησιν καὶ ἔντευξιν πεποίημαι, *1 Apol.* 1), a phrase that is neatly balanced at the very end by the claim that "we"—this time plural—"have made our address and explanation" (τὴν προσφώνησιν καὶ ἐξήγησιν πεποιήμεθα, *1 Apol.* 68.3).

12. Robert M. Grant, "Forms and Occasions of the Greek Apologists," *SMSR* 52 (1986): 213–26, at 216.

13. At *2 Apol.* 7(8).3 and 13.3.

14. That is true, I think, of the important and influential survey of Justin's thought by Sir Henry Chadwick in his *Early Christian Thought and the Classical Tradition: Studies in Justin, Clement, and Origen* (Oxford: Clarendon, 1966).

15. At this point—though not in our general theory of the history of the text—I am taking a different tack from that taken by my colleague Denis Minns.

16. So Schmid, "Inversionsphänomen," 346–47; Grant, "Forms," 215–16; W. R. Schoedel, "Apologetic Literature and Ambassadorial Activities," *HTR* 82 (1989): 55–78, at 76. See esp. Wolfram Kinzig, "Der 'Sitz im Leben' der Apologie in der Alten Kirche," *ZKG* 100 (1989): 291–317.

17. The first serviceable edition of the text was by A. Kontoleon, in *Mitteilungen des kaiserlichen Deutschen archäologischen Instituts, Athenische Abteilung* 16 (1891): 267–79, to which Mommsen added a short commentary, 279–82. The standard edition is Georgius Mihailov, ed., *Inscriptiones Graecae in Bulgaria Repertae*, vol. 4 (Serdica/Sofia: Academia Litterarum Bulgarica, 1966), no. 2236 = pp. 198–229.

18. So also *1 Apol.* 12.1: "The things we ask [ἀξιοῦμεν] are right and true."

19. See *Menander Rhetor*, ed. D. A. Russell and N. G. Wilson (Oxford: Clarendon, 1981), Treatise II, xii and xiii (pp. 180–81). Russell and Wilson very tentatively conclude that Menander's work may be placed in "the reign of Diocletian" (xl).

20. See the list of correspondences in Charles Munier, *L'Apologie de saint Justin, philosophe et martyre* (Paradosis 38; Fribourg: Éditions universitaires, 1994), 181.

21. Fergus Millar, "Emperors at Work," *JRS* 57 (1967): 9–19, at 10–11; idem, *The Emperor in the Roman World*, 2nd ed. (London: Duckworth, 1992), 240–42; Wynne Williams, "Individuality in the Imperial Constitutions: Hadrian and the Antonines," *JRS* 66 (1976): 67–83, at 69, with n. 12.

22. The text as it stands begins with a vocative ὦ Ῥωμαῖοι (1.1)—deleted, surely correctly, as a gloss by Boll, Schwartz, and Marcovich—but 2.8 already refers to the petition that the anonymous woman submitted to "you the autocrat," in the singular.

23. It is important to realize just how closed that world was. Even at the end of the century, Tertullian, speaking from the relatively heavily Christianized society of Roman North Africa, could still say that no one comes to our books unless he is already a Christian (*Tanto abest, ut nostris litteris annuant homines, ad quas nemo venit nisi jam Christianus, De Test. An.* 1).

24. The basis for this calculation is discussed in my essay, "The Textual Tradition of Justin's *Apologies*: A Modest Proposal," *StPat* 36 (2001): 54–60.

25. There are, of course, attempts to see coherence in the work. For very clever structures—which in the end, I think, succeed in imposing order rather than finding it—see Charles Munier, "La structure littéraire de l'Apologie de Justin," *RevScRel* 60 (1986): 34–54, at 49–54; reprinted in his *Autorité épiscopale et sollicitude pastorale IIe—VIe siècles* (Collected Studies CS 341; Aldershot: Variorum, 1990), no. IV; Munier, *L'Apologie*, 37–40; and, more briefly, Pouderon, *Apologistes grecs*, 138.

26. IV.8.3 refers to "the apology to Antoninus." There follow two citations from our *1 Apology*. There then follows a citation from our *2 Apology*, introduced by "in the same (work)," ἐν ταὐτῷ (IV.8.5). This is sometimes taken to be another explicit attribution of a passage from our *2 Apology* to what Eusebius thinks of as "the former apology" (so, for example, Pouderon, *Apologistes grecs*, 137 n. 2). But it is ταὐτῷ (presumably neuter), not ταὐτῇ (feminine—that is, apology), and is too vague a description to bear much weight.

27. At least, it is normally so understood (see, for example, Adolf Harnack, *Die Überlieferung der griechischen Apologeten des zweiten Jahrhunderts in der alten Kirche und im Mittelalter* [TU 1,1; Leipzig: J. C. Hinrichs, 1882], 138 n. 91). Pouderon, however, takes it to refer, "selon toute vraisemblance," to Antoninus Pius and Marcus Aurelius (*Apologistes grecs*, 137 n. 4). This would be possible if the phrase is taken to mean "a *second* book addressed to the same rulers who received the first one," rather than "a second book addressed to the *same* rulers we are now talking about" (see IV.14.10). The position of δεύτερον might to some extent support that construal. But this would mean that (1) Eusebius thought there were *two* second apologies or second books—one addressed to Pius and Marcus, the other to Marcus as the successor of Pius, and (2) he is being careless, for heretofore he has presented "the former apology" only as being πρὸς Ἀντωνῖνον (II.13.2; IV. pinax 12; IV.8.3; IV.11.11 [Antoninus and the Senate]); Antoninus and his sons are not introduced as the recipients until IV.18.2.

28. See Harnack, *Überlieferung*, 134–45, esp. 144.

29. This is, I think, true for example of the discussion in Marcovich, *Apologiae*, 2–3.

30. Tatian, *Oratio ad Graecos* 19.1 (p. 21, ll. 1–6, Schwartz).

31. According to the *Thesaurus Linguae Graecae*.

32. See, for example, V.13.9, VI.2.9, IX.11.7.

33. See, for example, IV.8.3 (of Justin), VI.19.7, VII.32.27.

34. See, for example, III.39.4, V.11.3 (quotation from Clement), V.20.6.

35. See, for example, IV.16.5 (quotation from Justin about Crescens), VI.19.15, VI.37, VII.28.2.

36. See, for example, I.4.14, VII.30.12, X.4.33.

37. *Fragmenta vornicänischer Kirchenväter aus den Sacra Parallela*, ed. Karl Holl (TU 20,2; Leipzig: J. C. Hinrichs, 1899), 94, 95, 96, 98, 99, 100 (pp. 32–34)—πρὸς Ἀντωνῖνον in 95 and 98–100, εἰς Ἀντωνῖνον in 96.

38. For a discussion of Tertullian's title, see Simon Price, "Latin Christian Apologetics," in Edwards et al., *Apologetics*, 105–29, at 115–16. Price concludes that "the title *Apologeticus* thus has a Greek ring, but it does not have any forensic overtones" (116).

39. At *1 Apol.* 42.1 Justin undertakes to explain the idiosyncrasies of prophetic language, "lest it provide a cop out for readers," and at *2 Apol.* 12.5 he claims that oversexed pagans adduce "the writings of Epicurus and the poets as an excuse."

40. Menander II.10 (trans. Russell and Wilson, 165).

41. The full list, in order, is "the former apology to Antoninus on behalf of our doctrine" (τῇ προτέρα πρὸς Ἀντωνῖνον ὑπὲρ τοῦ καθ' ἡμᾶς δόγματος ἀπολογία, *H.E.* II.1.32); "the apology of Justin to Antoninus" (τῆς Ἰουστίνου πρὸς Ἀντωνῖνον ἀπολογίας, IV. Pinax 12); "the apology to Antoninus" (IV.8.3); "other discourses containing apology (which he addresses

[προσφωνεῖ]) to Antoninus who was called Pius and the senate of the Romans" (IV.11.11); "the apology" (IV.11.11); "the aforementioned apology" (IV.16.2); "the former apology" (IV.17.1); "address (λόγος ... προσφωνητικός) to Antoninus called Pius and his sons and the senate of the Romans on behalf of our doctrines" (IV.18.2).

42. Kinzig, "Sitz im Leben," 298: "Die überraschend konsistente Terminologie des Eusebius lässt kaum einen Zweifel daran zu, daß die von ihm angeführte Gruppe von Schriften, die er— mindestens teilweise—vor Augen gehabt hat, das Wort apologia im Titel trug."

43. It is tempting to think that Eusebius has simply extracted the word προσφωνητικός from Justin's use of προσφώνησις in 1 Apol. 1—which he has quoted in H.E. IV.12—since it is not a normal part of his vocabulary. This is the only occurrence of the adjective in the whole of Eusebius contained in TLG, and the adverb προσφωνητικῶς appears once—in Comm. in Isaiam I.93 (p. 182, l. 5, Ziegler), where there is a contrast between words (Isa. 28:10-11) addressed directly (προσφωνητικῶς) "to the apostles and disciples and evangelists" and words addressed prophetically to the Jews.

44. Harnack persuaded himself that it was actually Athenagoras's Supplicatio (Überliefer- ung, 171–90). Munier is nearer the mark when he says simply that Eusebius's "prétendue 'sec- onde Apologie' demeure obstinément insaisissable" (L'Apologie, 16).

45. A part of a citation from our First Apology, presented in the manuscript Holl calls R (Rupefucaldinus [Berolinensis], 1,450) as being from "To Antoninus," recurs in K under the rubric "from the first λόγος of his apology" (Holl, 94 [p. 32]). Unfortunately, Photius, codex 125, is no help: he seems not to have seen our Apologies. The second half of his notice, which mentions a work presented "to Antoninus, surnamed Pius, and his sons, and the Senate," is simply derived from Eusebius's catalogue in H.E. IV.18. The first half of Photius's notice lists works he actually knew firsthand, including an "apology on behalf of Christians and against Greeks and against Jews"; for other references to this work, see Harnack, Überlieferung, 192 (nos. 25 and 26).

46. On the titles in A and for the evidence that "in the rest of the tradition" apart from A itself, "so far as it is accessible, the documents must have been read in the other order—First Apology first," see my "Textual Tradition," 57–58.

47. Adolf von Harnack, Analecta zur ältesten Geschichte des Christentums in Rom, appended to Paul Koetschau, Beiträge zur Textkritik von Origines' Johannescommentar (TU 28,2; Leipzig: J. C. Hinrichs, 1905), 3–5. The identification has been defended by, for example, Gerd Lüdemann, "Zur Geschichte des ältesten Christentums in Rom. I. Valentin und Marcion, II. Ptolemäus und Justin," ZNW 70 (1979): 86–114, at 101–2, and Peter Lampe, From Paul to Valentinus: Christians at Rome in the First Two Centuries, trans. Michael Steinhauser (London: T&T Clark, 2003), 239–40, and is treated favorably by Munier, L'Apologie, 27–28. Christoph Markschies, "New Research on Ptolemaeus Gnosticus," Zeitschrift für antikes Christentum 4 (2000): 225–54, at 247–49, returns a Scotch verdict: "Harnack's suggestion is not more than a hypothesis: not out of the question, but by no means secure" (249).

48. This identification is suggested by Robert M. Grant, "A Woman of Rome: The Matron in Justin, 2 Apology 2.1–9," CH 54 (1985): 461–72, and vigorously maintained by Lampe.

49. See the references in Markschies, "New Research," 248 n. 96.

50. 1 Apol. 26.5; 58.1–2.

51. Trans. Harold W. Attridge and George W. MacRae, in Nag Hammadi Codex I (The Jung Codex): Introductions, Texts, Translations, Indices, ed. Harold W. Attridge (Nag Hammadi Stud- ies 22; Leiden: Brill, 1985), 113 = The Nag Hammadi Library in English, ed. James M. Robinson, 3rd ed. (Leiden: Brill, 1988), 50.

52. Nag Hammadi Codex I, 111 = Nag Hammadi Library in English, 49.

53. This is a slightly revised version of the translation offered in our edition, which obelizes the offending passage; see our commentary on the textual problems, ad loc.

54. Trans. Harold W. Attridge and Elaine H. Pagels, in *Nag Hammadi Codex I*, 315 = *Nag Hammadi Library in English*, 97. See the discussion of the school model in Einar Thomassen, *The Spiritual Seed: The Church of the "Valentinians"* (Nag Hammadi and Manichaean Studies 60; Leiden: Brill, 2006), 467–68.

55. *2 Apol.* 6(5).3. In our edition we have adopted and try to justify Scaliger's emendation of the passive "being anointed" to the active "anointing."

56. Oskar Skarsaune, *The Proof from Prophecy: A Study in Justin Martyr's Proof-Text Tradition; Text-Type, Provenance, Theological Profile* (NovTSup 56; Leiden: Brill, 1987), 369.

57. The fable of the choice of Heracles was a set-piece of the sophist Prodicus, first related by Xenophon, *Symposium* II.1.21–34.

58. It is a truth universally recognized that *1 Apology*, at least, must have been written shortly after 150. The guess of 153 comes from the rather surprising inclusion of Lucius Verus—a private citizen (though the adopted son of Antoninus Pius) until the accession of Marcus—in the address. Though adopted by Antoninus in 138 on Hadrian's insistence, he lived until his twenty-third year "as a private citizen in the house of the emperor" (Scriptores Historiae Augustae, *Vita Veri* 2.11) and "was conspicuously deprived by Pius in the glory of the imperial family" (T. D. Barnes, in an important analysis of the *Vita Veri*—"Hadrian and Lucius Verus," *JRS* 57 [1967]: 65–79, at 68). But in 152 he was nominated quaestor for 153, and he held his first consulship in 154, which might have led an observer in Rome to think that he was coming out politically.

59. Thus Kinzig can say simply, "Der Ort der Verteidigung ist im erster Linie das Gericht" ("Sitz im Leben," 300).

60. This last point I owe to Frances Young, who concludes, "It could be said, therefore, that 'apology' is not a genre, but properly the end or purpose of a speech, particularly a speech for the defence in court, and then more loosely a defence or excuse offered in a less precise context or genre" ("Greek Apologists," 91).

61. There is a Greek version of the martyrdom, agreeing in broad outline with the story in Eusebius, under the name of Apollos; Herbert Musurillo, *The Acts of the Christian Martyrs* (Oxford Early Christian Texts; Oxford: Clarendon, 1972), 90–105.

62. *Le Martyre de Pionios, Prête de Smyrne*, ed. Louis Robert with G. W. Bowersock and C. P. Jones (Washington: Dumbarton Oaks Research Library and Collection, 1994), 4.2–24 (pp. 22–23). The "apology" concludes with the remark, "Having said these and many other things, it was a long time till Pionius fell silent" (5.1).

63. I will not speculate on when in the manuscript the *Saint*, ἅγιος, was prefixed to Justin's name, but the *Letter from the Churches of Lyons and Vienne*—scarcely more than a decade after Justin's martyrdom—speaks of οἱ ἅγιοι μάρτυρες (ap. Eus., *H.E.* V.1.16).

3. The *Rescript* of Hadrian

1. Melito of Sardis, *On Pascha, and fragments*, ed. and trans. Stuart George Hall (Oxford: Clarendon, 1979), frag. 3* (= Eusebius, *H.E.* IV.27.10).

2. *Prosopographia Imperii Romani Saeculi I. II. III pars V*, editio altera (Berlin: Walter de Gruyter, 1970–87), L. 247.

3. *Prosopographia Imperii Romani*, M. 612.

4. W. H. Waddington, *Fastes des provinces asiatiques de l'Empire romain depuis leur origine jusqu'au règne de Dioclétien* (Paris: Firmin Didot, 1872), 197–99.

5. Schmid considered that the reference to the punishment of calumnious accusers at the end of the rescript was an early interpolation, made under the influence of the spurious *Letter*

of Antoninus Pius to the Commune of Asia, which follows the rescript in the manuscript of Justin, "The Christian Re-interpretation of the *Rescript* of Hadrian," *Maia* 7 (1955): 5–13 (reprinted in W. Schmid, *Ausgewählte philologische Schriften*, ed. H. Erbse and J. Küppers [Berlin: Walter de Gruyter, 1984], 325–32), at 12–13 [331–32].

6. J. B. Lightfoot had similarly noted that while Justin was "naturally anxious to make the most of it . . . the document itself does not go nearly so far as he represents": *The Apostolic Fathers*, part II, S. *Ignatius*, S. *Polycarp*, 2nd ed. (London: Macmillan, 1889), 2:478.

7. Schmid, "The Christian Re-interpretation," 9 [329].

8. W. Schmid, "Ein Inversionsphänomen und seine Bedeutung im Text der Apologie des Justin," in *Forma Futuri, Studi in onore del Cardinale M. Pellegrino* (Turin: Erasmo, 1975), 253–81 (reprinted in *Ausgewählte philologische Schriften*, 338–64) at 272 [356].

9. Schmid, "Ein Inversionsphänomen," 275 [358], referring to D. B. Capelle, "Le rescrit d'Hadrien et S. Justin," *RBén* 39 (1927): 365–68.

10. Schmid, "Inversionsphänomen," 275 [358]: "Einem nachjustinischen Rezensor sehr wohl zuzutrauen wäre."

11. H. U. Instinsky, "Zur Entstehung des Titels nobilissimus Caesar," in *Beiträge zur älteren Europäischen Kulturgeschichte, Festschrift für Rudolf Egger* (Klagenfurt: Geschichtsverein für Kärnten, 1952–54), 1:98–103.

12. Herodian I.17.12.

13. Schmid, "Inversionsphänomen," 276 [359] n. 60; 275 [358] n. 58.

14. *Ägyptische Urkunden aus dem Königlichen Museen zu Berlin, Griechische Urkunden* I (Berlin: Weidmann, 1895), P 6847, no. 19 (p. 30).

15. *Corpus Inscriptionum Graecarum* II, ed. A. Boeckhius (Berlin: Reimen, 1843), no. 2454.

16. Schmid, "Inversionsphänomen," 272 [354], 276–81 [359–64].

17. H. Nesselhauf, "Hadrians Reskript an Minicius Fundanus," *Hermes* 104 (1976): 348–61, at 348.

18. For the earlier view, A. Birley, *Marcus Aurelius: A Biography*, 2nd ed. (London: Batsford, 1987), 258, 262; for the later, *Hadrian: The Restless Emperor* (London: Routledge, 1997), 127.

19. Lightfoot, *Apostolic Fathers*, II.1:478; T. Mommsen, "Der Religionsfrevel nach römischem Recht," *Historische Zeitschrift* 64, n. F. 28 (1890): 389–429 (reprinted in Mommsen, *Gesammelte Schriften* 3 = *Juristische Schriften* 3 [Berlin: Weidmann, 1907], 389–422) at 420 [415]; C. Callewaert, "Le rescrit d'Hadrien à Minicius Fundanus," *Revue d'histoire et de littérature religieuses* 8 (1903): 152–89, at 179.

20. Mommsen, "Der Religionsfrevel," 420 [414–15]. Mommsen is still able to remark that the best evidence of the groundlessness of doubts about the authenticy of the *Rescript* is "wie wenig sich die Neueren in den Standpunkt der römischen Regierung dem Christenthum gegenüber zu finden vermögen" (420 [415], n. 1).

21. Nesselhauf, "Hadrians Reskript," 352.

22. Ibid., 349–50.

23. Ibid., 351.

24. Mommsen, "Der Religionsfrevel," 420 [415].

25. Nesselhauf, "Hadrians Reskript," 356–57 "ein Verfahren, das sich mit der römischen Auffassung von Rechtsstaatlichkeit durchaus vertrug."

26. A modern (nineteenth-century) designation of a method of judicial inquiry (*cognitio*) in which a governor was not restricted to consideration of a formal list or catalog (*ordo*) of statute law.

27. R. A. Bauman, *Crime and Punishment in Ancient Rome* (London: Routledge, 1996), 50ff.; J. L. Strachan-Davidson, *Problems of the Roman Criminal Law* (Oxford: Clarendon, 1912), 2:158ff.

28. Cf. Callewaert, "Le rescrit d'Hadrien," 165; Bauman, *Crime and Punishment*, 5–6.
29. Cf. Callewaert, "Le rescrit d'Hadrien," 162; G. E. M. de Ste. Croix, "Why Were the Early Christians Persecuted?" *Past and Present* 26 (1963): 6–37, at 11.
30. Nesselhauf, "Hadrians Reskript," 356.
31. Cf. O. F. Robinson, *The Criminal Law of Ancient Rome* (Baltimore: Johns Hopkins University Press, 1995), 11–12; Strachan-Davidson, *Problems of the Roman Criminal Law*, 2:164.
32. Callewaert, "Le rescrit d' Hadrien," 170–74, considered that the rescript included reference to penal legislation outlawing the *nomen Christianum*.
33. *In Pisonem* 30.
34. Bauman, *Crime and Punishment*, 50.
35. Cf. Callewaert, "Le rescrit d'Hadrien," 163, 174.
36. Justinus des Philosophen und Märtyrers, *Rechtfertigung des Christentums (Apologie I u. II)*, ed. H. Veil (Strassburg: Heitz, 1894), 140.
37. Birley, *Hadrian*, 125.
38. A translation of this text has been given above, at n. 5.
39. Text from *Eusebius Werke*, II, *Die Kirchengeschichte*, ed. Eduard Schwartz and Theodor Mommsen (GCS; Leipzig: J. C. Hinrichs, 1903–09), 1:319–21.
40. We separate with a forward slash alternative renderings that can be paralleled in Pliny's correspondence and that seem to us equally plausible.
41. Lightfoot, *Apostolic Fathers*, II.1:479.
42. Ibid., II.1:480.
43. Trans. Hall, *Melito*, frag. 1 (p. 63).
44. R. Weijenbourg, "Meliton de Sardes lecteur de la première Apologie et du Dialogue de Saint Justin," *Antoninianum* 49 (1974): 362–66. According to the compiler of the *Chronicon Paschale* (483), Melito said many of the things reported by Justin.
45. *Digest* XLVIII.xx.1. A little later in this chapter, Ulpian, commenting on a *Rescript* of Hadrian, remarks that even the *pannicularia*, the clothes, small change, and other effects a convict might have about him at the time of execution, if not sent to the fisc, should at least be used for official purposes and not appropriated by soldiers or magistrates.
46. *Oxford Latin Dictionary*, ed. P. G. W. Glare (Oxford: Clarendon, 1982), 1315.
47. Cf. W. Williams, "Two Imperial Pronouncements Reclassified," *Zeitschrift für Papyrologie und Epigraphik* 22 (1976): 235–40, at 239.
48. Justinus, *Rechtfertigung*, ed. Veil, 138.
49. Schmid, "Inversionsphänomen," 361; Justinus, *Rechtfertigung*, ed. Veil, 137.

4. Justin and His Bible

1. David Trobisch, *The First Edition of the New Testament* (Oxford: Oxford University Press, 2000).
2. Fragment 3 (= Eusebius, *H.E.* 4.26.13–14), in Stuart George Hall, *Melito of Sardis: On Pascha and Fragments* (Oxford Early Christian Texts; Oxford: Clarendon, 1979), 64–67.
3. This is taken more or less for granted by Trobisch, *First Edition*, 44: "Even if the term New Testament is not explicitly used, it is implied by the designation Old Testament, which is introduced without explanation." This is less obvious than it seems, however, especially since the exact meaning of the term "books of the Old Covenant/Testament" is not clear. It could mean "books containing, or pertaining to, the Old Covenant," or it could mean "the books contained in the Old Testament." For discussion of the issue, see Wolfram Kinzig, "*Hē kainē diathēkē*:

The Title of the New Testament in the Second and Third Centuries," *JTS*, n.s., 45 (1994): 519–44, esp. 527–28. See also Willem Cornelis van Unnik, "*Hē kainē diathēkē*—a Problem in the Early History of the Canon," in *Sparsa Collecta: The Collected Essays of W. C. van Unnik* (NovTSup 29–31; Leiden: Brill, 1980), 2:157–71.

4. Kinzig enumerates the following passages as certainly attesting "old/new testament" as referring to the book collections: *Strom.* 1.44.3, 3.71.3, 4.134.4, 5.85.1, 7.100.5. He deems the following as most likely having the same meaning: *Paed.* 1.59.2; *Strom.* 3.54.4, 3.82.4, 3.108.2, 4.134.2, 6.125.3. See "*Hē kainē diathēkē*," 529 nn. 46, 47.

5. *Adv. Marc.* 4.1.1, 4.6.1, 5.11.4; *Adv. Prax.* 15.1, 31.1; *Praescr.* 30.9; *Pud.* 1.5, 6.5; *Mon.* 6.3; *Cast.* 10.4. For this list, which is not exhaustive, see Kinzig, "*Hē kainē diathēkē*," 530 n. 51.

6. Kinzig, "*Hē kainē diathēkē*," 534–44.

7. On Christians preferring the codex, not the scroll, as book format for biblical books, see Colin H. Roberts, "The Christian Book and the Greek Papyri," *JTS* 50 (1949): 155–68; Roberts and Theodore C. Skeat, *The Birth of the Codex* (London: Oxford University Press, 1983); Martin Hengel, *The Four Gospels and the One Gospel of Jesus Christ: An Investigation of the Collection and Origin of the Canonical Gospels* (London: SCM, 2000), 118–22; Graham N. Stanton, "Why Were Early Christians Addicted to the Codex?" in Stanton, *Jesus and Gospel* (Cambridge: Cambridge University Press, 2004), 165–91. See now also Larry W. Hurtado, *The First Christian Artifacts* (Grand Rapids: Eerdmans, 2006).

8. This was suggested by Roberts and Skeat and is argued anew by Graham N. Stanton, "The Fourfold Gospel," *NTS* 43 (1997): 317–46; revised reprint in Stanton, *Jesus and Gospel*, 63–91, esp. 71–75. See also Stanton, "Jesus Traditions and Gospels in Justin Martyr and Irenaeus," in *Jesus and Gospel*, 92–109, esp. 93–105; and Hengel, *Four Gospels*, 19–21. For reservations against the idea that the four-Gospel codex reigned supreme in the early centuries, see Hurtado, *Artifacts*.

9. The oldest example is papyrus P[46] from c. 200 C.E. The front and end leaves are missing, but the preserved part contains and documents the order Romans, Hebrews, 1 and 2 Corinthians, Ephesians, Galatians, Philippians, Colossians, 1 Thessalonians (2 Thessalonians by implication). See discussion in David Trobisch, *Paul's Letter Collection: Tracing the Origins* (Minneapolis: Fortress Press, 1994), 13–17.

10. For example, *Dial.* 57.2; 86.2; 126.6; 135.1; 138.3; 140.1, 2.

11. For example, *Dial.* 9.1, 23.4b, 56.15a, 86.2. Justin's other term for the OT books is *tas biblous tōn prophētōn, 1 Apol.* 31 passim, 36.3, 44.12.

12. Giving unambiguous and easy-to-find references to specific verses and texts in the Septuagint is notoriously difficult, especially in Psalms and some of the Prophets. I have chosen the expedient solution of always giving the chapter/psalm and verse count of the New Revised Standard Version. My translations of Justin's biblical texts, and of his own text, are those of the two translations I have used for his works in general. The so-called *First Apology* is quoted according to Thomas B. Falls, trans., *The Writings of Justin Martyr* (Fathers of the Church 6; Washington, D.C.: Catholic University of America Press, 1948); the *Dialogue* according to Thomas B. Falls, trans., *St. Justin Martyr: Dialogue with Trypho*, rev. Thomas P. Halton, ed. Michael Slusser (Selections from the Fathers of the Church 3; Washington, D.C.: Catholic University of America Press, 2003).

13. The following is a condensed version of the more extensive analysis in Oskar Skarsaune, *The Proof from Prophecy: A Study in Justin Martyr's Proof-Text Tradition: Text-Type, Provenance, Theological Profile* (NovTSup 56; Leiden: Brill, 1987), 25–29, 140–43; I therefore refrain from detailed referencing in the following. See also Skarsaune, "From Books to Testimonies: Remarks on the Transmission of the Old Testament in the Early Church," in *The New Testament and*

Christian-Jewish Dialogue: Studies in Honor of David Flusser, ed. Malcolm Lowe (*Immanuel* 24/25; Jerusalem: Ecumenical Theological Research Fraternity in Israel, 1990), 207–19.

14. Trans. Falls, altered.

15. Trans. Falls and Halton, altered.

16. *Dial.* 131.1 on Deut. 32:8; 137.3 on Isa. 3:9; 43.8, 67.1, 71.3, and 84.3 on Isa. 7:14; 124.3–4 on Ps. 82:7; 73.1 on Ps. 96:10.

17. The only case of a long quotation directly from a complete LXX scroll in the *First Apology* appears to be the quotation of Psalms 1–2 in *1 Apol.* 40.8–19.

18. Skarsaune, *Proof from Prophecy*, 228–34.

19. *Dial.* 120.4 on Gen. 49:10; 131.1 on Deut. 32:8; 137.3 on Isa. 3:9; 43.8, 67.1, 71.3, and 84.3 on Isa. 7:14; 124.3–4 on Ps. 82:7; 73.1 on Ps. 96:10; 72 on three passages allegedly deleted.

20. See Eric G. Turner, *The Typology of the Early Codex* (Haney Foundation Series 18; Philadelphia: University of Pennsylvania Press, 1977), esp. 89–95. When Justin tells his readers that during Christian worship the books of the Prophets are read (*1 Apol.* 67.3), either he could have Christian lectionaries in mind, with Haftarah-like excerpts of selected prophecies, or the Roman community could simply use ordinary Jewish Septuagint manuscripts for this purpose without making any problem of textual variants. It seems this latter attitude was the universal Christian approach prior to Justin. He is the first Christian writer on record for whom different readings in supposed messianic prophecies have become a major problem.

21. Dominique Barthélemy, "Redécouverte d'un chaînon manquant de l'histoire de la Septante," *RB* 60 (1953): 18–29.

22. For example, in *Dialogue* 13–16 we find the following sequence of long LXX quotations: Isa. 52:10—54:6; 55:3-13; 58:1-11; 57:1-4. In *Dialogue* 25–26 we have Isa. 63:15—64:12; 62:10—63:6; in *Dialogue* 36–38, Pss. 24:1-10; 47:6-10; 99:1-9; 45:2-18; in *Dialogue* 63–64, Pss. 45:7-13; 99:1-7; 72:1-19; 19:1-7.

23. For this and the following statements, see Skarsaune, *Proof from Prophecy*, 454–71, "Appendix II."

24. Justin evinces some familiarity with the narrative material of 1 Samuel 5–6 in *Dial.* 132.2–3; 1 Samuel 28 in *Dial.* 105.4; 2 Samuel 11–12 in *Dial.* 141.3–4; 1 Kings 6–8 and 11 in *Dial.* 34.8 (cf. also *Dial.* 36.2), calling this book by its Septuagint name, *Kingdoms*; 1 Kings 18:25-29 in *Dial.* 69.1; and 2 Kings 6:1-6 in *Dial.* 86.6. It is quite likely, however, that Justin's knowledge of these biblical narratives sometimes came to him through intermediary sources, as is instanced in *Dial.* 39.1–2, where Justin's source for Elijah's complaint about the apostasy of Israel is not 1 Kings 19, but Rom. 11:3-4.

25. For example, Isa. 19:24-25 in *Dial.* 123.5; Isa. 42:8 in *Dial.* 65.1. See the comments in Skarsaune, *Proof from Prophecy*, 350–52.

26. Jer. 4:3-4 in *Dial.* 28.2; 9:24-25 in 28.3 (notice again the neat sequence of quotations from the same part of the book following each other); 11:19 in 72.2; and 31:31-32 in 11.3.

27. Ezek. 16:3 is quoted in *Dial.* 77.4; 20:19-26 in 21.2; 36:12 in 123.6.

28. For the *kaige* recension and Justin's quotations from it, see Barthélemy, "Redécouverte"; Barthélemy, *Les Devanciers d'Aquila: Première publication intégrale du texte des fragments du Dodécapropheton* (VTSup 10; Leiden: Brill, 1963), 203–13; Natalio Fernández Marcos, *The Septuagint in Context: Introduction to the Greek Version of the Bible* (Leiden: Brill, 2000), 142–54.

29. Concerning the rest of the historical books, see n. 24 above.

30. On the *Codex Parisinus graecus* 450, see Adolf von Harnack, *Die Überlieferung der griechischen Apologeten des zweiten Jahrhunderts in der Alten Kirche und im Mittelalter* (TU 1; Leipzig: J. C. Hinrichs, 1882–83), 73–79; Miroslav Marcovich, *Iustini Martyris Dialogus cum Tryphone* (PTS 47; Berlin: Walter de Gruyter, 1997), 1–7.

31. The major studies to date are Joost Smit Sibinga, *The Old Testament Text of Justin Martyr*, vol. 1, *The Pentateuch* (Leiden: Brill, 1963; no further volumes published); Barthélemy, *Les Devanciers d'Aquila*, 203–13.

32. The most recent treatment of this hypothesis, classically stated by Rendel Harris in *Testimonies*, 2 vols. (Cambridge: Cambridge University Press, 1916–20), is Martin C. Albl, "*And Scripture Cannot Be Broken": The Form and Function of the Early Christian Testimonia Collections* (NovTSup 96; Leiden: Brill, 1999), with full history of research at 7–69.

33. Wilhelm Bousset, *Jüdisch-Christlicher Schulbetrieb in Alexandria und Rom* (FRLANT, n. F. 6; Göttingen: Vandenhoeck & Ruprecht, 1915), esp. 282–308.

34. Helmut Koester, "Septuaginta und synoptischer Erzählungsstoff im Schriftbeweis Justins des Märtyrers" (Habilitationsschrift Ruprecht-Karl-Universität, Heidelberg, 1956).

35. I have developed this point in some detail in Skarsaune, "The Development of Scriptural Interpretation in the Second and Third Centuries—Except Clement and Origen," in *Hebrew Bible/Old Testament: The History of Its Interpretation*, vol. 1, *From the Beginnings to the Middle Ages (until 1300)*, part i, *Antiquity*, ed. Magne Sæbø (Göttingen: Vandenhoeck & Ruprecht, 1996), 373–442.

36. See Koester, "Septuaginta," 92–93.

37. Text and translation according to Moses Aberbach and Bernard Grossfeld, *Targum Onkelos to Genesis: A Critical Analysis Together with an English Translation of the Text* (Denver: Ktav Books, Center for Judaic Studies University of Denver, 1982), 284–86.

38. There is one notable exception to this, namely, the continuous commentary on Ps. 22:1-23 in *Dialogue* 97–107, on which see below.

39. For the concept of targumizing, see Roger le Deaut, "Un phénomene spontané de l'hermeneutique juive ancienne: le 'targumisme,'" *Bib* 52 (1971): 505–25.

40. Apart from Gen. 49:11 already treated, see also the same phenomenon in Zech. 9:9 (*1 Apol*. 35.11); Num. 24:17 (*1 Apol*. 32.12); Isa. 1:7 (*1 Apol*. 47.5); Isa. 1:11-15 (*1 Apol*. 37.5–8a); Isa. 58:6 (*1 Apol*. 37.8b); Ps. 22:16 (*1 Apol*. 35.5, 38.4); Ps. 22:18 (*1 Apol*. 35.5, 38.4); Ps. 24:7 (*1 Apol*. 51.7); Ps. 72:17 (*Dial*. 121.1).

41. *Dial*. 73.4. For the Greek text, see Marcovich, 196, and note *ad loc*. The text of Psalm 96 that Justin quotes in *Dial*. 73.3–4 may be characterized as a good LXX text-type. See detailed study and synopsis in Skarsaune, *Proof from Prophecy*, 35–42.

42. According to A. Rahlfs, *Der Text des Septuaginta-Psalters* (Septuaginta-Studien, Heft 2; Göttingen: Vandenhoeck & Ruprecht, 1965), 160, the reading "from the tree" is only to be found in Latin, Sahidic, and Bohairic psalters and lectionaries, and in Greek only in two lectionary texts made to accompany the Latin or Sahidic texts. In general on Justin's texts of the Psalms, see Rahlfs, *Der Text*, 203–6.

43. The catchword link leading from Isaiah 11 to this verse in Isaiah 51 is "the arm of the Lord," contained also in Isa. 11:11.

44. See, e.g., 4QTestim 175.1–8, in which Deut. 5:28-29 and 18:18-19 are combined into one quote. Text and translation in Florentino García Martínez and Eibert J. C. Tigchelaar, eds., *The Dead Sea Scrolls Study Edition* (Leiden: Brill, 1997), 1:356–57.

45. See le Deaut, "Un phénomene spontané," and le Deaut, "La tradition juive ancienne et l'exégèse chrétienne primitive," *RHPhR* 51 (1971): 31–50.

46. In this I agree with Marcovich; see his note *ad loc*., p. 161. In *Dial*. 56.12, 18 Justin says that he has quoted the *whole* passage previously.

47. Translation according to Isidore Epstein, ed., *The Babylonian Talmud: Seder Nezikin, Sanhedrin* (London: Soncino Press, 1935), 246.

48. The same anti-Marcion material may have been reused in *1 Apology* 60–64. Justin him-

self mentions a *Syntagma against All Heresies* that he had written previously to the *Apology* in *1 Apol.* 26.1. A Justinian *Syntagma against Marcion* quoted by Irenaeus (*Adv. Haer.* 4.6.2; and from him, Eusebius, *H.E.* 4.18.9) is probably the same work. See Pierre Prigent, *Justin et l'Ancien Testament* (ÉtB; Paris: J. Gabalda, 1964), 121–23.

49. And also, I believe, in *Dial.* 74.4—76.7; cf. the doublet in *Dialogue* 126–129, and Skarsaune, *Proof from Prophecy*, 409–24.

50. Skarsaune, *Proof from Prophecy*, 234–42. (On this suggestion, see also the study by Will Rutherford in this volume.)

51. 4QTestim 175, ed. Martínez and Tigchelaar, 1:354–57; cf. C. Newsom, "The 'Psalms of Joshua' from Qumran Cave 4," *Journal of Jewish Studies* 39 (1988): 56–73. Other quotes of this Joshua apocryphon are preserved in 4TestimQ 378, 379, and 397 fr. 22.

52. See Skarsaune, "The Question of Old Testament Canon and Text in the Early Greek Church," in *Hebrew Bible/Old Testament*, 1/i:443–50.

53. The two most comprehensive surveys to date are Theodor Zahn, *Geschichte des Neutestamentlichen Kanons*, 2 vols. in 4 (Erlangen: Andreas Deichert, 1888–92), 1/ii:463–585, and Édouard Massaux, *The Influence of the Gospel of Saint Matthew on Christian Literature before Saint Irenaeus*, trans. Norman J. Belval and Suzanne Hecht, ed. Arthur J. Bellinzoni (Macon, Ga.: Mercer University Press, 1993), 3:10–101. While Zahn tends toward regarding probable references in Justin (to New Testament writings) as certain, and possible references as probable, Massaux is much more circumspect.

54. Arthur J. Bellinzoni, *The Sayings of Jesus in the Writings of Justin Martyr* (NovTSup 17; Leiden: Brill, 1967), 49–100.

55. Massaux, *Influence*, 3.11-34 (esp. 20), preferred to see Justin himself as the producer of this harmony and is followed in this view by Wolf-Dietrich Köhler, *Die Rezeption des Matthäusevangeliums in der Zeit vor Irenäus* (WUNT 2. Reihe 24; Tübingen: Mohr, 1987), 166–212.

56. Bellinzoni's study was followed up by Leslie L. Kline, "Harmonized Sayings of Jesus in the Pseudo-Clementine Homilies and Justin Martyr," *ZNW* 66 (1975): 223–41. Kline posited a postsynoptic harmonistic source of Jesus *logia* used by Justin and the Pseudo-Clementine *Homilies*. (Cf. criticism of such theories in Georg Strecker, "Eine Evangelienharmonie bei Justin und Pseudoklemens?" *NTS* 24 [1978]: 297–316. In general I tend to find Strecker's criticism less convincing than the theories he criticizes.) William L. Petersen has taken Bellinzoni's and Kline's theses one step further by arguing that Justin's harmonistic source for Jesus *logia* was the precursor of Tatian's *Diatessaron*, "Textual Evidence of Tatian's Dependence upon Justin's 'ΑΠΟΜΝΗMONEYMATA,'" *NTS* 36 (1990): 512–34. Helmut Koester has taken this up and argued that Justin's main source for Gospel material was a full-fledged Gospel harmony, "The Text of the Synoptic Gospels in the Second Century," in *Gospel Traditions in the Second Century: Origins, Recensions, Text, and Transmission*, ed. William L. Petersen (Christianity and Judaism in Antiquity 3; Notre Dame: University of Notre Dame Press, 1989), 19–37, esp. 28–33. But there is no indication that Justin's harmonistic source or sources were anything even near complete Gospels, and, unlike Tatian, Justin never thought of his harmonistic sources as replacing the four Gospels. See Stanton, "Fourfold Gospel," 77. Donald A. Hagner, "The Sayings of Jesus in the Apostolic Fathers and Justin Martyr," in *The Jesus Tradition Outside the Gospels*, ed. D. Wenham (Gospel Perspectives 5; Sheffield: JSOT, 1985), 233–68, esp. 246–49, accords oral tradition a greater role than do Bellinzoni and his followers.

57. A pioneering study of Justin as an early witness to Matthew's text was made by Édouard Massaux, "The Text of Matthew's Sermon on the Mount Used by Saint Justin: A Contribution to the Textual Criticism of the First Gospel," in Massaux, *Influence*, 3:190–230; originally published as "Le texte du Sermon sur la Montagne de Matthieu utilize par Saint Justin," *EThL* 28

(1952): 411–48. To my knowledge, this type of study has not been followed up by other scholars. Barbara Aland ("Die Münsteraner Arbeit am Text des Neuen Testaments und ihr Beitrag für
die frühe Überlieferung des 2. Jahrhunderts: Eine methodologische Betrachtung," in Petersen,
Gospel Traditions in the Second Century, 55–70) said in 1989 that the *Münster Stiftung* for NT text
research had begun such work on the early Fathers but that only Irenaeus and Clement of
Alexandria had been surveyed at that time (p. 58). She added that "hier [steht] noch ein
fruchtbares Arbeitsfeld, geeignet auch für Dissertationen, offen."

58. For a demonstration of this in some detail, see Koester, "Septuaginta," 67–97. The fact
that these fulfillment reports on occasion contain noncanonical details should therefore not be
used as an argument concerning Justin's own Gospel canon. Koester is probably right in claiming that this is true also for Justin's postcanonical Gospel material, since the noncanonical details
are sufficiently explained as being called forth by the scriptural prophecies behind the fulfillment
reports. See n. 63 below.

59. *1 Apol.* 32.1 and 35.11, respectively. The reading *epi polon onon, hyion hypozygiou* in
35.11 should probably not be emended but kept as it is, an asyndetically plerophoric description
of one animal: "upon a foal, an ass, a son of the beast of burden." See Koester, "Septuaginta," 93,
esp. n. 3.

60. Köhler, *Die Rezeption des Matthäusevangeliums*, has an extensive review of all quotations and allusions to Matthew in Justin on pp. 161–265. In general, he tends to explain all deviations in wording between Justin and canonical Matthew as free quotations on the part of Justin.
In this case, however, Köhler admits that a postcanonical source cannot be excluded (222 n. 2).

61. Concerning the *Memoirs* in *Dialogue* 98–107, see the recent discussion in Craig D.
Allert, *Revelation, Truth, Canon, and Interpretation: Studies in Justin Martyr's Dialogue with
Trypho* (VCSup 64; Leiden: Brill, 2002), 188–220; and the further discussion of the *Memoirs*
below.

62. On this, see Paul Foster's essay in the present volume.

63. The most frequently mentioned case of a possible dependence on the *Gospel of the
Ebionites* is Justin's story of Jesus' baptism in *Dial.* 88.3, where we find the noncanonical detail
that "a fire ignited the waters of the Jordan" when Jesus *stepped down* into the water. In the *Gospel
of the Ebionites* it is said that when Jesus had *come up* from the water, "a great light shone round
about the place" (Epiphanius, *Pan.* 30.13.7–8). I believe we are dealing with two entirely different motives. In *Dial.* 88.3 we have a fulfillment report matching John the Baptizer's prophecy:
Jesus will baptize with Spirit and fire (Matt. 3:11b/Luke 3:16b, quoted by Justin in *Dial.* 49.3), and
accordingly his own baptism was accompanied by the Spirit and by fire. See Koester, "Septuaginta," 87. In the *Gospel of the Ebionites*, on the other hand, the great light is an "exteriorization"
of the *enlightenment* associated with baptism. See Daniel Vigne, *Christ au Jourdain: Le Baptême
de Jésus dans la tradition judéo-chrétienne* (Paris: J. Gabalda, 1992), 32–37 and 266–70; and
Skarsaune, "Jewish-Christian Gospels: Which and How Many?" in *Ancient Israel, Judaism, and
Christianity in Contemporary Perspective: Essays in Memory of Karl-Johan Illman*, ed. Jacob
Neusner et al. (Studies in Judaism; Lanham, Md.: University Press of America, 2006), 393–408,
esp. 400–402.

64. Nor in other second-century "orthodox" literature prior to Irenaeus. For a presentation
of the established consensus on this point, see Charles E. Hill, *The Johannine Corpus in the Early
Church* (Oxford: Oxford University Press, 2004), 11–59. The remainder of Hill's 500-page monograph is an effective deconstruction and refutation of this consensus.

65. The groundbreaking edition and study of the fragments is still Ernst von Dobschütz,
Das Kerygma Petri kritisch untersucht (TU 11.1; Leipzig: J. C. Hinrichs, 1893). See also Henning
Paulsen, "Das Kerygma Petri und die urchristliche Apologetik," *ZKG* 88 (1977): 1–37. I quote and
paraphrase the fragments according to the translation in E. Hennecke and W. Schneemelcher,

eds., *New Testament Apocrypha*, trans. and ed. R. McL. Wilson (London: SCM, 1974), 2:99–102. I also follow Hennecke and Schneemelcher in their numbering of the fragments.

66. James M. Robinson and Helmut Koester, *Trajectories through Early Christianity* (Philadelphia: Fortress Press, 1971).

67. For a more complete statement of this point of view, see Skarsaune, "Justin's Self-Understanding as an Exegete," in Skarsaune, *Proof from Prophecy*, 11–13.

68. The dominance of Matthew or Matthean material, not only in Justin, but in general in the second-century writers, has been demonstrated in great detail by Massaux, *Influence*, and more recently by Köhler, *Rezeption des Matthäusevangeliums*. See also Hengel, *Four Gospels*, 68–78.

69. Skarsaune, *Proof from Prophecy*, 228–34.

70. Scholars who deny that Justin used John tend to circumvent this passage by limiting the extent of what the *Memoirs* taught to the virginal birth of Jesus. See, for example, John Pryor, "Justin Martyr and the Fourth Gospel," *SecCent* 9 (1992): 153–69, esp. 156–57. But this reading of Justin's text is hardly convincing; see the detailed refutation of this view in Hill, *Johannine Corpus*, 320–25. Hill also demonstrates that this passage is not singular in Justin; there are several others in the *Dialogue* and in the *Apology* in which clear allusions to the Johannine prologue occur; *Johannine Corpus*, 316–20. Apart from the prologue, it is probably the free quotation of John 3:3-5 in *1 Apol.* 61.4–5 that is the clearest proof of Justin's direct use of John. Per se, the words on baptism of John 3:3, 5 could have been transmitted to Justin independently of John, but Nicodemus's objection toward a second birth, John 3:4, is echoed almost *verbatim* by Justin in *1 Apol.* 61.5—a fact that those scholars who deny dependence upon John simply ignore. See extensive discussion in Hill, *Johannine Corpus*, 325–28, and his contribution to the present volume.

71. The words *ha kaleitai evangelia* are deemed a later gloss by some commentators, but see the argument against this view in Luise Abramowski, "The 'Memoirs of the Apostles' in Justin," in *The Gospel and the Gospels*, ed. Peter Stuhlmacher (Grand Rapids: Eerdmans, 1991), 323–35, esp. 323.

72. C. H. Cosgrove, "Justin Martyr and the Emerging Christian Canon: Observations on the Purpose and Destination of the Dialogue with Trypho," *VC* 36 (1982): 209–32, claims, based on this expression ("so-called"), that Justin has a clear reserve with regard to the name "Gospel" for a written document. I think this is an overinterpretation; Cosgrove overlooks the constraints of Justin's fiction: a Jew is speaking, not Justin himself. By calling the Gospels "your so-called Gospel," Trypho is rather referring to their common name among Christians.

73. Justin is quoting Matthew rather than the Synoptic parallel in Luke 10:22, as shown by Massaux, *Influence*, 3:39–40 and 70.

74. *Mem.* 1.1 in *1 Apol.* 5.3 and *2 Apol.* 10.5 (the charge against Socrates). The closeness of the latter passage to the explicit reference in *2 Apol.* 11 indicates that Xenophon's *Memoirs* rather than Plato's *Apology* was the source of Justin's report on the accusation against Socrates.

75. Especially in the partly parallel passages *1 Apol.* 5 and *2 Apol.* 10. See E. Benz, "Christus und Socrates in der alten Kirche: Ein Beitrag zum altkirchlichen Verständnis des Märtyrers und des Martyriums," *ZNW* 43 (1950–51): 195–224; and Skarsaune, "Judaism and Hellenism in Justin Martyr, Elucidated from His Portrait of Socrates," in *Geschichte—Tradition—Reflexion. Festschrift für Martin Hengel zum 70. Geburtstag*, III, *Frühes Christentum*, ed. H. Cancik, H. Lichtenberger, and P. Schäfer (Tübingen: Mohr Siebeck, 1996), 585–611.

76. On the literary genre of *Memoirs* in Antiquity, see the still very useful remarks of Zahn, *Geschichte des neutestamentlichen Kanons*, 1/ii:471–76.

77. Richard Heard, "The *Apomnēmoneumata* in Papias, Justin, and Irenaeus," *NTS* 1 (1954–55): 122–29.

78. Papias according to Eusebius, *H.E.* 3.39.15–16.
79. *1 Apol.* 66.3; *Dial.* 88.3.
80. *Dial.* 103.8; cf. *egrapsan* in *Dial.* 88.3.
81. *1 Apol.* 33.5.
82. *Dial.* 105.5.
83. *1 Apol.* 33.5, 66.3; *Dial.* 18.1.
84. *Dial.* 102.5, 103.8, 106.3.
85. The subject of *emnēmoneusen* in *H.E.* 3.39.15 could as well be Peter as Mark.
86. For this and the foregoing, see in particular Charles E. Hill, "What Papias Said about John (and Luke): A 'New' Papian Fragment," *JTS*, n.s., 49 (1998): 582–629; and Hill, "John and the Apostolic Memoirs," in *Johannine Corpus*, 337–42. Hill here demonstrates that Justin is almost pedantically careful in not ascribing direct apostolic authorship to the *Memoirs* in any case in which Luke or Mark is involved in the quotations.
87. This understanding, so ably defended by Hill, is by no means new. See, for example, S. P. Tregelles, *Canon Muratorianus* (Oxford: Clarendon, 1867), 71; Zahn, *Geschichte*, 1/ii:476–534; Hugh J. Lawlor, "Eusebius on Papias," *Hermathena* 19 (1922): 167–222, esp. 202; D. M. Davey, "Justin Martyr and the Fourth Gospel," *Scr* 17 (1965): 117–22, esp. 119; and Robert M. Grant, *Greek Apologists of the Second Century* (Philadelphia: Westminster, 1988), 59. The same position has recently been restated by Stanton, "Fourfold Gospel," 63–91, esp. 75–78.
88. Cosgrove, "Justin Martyr," argues that since the intended readership of the *Dialogue* was a Christian one, Justin's failure to quote the Gospels as authoritative Scripture was intentional. Justin did not consider the Gospels as any more authoritative than other Christian texts. The only authority, in the final analysis, was the *Logos* himself. The latter point is no doubt true, but Cosgrove forgets that regardless of the *Dialogue*'s intended readership, Justin is constrained by the fiction consistently maintained throughout the entire *Dialogue*. In the *Dialogue* itself he is consistently *debating with a Jew* on terms acceptable to this Jew. He has committed himself to only quoting texts considered authoritative and authentic by his Jewish interlocutor (*Dial.* 28.2; 32.2; 39.7; 55.3, 16; 58.1; 68.1; and esp. 71.2–3), and when he once breaks this principle by quoting three sayings of Jesus (*Dial.* 17.3–4), he excuses himself for the fact (*Dial.*18.1). For an extensive discussion of the *Dialogue*'s audience, and Cosgrove's thesis, see Allert, *Revelation, Truth, Canon, and Interpretation*, 15–25 and 54–57.
89. I think there is much to be said for Luise Abramowski's argument that the commentary on Psalm 22 in *Dialogue* 97–107 was originally an anti-Gnostic and/or anti-Marcion composition. The emphasis on the authentic remembrances of the original twelve apostles would be very apposite in such a setting. See Abramowski, "Memoirs," 324–25.
90. See the emphatic statement of this point of view in Otto A. Piper, "The Nature of the Gospel according to Justin Martyr," *JR* 14 (1961): 155–68. Cosgrove, "Justin Martyr," makes much the same point, but overplays it to the point of claiming that Justin was *opposed* to the idea of Christian Scriptures. Cf. n. 88.
91. This was demonstrated in great detail by A. Thoma, "Justins literarisches Verhältnis zu Paulus und zum Johannesevangelium," *Wissenschaftliche Zeitung für Theologie* 18 (1875): 383–412, 490–565, esp. 383–412. See also Moritz von Engelhardt, *Das Christenthum Justins des Märtyrers: Eine Untersuchung über die Anfänge der Katholischen Glaubenslehre* (Erlangen: Andreas Deichert, 1878), 353–74; Theodor Zahn, *Geschichte des neutestamentlichen Kanons*, 1/ii:563–75; Eva Aleith, *Paulusverständnis in der alten Kirche* (BZNW 18; Berlin: Töpelmann, 1937), 34–39; Massaux, *Influence*, 3:47–49, 96–101; Willis A. Shotwell, *The Biblical Exegesis of Justin Martyr* (London: SPCK, 1965), 50–55; Andreas Lindemann, *Paulus im ältesten Christentum* (BHTh 58; Tübingen: Mohr, 1979), 353–67; and Skarsaune, *Proof from Prophecy*, 92–100.

92. Two particularly striking examples occur in *Dialogue* 39 and *Dialogue* 95–96. In the first of these, Justin has an almost verbatim paraphrase of Rom. 11:3–4, including Paul's non-LXX quotation of 1 Kings 19:10, 14, 18. In the second case, Justin has borrowed Paul's interpretation of how Deut. 21:23b was fulfilled by Jesus bearing the curse of all men vicariously. The non-LXX version of the text is taken directly from Gal. 3:13, and the interpretation of the quote is lifted directly out of Galatians 3. But interestingly, Justin has combined this Pauline interpretation with an entirely different one that he no doubt took from another source, one that he uses in many places in the *Dialogue*. But it is the Pauline interpretation that he prefers. For details, see Skarsaune, *Proof from Prophecy*, 95, 99, 118–19, 218–20. Concerning Romans, it is possible to demonstrate that Justin used the relevant material directly from Paul's letter, and not via intermediary sources. Thirteen of Paul's OT quotations are hidden quotations, not marked as such. Justin has only one of these (Ps. 19:5 in *Dial.* 42:1). Twenty-three of Paul's quotations are introduced by the general "as is written"; of these Justin has six, one-fourth. In the remaining thirteen quotations, Paul has a specific reference to which biblical book is being quoted; of these Justin has seven, more than half. For further arguments that Justin used Romans directly and not via intermediary sources, see Skarsaune, *Proof from Prophecy*, 95–98.

93. See references above to his passages concerning the apostles.

94. See on this Walter Bauer, "The Picture of the Apostle in Early Christian Tradition: Accounts," in *New Testament Apocrypha*, ed. Hennecke and Schneemelcher, 2:35–74, esp. 35–45; Jean-Daniel Kaestli, "Les scenes d'attribution des champs de mission et le depart de l'apôtre dans les actes apocryphes," in *Les actes apocryphes des Apôtres: Christianisme et monde païen*, ed. François Bovon et al. (Publications de la Faculté de Théologie de l'Université de Genève 4; Genève: Labor et Fides, 1981), 249–64; and Skarsaune, "Noen trekk ved apostel-bildet i den tidlig-kristne litteratur [Norwegian]," *Ichthys* 27 (2000): 3–13, 57–68.

95. Apart from his extensive use of Romans and Galatians, Justin seems to have taken one scriptural quotation directly from Ephesians: Justin's non-LXX quotations of Ps. 68:18 in *Dial.* 39.4 and 87.6 agree exactly with the quotation of this psalm verse in Eph. 4:8. There are certain or probable echoes of 1 Corinthians, Philippians, and Colossians in Justin, and possible allusions to 1 and 2 Thessalonians, 1 Timothy, and Titus. For details, see Massaux, *Influence*, 3:48 and 96–100.

96. For details, see Massaux, *Influence*, 3:47, 98, 100; Skarsaune, *Proof from Prophecy*, 72–73, 107–8, 126–27, 168, 179–80, 296.

97. In *Dial.* 45.4 there is a possible but by no means certain echo of Rev. 12:9.

98. See Skarsaune, *Proof from Prophecy*, 401–407.

99. See, in general, Franz Overbeck, "Über das Verhältniss Justins des Märtyrers zur Apostelgeschichte," *Wissenschaftliche Zeitung für Theologie* 15 (1872): 305–49; John C. O'Neill, *The Theology of Acts in Its Historical Setting* (London: SPCK, 1961), 10–53; Niels Hyldahl, *Philosophie und Christentum: Eine Interpretation der Einleitung zum Dialog Justins* (Acta theologica danica 9; Kopenhagen: Munksgaard, 1966), 261–72; W. S. Kurz, "The Function of Christological Proof from Prophecy for Luke and Justin" (diss. on microfilm, Yale University, 1976). For details, see Massaux, *Influence*, 3:94; Skarsaune, *Proof from Prophecy*, 104–5.

100. James 1:15 may be echoed in *Dial.* 100.5.

101. 1 Peter 2:6 is only one among several candidates as the source of *Dial.* 114.4 and 126.1; 1 Peter 3:19-21 may or may not be echoed in *Dial.* 138.1 (see Skarsaune, *Proof from Prophecy*, 338–40); 1 Peter 4:6 may have influenced the wording of Justin's Pseudo-Jeremiah logion in *Dial.* 72.4.

102. The *Biblia Patristica* 1 lists only one reference to 1 John, a reference to 3:8 in *Dial.* 45.4, but this is possible at best.

5. Justin and Israelite Prophecy

1. See the chronology of Miroslav Marcovich, *Iustini Martyris Dialogus cum Tryphone* (PTS 47; Berlin: Walter de Gruyter, 1997), 1. He places the *Dialogue* during the period 155–160, after the *Apology*, c. 150–155. I follow his Greek text of the *Dialogue*, as well as the two volumes of Philippe Bobichon, *Justin Martyr. Dialogue avec Tryphon*, édition critique, traduction, commentaire (Paradosis 47/1–2; Fribourg: Academic Press, 2003). For the *Apology*, I follow André Wartelle, *Saint Justin. Apologies*, introduction, texte critique, traduction, commentaire et index (Paris: Études augustiniennes, 1987), who places the *First Apology* in 153–154 (p. 35), and the *Second Apology* (which will briefly take up our attention) shortly thereafter. I refer here to the *First Apology* simply as the *Apology*, and the approach Dr. Paul Parvis represents in the present volume suggests that this might be the more accurate designation.

2. Oskar Skarsaune, "Judaism and Hellenism in Justin Martyr, Elucidated from His Portrait of Socrates," in *Geschichte—Tradition—Reflexion. Festschrift für Martin Hengel zum 70. Geburtstag*, III, *Frühes Christentum*, ed. H. Cancik, H. Lichtenberger, and P. Schäfer (Tübingen: Mohr Siebeck, 1996), 585–611, at 608.

3. See especially *Dial.* 44.2 ("Because no one of them by any means was able to receive [the good promised to Abraham], apart from those likened by thought [*gnome*] to the faith of Abraham who recognize all the mysteries: I mean that one command was appointed for piety and the practice of righteousness, and another command and action was in the same way spoken either as referring to the mystery of Christ or on account of the hardness of your people's heart") and *Dial.* 92.1 ("So if someone undertakes, without the help of an immense grace received of God, to appreciate what was done, said, or accomplished by the Prophets, it will not help him to wish to relate words or events, if he is not in a position to render their reason [*logos*] also").

4. Oskar Skarsaune, *The Proof from Prophecy: A Study in Justin Martyr's Proof-Text Tradition: Text-Type, Provenance, Theological Profile* (NovTSup 56; Leiden: Brill, 1987).

5. Dominic Barthelémy, *Les Devanciers d'Aquila: Première publication intégrale du texte des fragments du Dodécaprophéton* (VTSup 10; Leiden: Brill, 1963). For a more recent discussion, see George J. Brooke, "The Twelve Minor Prophets and the Dead Sea Scrolls," in *Congress Volume Leiden 2004*, ed. André Lemaire (Leiden: Brill, 2006) 19–43.

6. Skarsaune, *Proof*, 432.

7. Ibid., 46.

8. See Judith M. Lieu, "Justin Martyr and the Transformation of Psalm 22," in *Biblical Traditions in Transmission: Essays in Honour of Michael A. Knibb*, ed. Charlotte Hempel and Judith M. Lieu (JSJSup 111; Leiden: Brill, 2006), 195–211. Lieu nonetheless finds it "hard to resist the 'school' model that many have used to understand the development of early Christian scriptural interpretation," and she speaks of a "testimonia-tradition." See also Judith M. Lieu, "Accusations of Jewish Persecution in Early Christian Sources, with Particular Reference to Justin Martyr and the *Martyrdom of Polycarp*," in *Tolerance and Intolerance in Early Judaism and Christianity*, ed. Graham N. Stanton and Guy G. Stroumsa (Cambridge: Cambridge University Press, 1998), 279–95. The entire perspective relies upon Pierre Prigent, *Justin et l'Ancien Testament. L'argumentation scripturaire du Traité de Justin contre toutes les hérésies comme source principale du Dialogue avec Tryphon et la Première Apologie* (ÉtB; Paris: J. Gabalda, 1964), who together with Barthélemy offered a new perspective for the study of Justin that Skarsaune and those who have followed him have pursued.

9. J. R. Harris and V. Burch, *Testimonies* (Cambridge: Cambridge University Press, 1920). It is noteworthy that when Barnabas Lindars took up this model in *New Testament Apologetic* (London: SCM, 1961), he decisively distanced himself from conceiving of apologetic as mere

Auseinandersetzung or confrontation and explored the category of *pesher*. Cf. Bruce Chilton, "Commenting on the Old Testament (with Particular Reference to the Pesharim, Philo, and the Mekhilta," in *It Is Written: Scripture Citing Scripture; Essays in Honour of Barnabas Lindars*, ed. D. A. Carson and H. G. M. Williamson (Cambridge: Cambridge University Press, 1988), 122–40.

10. Tessa Rajak, "Talking at Trypho: Christian Apologetic as Anti-Judaism in Justin's *Dialogue with Trypho the Jew*," in *The Jewish Dialogue with Greece and Rome: Studies in Cultural and Social Interaction* (AGJU 48; Leiden: Brill, 2001), 511–33, at 531.

11. See Theodore Stylianopoulos, *Justin Martyr and the Mosaic Law* (SBLDS 20; Missoula, Mt.: Scholars, 1975), 50, who thinks that because Justin was a Samaritan, he believed tassels were scarlet rather than blue (*Dial.* 46.5) and that hot water should not be drunk on the Sabbath (19.3 [sic!]; this is 29.3). It seems risky, however, to base an argument about Justin's thought on his Samaritan background, both because second-century Samaritanism is not a known quantity (see Reinhard Pummer, *The Samaritans* [Iconography of Religions 23.5; Brill: Leiden, 1987]), and because it is not even clear that Justin had been a Samaritan by anything but race. Tessa Rajak reads *Dialogue* 29 to mean that Justin had been a pagan, so that the term *genos* should only be understood of his people (120), not his thought; Rajak, "Talking at Trypho," 512. In a brief but helpful treatment, Peter Pilhofer, "Von Jakobus zu Justin. Lernen in den spätschriften des Neues Testaments und bei den Apologeten," in *Religiöse Lernen in der biblischen, frühjüdischen und frühchristlichen Überlieferung*, ed. Beate Ego and Helmut Merkel (WUNT 180; Tübingen: Mohr Siebeck, 2005), 253–69, at 265, suggests, "Justin sieht sich in einer Schultradition: Er hat eine Lehre empfagen, die er seinerseits nun weitergibt."

12. See Bernard Grossfeld and Moses Aberbach, *Targum Onqelos on Genesis 49: Translation and Analytic Commentary* (SBL Aramaic Studies 1; Missoula, Mt.: Scholars, 1976). Grossfeld was an early advocate of what has since become a consensus, that the earliest Targumim represent Judaism during the second century, not only within rabbinic discussion, but as that discussion was intended to influence popular practice and belief; see Bruce Chilton, "The Targumim and Judaism of the First Century," in *Judaism in Late Antiquity*, part 3, *Where We Stand: Issues and Debates in Ancient Judaism*, vol. 2, ed. J. Neusner and A. J. Avery-Peck (Handbuch der Orientalistik 41; Leiden: Brill, 1999), 15–150.

13. Justin also uses this argument as a weapon in his dispute with Marcion. The theme as a whole is explored in J. C. M. van Winden, *An Early Christian Philosopher: Justin Martyr's Dialogue with Trypho, Chapters One to Nine* (Philosophia Patrum 1; Leiden: Brill, 1971).

14. Bobichon, *Dialogue*, 1:81–82.

15. Wartelle, *Apologies*, 246 cites the same theme among other apologists, as well as writers in the classical tradition.

16. See Ben Witherington III, "Not So Idle Thoughts about EIDOLOTHUTON," *Tyndale Bulletin* 44, no. 2 (1993): 237–54.

17. See Bruce Chilton with Jacob Neusner, *Judaism in the New Testament: Practices and Beliefs* (London and New York: Routledge, 1995).

18. To this extent, the rabbinic project is more Aristotelian than Platonic; see Jacob Neusner, *The Theology of the Oral Torah: Revealing the Justice of God* (Montreal: McGill-Queen's University Press, 1999).

19. Edward Kessler, *Bound by the Bible: Jews, Christians, and the Sacrifice of Isaac* (Cambridge: Cambridge University Press, 2004), 19.

20. On the necessary element of supercessionism in Paul, see Chilton, *Rabbi Paul: An Intellectual Biography* (New York: Doubleday, 2004).

21. Bobichon, *Dialogue, ad loc.*: "Nous ne sommes plus dans une logique d'accomplisse-

ment (comme dans le Nouveau Testament), mais de substitution." On the phrase "la race israélite (*israèlitikon genos*) véritable, spirituelle," see Bernard Meunier, "Le clivage entre Juifs et chrétiens vu part Justin (vers 150)," in *Le Judaïsme à l'aube de l'ère chrétienne. XVIIIe congres de l'ACFEB (Lyon, September 1999)*, ed. Philippe Abadie and Jean-Pierre Lémonon (LD 186; Paris: du Cerf, 2001), 333–44, at 336. This leads to his conclusion (344): "Le judiaisme est à la rigueur hébergé par le chrétiens, ce n'est en aucun case l'inverse."

22. See Philippe Bobichon, "Préceptes éternels de la Loi mosaïque et le *Dialogue avec Tryphon* de Justin Martyr," *RB* 111, no. 2 (2004): 238–54, at 238 (trans. from English summary at 239).

23. Stylianopoulos, *Justin Martyr and the Mosaic Law*, 55.

24. Peter Schäfer, *Die Vorstellung vom heiligen Geist in der rabbinischen Literatur* (SANT 28; München: Kösel, 1972).

25. A probable awareness of the Birkhat ha-Minim causes him to reinterpret Gal. 3:10 in *Dialogue* 95–96. As Lieu, "Accusations of Jewish Persecution," 291, says, "On the one hand, the scriptural 'cursed be everyone who hangs on a tree' anticipates how the Jews would treat both Christ and Christians, yet, on the other, it also sets into sharp relief the Christian response of steadfastness and forgiveness."

26. Rodney Werline, "The Transformation of Pauline Arguments in Justin Martyr's *Dialogue with Trypho*," *HTR* 92, no. 1 (1999): 79–93, at 90.

27. See Bruce Chilton, "Prophecy in the Targumim," in *Mediators of the Divine: Horizons of Prophecy, Divination, Dreams, and Theurgy in Mediterranean Antiquity*, ed. R. M. Berchman (South Florida Studies in the History of Judaism 163; Atlanta: Scholars, 1998), 185–201.

28. Sylvain Jean Gabriel Sanchez, *Justin Apologiste Chrétien: Travaux sur le Dialogue avec Tryphon de Justin Martyr* (Cahier de la Revue Biblique 50; Paris: J. Gabalda, 2000), 253.

29. Straightforwardly, a "word of encouragement," but Paul goes on to relate the coming of "a savior, Jesus," and proclaims that "the *logos* of this salvation was sent to us" (16:23, 26).

30. Eric Francis Osborn, *Justin Martyr* (BHTh 47; Tübingen: Mohr, 1973), 88, 89.

31. See Sanchez, *Justin Apologiste Chrétien*, 185–94.

32. Cf. Laura Nasrallah, "Mapping the World: Justin, Tatian, Lucian, and the Second Sophistic," *HTR* 98, no. 3 (2005): 283–314.

33. Skarsaune, "Judaism and Hellenism in Justin Martyr," 606.

34. See Bruce Chilton, "Typologies of Memra and the Fourth Gospel," *Targum Studies* 1 (1992): 89–100; and Chilton, *Judaic Approaches to the Gospels* (International Studies in Formative Christianity and Judaism 2; Atlanta: Scholars, 1994), 177–201.

35. See van Winden, *Early Christian Philosopher*, 118.

36. Bobichon, *Dialogue*, 1:500.

37. See Bruce Chilton, *A Feast of Meanings: Eucharistic Theologies from Jesus through Johannine Circles* (NovTSup 72; Leiden: Brill, 1994); and Graham Keith, "Justin Martyr and Religious Exclusivism," *Tyndale Bulletin* 43, no. 1 (1992): 57–80.

38. See Stylianopoulos, *Justin Martyr and the Mosaic Law*, 49, observing the specification in Yoma 6:1 that the two goats must be alike (cf. *Dial.* 40.4).

39. Graham N. Stanton, "Justin Martyr's *Dialogue with Trypho*: Group Boundaries, 'Proselytes,' and 'God-fearers,'" in *Tolerance and Intolerance in Early Judaism and Christianity*, ed. Stanton and Stroumsa, 263–78.

40. See Bruce Chilton, "James and the (Christian) Pharisees," in *When Judaism and Christianity Began: Essays in Memory of Anthony J. Saldarini*, vol. 1, *Christianity in the Beginning*, ed. A. J. Avery-Peck, D. Harrington, and J. Neusner (JSJSup 85; Leiden: Brill, 2004), 19–47.

6. Was John's Gospel among
Justin's *Apostolic Memoirs?*

1. J. W. Pryor, "Justin Martyr and the Fourth Gospel," *SecCent* 9 (1992): 153–69, at 157. Some, however, hold that Justin did not know the Fourth Gospel (for example, A. J. Bellinzoni, *The Sayings of Jesus in the Writings of Justin Martyr* [NovTSup 17; Leiden: Brill, 1967]; Helmut Koester, *Ancient Christian Gospels: Their History and Development* [Philadelphia: Fortress Press, 1990], 246). Peter Hofrichter, "Logoslehre und Gottesbild bei Apologeten, Modalisten und Gnostikern. Johanneische Christologie im Licht ihrer frühesten Rezeption," in *Monotheismus und Christologie. Zur Gottesfrage im hellenistischen Judentum und im Urchristentum*, ed. H.-J. Klauck (Quaestiones Disputatae 138; Freiburg: Herder, 1992), 186–217, at 193–97, thinks Justin relied on a form of the Johannine prologue that was still independent of the Fourth Gospel. He suggests Justin may have known but only conditionally accepted the Gospel itself.

2. G. N. Stanton, "Jesus Traditions and Gospels in Justin Martyr and Irenaeus," in *The Biblical Canons*, J.-M. Auwers and H. J. de Jonge (BEThL 163; Leuven: Peeters, 2003), 353–70, at 364. Craig D. Allert, *Revelation, Truth, Canon, and Interpretation: Studies in Justin Martyr's Dialogue with Trypho* (VCSup 64; Leiden: Brill, 2002), 100, says, "the Memoirs are the Synoptic Gospels (and possibly the Gospel of John)" and believes Justin's *Logos* doctrine relied on John, but later he voices agreement with Bellinzoni that the sayings of Jesus in Justin show absolutely no dependence on John and says that the same applies to Justin's use of narrative material (202). (See also Oskar Skarsaune's essay, "Justin and His Bible," in this volume.)

3. See C. E. Hill, *The Johannine Corpus in the Early Church* (Oxford: Oxford University Press, 2004; corrected pbk. ed. 2006), 325–28.

4. One example is *1 Apol.* 32.10, "And the first power after God the Father and Lord of all is the Word, who is also the Son; and of Him we will, in what follows, relate how He took flesh and became man [σαρκοποιηθεὶς ἄνθρωπος γέγονεν]" (trans. from *ANF* 1). Of this passage Wartelle says, "Ce texte semble bien être écrit avec le souvenir précis du Prologue de l'*Évangile de Jean*" (André Wartelle, *Saint Justin. Apologies*, introduction, texte critique, traduction, commentaire et index [Paris: Études augustiniennes, 1987], 271).

5. Hill, *Johannine Corpus*, 316–25.

6. My translation. As Hofrichter, "Logoslehre und Gottesbild," 194, says, "Auch den Titel des 'Eingeborenen', den Philo nicht kennt, kann Justin (Dial 105,1; 1 Apol 33,6) kaum von anderswo als aus dem 'Johannesprolog' übernommen haben, denn er gebraucht diesen Titel im Zusammenhang mit dem Ursprung des Logos aus dem Vater, und dieser Kontext entspricht nur Joh 1,14."

7. Grant, on the other hand, says, "It is hard to restrict what the apostles taught to the virgin birth," that is, to what he might have taken only from Matthew and Luke (R. M. Grant, *Greek Apologists of the Second Century* [Philadelphia: Westminster, 1988], 58). See also most recently Everett Ferguson, "Factors Leading to the Selection and Closure of the New Testament Canon: A Survey of Some Recent Studies," in *The Canon Debate*, ed. Lee Martin McDonald and James A. Sanders (Peabody, Mass.: Hendrickson, 2002), 295–320, at 302–3.

8. Pryor, "Justin Martyr," 156–57. Pryor is correct that chap. 78 summarizes events surrounding Jesus' birth taken from Matthew and Luke. But even here, Justin does not give his Christian sources by name. He returns to the incarnation in chap. 100, where the "Gospel" and the "memoirs of his apostles" are mentioned, but only Luke 1:35 is cited explicitly for attestation of the incarnation. In this section, however, we also seem to have Johannine allusions. In 100.2 Christ is "the firstborn of God and before all creatures; . . . since he was made flesh

[σαρκοποιηθείς] by the virgin . . . and submitted to become a man." As can be seen in *1 Apol.* 32.10, 66.2; *Dial.* 84.2, 87.2, this is based on John 1:14 and belongs to a whole vocabulary of ontological and incarnational terms that are indebted to John's prologue.

9. Ἐμάθομεν in 105.1, συνήκαμεν in 81.3, and νενοήκαμεν in 75.1 and 100.1 all refer to something Justin and other Christians have learned, understood, or perceived from the Scriptures, but which cannot be attributed to Trypho and his friends.

10. So also Hofrichter, "Logoslehre und Gottesbild," 194.

11. See esp. Hill, *Johannine Corpus*, 319–20.

12. Here he refers to some material from Luke and Matthew as the teaching of those "who have recorded [οἱ ἀπομνημονεύσαντες] all that concerns our Saviour Jesus Christ." I take this, too, to be a reference to the *Memoirs*.

13. In 34.2 he mentions "the registers of the things which took place under Cyrenius [ἐκ τῶν ἀπογραφῶν τῶν γενομένων ἐπὶ Κυρηνίου], your first procurator in Judea," referring to Luke 2:1-5.

14. Often mistranslated as "Acts of Pilate," the title could be either "Acts Drawn Up under Pontius Pilate" or "Acts Which Occurred under Pontius Pilate."

15. See Koester, *Ancient Christian Gospels*, 42; Wartelle, *Apologies*, 273, on 35.9.

16. So Leslie W. Barnard, *St. Justin Martyr: The First and Second Apologies* (Ancient Christian Writers 56; New York: Paulist Press, 1997), 151 n. 242.

17. Koester, *Ancient Christian Gospels*, 41–42.

18. This assumed accessibility ties in with an interesting comment made recently by J. Eldon Epp, "Issues in the Interrelation of New Testament Textual Criticism and Canon," in *The Canon Debate*, ed. McDonald and Sanders, 485–515, at 512. Commenting on the modest page sizes of the earliest NT papyri, Epp writes, "This suggests that the media commonly used by and most appealing to early Christians were codices in the earliest attested form and sizes, which, in turn, rated high in portability, a feature not only valuable to early Christian travelers in their mission, but also convenient and practical in the dissemination of the writings they carried and used."

19. Charles E. Hill, "What Papias Said about John (and Luke): A 'New' Papian Fragment," *JTS*, n.s., 49 (1998): 582–629, esp. 595–96, and see below.

20. The passive participle, aorist or perfect, of πράσσω is also used four times in this account.

21. We do not know just when the title "Acts of the Apostles" came into use (it is in the uncials, ℵ, B, D, Ψ; we do not have the beginning of Acts in a papyrus), but in all likelihood it was in use by Justin's time, for Irenaeus refers to it as such (*Adv. Haer.* 3.13.3).

22. Such a title would have been seen as coming from Luke's introductory words in Luke 1:1, "Inasmuch as many have undertaken to compile a narrative of the things [or acts, πραγμάτων] which have been accomplished among us . . ."

23. Matt. 27:19 mentions sitting on the judgment seat, but the rest of the sentence makes it clear that it must be Pilate who is sitting and not Jesus.

24. Justin uses the plural ἐκάθισαν, imputing the action to "the Jews."

25. Including von Harnack, Loisy, Macgregor, and Bonsirven. See the commentaries of Barrett and Brown.

26. Koester, *Ancient Christian Gospels*, 397. Koester posits that all three works are based on a common written source. But pending the discovery of that source, it is much simpler to suppose that it is John's account that has been developed by relating it to Isa. 58:2 in Christian schools like Justin's, and thus that the *Gospel of Peter* is either dependent upon Justin or simply using the same testimony tradition related to John 19:13. On the *Gospel of Peter*'s dependence

upon John, see Hill, *Johannine Corpus*, 306–9, and on its relationship to Justin, see further Paul Foster's essay in this volume.

27. "And they put upon him a purple robe and set him on the seat of judgment [ἐκάθισαν αὐτὸν ἐπὶ καθέδραν κρίσεως] and said, 'Judge righteously, O king of Israel'" (3.7). See Hill, *Johannine Corpus*, 330–31.

28. See the article "Crucifixion in Antiquity" by Joe Zias at http://www.centuryone.org/crucifixion2.html. The crucified man found in 1968 near Giv'at ha-Mivtar was nailed at the feet, but apparently his arms were tied to the crossbar. Zias points out that Christian art often portrays the two thieves on Jesus' sides as being tied to their crosses.

29. That John mentions them not in his account of the crucifixion but in the story of Thomas after the resurrection is hardly evidence, as Koester, *Ancient Christian Gospels*, 397 n. 2, seems to think, against John being the source for Justin and the *Gospel of Peter*. Justin refers to the nails in the context of the crucifixion, but to the *Gospel of Peter* in the descent from the cross. We have seen above that Celsus, perhaps in Rome, only a few years later knows John's account (Origen, *C. Cels.* 2.55).

30. Ps.-Barn. 5.14 cites a condensation of Ps. 119:120, "nail my flesh" (καθήλωσόν μου τὰς σάρκας), in reference to the crucifixion. Ign. *Smyrn.* 1.1–2 also refers to Christ's being nailed (καθηλωμένος) for us, and our being established in faith "as if nailed to the cross of the Lord Jesus Christ." See Koester, *Ancient Christian Gospels*, 397. Once again, the *Gospel of Peter*, like Justin, knows of the nails drawn out of Jesus' hands during his descent from the cross (6.21)

31. He does cite the entire verse in his exegesis of the Psalm in *Dialogue* 97, 104. His elaboration on the fulfillment in 97.3 is not inconsistent with John's account, pace Pryor. Indeed, Justin's mention of the nails and the λαχμός in this very section would seem to point to a knowledge of John's crucifixion narrative.

32. The *Gospel of Peter* 4.12 also refers only to plural garments, but uses another word, τὰ ἐνδύματα.

33. See Hill, *Johannine Corpus*, 328–30.

34. Ibid., 325–28.

35. See Martin Hengel, *Die johanneische Frage: Ein Lösungsversuch*, with a contribution on the Apocalpyse by Jörg Frey (WUNT 67; Tübingen: Mohr, 1993); Titus Nagel, *Die Rezeption des Johannesevangeliums im 2. Jahrhundert: Studien zur vorirenäischen Auslegung des vierten Evangeliums in christlicher und christlich-gnostischer Literatur* (Arbeiten zur Bibel und ihrer Geschichte 2; Leipzig: Evangelische Verlagsanstalt, 2000); Hill, *Johannine Corpus*.

36. Hill, *Johannine Corpus*, 309–11.

7. Interpreting the Descent of the Spirit

1. Rather than expecting the deliverance of the nation, Justin seems to anticipate that some individual Jews will receive grace from God (*Dial.* 64.2–3) by believing in Jesus as Messiah (see, for example, *Dial.* 32.2; 39.1–2; 55.3).

2. For further discussion of this motif in Justin's writings, see Jeffrey Siker, *Disinheriting the Jews: Abraham in Early Christian Controversy* (Louisville: Westminster John Knox, 1991), 184; Annette Yoshiko Reed, "The Trickery of the Fallen Angels and the Demonic Mimesis of the Divine: Aetiology, Demonology, and Polemics in the Writings of Justin Martyr," *Journal of Early Christian Studies* 12, no. 2 (2004): 141–71, at 156.

3. See Siker, *Disinheriting the Jews*, 192–95; Judith M. Lieu, *Image and Reality: The Jews in the World of Christians in the Second Century* (Edinburgh: T&T Clark, 1996), 103. For discussion

of the development of *Adversus Iudaeos* literature, see Guy G. Stroumsa, "From Anti-Judaism to Antisemitism in Early Christianity," in *Contra Iudaeos,* ed. Ora Limor and Guy G. Stroumsa (Texts and Studies in Medieval and Early Modern Judaism; Tübingen: Mohr, 1996), 1–26.

4. See, for example, Hans Conzelmann, *Acts of the Apostles,* trans. James Limburg et al. (Hermeneia; Philadelphia: Fortress Press, 1987); Lloyd Gaston, "Anti-Judaism and the Passion Narrative in Luke and Acts," in *Anti-Judaism in Early Christianity,* ed. Peter Richardson and David Granskou (Waterloo: Wilfred Laurier, 1986), 1:127–53; Jack T. Sanders, "The Jewish People in Luke-Acts," in *Luke-Acts and the Jewish People: Eight Critical Perspectives,* ed. Joseph B. Tyson (Minneapolis: Augsburg, 1988), 58–72.

5. Scholars still debate the form of the New Testament traditions that Justin uses. Most agree, however, that he relies on written material that has some relationship with the Gospels of Matthew and Luke, whether a Gospel harmony based on these texts or the texts themselves. See, for example, Helmut Koester, *Ancient Christian Gospels: Their History and Development* (London: SCM, 1990), 37–40; Graham N. Stanton, *Jesus and Gospel* (Cambridge: Cambridge University Press, 2004), 99–105; Craig D. Allert, *Revelation, Truth, Canon, and Interpretation* (VCSup 114; Leiden: Brill, 2002), 20–21, 100–101, 194–95; and Oskar Skarsaune's contribution to this volume.

6. Oskar Skarsaune, *Proof from Prophecy: A Study in Justin Martyr's Proof-Text Tradition: Text-Type, Provenance, Theological Profile* (NovTSup 106; Leiden: Brill, 1987), 256–59, 362.

7. See, for example, Erwin R. Goodenough, *The Theology of Justin Martyr* (Jena: Frommannsche Buchhandlung, 1923), 97; Willis A. Shotwell, *The Biblical Exegesis of Justin Martyr* (London: SPCK, 1965), 7; Eric Francis Osborn, *Justin Martyr* (BHTh 47; Tübingen: Mohr, 1973), 165–67; Marc Hirshman, *A Rivalry of Genius: Jewish and Christian Biblical Interpretation in Late Antiquity,* trans. Batya Stein-Hirshman (Albany: State University of New York Press, 1996), 19–21; Siker, *Disinheriting the Jews,* 184.

8. Luke opens his two-volume work by indicating that it is "a narrative concerning the things that have been fulfilled" (Luke 1:1—διήγησιν περὶ τῶν πεπληροφορημένων ἐν ἡμῖν πραγμάτων). For further discussion regarding the motif of fulfillment in Luke-Acts, see Charles H. Talbert, *Reading Acts: A Literary and Theological Commentary on the Acts of the Apostles* (Reading the New Testament; New York: Crossroad, 1997), 2–3; Darrell Bock, "Scripture and the Realisation of God's Promises," in *Witness to the Gospel: The Theology of Acts,* ed. I. Howard Marshall and David Peterson (Grand Rapids: Eerdmans, 1998), 41–62, at 46; William Kurz, "Promise and Fulfillment in Hellenistic Jewish Narratives and in Luke and Acts," in *Jesus and the Heritage of Israel,* ed. David P. Moessner (Harrisburg: Trinity Press International, 1999), 147–70, at 148.

9. As Gregory Sterling maintains, *Historiography and Self-Definition: Josephus, Luke-Acts and Apologetic Historiography* (NovTSup 114; Leiden: Brill, 1992), 381–88, Luke wrote in continuity with the LXX and intended his account to be read as sacred text. According to Kugel, in James L. Kugel and Rowan A. Greer, *Early Biblical Interpretation* (Library of Early Christianity; Philadelphia: Westminster, 1986), 47, this approach is consistent with the tendency of interpreters and writers of the Second Temple period to incorporate the present into biblical history by giving current events or recent history a biblical aura.

10. There is no scholarly consensus regarding the ultimate fate of the Jewish people in Luke-Acts, but it is more widely recognized that the opening chapters of Acts envisage positive expectations for Jews. In *The Theology of the Acts of the Apostles* (Cambridge: Cambridge University Press, 1996), 44–45, Jacob Jervell argues that Luke presents the descent of the Spirit as the restoration of Israel in Acts 1–2. Similarly, Max Turner argues that Luke portrays the first outpouring of the Spirit as an initial phase of Israel's renewal in *Power from On High: The Spirit in*

Israel's Restoration and Witness in Luke-Acts (Sheffield: Sheffield Academic Press, 1996), 309–10. Likewise, David L. Tiede asserts that Jesus' exaltation and the sending of the Spirit result in the restoration of Israel's vocation as the servant of the Lord, in "The Exaltation of Jesus and the Restoration of Israel in Acts 1," *HTR* 79 (1986): 279–86. Although Jack Sanders, "The Jewish People," 58–73, argues that the Jewish people ultimately reject the gospel and so are rejected in Luke-Acts, he recognizes that they receive the message of repentance positively in the early chapters of Acts. Robert C. Tannehill, *The Narrative Unity of Luke-Acts: A Literary Interpretation* (Foundations and Facets; Philadelphia: Fortress Press, 1986–90), 2:26–42, 344–456, also maintains that the majority of Jews reject the gospel, but he recognizes that God offers restoration to them in the narrative. Still others, such as Richard Bauckham, "The Restoration of Israel in Luke-Acts," in *Restoration: Old Testament, Jewish, and Christian Perspectives*, ed. James M. Scott (Boston: Brill, 2001), 435–87, suggest that Luke depicts the success of the gospel among Jews (e.g., Acts 21:20) as their restoration; cf. Jervell, *Theology*, 34–43. Furthermore, Bauckham maintains that Luke presents an open, and potentially positive, future for the Jewish people.

11. Justin's account of the Spirit-baptism of Jesus in *Dialogue* 87–88 appears to draw upon material from both Matthew and Luke.

12. In the context of Jesus' baptism in *Dial.* 88.8, Justin cites a phrase from Ps. 2:7: "You are my son: today I have begotten you," a statement paralleled in some "Western" readings of Luke 3:22 (for example, codex D). Other manuscript traditions of Luke 3:22 make the link to Ps. 2:7 less certain: "You are my beloved son, in whom I am well pleased" (cf. Mark 1:11; Matt. 3:17). In *Proclamation from Prophecy and Pattern: Lucan Old Testament Christology* (JSNTSup 12; Sheffield: JSOT, 1987), 99–104, Darrell Bock notes the numerous scholarly perspectives regarding the possible scriptural allusions in Luke 3:22 (for example, Ps. 2:7; Isaiah 42; Genesis 22; Exod. 4:22-23; Isa. 41:8, 42:1, and 44:2 together; or Ps. 2:7 and Isa. 41:8 and 42:1 together) and concludes that no single allusion is explicit. Notwithstanding this uncertainty, Luke's statement appears to highlight the status of Jesus as Messiah, prophet, and beloved Son of God, whereas Justin's citation of Ps. 2:7 emphasizes the messianic role of Christ. See also Francis Bovon, *A Commentary on the Gospel of Luke 1:1—9:50*, trans. Christine M. Thomas (Hermeneia; Minneapolis: Fortress Press, 2002), 128–31.

13. Luke places the imprisonment of John prior to his account of the baptism of Jesus but still indicates that Jesus was baptized when all the people were baptized, which may imply that John baptized him (Luke 3:18-20). Justin indicates that John was baptizing at the Jordan River when Jesus was baptized, but he does not specify that John was the baptizer of Jesus. Compare the descriptions of the baptism of Jesus by John in Matt. 3:13-17 and Mark 1:9-11.

14. Luke emphasizes the "power" of Jesus' ministry and links it more closely to the anointing of the Spirit than do the other Synoptic accounts. For example, Jesus returns from his wilderness temptations "in the power of the Spirit" (Luke 4:14; cf. Mark 1:14a and Matt. 4:12); the Spirit empowers Jesus' ministry (Luke 4:18-19, 36; cf. Mark 6:1-6a and Matt. 13:53-58); power (presumably from the Spirit) proceeds from Jesus and heals people (Luke 5:17; 6:19; 8:46; cf. Mark 3:10 and Matt. 9:21; 14:36); and Peter recounts Jesus' ministry by explaining how God anointed Jesus of Nazareth with the Holy Spirit and with power (Acts 10:38).

15. Justin also uses δύναμις in conjunction with λόγος to describe Christ prior to his incarnation (*1 Apol.* 23.3, 32.10, 33.6; *Dial.* 105.1, 125.3, 128.4); because he had/was "power," he did not need the "powers" of the Holy Spirit (τῶν δυνάμεων τοῦ πνεύματος τοῦ ἁγίου). See Demetrius C. Trakatellis's discussion of Justin's christological use of δύναμις in *The Pre-Existence of Christ in Justin Martyr: An Exegetical Study with Reference to the Humiliation and Exaltation Christology* (Missoula, Mt.: Scholars, 1976), 27–37.

16. Citations of the *Dialogue* are taken from Philippe Bobichon, *Justin Martyr. Dialogue*

avec Tryphon, édition critique, traduction, commentaire (Paradosis 47/1–2; Fribourg: Academic Press, 2003).

17. Cf. *Dial.* 87.5, where Justin states that it was necessary for the gifts to cease from operating "among you," that is, from among Jews.

18. The feminine genitive plural participle may best be interpreted as a genitive of destination. See Daniel B. Wallace, *Greek Grammar Beyond the Basics* (Grand Rapids: Zondervan, 1996), 100–101. Herbert Weir Smyth describes a similar use of the genitive, "genitive of the end attained," in *Greek Grammar* (Cambridge, Mass.: Harvard University Press, 1956), 321, no. 1349. Additionally, when μέλλω occurs with a present infinitive, it can "denote an action that necessarily follows a divine decree." See Frederick William Danker, *A Greek-English Lexicon of the New Testament and Other Early Christian Literature* (Chicago: University of Chicago Press, 2000), 628. For Justin, the destined resting place of the Spirit was Jesus rather than Jewish prophets.

19. If we interpret the τοῦ . . . γενήσεσθαι as an infinitive of purpose, Justin's account of the bestowal of the Spirit upon Jesus reads as an event that occurred for the very purpose of bringing an end to the activity of the Spirit among Israel's prophets.

20. Skarsaune, *Proof from Prophecy*, 196–99, suggests that Justin was working with two sources in *Dialogue* 87–88, one that linked LXX Isa. 11:2ff. with a messianic anointing (87.3—88.2) and another that portrayed Jesus as a second Adam who possessed the powers of the Spirit from birth (88.3–8). In his view, Justin resists making a connection between the baptism of Jesus and Isaiah 11 in order to avoid promoting an adoptionist theology.

21. Compare *Dialogue* 49–51, especially 51.1–2. In *Proof from Prophecy*, 196–97, Skarsaune notes that Justin does not focus upon what happens to Jesus, at the point of his baptism, but instead provides an account of what happens to John: "Just as Jesus made John cease prophesying and baptizing [in *Dialogue* 49–51], so he puts an end to the distribution of the gifts of the Spirit among the Jews" in *Dial.* 87.3–5 (197).

22. See Joseph A. Fitzmyer, *The Gospel according to Luke I–IX* (AB 28; Garden City, N.Y.: Doubleday, 1981), 213; N. T. Wright, *Jesus and the Victory of God* (Minneapolis: Fortress Press, 1996), 147–97; Scot McKnight, *A New Vision for Israel: The Teachings of Jesus in National Context* (Grand Rapids: Eerdmans, 1999), 4–5.

23. Despite the Nazareth crowd's rejection of Jesus in Luke 4:22-30, Jesus continues to minister primarily to Jews in Luke's narrative (e.g., 4:44). As Scot McKnight explains in his essay "Gentiles, Gentile Mission," in *Dictionary of the Later New Testament and Its Developments*, ed. Ralph P. Martin and Peter H. Davids (Downers Grove, Ill.: InterVarsity Press, 1997), 391, Luke 4:26-27 affirms the Gentile mission, but God's salvation was offered to all people only after it was offered to Jews throughout Luke-Acts (see, e.g., the Jew-first strategy in Acts 3:23, 26; 13:46).

24. These Christ-believers may be Jews as well as Gentiles, as is evident in *Dial.* 39.2, where Justin refers to Jews who become Christians and receive the gifts of the Spirit.

25. Regarding the use of μέλλω together with a present infinitive, see n. 18. The context of the fulfillment of prophecy also suggests that "is destined," "must," or "will certainly" would be a fitting translation.

26. Darrell Bock concludes, "The Spirit's coming represents the inauguration of the kingdom blessing promised by the Father in the OT"; *Luke* (Baker Exegetical Commentary on the New Testament 3; Grand Rapids: Baker Books, 1996), 2:1943. According to Luke Timothy Johnson, *The Gospel of Luke* (Sacra Pagina; Collegeville, Minn.: Liturgical Press, 1991), 403, the idea of the descent of the Spirit as "the promise" is also associated with the fulfillment of God's promises to Abraham. He maintains that Luke-Acts makes the concept of promise roughly equivalent to the "blessing" made by God to Abraham (Acts 2:39; 3:24-26; 13:32; 26:6).

27. Turner, *Power*, 309–10.

28. Note also the parallel wording in the two servant passages themselves: LXX Isa. 42:6 (ἔδωκά σε εἰς διαθήκην γένους, εἰς φῶς ἐθνῶν) and 49:6 (ἰδοὺ τέθεικά σε εἰς διαθήκην γένους, εἰς φῶς ἐθνῶν).

29. C. K. Barrett, *The Acts of the Apostles* (ICC; Edinburgh: T&T Clark, 1994), 1:79–80, notes the allusion to Isa. 43:10 in Acts 1:8 and the possibility of an allusion to Isa. 49:6. Similarly, Tannehill, *Narrative Unity*, 2:17–18, argues that Isa. 49:6 is the source of the allusion in Acts 1:8 and that the phrase ἕως ἐσχάτου τῆς γῆς implies an ethnic inclusion.

30. Tiede, "Restoration of Israel," 279–86.

31. Even in *1 Apology* 50, where we read that Jesus sent his power upon the disciples after his ascension, there is no mention of the Spirit.

32. In a recent essay, Graham Stanton describes Justin's understanding of the Spirit as being deeply rooted in New Testament texts, but observes that "Justin goes his own way" in the double claim that prophecy had ceased among Israel and the gifts of the Spirit were now only among Christians. This, Stanton suggests, may be a corollary of the conviction that Christians are the true Israel. See "The Spirit in the Writings of Justin Martyr," in *The Holy Spirit and Christian Origins: Essays in Honor of James D. G. Dunn*, ed. Graham N. Stanton, Bruce W. Longenecker, and Stephen C. Barton (Grand Rapids: Eerdmans, 2004), 321–34, at 334.

33. Skarsaune, *Proof from Prophecy*, 100, and Stanton, "The Spirit in the Writings of Justin Martyr," 332, indicate that Justin appears to follow the quotation of LXX Ps. 67:18 found in Eph. 4:8, suggesting his dependence on the latter.

34. Acts 2:17 situates Joel's prophecy in an eschatological context by referring to the "last days," whereas Justin uses the LXX phrase "after these things." Nevertheless, there is little doubt that both Luke and Justin cite the same passage. Justin's addition of "my" with male and female servants suggests that he was following Acts 2:17, or the same version of the LXX that Luke quotes. The addition of "my" to "servants" occurs in Acts, Justin, Tertullian, and Augustine, but not in extant versions of the LXX nor in the Masoretic Text. See Stanton's discussion in "The Spirit in the Writings of Justin Martyr," 332.

35. Stanton, "The Spirit in the Writings of Justin Martyr," 326–27, notes that Justin also uses the phrase "prophetic spirit" twenty-five times in the *Apologies*; cf. Leslie W. Barnard, *Justin Martyr: His Life and Thought* (Cambridge: Cambridge University Press, 1967), 102–5.

36. The discrepancies between LXX Joel 3:1-2 and the form of its citation in the Codex Bezae of Acts 2:17, 39 are noteworthy insofar as they bear some similarity to the changes made by Justin. The Codex Bezae rendering of Joel 3:1-2, however, takes the alteration to the LXX even further by changing the second-person plural pronouns to the third person when modifying "sons" and "daughters" and by removing the second-person plural pronouns from "young men" and "elders." This, in addition to the change of the phrase "upon all flesh" from the singular (ἐπὶ πᾶσαν σάρκα) to the plural (ἐπὶ πάσας σάρκας), makes the text read as a universalistic statement that has no particular application to Jews whatsoever: "I will pour out my Spirit upon all flesh and their sons and their daughters shall prophesy and young men shall see visions and elders shall dream dreams" (ἐκχεῶ ἀπὸ τοῦ πνεύματός μου ἐπὶ πάσας σάρκας, καὶ προφητεύσουσιν οἱ υἱοὶ αὐτῶν καὶ αἱ θυγατέρες αὐτῶν, καὶ οἱ νεανίσκοι ὁράσεις ὄψονται, καὶ οἱ πρεσβύτεροι ἐνυπνιασθήσονται). Furthermore, Codex Bezae renders Acts 2:39 as a promise for those who have already received the Spirit (that is, the apostles and their group), rather than a promise for the Jews in his audience: "For the promise is for us and for our children" (ἡμῖν γὰρ ἐστιν ἡ ἐπαγγελία καὶ τοῖς τέκνοις ἡμῶν). Regarding these adaptations, Eldon Jay Epp concludes that the Codex Bezae's "conception of Peter's address as envisioning Gentiles is contradictory to the Lucan conception that the sermon here was directed only toward Jews (though they were Jews from all over the world) and that the Gentile mission first began later with Cornelius." See *The Theological Tendency of Codex Bezae Cantabrigiensis in Acts* (SNTSMS 3; Cambridge:

Cambridge University Press, 1966), 69. For a more recent discussion of Acts 2:17-39 in the Bezan text, see Josep Rius-Camps and Jenny Read-Heimerdinger, *The Message of Acts in Codex Bezae: A Comparison with the Alexandrian Tradition* (JSNTSup 257; London: T&T Clark, 2004), 1:169–91.

37. In *Proof from Prophecy*, 122–23, Skarsaune expresses his uncertainty regarding this unusual citation—he wonders if it is the unique work of Justin, a composition from someone who used the Hebrew text rather than the LXX, or a condensed version of the Acts citation. Stanton, "The Spirit in the Writings of Justin Martyr," 332–33, suggests that Justin used a condensed version of the Acts testimony.

38. Koester, *Ancient Christian Gospels*, 378.

8. The Relationship between the Writings of Justin Martyr and the So-Called *Gospel of Peter*

1. The term "reader" is here used as a shorthand both for those who read the text or epistle (in the case of Paul's writings) and for the probably larger group of auditors who had the text read to them by a lector.

2. Richard B. Hays, *Echoes of Scripture in the Letters of Paul* (New Haven: Yale University Press, 1989).

3. Christopher M. Tuckett, "Paul, Scripture, and Ethics: Some Reflections," *NTS* 46 (2000): 403–24.

4. Ibid., 406–7, esp. n. 11.

5. No claims for early notions of canonicity are being made here (especially in relation to the writings that formed the New Testament); rather, it is simply acknowledged that such writings probably carried a greater authority than a number of other Christian writings, although there were to be ongoing debates about which writings were to be considered authoritative.

6. G. M. Soares-Prabhu, *The Formulas Quotations in the Infancy Narrative of Matthew* (Rome: Biblical Institute Press, 1976).

7. One of the most striking examples of this phenomenon occurs in the address of John the Baptist to the "brood of vipers," Matt. 3:7-10//Luke 3:7-9. The actual words of the Baptist as they appear in the Greek of both Gospels are virtually identical, but the brief narrative introductions show that the evangelists saw these words addressed to different recipients: for Matthew, "Pharisees and Sadducees"; for Luke, "the crowds." This is strongly suggestive of the independent use of a common source. Thus, although the level of correspondence is extremely high (Matthew uses 76 words in his version and Luke 72, with 61 common words), other factors make direct literary borrowing unlikely.

8. John S. Kloppenborg Verbin, *Excavating Q: The History and Setting of the Sayings Gospel* (Edinburgh: T&T Clark, 2000), esp. 11–111.

9. For a fuller discussion of this problem, see P. Foster, "The Epistles of Ignatius of Antioch and the Writings That Later Formed the New Testament," in *The Reception of the New Testament in the Apostolic Fathers*, ed. A. F. Gregory and C. M. Tuckett (Oxford: Oxford University Press, 2005), 173–81.

10. Helmut Koester, *Synoptische Überlieferung bei den Apostolischen Vätern* (TU 65; Berlin: Akademie-Verlag, 1957), 3: "so hängt die Frage der Benutzung davon ab, ob sich in den angeführten Stücken Redaktionsarbeit eines Evangelisten findet."

11. Eusebius, *H.E.* 6.12.

12. P. Pilhofer, "Justin und das Petrusevangelium," *ZNW* 81 (1990): 60–78: "Der *terminus*

ad quem für das Petrusevangelium liegt in den Schriften des Justin (ca. 150/160) vor. Die Entstehung des Petrusevangeliums ist daher m. E. spätestens um 130 anzusetzen."

13. H. B. Swete, *The Akhmîm Fragment of the Apocryphal Gospel of St. Peter* (London: Macmillan, 1893), xxxv.

14. Translations of Justin are taken from ANF 1.

15. W. R. Cassels argues extensively for the phrase ἀπομνημονεύμασιν αὐτοῦ being understood as a reference to the *Gospel of Peter*. See *The Gospel according to Peter: A Study by the Author of "Supernatural Religion"* (London: Longmans, Green, 1894), 20–25.

16. Pilhofer, "Justin und das Petrusevangelium," 68: "Justin hier in der Tat vom Petrusevangelium spricht; denn zieht man die Zitierweise des Justin in Betracht, so wird man es wohl für möglich halten, daß er eine Geschichte aus dem Petrusevangelium mit einer anderen zusammenbringt, die möglicherweise nicht aus dem Petrusevangelium stammt, ohne dies näher zu kennzeichnen."

17. *1 Apology* 66, 67; *Dialogue* 100, 101, 102, 103 (2x), 104, 105 (3x), 106 (3x), 107.

18. Graham N. Stanton, *Jesus and Gospel* (Cambridge: Cambridge University Press, 2004), 101.

19. Of this first possible example Swete says that "it has nothing in common with Peter which cannot be explained by the influence of Ps. ii. and Acts iv." Swete, *Akhmîm Fragment*, xxxiii.

20. Adolf Harnack, *Bruchstücke des Evangeliums und der Apokalypse des Petrus* (Leipzig: J. C. Hinrichs, 1893), 37–40.

21. T. Zahn, *Das Evangelium des Petrus* (Erlangen: Deichert, 1893), 66–70.

22. Pilhofer, "Justin und das Petrusevangelium," 68–72.

23. Harnack, *Bruchstücke*, 39: "Damit scheint Justins Quelle unwidersprechlich aufgedeckt."

24. Swete, *Akhmîm Fragment*, xxxv.

25. See Henry George Liddell and Robert Scott, *A Greek-English Lexicon*, new (9th) ed., ed. Henry Stewart Jones (Oxford: Clarendon, 1940), 413; although G. W. H. Lampe, *A Patristic Greek Lexicon* (Oxford: Clarendon, 1969), 361, provides a meaning closer to that of the simplex form. He offers the translation "to drag roughly."

26. Swete, *Akhmîm Fragment*, xxxv.

27. E. P. Sanders, *The Tendencies of the Synoptic Tradition* (SNTSMS 9; Cambridge: Cambridge University Press, 1969); see chap. 3, "Increasing Detail as a Possible Tendency of the Tradition," 88–189.

28. Swete, *Akhmîm Fragment*, xxxv.

29. Harnack, *Bruchstücke*, 39: "Dial. 97 bietet Justin den Ausdruck λαχμὸν βάλλοντες bei den Vertheilung der Kleider des Herrn. Kein kanonisches Ev. bietet ihn; aber im Petrusev. lesen wir v. 12: λαχμὸν ἔβαλον ἐπ' αὐτοῖς."

30. Pilhofer, "Justin und das Petrusevangelium," 74–75: "Dieser Befund ist m. E. das stärkste Argument für eine literarische Abhängigkeit des Justin vom dem Petrusevangelium."

31. Swete, *Akhmîm Fragment*, xxxiv.

32. See Harnack, *Bruchstücke*, 38; and Cassels, *Gospel according to Peter*, 28.

33. Cassels, *Gospel according to Peter*, 28.

34. See Harnack, *Bruchstücke*, 38, and Cassels, *Gospel according to Peter*, 28.

35. Cassels, *Gospel according to Peter*, 28.

36. Harnack, *Bruchstücke*, 39.

37. See R. E. Brown, "The *Gospel of Peter* and Canonical Gospel Priority," *NTS* 33 (1987): 321–43; *The Death of the Messiah: From Gethsemane to the Grave; A Commentary on the Passion Narratives in the Four Gospels* (New York: Doubleday, 1994), 2:1332–37.

38. Pilhofer, "Justin und das Petrusevangelium," 63–68.
39. A. J. Bellinzoni, *The Sayings of Jesus in the Writings of Justin Martyr* (Leiden: Brill, 1967), 139.
40. Paul Foster was supported by the Arts and Humanities Research Council for a period of research leave during which this article was written. The AHRC funds postgraduate training and research in the arts and humanities, from archaeology and English literature to design and dance. The quality and range of research supported not only provides social and cultural benefits but also contributes to the economic success of the UK. For further information on the AHRC, please see its Web site, http://www.ahrc.ac.uk.

9. Justin Martyr and the Apologetic Tradition

1. Bernard Pouderon, *Les apologistes grecs du IIe siècle* (Initiations aux pères de l'église; Paris: du Cerf, 2005), 14–15.
2. Pouderon adds the *Sentences* of Sextus (*Apologistes*, chap. 15).
3. Mark Edwards, Martin Goodman, and Simon Price, eds., *Apologetics in the Roman Empire: Pagans, Jews, and Christians* (Oxford: Oxford University Press, 1999); the quotation is from Edwards, Goodman, Price, and Christopher Rowland, "Introduction: Apologetics in the Roman World," 1–13, at 1.
4. Martin Goodman, "Josephus' Treatise *Against Apion*," in *Apologetics*, ed. Edwards, Goodman, and Price, 45–58, at 58.
5. On the source of the mistranslation of Tertullian's addressees, see Timothy David Barnes, *Tertullian: A Historical and Literary Study*, rev. ed. (Oxford: Clarendon, 1985), 25.
6. For Tatian, see *H.E.* IV.29.7 and VI.13.7; the three books to Autolycus are "three . . . συγγράμματα" in IV.24.
7. Frances Young, "Greek Apologists of the Second Century," in *Apologetics*, ed. Edwards, Goodman, and Price, 81–104, at 90–92.
8. Michael Frede argues in his essay "Eusebius' Apologetic Writings," in *Apologetics*, ed. Edwards, Goodman, and Price, 223–50, at 225–31, that Eusebius's use of the term *apologia* in his *Preparation for the Gospel* is a good deal looser than that which he employs in the *Ecclesiastical History*, and that he sometimes uses it to describe the *Preparation* itself. Nonetheless, careful examination of all Eusebius's uses of the term in this work shows that he never uses it to describe the genre of this writing as a whole, merely the nature of a section of argument. In the case of his two quotations of 1 Peter 3:14, Eusebius picks up the word *logos* rather than the word *apologia* to describe the looser category of general writings in defense of Christianity (*Praeparatio Evangelica* I.3.6 and I.5.2).
9. Frede, "Eusebius' Apologetic Writings," 224.
10. The Syriac text includes a brief reference to arrests and trials for the name of Christ (15.7), without any reference to the emperor's ability to change the situation. I use the edition of Bernard Pouderon and Marie-Joseph Pierre, *Aristide, Apologie* (SC 470; Paris: du Cerf, 2003).
11. Aristides, *Apology* 17.3 (Syriac).
12. For the evidence, see Pouderon and Pierre, *Aristide*, 25–43.
13. *Eusebius Werke*, V, *Die Chronik aus dem armenischen übersetzt*, trans. Josef Karst (Griechischen Christlichen Schriftsteller 20; Leipzig: J. C. Hinrichs, 1911), 220 (a French translation [based on Karst] is in Pouderon and Pierre, *Aristide*, 26), and *Eusebius Werke*, VII, *Die Chronik des Hieronymus*, ed. Rudolf Helm, 3rd ed. Ursula Treu (Griechischen Christlichen Schriftsteller; Berlin: Akademie-Verlag, 1984), 199.

14. In the *Chronicon* Eusebius does, in fact, claim some sort of causal connection between the rescript and a Hadrianic dating. The reference to Quadratus and Aristides is followed, in the same sentence in Jerome's Latin version, by ". . . and Serenus Granianus, legate and a very noble man, wrote to the emperor. . . . Moved by *these things* [*quibus*, in the plural], Hadrian writes to Minicius Fundanus, Proconsul of Asia" (Hadrian 8, in *Chronik*, ed. Helm, 199).

15. In the *Chronicon*, the only reference to Montanus or Montanism is to the "outbreak" of the movement in, he thinks, 171 (Marcus 11, in *Chronik*, ed. Helm, 206). In the *Historia Ecclesiastica*, he had much fuller information at his disposal.

16. Christine Trevett, *Montanism: Gender, Authority, and the New Prophecy* (Cambridge: Cambridge University Press, 1996), 35–36. William Tabbernee, *Montanist Inscriptions and Testimonia* (Macon, Ga.: Mercer University Press, 1997), 42–44, sees the reference as being rather to an early associate of the three prophets, perhaps Theodotus or Themiso, who is being described as a κριτής, though the term seems to be unattested elsewhere as a Montanist title, and in the context we would surely expect a proper name here.

17. See the discussion in Robert M. Grant, "Quadratus, the First Christian Apologist," in *A Tribute to Arthur Voobus: Studies in Early Christian Literature and Its Environment, Primarily in the Syrian East*, ed. Robert H. Fischer (Chicago: Lutheran School of Theology, 1977), 177–83.

18. Paul Foster ("The Apology of Quadratus," in *The Writings of the Apostolic Fathers*, ed. Paul Foster [London: T&T Clark, 2007], 52–62, at 54–55) points out that the dating of Quadratus's apology assumed in the *Ecclesiastical History* seems now to be earlier than that given in the *Chronicon*, that is, right at the beginning of Hadrian's reign rather than 124–125. This, of course, moves it nearer the reign of Trajan in which the prophet Quadratus is first introduced.

19. Irenaeus, in *Against the Heresies* (II.32.3–4), discusses the practices of people he designates as followers of Simon and Carpocrates, who do deeds of power (healings and castings-out of demons) that are really illusions and magic tricks—unlike the true disciples of Jesus, whose miracles really do good to those who receive them by really healing and helping them. "But even if they do something, working through magic, as we have said, they fraudulently strive to seduce the foolish. Presenting no useful fruit for those for whom they say they perform deeds of power, but bringing beardless boys and deluding the eyes and showing phantasms which immediately cease and do not persevere for any time, they show themselves similar not to Jesus our Lord but to Simon Magus" (II.32.3). "If they say that the Lord also did these sorts of things by phantasms, we, leading them back to the prophecies, will demonstrate from them that all these things were both predicted about him and confirmed as having happened, and that he alone is Son of God. This is why also those who truly are his disciples perform in his name, accepting grace from him, for the benefit of the rest of humankind, as each has received the gift from him. For some cast out demons really and truly, so that often those very people who have been cleansed from the evil spirits believe and are in the church, and some even have foreknowledge of future events, and visions and prophetic sayings, and others, through the laying on of hands, heal those who suffer and restore them to health, and still, as we have said, dead have been raised and remained with us a good number of years" (II.32.4). A further parallel is to be found in the fragments of Papias: "Concerning those who were raised from the dead by Christ, that they were alive until the time of Hadrian" (frag. 10, in Ulrich H. J. Körtner and Martin Leutzsch, *Papiasfragmente, Hirt des Hermas* [Schriften des Urchristentums 3; Darmstatt: Wissenschaftliche Buchgesellschaft, 1998], 62–63). It is found in one of a series of extracts from the work of the fifth-century church historian Philip of Side discovered and edited by C. de Boor, *Neue Fragmente des Papias, Hegesippus und Pierius in bisher unbekannten Excerpten aus der Kirchengeschichte des Philippus Sidetes* (TU V.2; Leipzig: J. C. Hinrichs, 1888), 165–84, there numbered frag. 6, p. 170.

20. For Apolinarius against the Montanists, see *H.E.* IV.27; V.16.1; and V.19.1–2. For the

anti-Montanist Miltiades, see V.17.1, and for the Montanist Miltiades, V.16.3 (from the account of the "Anonymous." For the fragments of Melito of Sardis, see Stuart George Hall, ed. and trans., *Melito of Sardis: On Pascha and Fragments* (Oxford Early Christian Texts; Oxford: Clarendon, 1979).

21. For Justin, the edition I primarily use is Miroslav Marcovich, ed., *Iustini Martyris Apologiae pro Christianis* (PTS 38; Berlin: Walter de Gruyter, 1994), but I have also consulted the draft of the edition being prepared by Denis Minns and Paul Parvis.

22. One can find a modern parallel to the process I am envisaging with the popular British children's writer Enid Blyton, whose books were enormously successful in the 1930s, '40s, and '50s but have had to be bowdlerized to suit the palates of a modern audience (or at least their parents'): so gollywogs have been removed from the Noddy stories, the word "queer" has been replaced with "strange," and all the children now do the washing up, not just the girls.

23. On the use of formal embassies by institutions such as cities to present requests to the emperor, see in particular Fergus Millar, *The Emperor in the Roman World (31 BC—AD 337)*, 2nd ed. (London: Duckworth, 1992), 217–18, and on the *libellus*, see the essay by Paul Parvis in the present volume.

24. For a list of specific parallels between Athenagoras's *Supplicatio* and Justin's *First Apology*—some more probative than others—see Bernard Pouderon, *Athénagore d'Athènes, philosophe Chrétien* (ThH 82; Paris: du Cerf, 1989), 348–49.

25. See, for example, *Supp.* 15.1 ("Since the multitude, being unable to distinguish what matter is and what God is and how vast a difference there is between them—since *they* approach idols formed of matter, are we, who distinguish and separate the ingenerate and the generate, that which is and that which is not, the intelligible and the perceptible and allot to each of them the appropriate name—are *we*, on their account, to approach and worship statues?"); 15.4 ("So, if we were to consider forms of matter to be gods, we would seem to be without perception of the one who is God, equating things that are dissolve and corrupt with the eternal"). The edition I have used of the *Supplicatio* is Athenagoras, *Legatio and De Resurrectione*, ed. and trans. William R. Schoedel (Oxford Early Christian Texts; Oxford: Clarendon, 1972).

26. The Genesis 6 myth appears in Justin at *2 Apol.* 4(5).2–4.

27. The manuscript tradition of the *Apology* is rich and complex, and there is no fully satisfactory edition. I have used the convenient edition of T. R. Glover (Tertullian, *Apology, De Spectaculis*, ed. and trans. Glover; Minucius Felix, ed. and trans. Gerald H. Rendall [LCL; London: William Heinemann, 1931], which reproduces the text of Oehler [1853]), but with the occasional look at Quintus Septimius Florens, *Tertulliani Apologeticum*, ed. Heinrich Hoppe (CSEL 69; Vienna: Hoelder–Pichler–Tempsky, 1939).

28. This is the source of the tag "If the Tiber reaches the walls, if the Nile doesn't reach the fields . . ." (40.2).

29. The manuscripts (as cited by Hoppe) offer *Apologeticum* (in various spellings), *Liber apologeticus*, or simply *Apologeticus*. Jerome, *Ep.* 70.5, knows it as *apologeticus (liber)*. See the discussion in Simon Price, "Latin Christian Apologetics: Minucius Felix, Tertullian, and Cyprian," in *Apologetics*, ed. Edwards, Goodman, and Price, 105–29, at 115–16.

10. "Jesus" as God's Name, and Jesus as God's Embodied Name in Justin Martyr

1. I have offered my own modest analysis of Justin's effort along these lines in *Lord Jesus Christ: Devotion to Jesus in Earliest Christianity* (Grand Rapids: Eerdmans, 2003), 640–48.

Among more in-depth treatments, see Eric Osborn, *Justin Martyr* (BHTh 47; Tübingen: Mohr [Paul Siebeck], 1973).

2. Jean Daniélou, *The Theology of Jewish Christianity*, trans. J. A. Baker (London: Darton, Longman & Todd; Chicago: Henry Regnery, 1964), 147–63. See also Richard N. Longenecker, *The Christology of Early Jewish Christianity* (SBT, 2nd ser. 17; London: SCM, 1970), 41–46 (heavily dependent on Daniélou); and Adelheid Ruck-Schröder, *Der Name Gottes und der Name Jesu: Eine neutestamentliche Studie* (WMANT 80; Neukirchen-Vluyn: Neukirchener, 1999). Among earlier studies, see, for example, Joseph Ponthot, *La signification religieuse du "Nom" chez Clément de Rome et dans la Didaché* (ALBO 3/12; Louvain: Publications universitaires de Louvain, 1959); and Lucien Cerfaux, "La première communauté chrétienne," in *Recueil Lucien Cerfaux, Tome II* (Gembloux: J. Duculot, 1954), 125–56, esp. 148–49.

3. Daniélou, *Theology of Jewish Christianity*, 150.

4. C. J. Davis, *The Name and Way of the Lord* (JSNTSup 129; Sheffield: JSOT, 1996).

5. See, for example, Silva New, "The Name, Baptism, and the Laying On of Hands," in *The Beginnings of Christianity*, part 1, *The Acts of the Apostles*, ed. F. J. Foakes Jackson and Kirsopp Lake (London: Macmillan, 1932; repr., Grand Rapids: Baker, n.d.), 5:121–40. On the use of Jesus' name in baptism, the classic discussion is Wilhelm Heitmüller, *"Im Namen Jesu": Eine sprach- und religionsgeschichtliche Untersuchung zum Neuen Testament, speziell zur altchristlichen Taufe* (FRLANT 1/2; Göttingen: Vandenhoeck & Ruprecht, 1903); and more recently, Lars Hartman, *"Into the Name of the Lord Jesus": Baptism in the Early Church* (Edinburgh: T&T Clark, 1997).

6. Daniélou, *Theology of Jewish Christianity*, 147 n. 2.

7. See, for example, H. Bietenhard, "Name," *New International Dictionary of New Testament Theology*, 2:648–55, esp. 649–50.

8. Larry W. Hurtado, "The Binitarian Shape of Early Christian Worship," in *The Jewish Roots of Christological Monotheism: Papers from the St. Andrews Conference on the Historical Origins of the Worship of Jesus*, ed. Carey C. Newman, James R. Davilia, and Gladys S. Lewis (Leiden: Brill, 1999), 187–213.

9. "Jesus" (Ιησους) comes from the Greek rendering of the Hebrew name *Joshua* (more specifically, from *Yeshua*, the shortened form of the name *Yehoshua* preferred in postexilic Hebrew), a theophoric name meaning "Yahweh saves" or "Yahweh is salvation." The first bearer of the name in the Old Testament is Joshua, the chief aide to Moses, but there are several other Old Testament figures with the name, and in postbiblical usage it was a common Jewish name. See, for example, George W. Ramsey, "Joshua," *Anchor Bible Dictionary*, 3:999–1000. Among the more well-known bearers is "Jesus, son of Sirach," the author of Ecclesiasticus. Adolf Deissmann's fascinating discussion is still worth reading: "The Name 'Jesus,'" in *Mysterium Christi: Christological Studies by British and German Theologians*, ed. G. K. A. Bell and D. Adolf Deissmann (London: Longmans, Green, 1930), 3–27.

10. Interestingly, Philo also (but independently) shows awareness of the etymology in *Mut. Nom.* 121.

11. Of course, the key study of Justin's use of Old Testament material remains Oskar Skarsaune, *The Proof from Prophecy: A Study in Justin Martyr's Proof-Text Tradition; Text-Type, Provenance, Theological Profile* (NovTSup 66; Leiden: Brill, 1987). However, Skarsaune focuses heavily on questions about the kind of text(s) used by Justin, and what prior proof-texting traditions and collections he may have known, whereas I focus here on attempting to grasp Justin's christological appropriation of certain Old Testament passages.

12. Translations of the *Dialogue* are adapted from Marcus Dods and George Reith in ANF 1 unless otherwise indicated.

13. Alan Segal noted that Exod. 23:20-21 figures in rabbinic reports about "two powers" heretics, and Segal judged that it is highly likely that Jewish Christians are the target (or at least

prominent among those targeted); *Two Powers in Heaven: Early Rabbinic Reports about Christianity and Gnosticism* (SJLA 25; Leiden: Brill, 1977), esp. 68–73.

14. Cf. Skarsaune, *Proof from Prophecy*, 209–13, who proposed that Justin's argument was originally directed against Marcion, and, in my view, treats rather lightly the christological argument here.

15. It is interesting that the LXX of the Old Testament account has the figure named Οσηε, whereas the Masoretic/Hebrew text of the passage has the name as *Yehoshua* (Joshua/Jesus). In Justin's citation of the passage, the figure's name is Αυση, the form of the birth-name of Moses' adjutant in LXX Num. 13:16.

16. On ancient Jewish exegesis, see, for example, David Instone Brewer, *Techniques and Assumptions in Jewish Exegesis Before 70 CE* (Texte und Studien zum antiken Judentum 30; Tübingen: Mohr [Paul Siebeck], 1992).

17. Note, for example, Origen's response to Celsus's charge that Christians used incantations in their exorcisms. Origen insists that Christians use only the name of Jesus: "It is clear that Christians make no use of spells, but only of the name of Jesus and certain other words which are believed to be effective, taken from the divine scripture" (*C. Cels.* 1.6, trans. Henry Chadwick [Cambridge: Cambridge University Press, 1953], 10). Cf. Charles A. Gieschen, "The Divine Name in Ante-Nicene Christology," *VC* 57 (2003): 115–58, who claimed that to "call upon the name of the Lord" originally did not involve invoking Jesus by name, but instead referred to the notion that he bears the divine name in his person. But Gieschen seems to me to ignore the numerous indications that Ιησους was itself used in cultic/liturgical settings, especially baptism, and also gathered worship. For a broad-ranging study, see William Q. Parkinson, "'In the Name of Jesus': The Ritual Use and Christological Significance of the Name of Jesus in Early Christianity" (Ph.D. diss., University of Edinburgh, 2003).

18. For example, Irenaeus, *Adv. Haer.* 1.15.1–3.

19. Larry W. Hurtado, "The Origin of the *Nomina Sacra*: A Proposal," *JBL* 117 (1998): 655–73.

20. Cf. Skarsaune (*Proof from Prophecy*, e.g., 208), who proposes that in this and a few other matters Justin is an innovator. I do not question Justin's own ability, but I think that in his handling of Jesus' name he is more indebted to prior Christian tradition than Skarsaune seems to grant.

21. For example, P. Chester Beatty VI (Numbers and Deuteronomy), where Joshua's name is written as Ις or Ιης (or with the appropriate final letter in accusative or dative cases of the name), and the customary supralinear stroke placed over *nomina sacra*. Frederic G. Kenyon, *The Chester Beatty Biblical Papyri, Fasciculus V, Numbers and Deuteronomy, Text* (London: Emery Walker Ltd., 1935), esp. ix–x.

22. See, for example, 2 Cor. 3:7—4:6 and John 1:14; 17:1-5, 22-24. In John 17, we see how notions of Jesus as God's glory and God's name are associated (God's name in 17:6, 11-12). On Paul's christological usage (our earliest) of this category and its Jewish background, see esp. Carey C. Newman, *Paul's Glory-Christology: Tradition and Rhetoric* (NovTSup 69; Leiden: Brill, 1992).

23. The LXX reading here is καὶ ἐπὶ τῷ ὀνόματι αὐτοῦ ἔθνη ἐλπιοῦσιν, whereas the Masoretic Text has "and the coastlands wait for his teaching (לתורתו)."

24. My translation reflects the Goodspeed text of Justin here, following the reading of the manuscript (*Parisinus graecus* 450), Ὑμνήσατε τῷ θεῷ, whereas the Rahlfs LXX text at Isa. 42:10 prefers Ὑμνήσατε τῷ κυρίῳ, which the ANF translation appears to reflect ("Sing unto the LORD a new song"). But the Rahlfs apparatus lists θεῷ as the reading supported here by the original hand of Codex Sinaiticus (S*) and also by Codex Purpureus Vindobonensis (L). The

Stuttgart edition of the Hebrew text has "Sing unto *YHWH* (יהוה)" here. There is good evidence indicating that Greek-speaking Jews customarily used Κύριος as an oral substitute for the Tetragrammaton.

25. Interestingly, the LXX text of Ps. 95:1 (MT 96:1) has Ἄισατε τῷ κυρίῳ ᾆσμα καινόν, synonymous with the LXX wording of Isa. 42:10, but not identical. In the MT, however, the opening words of Ps. 96:1 and the first words of Isa. 42:10 are the same, exhorting a new song to *Yahweh*.

26. My translation varies here—apart from the added emphasis—from ANF, which I think does not adequately render the binitarian interpretation of the passage that Justin was urging.

27. Again, I refer readers particularly to Daniélou, *Theology of Jewish Christianity*, 147–63, and Longenecker, *Christology of Early Jewish Christianity*, 41–46, for fuller discussion and further references to primary texts and previous scholarship. More recently, see the provocative discussion by Jarl E. Fossum, "In the Beginning Was the Name," in Fossum, *The Image of the Invisible God: Essays on the Influence of Jewish Mysticism on Early Christology* (Novum Testamentum et Orbis Antiquus 30; Göttingen: Vandenhoeck & Ruprecht, 1995), 109–33, esp. 109–16. Cf. Ponthot, *La signification religieuse du "Nom*," but Ponthot reads *1 Clement* and *Didache* in the context of Jewish references to the divine name, playing down the significance of other early Christian evidence about reverence for Jesus. This seems to me a curious interpretative procedure. Obviously, the more relevant interpretative context for these writings is early Christian evidence.

28. Daniélou, *Theology of Jewish Christianity*, 151.

29. Kurt Niederwimmer, *The Didache: A Commentary*, trans. Linda M. Maloney (Hermeneia; Minneapolis: Fortress Press, 1998), 156. I echo here a view of the prayer taken by Fossum, "Beginning," 122–23.

30. Daniélou, *Theology of Jewish Christianity*, 148.

11. *Altercatio Jasonis et Papisci* as Testimony Source for Justin's "Second God" Argument?

1. *Dialogue* 56–62, 125–29; *1 Apology* 63; cf. *Dial.* 37.4–38.1; 75; 86.2–5; 113.4, 7; 114.3.

2. Or "another God." Justin also prefers ἄλλος θεός. As a matter of course he interprets all OT theophanies christologically (cf. *Dial.* 127.1–3).

3. It is not insignificant that Trypho explicitly formulates the problem (*Dial.* 55.1).

4. Justin himself may indicate his uniqueness (*Dial.* 56.16). Demetrius Trakatellis, *The Preexistence of Christ in the Writings of Justin Martyr: An Exegetical Study with Reference to the Humiliation and Exaltation Christology* (HDR 6; Missoula, Mt.: Scholars, 1976), 53–60; Benedict Kominiak, *The Theophanies of the Old Testament in the Writings of St. Justin* (Studies in Sacred Theology, 2nd ser., 14; Washington, D.C.: Catholic University of America Press, 1948), 4.

5. Philo, *Mut. Nom.* 15; *Abr.* 107–66 (Abraham); *Som.* 1.120–32 (Jacob); and *Vit. Mos.* 1.65–84; *Agric.* 51; *Migr.* 174 (Moses). Philo does not mention the theophany to Joshua. Paul Heinisch, *Der Einfluss Philos auf die älteste christliche Exegese (Barnabas, Justin u. Clemens von Alexandria)* (Alttestamentliche Abhandlungen 1/2; Münster: Aschendorff, 1908), 195–211; Erwin R. Goodenough, *The Theology of Justin Martyr* (Jena: Frommannsche Buchhandlung, 1923), 141–47; Trakatellis, *Pre-Existence*, 53–92.

6. Justin never explicitly cites or references Philo, draws entirely different conclusions, utilizes theophanic passages in an altogether different manner, has a much more literal approach

to theophanic material, and has an unabashedly personal *Logos*. The Jewish interpretations of theophany of which Justin is aware know only the appearance of God the Father and/or his angels, never the *Logos* (*1 Apol.* 63.1; Jules Lebreton, *Histoire du dogme de la Trinité* [Paris: Gabriel Beauchesne, 1928], 2:672–73).

7. Oskar Skarsaune, *The Proof from Prophecy: A Study in Justin Martyr's Proof-Text Tradition: Text-Type, Provenance, Theological Profile* (NovTSup 66; Leiden: Brill, 1987), 409–24; Lebreton, *Histoire*, 2:667–72; R. P. C. Hanson, *Allegory and Event: A Study of the Sources and Significance of Origen's Interpretation of Scripture* (Louisville: Westminster John Knox, 2002), 107–8; Leslie W. Barnard, *Justin Martyr: His Life and Thought* (Cambridge: Cambridge University Press, 1967), 92–96; Willis A. Shotwell, *The Biblical Exegesis of Justin Martyr* (London: SPCK, 1965), 45-47, 96-100.

8. Skarsaune, *Proof from Prophecy*, 206–13.

9. Skarsaune, *Proof from Prophecy*, 234–42; cf. 380–91. F. C. Conybeare suggested some dependence of *Dialogue* on *JP* (*The Dialogues of* Athanasius and Zacchaeus *and* Timothy and Aquila *Edited with Prolegomena and Facsimiles* [Anecdota Oxoniensia, Classical Series 8; Oxford: Clarendon, 1898], xxxv–xxxvii, xlvii–l; cf. li–lvii). Also P. Nautin ("Histoire des dogmes et des sacrements chrétiens," in *Annuaire de l'École pratique des Hautes Études—(Ve Section) Section des Sciences religieuses* 1967–68 [Paris], 162–67), followed by Pierre Monat (*Lactance et la Bible: Une propédeutique latine à la lecture de la Bible dans l'Occident constantinien* [Paris: Études augustiniennes, 1982], 1:272–73). Bernd Reiner Voss (*Der Dialog in der frühchristlichen Literatur* [Studia et testimonia antiqua 9; München: W. Fink, 1970], 24, 322–25) allowed dependence on *JP* (or at least the *Gattung* beginning to appear in *JP*).

10. Justin may have already developed his Christophany theory in his *Syntagma* as Pierre Prigent proposed (*Justin et l'Ancien Testament. L'argumentation scripturaire du Traité de Justin contre toutes les hérésies comme source principale du Dialogue avec Tryphon et la Première Apologie* [ÉtB; Paris: Librairie Lecoffre, 1964], 11–13, 117–33). If correct this only transposes the problem of sources (Trakatellis, *Pre-existence*, 59), and there is no reason to suspect the "two powers" proof-texts in *Syntagma* were different from those in *Dialogue*.

11. Cf. *Dial.* 61.1: "another testimony" (μαρτύριον ἄλλο). Form- and source-critical readings confirm distinguishable types of material in these passages (Prigent, *Justin*, 121; Skarsaune, *Proof from Prophecy*, 388), yet the inclusion of the Joshua theophany (62.4) and Trypho's response to the entire "second God" proof (63.1) indicate these units constitute the same demonstration.

12. *Dial.* 56.5, 9–10.

13. "[*Dial.* 56.14] semble bien être une petite parenthèse" (Prigent, *Justin*, 123).

14. The messianic connection in *Dial.* 56.15 linking Psalms 109 and 44 to "Christ" is secondary, anticipatory of the extended argument in 63.5 and 68.3.

15. Wilhelm Bousset, *Jüdisch-Christlicher Schulbetrieb in Alexandria und Rom: literarische Untersuchungen zu Philo und Clemens von Alexandria, Justin und Irenäus* (FRLANT, n. F. 6; Göttingen: Vandenhoeck & Ruprecht, 1915), 304–8.

16. Later theophanies are simply "some other proofs on this rubric" (*Dial.* 57.4; cf. 58.2).

17. *Dial.* 58.3; 59.1, 3; 60.2, 4–5.

18. J. Rendel Harris and V. Burch (*Testimonies* [Cambridge: Cambridge University Press, 1916], 1:1–4); B. P. W. Stather Hunt (*Primitive Gospel Sources* [London: James Clarke, 1951], vii–viii, 3–13); and Barnabas Lindars (*New Testament Apologetic: The Doctrinal Significance of the Old Testament* [London: SCM, 1961], 13, 23–24) noted the apologetic context with Judaism as a key impetus for early Christian collections of testimony texts.

19. Martin C. Albl, *"And Scripture Cannot Be Broken": The Form and Function of the Early Christian Testimonia Collections* (NovTSup 96; Leiden: Brill, 1999), 216–36, esp. 232–33.

20. T. F. Glasson, "'Plurality of Divine Persons' and the Quotations in Hebrews 1.6ff.," *NTS* 12 (1965–66): 271–72.

21. Albl, *"Scripture,"* 190–207.

22. Reading "Lord" (κυρίῳ) for "Cyrus" (Κύρῳ: LXX Isa. 45:1).

23. Albl, *"Scripture,"* 232 n. 98.

24. Cf. Alan Segal, *Two Powers in Heaven: Early Rabbinic Reports about Christianity and Gnosticism* (SJLA 25; Leiden: Brill, 1977).

25. It appears no less than six times in *Dialogue.*

26. Skarsaune, *Proof from Prophecy,* 412–13.

27. The concentration of temporal markers intensifies the themes of Christ's begetting ("before" [πρό]: Prov. 8:24-25) and pre-existence ("when" [ἡνίκα and ὅτε]: 8:27-31).

28. *Dial.* 61.1, 3.

29. Similar speculation appears to lie behind John 1:1-3 and Col. 1:15-20.

30. Trakatellis, *Pre-existence,* 65–66; Skarsaune, *Proof from Prophecy,* 209 n. 62.

31. For fragments and descriptions see J. C. T. Otto, ed., *Corpus Apologetarum Christianorum Saeculi Secundi* (Jena: Mauke [Herm. Dufft], 1872), 9:356–57.

32. More than two centuries separate Justin's *Dialogue* and the next intact dialogue, *AZ*. We possess fragments of a third-century dialogue (POxy 2070); others (possibly dialogic) works are lost entirely (*Pros Ioudaious* of Miltiades and of Apollinaris [Eusebius, *H.E.* 5.17.5; 4.27]).

33. Conybeare, *Dialogues,* and "A New Second-Century Christian Dialogue," *Expositor,* 5th ser., 5 (1897): 300–320, 443–63 (translation of *AZ* from Armenian). Lawrence Lanzi Lahey, "The *Dialogue of Timothy and Aquila*: Critical Greek Text and English Translation of the Short Recension with an Introduction Including a Source-Critical Study" (Ph.D. diss., University of Cambridge, 2000); Adolf Harnack, *Die Altercatio Simonis Iudaei et Theophili Christiani* (TU 1.3; Leipzig: J. C. Hinrichs'sche Buchhandlung, 1883). William Varner, *Ancient Jewish-Christian Dialogues: Athanasius and Zacchaeus, Simon and Theophilus, Timothy and Aquila; Introductions, Texts, and Translations* (Studies in the Bible and Early Christianity 58; Lewiston, N.Y.: Edwin Mellen, 2004).

34. Anticipated in "Second-Century Dialogue," 300–301, but developed at greater length in Conybeare, *Dialogues* (xxxiv, li–lvii).

35. Lahey, "Short Recension," 74–89. The suggestion of dependence has received greatest attention in regard to *STh*; Vacher Burch (in Harris, *Testimonies*, 1:94–96) and Harnack (*Altercatio*, 115–30), who later (review of Corssen's *Altercatio*, in *Theologische Literaturzeitung* 15 [1890], coll. 624–25) sympathized somewhat with Peter Corssen's conclusion that *STh* depends on Tertullian's *Adv. Jud.*, Cyprian's *Test.*, and *JP* (*Die Altercatio Simonis Iudaei et Theophili Christiani auf ihre Quellen geprüft* [Jever: C. L. Mettcker u. Söhne, 1890]). More cautiously, Voss (*Dialog* 24 and esp. n. 10) and Zahn ("Über die 'Altercatio,'" 308–29).

36. A. Lukyn Williams, *Adversus Judaeos: A Bird's-Eye View of Christian Apologiae until the Renaissance* (Cambridge: Cambridge University Press, 1935), 30, 117 n. 2. Eduard Bratke, "Epilegomena zur Wiener Ausgabe der Altercatio legis inter Simonem Judaeum et Theophilum Christianum" (*Sitzungsberichte der philosophisch-historischen Klasse der kaiserlichen Akademie der Wissenschaften* 148; Wien: Carl Gerold's Sohn, 1904), 131–33, 158–78. Patrick Andrist, "Le *Dialogue d'Athanase et Zachée*: étude des sources et du contexte littéraire" (Ph.D. diss., Université de Genève, 2001), 289–91.

37. Varner, *Ancient Jewish-Christian Dialogues,* 11-12.

38. Lahey, "Short Recension," 74.

39. Ibid.

40. *AZ* does not depend directly on *Dialogue* (Andrist, "Le *Dialogue*," 199–201, 274). *STh*

is more directly related to Tertullian's *Adv. Jud.*, Cyprian's *Test.*, and a collection of allegorical interpretations of Scripture (possibly Origen's *Tractatus de libris Scripturarum*; Pierre Battifol, "Une source nouvelle de l'Altercatio Simonis Judaei et Theophili Christiani," *RB* 8 [1899]: 337–45; cf. Bratke, "Epilegomena," 109–58; Harnack, *Altercatio*, 110–15) than to *Dialogue*. The later dialogues conclude with a baptismal scene and begin with a discussion on divine unity containing common order and elements (see below) not shared by *Dialogue*, suggesting a source other than *Dialogue* for their framework.

41. *AZ* 130a–b (Armenian); *STh* 29–30; *LR* 57.5–6 [SR XXVI.1–2], 16–17 [XXVII.2, 4].

42. Ps.-Cyprian, *Ad Vig.* 8.

43. Lahey, "Short Recension," 87–89.

44. *Qu. hebr. Gen.* (Otto, fr. 3).

45. Tertullian, *Adv. Prax.* 5.1; Hilary, *Comm. Ps.* 2.

46. *Comm. Gal.* 3.13 (Otto, fr. 2): *Memini me.*

47. Conybeare, *Dialogues*, xliv.

48. Maximus's *Contra Iudaeos* closely links Gen. 1:1 with Prov. 8:22ff. and Gen. 1:26.

49. Lahey, "Short Recension," 81.

50. Cf. Harnack's balanced assessment (*Die Überlieferung der griechischen Apologeten des zweiten Jahrhunderts in der alten Kirche und im Mittelalter* [TU 1.2; Leipzig: J. C. Hinrichs'sche Buchhandlung, 1882], 119). This interpretation appears in Irenaeus, *Epid.* 43 (cf. J. P. Smith, "Hebrew Christian Midrash in Iren. Epid. 43," *Bib.* 38 [1957]: 24–34; P. Nautin, "Genèse 1,1-2, de Justin à Origène," in *In Principio. Interprétations des premiers versets de la Genèse* [École pratique des Hautes Études—(Ve Section) Section des Sciences religieuses 152; Paris: Études augustiniennes, 1973], 83–86).

51. *AZ* 3; *TA* 4.7.

12. Justin and the Pontic Wolf

1. There is, of course, the never-ending discussion as to whether Justin actually wrote two *Apologies*, that is, two different, self-contained works. As the question is peripheral to this paper, however, I will stick to the conventional terms *First* and *Second Apology*. The edition I use is André Wartelle, *Saint Justin. Apologies*, introduction, texte critique, traduction, commentaire et index (Paris: Études augustiniennes, 1987). All translations of Justin's text are my own.

2. *1 Apol.* 1.1.

3. Cf., for example, Erwin R. Goodenough, *The Theology of Justin Martyr* (Jena: Frommannsche Buchhandlung, 1923), 82; Charles Munier, "A propos des Apologies de Justin," *RevScRel* 61 (1987): 177–86, at 182f.

4. Lorraine Buck, "Justin Martyr's *Apologies*: Their Number, Destination, and Form," *JTS*, n.s., 54 (2003): 45–59.

5. Ibid., 51.

6. On a personal note, I know quite a few well-educated people, yet none of them would be able to correctly fill in a British banking form.

7. Peter Lampe, *From Paul to Valentinus: Christians at Rome in the First Two Centuries*, trans. Michael Steinhauser, ed. Marshall D. Johnson (Minneapolis: Fortress Press, 2003), 268 = *Die stadtrömischen Christen in den ersten beiden Jahrhunderten*, 2nd ed. (Tübingen: Mohr, 1989), 230. Wartelle, on the other hand, argues that it is "peu probable que Justin fût mal informé des règles à suivre dans une adresse aux autorités gouvernementales" (Wartelle, *Apologies*, 32), without further explanation.

8. Buck, "Justin Martyr's *Apologies*," 56–57.

9. Ibid., 51.

10. *Dial.* 58.1.

11. For example, *Dial.* 118.4f. Ironically, he even repeats *this* insight again and again; cf. Lampe, *From Paul to Valentinus*, 270 = *Christen*, 231.

12. *1 Apol.* 45.6.

13. *1 Apol.* 1.3.

14. Buck, "Justin Martyr's *Apologies*," 54–55.

15. This does not, of course, mean that he would not have made his work also accessible for other people to read.

16. Lampe, *From Paul to Valentinus*, 268 = *Christen*, 230.

17. *1 Apol.* 26.5.

18. *1 Apol.* 58.1–2.

19. Marcionites (Μαρκιανοί) are included in—and in fact lead off—a bare list of those who falsely call themselves Christians, in *Dial.* 35.6.

20. Ἄλογος, as well as meaning "irrational," obviously has connotations of being separated from the *Logos*; ἀπόδειξις connotes a means of scientific demonstration, as well as "proof" in general.

21. Adolf von Harnack, *Marcion. Das Evangelium von fremden Gott*, 2nd ed. (TU 46; Leipzig: J. C. Hinrichs, 1924; repr., Darmstadt: Wissenschaftliche Buchgesellschaft, 1996), 8*. This is my own translation. The English version, *Marcion, the Gospel of the Alien God*, trans. John E. Steely and Lyle D. Blerma (Durham, N.C.: Labyrinth, 1990), does not contain the *Beilagen* from which this and subsequent quotations in this chapter are taken.

22. *1 Apol.* 26.2–4 + *1 Apol.* 56.

23. Harnack, *Marcion*, 7*.

24. Cf. *1 Apol.* 56.3: "if someone is still possessed by that man's [Simon's] teaching." Cf. also Karlmann Beyschlag, *Simon Magus und die christliche Gnosis* (Tübingen: Mohr, 1974), 12: "Ihre [the Simonians'] Zahl hält er [Justin]—abgesehen von Samarien (aber eine simonianische Volksreligion dürfte es dort nie gegeben haben!)—für verschwindend klein."

25. According to Irenaeus, Simon is the man "from whom all heresies came into being" (*ex quo universae haereses substiterunt*; *Adv. Haer.* I.23.2).

26. Cf. *1 Apol.* 56.2: "Simon . . . astounded the Sacred Senate and the Roman people to such an extent that he was thought to be a god."

27. See *1 Apol.* 58.1.

28. Cf., for example, *1 Apol.* 59–60.

29. Goodenough, *Theology*, 105.

30. *2 Apol.* 15.3.

31. Cf. *2 Apol.* 13.2.

32. *1 Apol.* 46.2–3.

33. Cf. Eric Osborn, *Justin Martyr* (BHTh 47; Tübingen: Mohr [Paul Siebeck], 1973), 1: "The imperial government objected to Christianity on one ground alone: the exclusiveness by which it refused to worship the gods of the Roman people."

34. Cf. *1 Apol.* 7.3 + 26.6.

35. Similar ideas can be found in the doctrine of Numenius of Apamea, for example; cf. John Dillon, *The Middle Platonists* (London: Duckworth, 1977), 366–72.

36. Cf. Enrico Norelli, "Marcion: ein christlicher Philosoph oder ein Christ gegen die Philosophie?" in Gerhard May and Katharina Greshat, eds., *Marcion und seine kirchengeschichtliche Wirkung; Marcion and His Impact on Church History* (TU 159; Berlin: Walter de

Gruyter, 2002), 113–30, at 128: "In sämtliche Formen des Platonismus ist der erste Gott . . . letzten Endes für die Schöpfung des Weltalls verantwortlich."

37. Osborn, *Justin*, 5.

38. Cf. *1 Apol.* 20.3.

39. *1 Apol.* 26.7.

40. *Adv. Haer.* IV.6.2. Lampe rightly observed, "Even if this work were Justin's lost *Syntagma* against all heresies . . . it would not change matters. Irenaeus would then be a witness that the *Syntagma* was directed primarily against Marcion" (Lampe, *From Paul to Valentinus*, 250 n. 52 = *Christen*, 213).

41. As all of these features are well attested and undisputed, I refrain from giving full references and refer to Barbara Aland's excellent summary of Marcion's theology: Barbara Aland, "Marcion/Marcioniten," *Theologische Realenzyklopädie* 22 (1992): 89–101.

42. It seems to me rash to conclude, for example, from the fact that Justin did not mention Marcion's "Bible" in his *Apology* that he did not know of it—as does Hildegard König in her article "Marcion von Sinope," in *Lexikon der antiken christlichen Literatur*, ed. Siegmar Döpp with Peter Bruns, 3rd ed. (Freiburg: Herder, 2002), 483.

43. See above at n. 34.

44. This is all the more striking as the law occupies significant attention in Justin's *Dialogue with Trypho*; cf. Theodore Stylianopoulos, *Justin Martyr and the Mosaic Law* (SBLDS 20; Missoula, Mt.: Scholars, 1975), 17.

45. *1 Apol.* 32.1.

46. Stylianopoulos, *Justin*, 131.

47. *C. Cels.* V.14 (trans. H. Chadwick).

48. Goodenough, *Theology*, 290.

49. Origen, *Hom. in Ezech.* 7.3.

50. Stylianopoulos, *Justin*, 17.

13. Questions Liturgists Would Like to Ask Justin Martyr

1. *Lambeth Conference 1958* (London: SPCK, 1958), Committee Report 2.80.

2. The Justin passage concerned is *1 Apology* 66–67. It is originally cited (and attributed to Justin's "second apology") in Cranmer's *A Defence of the True and Catholic Doctrine of the Sacrament of the Body and Blood of Our Saviour Christ*, which Diarmaid MacCulloch (*Thomas Cranmer: A Life* [New Haven: Yale University Press, 1996], 462) reckons was published in "high summer 1550," but had been drafted up to two years earlier. It is taken up by Gardiner in his *Explication* and by Cranmer again in his *Answer* (see *On the Lord's Supper* [Cambridge: Parker Society, 1844], 263–65). There is reference back to it also at his trial (*On the Lord's Supper*, 420). I would be grateful for secure information about how much of Justin's works may plausibly be said to have been available to Cranmer before 1551. The evidence for the independent circulation of this section of the *Apology* is that chapters 65–67 are found in detached form, in Greek, in the sixteenth-century manuscripts *Ottobonianus graecus* 274, and Athos, *Vatopedi, Skete Demetriu* 33, and, in Latin, in *Codex Ambrosianus (latinus)* H. 142 *infer.*, of the year 1564, and in the roughly contemporary *Codex monacensis latinus* 132. (For these Greek manuscripts see Miroslav Marcovich, ed., *Justini Martyris Apologiae pro Christianis* [PTS 38; Berlin: Walter de Gruyter, 1966], 7 with n. 15, and for the Latin, J. C. Th. von Otto, ed., *Justini Philosophi et Martyris Opera Quae Feruntur Omnia*, I.i, *Opera Justini Indubitata*, 3rd ed. [Jena: Hermann Dufft, 1876], xxxi.)

3. I say "Antonine Wall," rather than "Hadrian's," not only because Antoninus was the emperor whom Justin addressed, and thus this was the one period when the northern boundary of the Empire was drawn from the Forth to the Clyde, but also because the conference for which this essay was originally prepared was itself being held—and knew itself to be held—barely a stone's throw from that very boundary.

4. Leslie W. Barnard, *St. Justin Martyr: The First and Second Apologies* (Ancient Christian Writers 56; New York: Paulist, 1997), 101 n. 61.

5. *1 Apol.* 61.2.

6. See Paul F. Bradshaw, *The Search for the Origins of Christian Worship: Sources and Methods for the Study of Early Liturgy*, 2nd ed. (Oxford: Oxford University Press, 2002), where, in his preface (ix–x), he traces his use of "lumpers" and "splitters" in his first edition (London: SPCK) ten years before and modestly suggests that the splitters have been gaining ground since. He summarizes with a note that we cannot now talk *tout simple* about "what the early church did."

7. Joachim Jeremias, *Infant Baptism in the First Four Centuries*, trans. David Cairns (London: SCM, 1960), 60.

8. See Kurt Aland, *Did the Early Church Baptize Infants?* trans. G. R. Beasley-Murray (London: SCM, 1963), 71, 73.

9. Joachim Jeremias, *The Origins of Infant Baptism: A Further Study in Reply to Kurt Aland*, trans. Dorothea M. Barton (London: SCM, 1963), 56–57.

10. The particular issue of infant baptism provides a further illustration of how the answers to liturgical questions addressed to Justin may be called in aid as relevant to twentieth-century liturgical practice.

11. See his "Justin Martyr and Confirmation," originally published in *Theology* 51, no. 334 (April 1948), and reprinted in his collected works: E. C. Ratcliff, *Liturgical Studies*, ed. A. H. Couratin and D. H. Tripp (London: SPCK, 1976), 110–17, from which it is cited here.

12. This issue does, of course, have to take us back to the New Testament—but it is the lack of any invariable or even regular use of a postbaptismal ceremony in the New Testament that has led to scholars working backwards from later evidence in the interests of a "two-staging" answer. See J. D. G. Dunn, *Baptism in the Holy Spirit: A Re-examination of the New Testament Teaching on the Gift of the Spirit in Relation to Pentecostalism Today* (London: SCM, 1970), for a thorough sifting of the New Testament evidence in its own right, and Colin Buchanan, *Anglican Confirmation* (Grove Liturgical Study 48; Nottingham: Grove Books, 1986), for its relation to the early church.

13. This distinguishing of two central features of consecration by a simple reversal of the central words provides in my judgment the easiest separation of strands of thought that are often confused. It does not prejudge whether Justin would have recognized such a latter-day question. See Colin Buchanan, *Eucharistic Consecration* (Grove Worship Series 148; Cambridge: Grove Books, 1998).

14. See Barnard, *Apologies*, 179 n. 399.

15. Paul F. Bradshaw, *Eucharistic Origins* (Alcuin Club Collections 80; London: SPCK, 2004), 75–76.

16. John Austin Baker interestingly opines that although in Paul the narrative was simply catechetical, "Justin . . . shows that in his day the words of institution had become part of the thanksgiving over the bread and wine" (in "The 'Institution' Narrative and the Christian Eucharist," in the Church of England Doctrine Commission symposium, *Thinking about the Eucharist: Essays by Members of the Archbishops' Commission on Christian Doctrine* [London: SCM, 1972], 54).

17. Cf., for example, *Didache* 14.3; Irenaeus, *Adv. Haer.* IV.17.5; Tertullian, *Adv. Marc.* III.22.6.

18. This is very tangential to the liturgical questions, but my point is that the text of the letter of "Clement" only claims to be from the *church* at Rome (and is written in the first-person plural), that no reference is made to any bishop of Rome, and that mention of Peter (in chap. 5), while apparently referring not only to his apostleship but also to his martyrdom, does not connect him with Rome at all (and gives far more space to Paul). The attribution to Clement is by later authors.

19. There is the intriguing reference in Ign. *Smyrn.* 8.1 to the bishop delegating eucharistic presidency. If Rome had in Justin's day various congregations at different locations, was a single bishop overseeing them, and even authorizing their presiders?

14. Justin and Hellenism

1. Judith Lieu, *Christian Identity in the Jewish and Graeco-Roman World* (Oxford: Oxford University Press, 2004), 310.

2. Kathryn Tanner, *Theories of Culture: A New Agenda for Theology* (Guides to Theological Inquiry; Minneapolis: Fortress Press, 1997).

3. Gayati Spivak, "Can the Subaltern Speak? Speculations on Widow Sacrifice," in *Marxism and the Interpretation of Culture*, ed. C. Nelson and L. Grossberg (London: Macmillan, 1988), 271–313. For a recent discussion of the history and problems of "subaltern studies," see Dipesh Chakrabarty, *Habitations of Modernity: Essays in the Wake of Subaltern Studies* (Chicago: University of Chicago Press, 2002), 3–47.

4. Homi Bhabha, *The Location of Culture* (London: Routledge, 1994). See also the discussion in Robert Young, *Colonial Desire: Hybridity in Theory, Culture, and Race* (London: Routledge, 1995), 20–28.

5. Chakrabarty, *Habitations*, 36.

6. G. Bowersock, *Hellenism in Late Antiquity* (Ann Arbor: University of Michigan Press, 1996); Simon Swain, *Hellenism and Empire: Language, Classicism, and Power in the Greek World AD 50–250* (Oxford: Clarendon, 1996); Simon Goldhill, ed., *Being Greek under Rome: Cultural Identity, the Second Sophistic, and the Development of Empire* (Cambridge: Cambridge University Press, 2001); Tim Whitmarsh, *Greek Literature and the Roman Empire: The Politics of Imitation* (Oxford: Oxford University Press, 2001).

7. Shaye J. D. Cohen, *The Beginnings of Jewishness: Boundaries, Varieties, Uncertainites* (Berkeley: University of California Press, 1999); Erich Gruen, *Heritage and Hellenism: The Reinvention of Jewish Tradition* (Berkeley: University of California Press, 1998); Daniel Boyarin, *Border Lines: The Partition of Judaeo-Christianity* (Philadelphia: University of Pennsylvania Press, 2004).

8. Whitmarsh, *Greek Literature*, 15.

9. Ibid., 25.

10. A very helpful summary of current methodologies (and their conflicts) in the history of ancient Christianity may be found in David Brakke, "The Early Church in North America: Late Antiquity, Theory, and the History of Christianity," *Church History* 71, no. 3 (2002): 473–91.

11. See the analysis of Justin as "polemicist" by Karen King, *What Is Gnosticism?* (Cambridge: Harvard University Press, 2003), 27.

12. Whitmarsh discusses the issues of performance, identity, and interpretation in *Greek Literature*, 31–33.

13. Rebecca Lyman, "The Politics of Passing: Justin Martyr's Conversion as a Problem of

'Hellenization,'" in *Conversion in Late Antiquity and the Early Middle Ages: Seeing and Believing*, ed. Kenneth Mills and Anthony Grafton (Rochester: University of Rochester Press, 2003), 36–60.

14. Fergus Millar, *The Roman Near East, 31 BC–AD 337*, 2nd ed. (Cambridge: Harvard University Press, 1993), 227.

15. Lyman, "Politics of Passing," 38–41; see also on "geographical thinking" and identity, Laura Nasrallah, "Mapping the World: Justin, Tatian, Lucian, and the Second Sophistic," *HTR* 98, no. 3 (2005): 283–314.

16. Simon Swain, "Defending Hellenism: Philostratus, *In Honour of Apollonius*," in *Apologetics in the Roman Empire: Pagans, Jews, and Christians*, ed. Mark Edwards, Martin Goodman, and Simon Price (Oxford: Oxford University Press, 1999), 185; Richard Lim, *Public Disputation, Power, and Social Order in Late Antiquity* (Berkeley: University of California, 1995), 8.

17. W. H. C. Frend, *The Rise of Christianity* (Philadelphia: Fortress Press, 1984), 237.

18. G. C. Stead, *Philosophy in Christian Antiquity* (Cambridge: Cambridge University Press, 1994), 81–82.

19. Frances Young, "Greek Apologists of the Second Century," in *Apologetics in the Roman Empire*, ed. Edwards, Goodman, and Price, 85.

20. Tessa Rajak, "Talking at Trypho: Christian Apologetic as Anti-Judaism in Justin's *Dialogue with Trypho the Jew*," in *Apologetics in the Roman Empire*, ed. Edwards, Goodman, and Price, 67.

21. Frances Young, *Biblical Exegesis and the Formation of Christian Culture* (Cambridge: Cambridge University Press, 1997), 53–54.

22. Rajak, "Talking at Trypho," 66.

23. M. J. Edwards, "On the Platonic Schooling of Justin Martyr," *JTS*, n.s., 42 (1991): 32; he also notes that scholars often see Justin as "two people" in evaluating his authorship of the *Apologies* and *Dialogue*: "Justin's Logos and the Word of God," *Journal of Early Christian Studies* 3 (1995): 261.

24. See references in my "Politics of Passing," 51 n. 9.

25. Leslie W. Barnard, *Justin Martyr: His Life and Thought* (Cambridge: Cambridge University Press, 1967), 11.

26. Lim, *Public Disputation*, 7.

27. Rajak, "Talking at Trypho," 67.

28. Bhabha, *Location of Culture*, 86.

29. On Harnack see Dale Martin, "Paul and the Judaism/Hellenism Dichotomy: Toward a Social History of the Question," in *Paul Beyond the Judaism/Hellenism Divide*, ed. T. Engberg-Pedersen (Louisville: Westminster John Knox, 2001), 34–35.

30. William V. Rowe, "Adolf von Harnack and the Concept of Hellenization," in *Hellenization Revisited: Shaping a Christian Response within the Greco-Roman World*, ed. Wendy Helleman (Lanham, Md.: University Press of America, 1994), 69–98.

31. J. C. M. van Winden, *An Early Christian Philosopher: Justin Martyr's Dialogue with Trypho, Chapters One to Nine* (Philosophia Patrum 1; Leiden: Brill, 1971), 2–3. Simon Swain characterizes a divide between Christianity and Hellenic authors until the third century, so that Celsus for unknown reasons has a tone of one "picking holes in the views of an idiot minority"; "Defending Hellenism," 157.

32. Young, *Colonial Desire*, 162.

33. Adolf Harnack, *The Mission and Expansion of Christianity in the First Three Centuries*, trans. James Moffatt, 2nd ed. (London: Williams & Norgate, 1908), 1:254.

34. Bhabha, *Location of Culture*, 114.

35. Ibid., 113.

36. Ibid., 36–39; Young, *Colonial Desire*, 23.

37. Gayati Spivak, *The Critique of Post-Colonial Reason: Toward a History of the Vanishing Present* (Cambridge: Harvard University Press, 1999), 65.

38. Chakrabarty, *Habitations*, 140; see also comments by Bhabha in the introduction, ix–xiii.

39. Ibid., 140–45.

40. Justin's reputation as an original thinker was recently defended by Edwards, "Platonic Schooling," and "Justin's Logos." On this long debate see references helpfully collected in Oskar Skarsaune, "Judaism and Hellenism in Justin Martyr, Elucidated from His Portrait of Socrates," in *Geschichte—Tradition—Reflexion. Festschrift für Martin Hengel zum 70. Geburtstag*, III, *Frühes Christentum*, ed. H. Cancik, H. Lichtenberger, and P. Schäfer (Tübingen: Mohr, 1996), 585–611, at 586.

41. On the relation of Greek authors to Roman power, see Whitmarsh, *Greek Literature*, 23–26.

42. Skarsaune, "Judaism and Hellenism"; M. D. Young, "Justin, Socrates, and the Middle Platonists," *StPat* 15 (1989): 161–70.

43. Edwards, "Justin's Logos," 272–80.

44. Arthur J. Droge, *Homer or Moses? Early Christian Interpretation of the History of Culture* (Tübingen: Mohr, 1989).

45. On this question see now Denice Kimber Buell, *Why This New Race? Ethnic Reasoning in Early Christianity* (New York: Columbia University Press, 2005).

46. John Dillon, "'Orthodoxy' and 'Eclecticism': Middle Platonists and Neo-Pythagoreans," in *The Question of "Eclecticism": Studies in Later Greek Philosophy*, ed. J. M. Dillon and A. A. Long (Berkeley: University of California Press, 1988), 116–24.

47. See Simon Goldhill, "Setting an Agenda: 'Everything Is Greece to the Wise,'" in *Being Greek Under Rome*, ed. Goldhill, 1–28.

48. Droge, *Homer or Moses?* 62–63; Edwards, "Platonic Schooling," 29–33.

49. Whitmarsh, *Greek Literature*, 21.

Bibliography

Aberbach, Moses, and Bernard Grossfeld. *Targum Onkelos to Genesis: A Critical Analysis Together with an English Translation of the Text.* Denver: Ktav Books, Center for Judaic Studies University of Denver, 1982.

Abramowski, Luise. "The 'Memoirs of the Apostles' in Justin." In *The Gospel and the Gospels*, ed. Peter Stuhlmacher, 323–35. Grand Rapids: Eerdmans, 1991.

Ägyptische Urkunden aus dem Königlichen Museen zu Berlin, Griechische Urkunden I. Berlin: Weidmann, 1895.

Aland, Barbara. "Die Münsteraner Arbeit am Text des Neuen Testaments und ihr Beitrag für die frühe Überlieferung des 2. Jahrhunderts: Eine methodologische Betrachtung." In *Gospel Traditions in the Second Century: Origins, Recensions, Text, and Transmission*, ed. William L. Petersen, Christianity and Judaism in Antiquity 3, 55–70. Notre Dame: University of Notre Dame Press, 1989.

———. "Marcion/Marcioniten." *Theologische Realenzyklopädie* 22 (1992): 89–101.

Aland, Kurt. *Did the Early Church Baptize Infants?* Trans. G. R. Beasley-Murray. London: SCM, 1963.

Albl, Martin C. *"And Scripture Cannot Be Broken": The Form and Function of the Early Christian* Testimonia *Collections.* NovTSup 96. Leiden: Brill, 1999.

Aleith, Eva. *Paulusverständnis in der alten Kirche.* BZNW 18. Berlin: Töpelmann, 1937.

Allert, Craig D. *Revelation, Truth, Canon, and Interpretation: Studies in Justin Martyr's Dialogue with Trypho.* VCSup 64. Leiden: Brill, 2002.

Andresen, Carl. "Justin und die mittlere Platonismus." *ZNW* 44 (1952–53): 157–95.

———. *Logos und Nomos. Die Polemik des Kelsos wider das Christentum.* Arbeiten zur Kirchengeschichte 30. Berlin: Walter de Gruyter, 1955.

Andrist, Patrick. "Le *Dialogue d'Athanase et Zachée*: étude des sources et du contexte littéraire." Ph.D. diss., Université de Genève, 2001.

Armstrong, A. H., ed. *The Cambridge History of Later Greek and Early Medieval Philosophy.* Cambridge: Cambridge University Press, 1970.

Athenagoras. Legatio *and* De Resurrectione. Ed. and trans. William R. Schoedel. Oxford Early Christian Texts. Oxford: Clarendon, 1972.

Attridge, Harold W., ed. *Nag Hammadi Codex I (the Jung Codex): Introductions, Texts, Translations, Indices.* Trans. Harold W. Attridge and George W. MacRae. Nag Hammadi Studies 22. Leiden: Brill, 1985.

Baker, John Austin. "The 'Institution' Narrative and the Christian Eucharist." In *Thinking about the Eucharist: Essays by Members of the Archbishops' Commission on Christian Doctrine.* Church of England Doctrine Commission symposium. London: SCM, 1972.

Barclay, John M. G. "Who Was Considered an Apostate in the Jewish Diaspora?" In *Tolerance and Intolerance in Early Judaism and Christianity*, ed. Graham N. Stanton and Guy G. Stroumsa, 80–98. Cambridge: Cambridge University Press, 1998.

Barnard, L. W. *Justin Martyr: His Life and Thought*. Cambridge: Cambridge University Press, 1967.

———. *St. Justin Martyr: The First and Second Apologies*. Ancient Christian Writers 56. New York: Paulist Press, 1997.

Barnes, T. D. "Hadrian and Lucius Verus." *JRS* 57 (1967): 65–79.

———. *Tertullian: A Historical and Literary Study*. Rev. ed. Oxford: Clarendon, 1985.

Barrett, C. K. *The Acts of the Apostles*. 2 vols. ICC. Edinburgh: T&T Clark, 1994–2002.

Barthélemy, Dominique. *Les Devanciers d'Aquila: Première publication intégrale du texte des fragments du Dodécaprophéton*. VTSup 10. Leiden: Brill, 1963.

———. "Redécouverte d'un chaînon manquant de l'histoire de la Septante." *RB* 60 (1953): 18–29.

Battifol, Pierre. "Une source nouvelle de l'Altercatio Simonis Judaei et Theophili Christiani." *RB* 8 (1899): 337–45.

Bauckham, Richard. "The Restoration of Israel in Luke-Acts." In *Restoration: Old Testament, Jewish, and Christian Perspectives*, ed. James M. Scott, 435–87. Leiden: Brill, 2001.

Bauer, Walter. "The Picture of the Apostle in Early Christian Tradition: Accounts." In *New Testament Apocrypha*, ed. E. Hennecke and W. Schneemelcher, trans. and ed. R. McL. Wilson, 2:35–74. London: SCM, 1973–74.

Bauman, R. A. *Crime and Punishment in Ancient Rome*. London: Routledge, 1996.

Bellinzoni, Arthur J. *The Sayings of Jesus in the Writings of Justin Martyr*. NovTSup 17. Leiden: Brill, 1967.

Benz, E. "Christus und Socrates in der alten Kirche: Ein Beitrag zum altkirchlichen Verständnis des Märtyrers und des Martyriums." *ZNW* 43 (1950–51): 195–224.

Beyschlag, Karlmann. *Simon Magus und die christliche Gnosis*. Tübingen: Mohr, 1974.

Bhabha, Homi. *The Location of Culture*. London: Routledge, 1994.

Birley, A. *Hadrian: The Restless Emperor*. London: Routledge, 1997.

———. *Marcus Aurelius. A Biography*. 2nd ed. London: Batsford, 1987.

Blanchard, Yves-Marie. *Aux sources du Canon, le témoignage d'Irénée*. Cogitatio Fidei 175. Paris: du Cerf, 1993.

Blunt, A. W. F. *The Apologies of Justin Martyr*. Cambridge Patristic Texts. Cambridge: Cambridge University Press, 1911.

Bobichon, Philippe. *Justin Martyr. Dialogue avec Tryphon*, édition critique, traduction, commentaire. Paradosis 47/1–2. 2 vols. Fribourg: Academic Press, 2003.

———. "Justin martyr: étude stylistique du *Dialogue avec Tryphon*, suivie d'une comparaison avec l'*Apologie* et le *De resurrectione*." *Recherches augustiniennes et patristiques* 34 (2005): 1–61.

———. "Préceptes éternels de la Loi mosaïque et le *Dialogue avec Tryphon* de Justin Martyr." *RB* 111 (2004): 238–54.

Bock, Darrell. *Luke*. 2 vols. Baker Exegetical Commentary on the New Testament 3. Grand Rapids: Baker Books, 1994–96.

———. *Proclamation from Prophecy and Pattern: Lucan Old Testament Christology.* JSNTSup 12. Sheffield: JSOT, 1987.

———. "Scripture and the Realisation of God's Promises." In *Witness to the Gospel: The Theology of Acts,* ed. I. Howard Marshall and David Peterson, 41–62. Grand Rapids: Eerdmans, 1998.

Boeckhius, A., ed. *Corpus Inscriptionum Graecarum* II. Berlin: Reimen, 1843.

Boll, F. C. "Über das Verhältnis der beiden Apologien Justins des Märtyrers zu einander." *Zeitschrift für die historische Theologie* 12.3 (1842): 3–47.

Boor, C. de, ed. *Neue Fragmente des Papias, Hegesippus und Pierius in bisher unbekannten Excerpten aus der Kirchengeschichte des Philippus Sidetes.* TU V.2. Leipzig: J. C. Hinrichs, 1888.

Bousset, Wilhelm. *Jüdisch-Christlicher Schulbetrieb in Alexandria und Rom. Literarische Untersuchungen zu Philo und Clemens von Alexandria, Justin und Irenäus.* FRLANT, Neue Folge 6. Göttingen: Vandenhoeck & Ruprecht, 1915.

Bovon, Francis. *A Commentary on the Gospel of Luke 1:1—9:50.* Trans. Christine M. Thomas. Hermeneia. Minneapolis: Fortress Press, 2002.

Bowersock, G. *Hellenism in Late Antiquity.* Ann Arbor: University of Michigan Press, 1996.

Boyarin, Daniel. *Border Lines: The Partition of Judaeo-Christianity.* Philadelphia: University of Pennsylvania Press, 2004.

———. *Dying for God: Martyrdom and the Making of Christianity and Judaism.* Stanford: Stanford University Press, 1999.

Bradshaw, Paul F. *Eucharistic Origins.* Alcuin Club Collections 80. London: SPCK, 2004.

———. *The Search for the Origins of Christian Worship: Sources and Methods for the Study of Early Liturgy.* 2nd ed. Oxford: Oxford University Press, 2002.

Brakke, David. "The Early Church in North America: Late Antiquity, Theory, and the History of Christianity." *Church History* 71 (2002): 473–91.

Bratke, Eduard. "Epilegomena zur Wiener Ausgabe der Altercatio legis inter Simonem Judaeum et Theophilum Christianum." In *Sitzungsberichte der philosophisch-historischen Klasse der kaiserlichen Akademie der Wissenschaften,* 148:131–33, 158–78. Wien: Carl Gerold's Sohn, 1904.

Brewer, David Instone. *Techniques and Assumptions in Jewish Exegesis Before 70 CE.* Texte und Studien zum antiken Judentum 30. Tübingen: Mohr [Paul Siebeck], 1992.

Brooke, George J. "The Twelve Minor Prophets and the Dead Sea Scrolls." In *Congress Volume Leiden 2004,* ed. André Lemaire, 19–43. Leiden: Brill, 2006.

Brown, R. E. *The Death of the Messiah: From Gethsemane to the Grave; A Commentary on the Passion Narratives in the Four Gospels.* 2 vols. New York: Doubleday, 1994.

———. "The Gospel of Peter and Canonical Gospel Priority." *NTS* 33 (1987): 321–43.

Buchanan, Colin. *Anglican Confirmation.* Grove Liturgical Study 48. Nottingham: Grove Books, 1986.

Buck, P. Lorraine. "Justin Martyr's *Apologies*: Their Number, Destination, and Form." *JTS,* n.s. 54 (2003): 45–59.

Buell, Denice Kimber. *Why This New Race? Ethnic Reasoning in Early Christianity.* New York: Columbia University Press, 2005.

Bueno, Daniel Ruiz. *Padres Apologistas griegos (s. II).* Madrid: Biblioteca de Autores Cristianos, 1954.

Callewaert, C. "Le rescrit d'Hadrien à Minicius Fundanus." *Revue d'histoire et de littérature religieuses* 8 (1903): 152–89.

Capelle, D. B. "Le rescrit d'Hadrien et S. Justin." *RBen* 39 (1927): 365–68.

Cassels, W. R. *The Gospel according to Peter: A Study by the Author of "Supernatural Religion."* London: Longmans, Green, 1894.

Cerfaux, Lucien. "La première communauté chrétienne." In *Recueil Lucien Cerfaux, Tome II*, 125–56. Gembloux: J. Duculot, 1954.

Chadwick, Henry. *Early Christian Thought and the Classical Tradition: Studies in Justin, Clement, and Origen.* Oxford: Oxford University Press, 1966.

———. "Justin Martyr's Defence of Christianity." *BJRL* 47 (1964–65): 275–97.

———. "Philo and the Beginnings of Christian Thought." Part 2 in *The Cambridge History of Later Greek and Early Medieval Philosophy*, ed. A. H. Armstrong, 137–92. Cambridge: Cambridge University Press, 1970.

———, trans. *Origen: Contra Celsum.* Cambridge: Cambridge University Press, 1953.

Chakrabarty, Dipesh. *Habitations of Modernity: Essays in the Wake of Subaltern Studies.* Chicago: University of Chicago Press, 2002.

Chilton, Bruce. "Commenting on the Old Testament (with Particular Reference to the Pesharim, Philo, and the Mekhilta)." In *It Is Written: Scripture Citing Scripture; Essays in Honour of Barnabas Lindars*, ed. D. A. Carson and H. G. M. Williamson, 122–40. Cambridge: Cambridge University Press, 1988.

———. *A Feast of Meanings: Eucharistic Theologies from Jesus through Johannine Circles.* NovTSup 72. Leiden: Brill, 1994.

———. "James and the (Christian) Pharisees." In *When Judaism and Christianity Began: Essays in Memory of Anthony J. Saldarini*, vol. 1, *Christianity in the Beginning*, ed. A. J. Avery-Peck, D. Harrington, and J. Neusner, 19–47. JSJSup 85. Leiden: Brill, 2004.

———. *Judaic Approaches to the Gospels.* International Studies in Formative Christianity and Judaism 2. Atlanta: Scholars, 1994.

———. "Prophecy in the Targumim." In *Mediators of the Divine: Horizons of Prophecy, Divination, Dreams, and Theurgy in Mediterranean Antiquity*, ed. R. M. Berchman, 185–201. South Florida Studies in the History of Judaism 163. Atlanta: Scholars, 1998.

———. *Rabbi Paul: An Intellectual Biography.* New York: Doubleday, 2004.

———. "The Targumim and Judaism of the First Century." In *Judaism in Late Antiquity, part 3, Where We Stand: Issues and Debates in Ancient Judaism*, ed. J. Neusner and A. J. Avery-Peck, 2:15–150. Handbuch der Orientalistik 41. Brill: Leiden, 1999.

———. "Typologies of Memra and the Fourth Gospel." *Targum Studies* 1 (1992): 89–100.

Chilton, Bruce, and Jacob Neusner. *Judaism in the New Testament: Practices and Beliefs.* London and New York: Routledge, 1995.

Cohen, Shaye J. D. *The Beginnings of Jewishness: Boundaries, Varieties, Uncertainties.* Berkeley: University of California Press, 1999.

Collins, John J. *Between Athens and Jerusalem: Jewish Identity in the Hellenistic Diaspora.* 2nd ed. Grand Rapids: Eerdmans, 2000.

Conybeare, F. C. *The Dialogues of* Athanasius and Zacchaeus *and* Timothy and Aquila, *Edited with Prolegomena and Facsimiles.* Anecdota Oxoniensia, Classical Series 8. Oxford: Clarendon, 1898.

———. "A New Second-Century Christian Dialogue." *Expositor*, 5th ser., 5 (1897): 300–20, 443–63.

Conzelmann, Hans. *Acts of the Apostles.* Trans. James Limburg et al. Hermeneia. Philadelphia: Fortress Press, 1987.

Corssen, Peter. *Die Altercatio Simonis Iudaei et Theophili Christiani auf ihre Quellen geprüft.* Jever: C. L. Mettcker u. Söhne, 1890.

Cosgrove, C. H. "Justin Martyr and the Emerging Christian Canon: Observations on the Purpose and Destination of the *Dialogue with Trypho.*" *VC* 36 (1982): 209–32.

Cranmer, Thomas. *On the Lord's Supper.* Cambridge: Parker Society, 1844.

Daniélou, Jean. *The Theology of Jewish Christianity.* Trans. J. A. Baker. London: Darton, Longman & Todd; Chicago: Henry Regnery, 1964.

Davey, D. M. "Justin Martyr and the Fourth Gospel." *Scr* 17 (1965): 117–22.

Davis, C. J. *The Name and Way of the Lord.* JSNTSup 129. Sheffield: JSOT, 1996.

Deaut, Roger le. "La tradition juive ancienne et l'exégèse chrétienne primitive." *RHPhR* 51 (1971): 31–50.

———."Un phénomene spontané de l'hermeneutique juive ancienne: le 'targumisme.'" *Bib* 52 (1971): 505–25.

Deissmann, Adolf. "The Name 'Jesus.'" In *Mysterium Christi: Christological Studies by British and German Theologians*, ed. G. K. A. Bell and D. Adolf Deissmann, 3–27. London: Longmans, Green, 1930.

Dillon, John. *The Middle Platonists.* London: Duckworth, 1977.

———. "'Orthodoxy' and 'Eclecticism': Middle Platonists and Neo-Pythagoreans." In *The Question of "Eclecticism": Studies in Later Greek Philosophy*, ed. J. M. Dillon and A. A. Long, 116–24. Berkeley: University of California Press, 1988.

Dobschütz, Ernst von. *Das Kerygma Petri kritisch untersucht.* TU 11.1. Leipzig: J. C. Hinrichs, 1893.

Dörrie, Heinrich. "Die platonische Theologie des Kelsos in ihrer Auseinandersetzung mit der christlicher Theologie." *Nachrichten der Akademie der Wissenschaften zu Göttingen, philologisch-historische Klasse* (1967), 2:19–55.

Droge, Arthur J. *Homer or Moses? Early Christian Interpretation of the History of Culture.* Tübingen: Mohr, 1989.

Dunn, James D. G. *Baptism in the Holy Spirit: A Re-examination of the New Testament Teaching on the Gift of the Spirit in Relation to Pentecostalism Today.* London: SCM, 1970.

———. *The Parting of the Ways between Christianity and Judaism and Their Significance for the Character of Christianity.* London: SCM, 1991.

————, ed. *Jews and Christians: The Parting of the Ways, AD 70 to 135.* Tübingen: Mohr (Paul Siebeck), 1992.

Edelstein, Ludwig. *The Meaning of Stoicism.* Martin Classical Lectures 21. Cambridge: Harvard University Press, 1966.

Edwards, M. J. " Justin's Logos and the Word of God." *Journal of Early Christian Studies* 3 (1995): 261–80.

————. "On the Platonic Schooling of Justin Martyr." *JTS,* n.s., 42 (1991): 17–34.

Edwards, M. J., Martin Goodman, and Simon Price, eds. *Apologetics in the Roman Empire.* Oxford: Oxford University Press, 1999.

Engelhardt, Moritz von. *Das Christenthum Justins des Märtyrers: Eine Untersuchung über die Anfänge der Katholischen Glaubenslehre.* (Erlangen: Andreas Deichert, 1878.

Epp, J. Eldon. "Issues in the Interrelation of New Testament Textual Criticism and Canon." In *The Canon Debate,* ed. Lee Martin McDonald and James A. Sanders, 485–515. Peabody, Mass.: Hendrickson, 2002.

————. *The Theological Tendency of Codex Bezae Cantabrigiensis in Acts.* SNTSMS 3. Cambridge: Cambridge University Press, 1966.

Epstein, Isidore, ed. *The Babylonian Talmud: Seder Nezikin, Sanhedrin.* London: Soncino Press, 1935.

Eusebius Werke, II, *Die Kirchengeschichte.* Ed. Eduard Schwartz and Theodor Mommsen. Griechischen Christlichen Schriftsteller 9. 3 vols. Leipzig: J. C. Hinrichs, 1903–09.

Eusebius Werke, V, *Die Chronik aus dem armenischen übersetzt.* Trans. Josef Karst. Griechischen Christlichen Schriftsteller 20. Leipzig: J. C. Hinrichs, 1911.

Eusebius Werke, VII, *Die Chronik des Hieronymus.* Ed. Rudolf Helm. 3rd ed. Ursula Treu. Griechischen Christlichen Schriftsteller, Berlin: Akademie-Verlag, 1984.

Falls, Thomas B., trans. *St. Justin Martyr: Dialogue with Trypho.* Rev. Thomas P. Halton. Ed. Michael Slusser. Selections from the Fathers of the Church 3. Washington, D.C.: Catholic University of America Press, 2003.

————, trans. *The Writings of Justin Martyr.* Fathers of the Church 6. Washington, D.C.: Catholic University of America Press, 1948.

Ferguson, Everett. "Factors Leading to the Selection and Closure of the New Testament Canon: A Survey of Some Recent Studies." In *The Canon Debate,* ed. Lee Martin McDonald and James A. Sanders, 295–320. Peabody, Mass.: Hendrickson, 2002.

Fitzmyer, Joseph A. *The Gospel According to Luke I–IX.* AB 28. Garden City, N.Y.: Doubleday, 1981.

Fossum, Jarl E. "In the Beginning Was the Name." In Jarl E. Fossum, *The Image of the Invisible God: Essays on the Influence of Jewish Mysticism on Early Christology,* 109–33. Novum Testamentum et Orbis Antiquus 30. Göttingen: Vandenhoeck & Ruprecht, 1995.

Foster, Paul. "The Apology of Quadratus." In *The Writings of the Apostolic Fathers,* ed. Paul Foster, 52–62. London: T&T Clark, 2007.

————. "The Epistles of Ignatius of Antioch and the Writings That Later Formed the New Testament." In *The Reception of the New Testament in the Apostolic Fathers*, ed. A. F. Gregory and C. M. Tuckett, 173–81. Oxford: Oxford University Press, 2005.

Frede, Michael. "Eusebius' Apologetic Writings." In *Apologetics in the Roman Empire*, ed. M. J. Edwards, Martin Goodman, and Simon Price, 223–50. Oxford: Oxford University Press, 1999.

Frend, W. H. C. *The Rise of Christianity.* Philadelphia: Fortress Press, 1984.

Gaston, Lloyd. "Anti-Judaism and the Passion Narrative in Luke and Acts." In *Anti-Judaism in Early Christianity*, vol. 1, ed. Peter Richardson and David Granskou, 127–53. Waterloo: Wilfred Laurier, 1986.

Gieschen, Charles A. "The Divine Name in Ante-Nicene Christology." *VC* 57 (2003): 115–58.

Glasson, T. F. "'Plurality of Divine Persons' and the Quotations in Hebrews 1.6ff." *NTS* 12 (1965–66): 271–72.

Goldhill, Simon, ed. *Being Greek under Rome: Cultural Identity, the Second Sophistic, and the Development of Empire.* Cambridge: Cambridge University Press, 2001.

Goodenough, Erwin R. *The Theology of Justin Martyr.* Amsterdam: Philo, 1968 [= Jena: Frommannsche Buchhandlung, 1923].

Goodman, Martin. "Josephus' Treatise *Against Apion*." In *Apologetics in the Roman Empire*, ed. M. J. Edwards, Martin Goodman, and Simon Price, 45–58. Oxford: Oxford University Press, 1999.

Goodspeed, Edgar J., ed. *Die älteste Apologeten.* Göttingen: Vandenhoeck & Ruprecht, 1914.

Grant, Robert M. "Forms and Occasions of the Greek Apologists." *Studi e materiali di storia delle religioni* 52 (1986): 213–26.

————. *Greek Apologists of the Second Century.* Philadelphia: Westminster, 1988.

————. "Quadratus, the First Christian Apologist." In *A Tribute to Arthur Vööbus: Studies in Early Christian Literature and Its Environment, Primarily in the Syrian East*, ed. Robert H. Fischer, 177–83. Chicago: Lutheran School of Theology, 1977.

————. "A Woman of Rome: The Matron in Justin, 2 *Apology* 2.1–9." *CH* 54 (1985): 461–72.

Grossfeld, Bernard, and Moses Aberbach. *Targum Onqelos on Genesis 49: Translation and Analytic Commentary.* SBL Aramaic Studies 1. Missoula, Mt.: Scholars, 1976.

Gruen, Erich. *Heritage and Hellenism: The Reinvention of Jewish Tradition.* Berkeley: University of California Press, 1998.

Hagner, Donald A. "The Sayings of Jesus in the Apostolic Fathers and Justin Martyr." In *The Jesus Tradition Outside the Gospels*, ed. D. Wenham, 233–68. Gospel Perspectives 5. Sheffield: JSOT, 1985.

Hall, Stuart George, ed. and trans. *Melito of Sardis: On Pascha and Fragments.* Oxford Early Christian Texts. Oxford: Clarendon, 1979.

Hanson, R. P. C. *Allegory and Event: A Study of the Sources and Significance of Origen's Interpretation of Scripture.* Louisville: Westminster John Knox, 2002.

Harnack, Adolf. *Die Altercatio Simonis Iudaei et Theophili Christiani*. TU 1.3. Leipzig: J. C. Hinrichs, 1883.

——. *Analecta zur ältesten Geschichte des Christentums in Rom*, appended to Paul Koetschau, *Beiträge zur Textkritik von Origines' Johannescommentar*. TU 28.2. Leipzig: J. C. Hinrichs, 1905.

——. *Bruchstücke des Evangeliums und der Apokalypse des Petrus*. Leipzig: J. C. Hinrichs, 1893.

——. *Geschichte der altchristlichen Litteratur bis Eusebius*, Zweiter Theil, *Die Chronologie*, i., *Die Chronologie der Litteratur bis Irenäus*. Leipzig: J. C. Hinnrichs, 1897.

——. *Marcion. Das Evangelium von fremden Gott*. 2nd ed. TU 46. Leipzig: J.C. Hinrichs, 1924; repr., Darmstadt: Wissenschaftliche Buchgesellschaft, 1996 = *Marcion, the Gospel of the Alien God*. Trans. John E. Steely and Lyle D. Blerma. Durham, N.C.: Labyrinth, 1990.

——. *The Mission and Expansion of Christianity in the First Three Centuries*. Trans. James Moffatt. 2nd ed. London: Williams & Norgate, 1908.

——. *Die Überlieferung der griechischen Apologeten des zweiten Jahrhunderts in der alten Kirche und im Mittelalter*. TU 1.1, 2. Leipzig: J. C. Hinrichs, 1882.

Harris, J. Rendel, and V. Burch. *Testimonies*. 2 vols. Cambridge: Cambridge University Press, 1916–20.

Hartman, Lars. *"Into the Name of the Lord Jesus": Baptism in the Early Church*. Edinburgh: T&T Clark, 1997.

Hays, Richard B. *Echoes of Scripture in the Letters of Paul*. New Haven: Yale University Press, 1989.

Heard, Richard. "The *Apomnēmoneumata* in Papias, Justin, and Irenaeus." *NTS* 1 (1954–55): 122–29.

Heinisch, Paul. *Der Einfluss Philos auf die älteste christliche Exegese (Barnabas, Justin u. Clemens von Alexandria)*. Alttestamentliche Abhandlungen 1/2. Münster: Aschendorff, 1908.

Heitmüller, Wilhelm. *"Im Namen Jesu": Eine sprach- und religionsgeschichtliche Untersuchung zum Neuen Testament, speziell zur altchristlichen Taufe*. FRLANT 1/2. Göttingen: Vandenhoeck & Ruprecht, 1903.

Hengel, Martin. *The Four Gospels and the One Gospel of Jesus Christ: An Investigation of the Collection and Origin of the Canonical Gospels*. London: SCM, 2000.

——. *Die Johanneische Frage: Ein Lösungsversuch*, with a contribution on the Apocalypse by Jörg Frey. WUNT 67. Tübingen: Mohr, 1993.

——. *Judentum und Hellenismus. Studien zu ihrer Begegnung unter besonderer Berücksichtigung Palästinas bis zur Mitte des 2. Jh.s vor Christus*. 2nd ed. Tübingen: Mohr, 1973 = *Judaism and Hellenism*. Trans. John Bowden. Minneapolis: Fortress Press, 1974.

Hennecke, E. and W. Schneemelcher, eds. *New Testament Apocrypha*. Trans. and ed. R. McL. Wilson. 2 vols. London: SCM, 1973–74.

Hilgenfeld, A. "Die alttestamentliche Citate Justins in ihrer Bedeutung für die Untersuchung über seine Evangelien." *Theologische Jahrbücher* 9 (1850): 385–439, 567–78.

Hill, Charles E. *The Johannine Corpus in the Early Church.* Oxford: Oxford University Press, 2004.

———. "What Papias Said about John (and Luke): A 'New' Papian Fragment." *JTS*, n.s., 49 (1998): 582–629.

Hirshman, Marc. *A Rivalry of Genius: Jewish and Christian Biblical Interpretation in Late Antiquity.* Trans. Batya Stein-Hirshman. Albany: State University of New York Press, 1996.

Hofrichter, Peter. "Logoslehre und Gottesbild bei Apologeten, Modalisten und Gnostikern. Johanneische Christologie im Licht ihrer frühesten Rezeption." In *Monotheismus und Christologie. Zur Gottesfrage im hellenistischen Judentum und im Urchristentum,* cd. II.-J. Klauck, 186–217. Quaestiones Disputatae 138. Freiburg: Herder, 1992.

Holfelder, H. H. "Εὐσέβεια καὶ φιλοσοφία. Literarische Einheit und politischer Kontext von Justins Apologie." *ZNW* 68 (1977): 48–66, 231–51.

Holl, Karl, ed. *Fragmenta vornicänischer Kirchenväter aus den Sacra Parallela.* TU 20.2. Leipzig: J. C. Hinrichs, 1899.

Holte, Ragnar. "*Logos spermatikos*: Christianity and Ancient Philosophy according to St. Justin's Apologies." *StTh* 12 (1958): 109–68.

Horbury, William. "The Benediction of the *Minim* and Jewish-Christian Controversy." *JTS*, n.s., 33 (1982): 19–61.

Horner, Timothy J. *"Listening to Trypho": Justin Martyr's* Dialogue *Reconsidered.* Contributions to Biblical Exegesis and Theology 28. Leuven: Peeters, 2001.

Hurtado, Larry W. "The Binitarian Shape of Early Christian Worship." In *The Jewish Roots of Christological Monotheism: Papers from the St. Andrews Conference on the Historical Origins of the Worship of Jesus,* ed. Carey C. Newman, James R. Davilia, and Gladys S. Lewis, 187–213. Leiden: Brill, 1999.

———. *The First Christian Artifacts.* Grand Rapids: Eerdmans, 2006.

———. *Lord Jesus Christ: Devotion to Jesus in Earliest Christianity.* Grand Rapids: Eerdmans, 2003.

———. "The Origin of the *Nomina Sacra*: A Proposal." *JBL* 117 (1998): 655–73.

Hyldahl, Niels. *Philosophie und Christentum. Eine Interpretation der Einleitung zum Dialog Justins.* Acta theologica danica 9. Kopenhagen: Munksgaard, 1966.

Instinsky, H. U. "Zur Entstehung des Titels nobilissimus Caesar." In *Beiträge zur älteren Europäischen Kulturgeschichte, Festschrift für Rudolf Egger,* 1:98–103. Klagenfurt: Geschichtsverein für Kärnten, 1952–54.

Janowski, Bernd, and Peter Stuhlmacher, eds. *The Suffering Servant: Isaiah 53 in Jewish and Christian Sources.* Trans. Daniel P. Bailey. Grand Rapids: Eerdmans, 2004.

Jeremias, Joachim. *Infant Baptism in the First Four Centuries.* Trans. David Cairns. London: SCM, 1960.

———. *The Origins of Infant Baptism: A Further Study in Reply to Kurt Aland.* Trans. Dorothea M. Barton. London: SCM, 1963.

Jervell, Jacob. *The Theology of the Acts of the Apostles.* Cambridge: Cambridge University Press, 1996.

Johnson, Luke Timothy. *The Gospel of Luke*. Sacra Pagina. Collegeville, Minn.: Liturgical Press, 1991.

Joly, Robert. *Christianisme et philosophie: Études sur Justin et les Apologistes grecs du deuxième siècle*. Bruxelles: Éditions de l'Université Libre de Bruxelles, 1973.

Jones, F. Stanley. "Jewish Christianity of the *Pseudo-Clementines*." In *A Companion to Second-Century Christian "Heretics*," ed. Antti Marjanen and Petri Luomanen, 315–34. VCSup 76. Leiden: Brill, 2005.

Justin. *Apologie. Prima apologia per i cristiani ad Antonio il Pio; Seconda apologia per i cristiani al Senato romano; Prologo al Dialogo con Trifone*, intoduzione, traduzione, note e apparati di Giuseppe Girgenti. Testi a fronte 25. Milano: Rusconi, 1995.

———. *Apologies*, texte grec, traduction française, introduction et index de Louis Pautigny. Textes et documents pour l'étude historique du christianisme 1. Paris: A. Picard, 1904.

———. *Dialogue avec Tryphon*, texte grec, traduction française, introduction, notes et index de Georges Archambault. Textes et documents pour l'étude historique du christianisme 8 et 11. Paris: A. Picard, 1909.

Kaestli, Jean-Daniel. "Les scenes d'attribution des champs de mission et le depart de l'apôtre dans les actes apocryphes." In *Les actes apocryphes des Apôtres: Christianisme et monde païen*, ed. François Bovon et al., 249–64. Publications de la Faculté de Théologie de l'Université de Genève 4. Genève: Labor et Fides, 1981.

Keith, Graham. "Justin Martyr and Religious Exclusivism." *Tyndale Bulletin* 43 (1992): 57–80.

Kenyon, Frederic G. *The Chester Beatty Biblical Papyri, Fasciculus V, Numbers and Deuteronomy, Text*. London: Emery Walker Ltd., 1935.

Kessler, Edward. *Bound by the Bible: Jews, Christians, and the Sacrifice of Isaac*. Cambridge: Cambridge University Press, 2004.

King, Karen. *What Is Gnosticism?* Cambridge, Mass.: Harvard University Press, 2003.

Kinzig, Wolfram. "Der 'Sitz im Leben' der Apologie in der Alten Kirche." *ZKG* 100 (1989): 291–317.

———. "*Hē kainē diathēkē*: The Title of the New Testament in the Second and Third Centuries." *JTS*, n.s., 45 (1994): 519–44.

Kline, Leslie L. "Harmonized Sayings of Jesus in the Pseudo-Clementine Homilies and Justin Martyr." *ZNW* 66 (1975): 223–41.

Kloppenborg Verbin, John S. *Excavating Q: The History and Setting of the Sayings Gospel*. Edinburgh: T&T Clark, 2000.

Koester, Helmut. *Ancient Christian Gospels: Their History and Development*. London/Philadelphia: SCM/Fortress Press, 1990.

———. "Septuaginta und synoptischer Erzählungsstoff im Schriftbeweis Justins des Märtyrers." Habilitationsschrift Ruprecht–Karl–Universität. Heidelberg, 1956.

———. *Synoptische Überlieferung bei den Apostolischen Vätern*. TU 65. Berlin: Akademie-Verlag, 1957.

Koetschau, Paul. *Beiträge zur Textkritik von Origines' Johannescommentar*. TU 28.2. Leipzig: J. C. Hinrichs, 1905.

Köhler, Wolf-Dietrich. *Die Rezeption des Matthäusevangeliums in der Zeit vor Irenäus.* WUNT 2. Reihe 24. Tübingen: Mohr, 1987.

Kominiak, Benedict. *The Theophanies of the Old Testament in the Writings of St. Justin.* Studies in Sacred Theology, 2nd ser., 14. Washington, D.C.: Catholic University of America Press, 1948.

König, Hildegard. "Marcion von Sinope." In *Lexikon der antiken christlichen Literatur,* ed. Siegmar Döpp with Peter Bruns, 3rd ed., 483. Freiburg: Herder, 2002.

Kontoleon, A. [Edition of Scaptopara petition.] In *Mitteilungen des kaiserlichen Deutschen archäo-logischen Instituts, Athenische Abteilung* 16 (1891): 267–79.

Körtner, Ulrich H. J., and Martin Leutzsch. *Papiasfragmente, Hirt des Hermas.* Schriften des Urchristentums 3. Darmstatt: Wissenschaftliche Buchgesellschaft, 1998.

Kugel, James L., and Rowan A. Greer. *Early Biblical Interpretation.* Library of Early Christianity. Philadelphia: Westminster, 1986.

Kurz, W. S. "The Function of Christological Proof from Prophecy for Luke and Justin." Ph.D. diss. on microfilm, Yale University, 1976.

———. "Promise and Fulfillment in Hellenistic Jewish Narratives and in Luke and Acts." In *Jesus and the Heritage of Israel,* ed. David P. Moessner, 147–70. Harrisburg, Pa.: Trinity Press International, 1999.

Lahey, Lawrence Lanzi. "The *Dialogue of Timothy and Aquila*: Critical Greek Text and English Translation of the Short Recension with an Introduction Including a Source-Critical Study." Ph.D. diss., University of Cambridge, 2000.

Lampe, G. W. H. *A Patristic Greek Lexicon.* Oxford: Clarendon, 1969.

Lampe, Peter. *From Paul to Valentinus: Christians at Rome in the First Two Centuries.* Trans. Michael Steinhauser. Ed. Marshall D. Johnson. London: T&T Clark, 2003 = *Die stadtrömischen Christen in den ersten beiden Jahrhunderten.* 2nd ed. Tübingen: Mohr, 1989.

Lawlor, Hugh J. "Eusebius on Papias." *Hermathena* 19 (1922): 167–222.

Lebreton, Jules. *Histoire du dogme de la Trinité.* 2 vols. Paris: Gabriel Beauchesne, 1928.

Lieu, Judith M. "Accusations of Jewish Persecution in Early Christian Sources, with Particular Reference to Justin Martyr and the *Martyrdom of Polycarp*." In *Tolerance and Intolerance in Early Judaism and Christianity,* ed. Graham N. Stanton and Guy G. Stroumsa, 279–95. Cambridge: Cambridge University Press, 1998.

———. *Christian Identity in the Jewish and Graeco-Roman World.* Oxford: Oxford University Press, 2004.

———. *Image and Reality: The Jews in the World of the Christians in the Second Century.* Edinburgh: T&T Clark, 1996.

———. "Justin Martyr and the Transformation of Psalm 22." In *Biblical Traditions in Transmission: Essays in Honour of Michael A. Knibb,* ed. Charlotte Hempel and Judith M. Lieu, 195–211. JSJSup 111. Leiden: Brill, 2006.

———. *Neither Jew nor Greek? Constructing Early Christianity.* London: T&T Clark, 2002.

Lieu, Judith M., John A. North, and Tessa Rajak, eds. *The Jews among Pagans and Christians in the Roman Empire.* London: Routledge, 1992.

Lightfoot, J. B. *The Apostolic Fathers*, part 2, *S. Ignatius, S. Polycarp*. 3 vols. 2nd ed. London: Macmillan, 1889.

Lightstone, Jack. "Christian Anti-Judaism in Its Judaic Mirror: The Judaic Context of Early Christianity Revised." In *Anti-Judaism in Early Christianity*, Studies in Christianity and Judaism 2: Separation and Polemic, ed. Stephen G. Wilson, 103–32. Waterloo: Wilfrid Laurier, 1986.

Lindars, Barnabas. *New Testament Apologetic: The Doctrinal Significance of the Old Testament*. London: SCM, 1961.

Lindemann, Andreas. *Paulus im ältesten Christentum*. BHTh 58. Tübingen: Mohr, 1979.

Longenecker, Richard N. *The Christology of Early Jewish Christianity*. SBT, 2nd ser., 17. London: SCM, 1970.

Lüdemann, Gerd. "Zur Geschichte des ältesten Christentums in Rom. I. Valentin und Marcion, II. Ptolemäus und Justin." *ZNW* 70 (1979): 86–114.

Lyman, Rebecca. "The Politics of Passing: Justin Martyr's Conversion as a Problem of 'Hellenization.'" In *Conversion in Late Antiquity and the Early Middle Ages: Seeing and Believing*, ed. Kenneth Mills and Anthony Grafton, 36–60. Rochester, N.Y.: University of Rochester Press, 2003.

MacCulloch, Diarmid. *Thomas Cranmer: A Life*. New Haven: Yale University Press, 1996.

Marcos, Natalio Fernández. *The Septuagint in Context: Introduction to the Greek Version of the Bible*. Leiden: Brill, 2000.

Marcovich, Miroslav, ed. *Iustini Martyris Apologiae pro Christianis*. PTS 38. Berlin: Walter de Gruyter, 1994.

———. *Iustini Martyris Dialogus cum Tryphone*. PTS 47. Berlin: Walter de Gruyter, 1997.

———. *Pseudo-Justinus. Cohortatio ad Graecos, De Monarchia, Oratio ad Graecos*. PTS 32. Berlin: Walter de Gruyter, 1990.

Markschies, Christoph. "New Research on Ptolemaeus Gnosticus." *Zeitschrift für antikes Christentum* 4 (2000): 225–54.

Martin, Dale. "Paul and the Judaism/Hellenism Dichotomy: Toward a Social History of the Question." In *Paul beyond the Judaism/Hellenism Divide*, ed. T. Engberg-Pedersen, 26–61. Louisville: Westminster John Knox, 2001.

Martínez, Florentino García, and Eibert J. C. Tigchelaar, eds. *The Dead Sea Scrolls Study Edition*. 2 vols. Leiden: Brill, 1997–98.

Massaux, Édouard. *The Influence of the Gospel of Saint Matthew on Christian Literature before Saint Irenaeus*. Trans. Norman J. Belval and Suzanne Hecht. Ed. Arthur J. Bellinzoni. 3 vols. Macon, Ga.: Mercer University Press, 1990–93.

———. "The Text of Matthew's Sermon on the Mount Used by Saint Justin: A Contribution to the Textual Criticism of the First Gospel." In Massaux, *Influence*, 3:190–230. Originally published as "Le texte du Sermon sur la Montagne de Matthieu utilize par Saint Justin." *EThL* 28 (1952): 411–48.

McKnight, Scot. "Gentiles, Gentile Mission." In *Dictionary of the Later New Testament and Its Developments*, ed. Ralph P. Martin and Peter H. Davids, 391. Downers Grove, Ill.: InterVarsity Press, 1997.

———. *A New Vision for Israel: The Teachings of Jesus in National Context.* Grand Rapids: Eerdmans, 1999.

Meecham, Henry G. *The Epistle to Diognetus.* Manchester: Manchester University Press, 1949.

Meunier, Bernard. "Le Clivage entre Juifs et chrétiens vu part Justin (vers 150)." In *Le Judaïsme à l'aube de l'ère chrétienne. XVIIIᵉ congres de l'ACFEB (Lyon, September 1999)*, ed. Philippe Abadie and Jean-Pierre Lémonon, 333–44. LD 186. Paris: du Cerf, 2001.

Mihailov, Georgius, ed. *Inscriptiones Graecae in Bulgaria Repertae.* Vol. 4. Serdica/Sofia: Academia Litterarum Bulgarica, 1966.

Millar, Fergus. *The Emperor in the Roman World (31 BC–AD 337).* 2nd ed. London: Duckworth, 1992.

———. "Emperors at Work." *JRS* 57 (1967): 9–19.

Mommsen, T. "Der Religionsfrevel nach römischem Recht." *Historische Zeitschrift*, 64, n. F. 28 (1890): 389–429.

Monat, Pierre. *Lactance et la Bible: Une propédeutique latine à la lecture de la Bible dans l'Occident constantinien.* 2 vols. Paris: Études augustiniennes, 1982.

Munier, Charles. *L'Apologie de saint Justin, philosophe et martyre.* Paradosis 38. Fribourg: Éditions Universitaires, 1994.

———. *Autorité épiscopale et sollicitude pastorale IIᵉ—VIᵉ siècles.* Collected Studies CS 341. Aldershot: Variorum, 1990.

———. *Justin martyr, apologie pour les chrétiens.* Patrimoines, christianisme. Paris: du Cerf, 2006.

———. "A propos des Apologies de Justin." *RevScRel* 61 (1987): 177–86.

———. "La structure littéraire de l'Apologie de Justin." *RevScRel* 60 (1986): 34–54.

———, ed. *Justin, Apologie pour les Chrétiens,* introduction, texte critique, traduction et notes. Sources chrétiennes 507. Paris: du Cerf, 2006.

———, ed. *Saint Justin. Apologie pour les chrétiens*, édition et traduction. Paradosis 39. Fribourg: Éditions Universitaires, 1995.

Musurillo, Herbert. *The Acts of the Christian Martyrs.* Oxford Early Christian Texts. Oxford: Clarendon, 1972.

Nagel, Titus. *Die Rezeption des Johannesevangeliums im 2. Jahrhundert: Studien zur vorirenäischen Auslegung des vierten Evangeliums in christlicher und christlich-gnostischer Literatur.* Arbeiten zur Bibel und ihrer Geschichte 2. Leipzig: Evangelische Verlagsanstalt, 2000.

Nasrallah, Laura. "Mapping the World: Justin, Tatian, Lucian, and the Second Sophistic." *HTR* 98, no. 3 (2005): 283–314.

Nautin, P. "Genèse 1,1–2, de Justin à Origène." In *In Principio. Interprétations des premiers versets de la Genèse*, 83–86. École pratique des Hautes Études—(Vᵉ Section). Section des Sciences religieuses 152. Paris: Études Augustiennes, 1973.

———. "Histoire des dogmes et des sacrements chrétiens." In *Annuaire de l'École pratique des Hautes Études—(Vᵉ Section) Section des Sciences religieuses* 1967/68: 162–67.

Nesselhauf, H. "Hadrians Reskript an Minicius Fundanus." *Hermes* 104 (1976): 348–61.

Neusner, Jacob. *The Theology of the Oral Torah: Revealing the Justice of God*. Montreal: McGill-Queen's University Press, 1999.

New, Silva. "The Name, Baptism, and the Laying On of Hands." In *The Beginnings of Christianity*, part 1, *The Acts of the Apostles*, ed. F. J. Foakes Jackson and Kirsopp Lake, 5:121–40. London: Macmillan, 1932; repr., Grand Rapids: Baker, n.d.

Newman, Carey C. *Paul's Glory-Christology: Tradition and Rhetoric*. NovTSup 69. Leiden: Brill, 1992.

Newsom, C. "The 'Psalms of Joshua' from Qumran Cave 4." *Journal of Jewish Studies* 39 (1988): 56–73.

Niederwimmer, Kurt. *The Didache: A Commentary*. Trans. Linda M. Maloney. Hermeneia. Minneapolis: Fortress Press, 1998.

Norelli, Enrico. "Marcion: ein christlicher Philosoph oder ein Christ gegen die Philosophie?" In *Marcion und seine kirchengeschichtliche Wirkung; Marcion and His Impact on Church History*, ed. Gerhard May and Katharina Gresham, 113–30. TU 159. Berlin: Walter de Gruyter, 2002.

O'Neill, John C. *The Theology of Acts in Its Historical Setting*. London: SPCK, 1961.

Osborn, Eric Francis. *Justin Martyr*. BHTh 47. Tübingen: J. C. B. Mohr (Paul Siebeck), 1973.

Otto, J. C. T. von, ed. *Corpus Apologetarum Christianorum Saeculi Secundi*. Vol. 9. Jena: Mauke (Herm. Dufft), 1872.

———. *S. Iustini Philosophi et Martyris Opera quae feruntur omnia*, T. II, editio altera. Iena: Frider. Mauke, 1869; 3rd. ed., 1876.

Overbeck, Franz. "Über das Verhältniss Justins des Märtyrers zur Apostelgeschichte." *Wissenschaftliche Zeitung für Theologie* 15 (1872): 305–49.

Parkinson, William Q. "'In the Name of Jesus': The Ritual Use and Christological Significance of the Name of Jesus in Early Christianity." Ph.D. diss., University of Edinburgh, 2003.

Parvis, Paul. "The Textual Tradition of Justin's *Apologies*: A Modest Proposal." *StPat* 36 (2001): 54–60.

Paulsen, Henning. "Das Kerygma Petri und die urchristliche Apologetik." *ZKG* 88 (1977): 1–37.

Pearson, Birger A. "On Rodney Stark's Foray into Early Christian History." *Religion* 29 (1999): 171–76.

Perrone, Lorenzo. "Eine 'verschollende Bibliothek'? Das Schicksal frühchristlicher Schriften (2.–3. Jahrhundert) am Beispiel des Irenäus von Lyon." *ZKG* 116 (2005): 1–29.

Petersen, William L. "The Text of the Synoptic Gospels in the Second Century." In *Gospel Traditions in the Second Century: Origins, Recensions, Text, and Transmission*, ed. William L. Petersen, 19–37. Christianity and Judaism in Antiquity 3. Notre Dame: University of Notre Dame Press, 1989.

———. "Textual Evidence of Tatian's Dependence upon Justin's 'ΑΠΟΜΝΗΜΟΝΕΥΜΑΤΑ.'" *NTS* 36 (1990): 512–34.

Pilhofer, Peter. "Justin und das Petrusevangelium." *ZNW* 81 (1990): 60–78.

———. "Von Jakobus zu Justin. Lernen in den spätschriften des Neues Testaments und bei den Apologeten." In *Religiöse Lernen in der biblischen, frühjüdischen und frühchristlichen Überlieferung*, ed. Beate Ego and Helmut Merkel, 253–69. WUNT 180. Tübingen: Mohr Siebeck, 2005.

Piper, Otto A. "The Nature of the Gospel according to Justin Martyr." *JR* 14 (1961): 155–68.

Ponthot, Joseph. *La signification religieuse du "Nom" chez Clément de Rome et dans la Didaché.* ALBO 3/12. Louvain: Publications universitaires de Louvain, 1959.

Pouderon, Bernard. *Les Apologistes grecs du II*^e *siècle*. Initiations aux pères de l'église. Paris: du Cerf, 2005.

———. *Athénagore d'Athènes, philosophe Chrétien.* ThH 82. Paris: du Cerf, 1989.

Pouderon, Bernard, and Marie-Joseph Pierre, eds. *Aristide, Apologie.* SC 470. Paris: du Cerf, 2003.

Price, Simon. "Latin Christian Apologetics." In *Apologetics in the Roman Empire: Pagans, Jews, and Christians*, ed. Mark Edwards, Martin Goodman, and Simon Price, 105–29. Oxford: Oxford University Press, 1999.

Prigent, Pierre. *Justin et l'Ancien Testament. L'argumentation scripturaire du Traité de Justin contre toutes les hérésies comme source principale du Dialogue avec Tryphon et la Première Apologie.* ÉtB; Paris: J. Gabalda, 1964.

Prosopographia Imperii Romani Saeculi I. II. III pars V, editio altera. Berlin: Walter de Gruyter, 1970–1987.

Pryor, John. "Justin Martyr and the Fourth Gospel." *SecCent* 9 (1992): 153–69.

Pummer, Reinhard. *The Samaritans.* Iconography of Religions 23.5. Leiden: Brill, 1987.

Quasten, Johannes. *Patrology*, vol. 1, *The Beginnings of Patristic Literature.* Utrecht: Spectrum, 1966.

Rahlfs, A. *Der Text des Septuaginta-Psalters.* Septuaginta-Studien, Heft 2. Göttingen: Vandenhoeck & Ruprecht, 1965.

Rajak, Tessa. "Talking at Trypho: Christian Apologetic as Anti-Judaism in Justin's *Dialogue with Trypho the Jew*." In *The Jewish Dialogue with Greece and Rome: Studies in Cultural and Social Interaction*, 511–33. AGJU 48. Leiden: Brill, 2001.

Ratcliff, E. C. "Justin Martyr and Confirmation." In *Liturgical Studies*, ed. A. H. Couratin and D. H. Tripp, 110–17. London: SPCK, 1976. Originally published in *Theology* 51, no. 334 (April 1948).

Reed, Annette Yoshiko. "The Trickery of the Fallen Angels and the Demonic Mimesis of the Divine: Aetiology, Demonology, and Polemics in the Writings of Justin Martyr." *Journal of Early Christian Studies* 12, no. 2 (2004): 141–71.

Remus, Harold. "Justin Martyr's Argument with Judaism." In *Anti-Judaism in Early Christianity*, Studies in Christianity and Judaism 2: Separation and Polemic, ed. Stephen G. Wilson, 59–80. Waterloo: Wilfrid Laurier, 1986.

Rist, John. *Stoic Philosophy.* Cambridge: Cambridge University Press, 1969.

Rius-Camps, Josep, and Jenny Read-Heimerdinger. *The Message of Acts in Codex Bezae: A Comparison with the Alexandrian Tradition.* Vol. 1. JSNTSup 257. London: T&T Clark, 2004.

Robert, Louis, ed., with G. W. Bowersock and C. P. Jones. *Le Martyre de Pionios, Prête de Smyrne.* Washington, D.C.: Dumbarton Oaks Research Library and Collection, 1994.

Roberts, Colin H. "The Christian Book and the Greek Papyri." *JTS* 50 (1949): 155–68.

Roberts, Colin H., and Theodore C. Skeat. *The Birth of the Codex.* London: Oxford University Press, 1983.

Robinson, James M., ed. *The Nag Hammadi Library in English.* 3rd ed. Leiden: Brill, 1988.

Robinson, James M., and Helmut Koester. *Trajectories through Early Christianity.* Philadelphia: Fortress Press, 1971.

Robinson, O. F. *The Criminal Law of Ancient Rome.* Baltimore: Johns Hopkins University Press, 1995.

Rokéah, David. *Justin Martyr and the Jews.* Leiden: Brill, 2002.

Rowe, William V. "Adolf von Harnack and the Concept of Hellenization." In *Hellenization Revisited: Shaping a Christian Response within the Greco-Roman World,* ed. Wendy Helleman, 69–98. Lanham, Md.: University Press of America, 1994.

Ruck-Schröder, Adelheid. *Der Name Gottes und der Name Jesu: Eine neutestamentliche Studie.* WMANT 80. Neukirchen-Vluyn: Neukirchener, 1999.

Rudolph, Anette. *"Denn wir sind jenes Volk . . .": Die neue Gottesverehrung in Justins Dialog mit dem Juden Trypho in historisch-theologischer Sicht.* Hereditas 15. Bonn: Borengässer, 1999.

Russell, D. A., and N. G. Wilson, eds. *Menander Rhetor.* Oxford: Clarendon, 1981.

Sanchez, Jean Gabriel. *Justin Apologiste chrétien: Travaux sur le* Dialogue avec Tryphon *de Justin Martyr.* Cahiers de la Revue Biblique 50. Paris: J. Gabalda, 2000.

Sanders, E. P., ed. *Jewish and Christian Self-Definition.* 3 vols. Philadelphia: Fortress Press, 1980–82.

———. *The Tendencies of the Synoptic Tradition.* SNTSMS 9. Cambridge: Cambridge University Press, 1969.

Sanders, Jack T. "The Jewish People in Luke-Acts." In *Luke-Acts and the Jewish People: Eight Critical Perspectives,* ed. Joseph B. Tyson, 58–72. Minneapolis: Augsburg, 1988.

———. *Schismatics, Sectarians, Dissidents, Deviants: The First One Hundred Years of Jewish Christian Relations.* Valley Forge, Pa.: Trinity Press International, 1993.

Schäfer, Peter. *Die Vorstellung vom heiligen Geist in der rabbinischen Literatur.* SANT 28. München: Kösel, 1972.

Schmid, Wolfgang. *Ausgewählte philologische Schriften.* Ed. H. Erbse and J. Küppers. Berlin: Walter de Gruyter, 1984.

———. "The Christian Re-interpretation of the *Rescript* of Hadrian." *Maia* 7 (1955): 5–13.

———. "Ein Inversionsphänomen und seine Bedeutung im Text der Apologie des Justin." In *Forma Futuri: Studi in onore del Cardinale M. Pellegrino,* 253–81. Turin: Erasmo, 1975.

Seeberg, Bengt. "Die Geschichtstheologie Justins des Märtyrers." *ZKG* 58 (1939): 1–81.

———. *Die Geschichtstheologie Justins des Märtyrers.* Stuttgart, 1939.

Segal, Alan F. *Rebecca's Children: Judaism and Christianity in the Roman World.* Cambridge, Mass.: Harvard University Press, 1986.

———. *Two Powers in Heaven: Early Rabbinic Reports about Christianity and Gnosticism.* SJLA 25. Leiden: Brill, 1977.

Setzer, Claudia J. *Jewish Responses to Early Christians: History and Polemics, 30–150 A.D.* Minneapolis: Fortress Press, 1994.

Shotwell, W. A. *The Biblical Exegesis of Justin Martyr.* London: SPCK, 1965.

Sibinga, J. Smit. *The Old Testament Text of Justin Martyr 1: The Pentateuch.* Leiden: Brill, 1963.

Siker, Jeffrey. *Disinheriting the Jews: Abraham in Early Christian Controversy.* Louisville: Westminster John Knox, 1991.

Skarsaune, Oskar. "The Development of Scriptural Interpretation in the Second and Third Centuries—except Clement and Origen." In *Hebrew Bible/Old Testament: The History of Its Interpretation*, vol. 1, *From the Beginnings to the Middle Ages (until 1300)*, Part i, *Antiquity*, ed. Magne Sæbø, 373–442. Göttingen: Vandenhoeck & Ruprecht, 1996.

———. "From Books to Testimonies: Remarks on the Transmission of the Old Testament in the Early Church." In *The New Testament and Christian-Jewish Dialogue: Studies in Honor of David Flusser*, ed. Malcolm Lowe, 207–19. *Immanuel* 24/25. Jerusalem: Ecumenical Theological Research Fraternity in Israel, 1990.

———. "Jewish-Christian Gospels: Which and How Many?" In *Ancient Israel, Judaism, and Christianity in Contemporary Perspective: Essays in Memory of Karl-Johan Illman*, ed. Jacob Neusner et al., 393–408. Studies in Judaism. Lanham, Md.: University Press of America, 2006.

———. "Judaism and Hellenism in Justin Martyr, Elucidated from His Portrait of Socrates." In *Geschichte—Tradition—Reflexion. Festschrift für Martin Hengel zum 70. Geburtstag, III, Frühes Christentum*, ed. H. Cancik, H. Lichtenberger, and P. Schäfer, 585–611. Tübingen: Mohr Siebeck, 1996.

———. "Noen trekk ved apostel-bildet i den tidlig-kristne litteratur." *Ichthys* 27 (2000): 3–13, 57–68.

———. *The Proof from Prophecy: A Study in Justin Martyr's Proof-Text Tradition; Text-Type, Provenance, Theological Profile.* NovTSup 66. Leiden: Brill, 1987.

Smith, J. P. "Hebrew Christian Midrash in Iren. Epid. 43." *Bib.* 38 (1957): 24–34.

Soares-Prabhu, G. M. *The Formulas Quotations in the Infancy Narrative of Matthew.* Rome: Biblical Institute Press, 1976.

Spanneut, Michel. *Le stoïcisme des Pères.* Patristica Sorbonensia. Paris: Seuil, 1957.

Spivak, Gayati. "Can the Subaltern Speak? Speculations on Widow Sacrifice." In *Marxism and the Interpretation of Culture*, ed. C. Nelson and L. Grossberg, 271–313. London: Macmillan, 1988.

———. *The Critique of Post-Colonial Reason: Toward a History of the Vanishing Present.* Cambridge, Mass.: Harvard University Press, 1999.

Stanton, Graham N. "The Fourfold Gospel." *NTS* 43 (1997): 317–46; revised reprint in Stanton, *Jesus and Gospel*, 63–91.

———. *Jesus and Gospel.* Cambridge: Cambridge University Press, 2004.

———. "Jesus Traditions and Gospels in Justin Martyr and Irenaeus." In Stanton, *Jesus and Gospel*, 92–109. Also in *The Biblical Canons*, ed. J.-M. Auwers and H. J. de Jonge, 353–70. BEThL 163. Leuven: Peeters, 2003.

———. "Justin Martyr's *Dialogue with Trypho*: Group Boundaries, 'Proselytes' and 'God-fearers.'" In *Tolerance and Intolerance in Early Judaism and Christianity*, ed. Graham N. Stanton and Guy G. Stroumsa, 263–78. Cambridge: Cambridge University Press, 1998.

———. "The Spirit in the Writings of Justin Martyr." In *The Holy Spirit and Christian Origins: Essays in Honor of James D. G. Dunn*, ed. Graham N. Stanton, Bruce W. Longenecker, and Stephen C. Barton, 321–34. Grand Rapids: Eerdmans, 2004.

———. "Why Were Early Christians Addicted to the Codex?" In Stanton, *Jesus and Gospel*, 165–91. Cambridge: Cambridge University Press, 2004.

Stark, Rodney. *The Rise of Christianity*. Princeton: Princeton University Press, 1996; paper ed., San Francisco: HarperSanFrancisco, 1997.

Ste. Croix, G. E. M. de. "Why Were the Early Christians Persecuted?" *Past and Present* 26 (1963): 6–37.

Stead, G. C. *Philosophy in Christian Antiquity*. Cambridge: Cambridge University Press, 1994.

Sterling, Gregory. *Historiography and Self-Definition: Josephus, Luke-Acts, and Apologetic Historiography*. NovTSup 114. Leiden: Brill, 1992.

Strachan-Davidson, J. L. *Problems of the Roman Criminal Law*. 2 vols. Oxford: Clarendon, 1912.

Strecker, Georg. "Eine Evangelienharmonie bei Justin und Pseudoklemens?" *NTS* 24 (1978): 297–316.

Stroumsa, Guy G. "From Anti-Judaism to Antisemitism in Early Christianity." In *Contra Iudaeos*, ed. Ora Limor and Guy G. Stroumsa, 1–26. Texts and Studies in Medieval and Early Modern Judaism. Tübingen: Mohr, 1996.

Stylianopoulos, Theodore. *Justin Martyr and the Mosaic Law*. SBLDS 20. Missoula, Mt.: Scholars, 1975.

Swain, Simon. "Defending Hellenism: Philostratus, *In Honour of Apollonius*." In *Apologetics in the Roman Empire: Pagans, Jews, and Christians*, ed. Mark Edwards, Martin Goodman, and Simon Price, 157–96. Oxford: Oxford University Press, 1999.

———. *Hellenism and Empire: Language, Classicism, and Power in the Greek World AD 50–250*. Oxford: Clarendon, 1996.

Swete, H. B. *The Akhmîm Fragment of the Apocryphal Gospel of St. Peter*. London: Macmillan, 1893.

Tabbernee, William. *Montanist Inscriptions and Testimonia*. Macon, Ga.: Mercer University Press, 1997.

Talbert, Charles H. *Reading Acts: A Literary and Theological Commentary on the Acts of the Apostles*. Reading the New Testament. New York: Crossroad, 1997.

Tannehill, Robert C. *The Narrative Unity of Luke-Acts: A Literary Interpretation*. 2 vols. Foundations and Facets. Philadelphia: Fortress Press, 1986–90.

Tanner, Kathryn. *Theories of Culture: A New Agenda for Theology*. Guides to Theological Inquiry. Minneapolis: Fortress Press, 1997.

Tertullian. *Apology, De Spectaculis.* Ed. and trans. T. R. Glover. *Minucius Felix.* Ed. and trans. Gerald H. Rendall. Loeb Classical Library. London: William Heinemann, 1931.

———. *Apologeticum.* Ed. Heinrich Hoppe. CSEL 69. Vienna: Hoelder–Pichler–Tempsky, 1939.

Thoma, A. "Justins literarisches Verhältnis zu Paulus und zum Johannesevangelium." *Wissenschaftliche Zeitung für Theologie* 18 (1875): 383–412, 490–565.

Thomassen, Einar. *The Spiritual Seed: The Church of the "Valentinians."* Nag Hammadi and Manichaean Studies 60. Leiden: Brill, 2006.

Tiede, David L. "The Exaltation of Jesus and the Restoration of Israel in Acts 1." *HTR* 79 (1986): 279–86.

Trakatellis, Demetrius C. *The Pre-existence of Christ in Justin Martyr: An Exegetical Study with Reference to the Humiliation and Exaltation Christology.* HDR 6. Missoula, Mt.: Scholars, 1976.

Tregelles, S. P. *Canon Muratorianus.* Oxford: Clarendon, 1867.

Trevett, Christine. *Montanism: Gender, Authority, and the New Prophecy.* Cambridge: Cambridge University Press, 1996.

Trobisch, David. *The First Edition of the New Testament.* Oxford: Oxford University Press, 2000.

———. *Paul's Letter Collection: Tracing the Origins.* Minneapolis: Fortress Press, 1994.

Tuckett, Christopher M. "Paul, Scripture, and Ethics: Some Reflections." *NTS* 46 (2000): 403–24.

Turner, Eric G. *The Typology of the Early Codex.* Haney Foundation Series 18. Philadelphia: University of Pennsylvania Press, 1977.

Turner, Max. *Power from On High: The Spirit in Israel's Restoration and Witness in Luke-Acts* (Sheffield: Sheffield Academic Press, 1996)

Unnik, Willem Cornelis van. "*Hē kainē diathēkē*—a Problem in the Early History of the Canon." In *Sparsa Collecta: The Collected Essays of W. C. van Unnik*, 2:157–71. NovTSup 29–31. Leiden: Brill, 1973, 1980, 1983.

Varner, William. *Ancient Jewish-Christian Dialogues: Athanasius and Zacchaeus, Simon and Theophilus, Timothy and Aquila; Introductions, Texts, and Translations.* Studies in the Bible and Early Christianity 58. Lewiston, N.Y.: Edwin Mellen, 2004.

Veil, H., ed. *Justinus des Philosophen und Märtyrers, Rechtfertigung des Christentums (Apologie I u. II).* Strassburg: Heitz, 1894.

Vigne, Daniel. *Christ au Jourdain: Le Baptême de Jésus dans la tradition judéo-chrétienne.* Paris: J. Gabalda, 1992.

Vogel, C. J. de. *Greek Philosophy: A Collection of Texts.* Vol. 3, *The Hellenistic-Roman Period.* 2nd ed. Leiden: E. J. Brill, 1964.

Voss, Bernd Reiner. *Der Dialog in der frühchristlichen Literatur.* Studia et testimonia antiqua 9. München: W. Fink, 1970.

Waddington, W. H. *Fastes des provinces asiatiques de l'Empire romain depuis leur origine jusqu'au règne de Dioclétien.* Paris: Firmin Didot, 1872.

Wartelle, André. *Bibliographie historique et critique de saint Justin, philosophe et martyre, et des apologistes grecs du IIe siècle, 1494–1994, avec un supplement.* Paris: Lanore, 2001.

————. *Saint Justin. Apologies*, introduction, texte critique, traduction, commentaire et index. Paris: Études augustiniennes, 1987.

Weijenbourg, R. "Meliton de Sardes lecteur de la première Apologie et du Dialogue de Saint Justin." *Antoninianum* 49 (1974): 362–66.

Werline, Rodney. "The Transformation of Pauline Arguments in Justin Martyr's *Dialogue with Trypho*." *HTR* 92 (1999): 79–93.

Whitmarsh, Tim. *Greek Literature and the Roman Empire: The Politics of Imitation.* Oxford: Oxford University Press, 2001.

Williams, A. Lukyn. *Adversus Judaeos: A Bird's-Eye View of Christian* Apologiae *until the Renaissance.* Cambridge: Cambridge University Press, 1935.

Williams, Wynne. "Individuality in the Imperial Constitutions: Hadrian and the Antonines." *JRS* 66 (1976): 67–83.

————. "Two Imperial Pronouncements Reclassified." *Zeitschrift für Papyrologie und Epigraphik* 22 (1976): 235–40.

Wilson, Stephen G. *Related Strangers: Jews and Christians 70–170 C.E.* Minneapolis: Fortress Press, 1995.

Winden, J. C. M. van. *An Early Christian Philosopher: Justin Martyr's Dialogue with Trypho, Chapters One to Nine.* Philosophia Patrum 1. Leiden: Brill, 1971.

Witherington, Ben, III. "Not So Idle Thoughts about EIDOLOTHUTON." *Tyndale Bulletin* 44, no. 2 (1993): 237–54.

Wright, N. T. *Jesus and the Victory of God.* Minneapolis: Fortress Press, 1996.

Young, Frances. *Biblical Exegesis and the Formation of Christian Culture.* Cambridge: Cambridge University Press, 1997.

————. "Greek Apologists of the Second Century." In *Apologetics in the Roman Empire: Pagans, Jews, and Christians*, ed. Mark Edwards, Martin Goodman, and Simon Price, 81–104. Oxford: Oxford University Press, 1999.

Young, M. D. "Justin, Socrates, and the Middle Platonists." *StPat* 15 (1989): 161–70.

Young, Robert. *Colonial Desire: Hybridity in Theory, Culture, and Race.* London: Routledge, 1995.

Zahn, Theodor. *Geschichte des Neutestamentlichen Kanons.* 2 vols. in 4. Erlangen: Andreas Deichert, 1888–92.

Index of Names

Ancient Names

Abercius Marcellus, 121
Antoninus Pius, 23, 24, 26, 29–32, 38, 40, 116, 119, 122, 146
Apolinarius of Hierapolis, 7, 116, 117, 122, 126
Apollonius, 36
Aristides, 7, 27, 116–22
Aristo of Pella, 16, 63, 75
Arnobius, 117
Athenagoras, 7, 116, 118, 119, 123–27
Atticus, 167
Aurelius Pyrrus, 26

Caesar (son of Urbicus), 47
Celsus, 1, 2, 10, 15, 94, 141, 151, 160, 165
Chrysostom, 95
Cicero, 42
Clement of Alexandria, 30, 33, 54, 56, 64, 69, 82, 116, 134
Clement of Rome, 123, 153, 158
Commodus, 40, 116, 126
Constantine, 117
Crescens the Cynic, 29, 34, 48
Cyprian, 117, 141, 143

Diocletian, 39
Dionysius of Corinth, 120
Domitian, 45

Eusebius of Caeserea, 3, 4, 22, 23, 24, 28–32, 34–36, 38, 42–48, 90, 115–23, 126, 127

Gordian III, 25, 26

Hadrian, 3, 4, 7, 24, 26, 27, 38–49, 81, 116, 118–22, 146
Hamilcar, 124
Heraclitus, 34, 151
Hermias, 116
Herod Antipas, 61, 78, 108, 111
Herodian, 40
Hilary, 143
Hippolytus, 153, 156

Ignatius of Antioch, 90, 121, 123, 153, 158
Irenaeus of Lyon, 5, 13–14, 53, 76, 94, 122, 149, 153

Jeremias, 155–56
Jerome, 120, 143
John of Damascus, 35
Josephus, 111, 117

Lactantius, 117
Licinius Silvanus Granianus, 38, 46
Lollicus Urbicus (Urban Prefect), 22, 27, 32, 33, 39, 47, 48
Lucian of Antioch, 36
Lucian of Samosata, 20, 35, 165, 167
Lucius Verus, 29, 40, 47, 48, 116, 146

Marcellus of Ancyra, 8, 117
Marcion, 8, 9, 14, 32, 53, 54, 63, 76, 145, 147–51
Marcus Aurelius, 29, 38, 45, 116, 120, 126, 146
Maximian, 39
Maximus of Turin, 143
Melito of Sardis, 3, 7, 38, 40, 45, 46, 53, 116, 117, 122, 126

Menander Rhetor, 26, 30, 148
Menelaus, 124
Miltiades, 7, 116, 117, 118, 122, 126
Minucius Felix, 117
Minucius Fundanus, 3, 24, 26, 38, 39, 41, 42,
    43, 44, 45
Musonius, 34

Numenius, 167

Origen, 30, 58, 62, 64, 117, 118, 127, 151

Papias of Hierapolis, 14, 30, 72, 90, 107, 121,
    122
Perennis, 36
Philo, 15, 81, 85, 137
Philostratus, 117
Pionius, 36
Plato, 24, 81, 149, 167
Pliny, 4, 25, 41, 43, 45, 47, 153, 155
Plutarch, 165, 167
Polycarp, 121, 123
Polycrates, 121, 122
Ptolemaeus, 40
Ptolemy, 22, 32, 33, 47, 48
Pythagoras, 167

Quadratus, 7, 116–23

Rufinus, 3, 4, 38, 42– 47

Serapion, 106
Serenius Granianus, 38, 39, 43, 44
Simon Magus, 32
Socrates, 34, 72, 77, 81, 85, 125, 164, 166,
    167, 168

Tatian, 7, 29, 67, 94, 116, 118, 120, 127
Tertullian, 7, 30, 31, 36, 47, 54, 82, 94, 95,
    116, 117, 118, 122, 124, 126–27, 141,
    143, 153, 156, 157
Theophilus, 7, 116, 118, 120, 127
Trajan, 4, 25, 26, 39, 40–43, 45, 47, 120, 121,
    122
Trypho, 8, 15, 17, 34, 56, 71, 79, 80, 82, 83,
    85, 87, 89, 91, 92, 97, 98, 130, 132,
    133, 134, 138, 157, 167

Ulpian, 44

Urban Prefect, Urbicus (see Lollicus
    Urbicus)

Valentinus, 35

Xenophon, 24, 35, 72

Modern Names

Andresen, Carl, 2, 15
Archambault, Georges, 14
Armstrong, A. H., 15

Barnard, Leslie, 16, 21, 154, 164
Barthélemy, Dominic, 57, 78
Bellinzoni, Arthur J., 64, 112
Bhabha, Homi, 161, 164–66
Birley, A., 41, 43
Blunt, A. W. F., 14
Bobichon, Philippe, 14, 17, 83, 86
Boll, F. C., 23, 24
Bousset, Wilhelm, 58
Bowersock, G., 162
Boyarin, Daniel, 3, 18, 162
Bradshaw, Paul F., 157
Buchanan, Colin, 9, 10
Buck, Lorraine, 9, 146–47

Callewaert, C., 41
Capelle, D. B., 40
Cassels, W. R., 111
Chakrabarty, Dipesh, 161, 165, 166
Chilton, Bruce, 5, 6
Cohen, Shaye J. D., 19, 162
Conybeare, Frederick, 8, 141, 143
Cranmer, Thomas, 152–53

Daniélou, Jean, 18, 128, 129, 134, 135
Dix, Gregory, 156, 157
Droge, Arthur, 167
Dunn, James D. G., 2, 17–18

Edelstein, Ludwig, 15
Edwards, Mark, 164, 167
Estienne, Robert, 14

Foster, Paul, 6

Frede, Michael, 118
Frend, William, 163

Gibbon, Edward, 161
Goodenough, Charles R., 14, 15, 16, 21
Goodman, Martin, 117
Goodspeed, Edgar, 14, 24
Grabe, John Ernest, 24
Grant, Robert M., 24
Gruen, Erich, 162

von Harnack, Adolf, 10, 23, 24, 29, 30, 32,
       108, 109, 110, 111, 148, 157, 164, 165
Harris, Rendel, 78
Hays, Richard, 104
Heard, Richard, 72
Heid, Stefan, 21
Hengel, Martin, 18
Hill, Charles, 5, 6
Hirshman, Marc, 3, 18
Horner, Timothy, 2, 17
Hurtado, Larry, 7–8, 10
Hyldahl, Niels, 15

Instinsky, Hans Ulrich, 40

Jeremias, Joachim, 155–56
Joly, Robert, 15
Jones, F. Stanley, 20

Kessler, Edward, 82
Kinzig, Wolfram, 31, 54
Koester, Helmut, 5, 58, 59, 66, 69, 90, 91, 95,
       103, 106

Lahey, Lawrence, 8, 141, 142, 144
Lampe, Peter, 146
Lieu, Judith, 2, 18, 78, 160
Lightfoot, J. B., 41, 44
Lim, Richard, 164, 165
Lyman, Rebecca, 2, 3, 9–10

Marcovich, Miroslav, 14, 24
Millar, Fergus, 163
Minns, Denis, 3, 4, 14
Moll, Sebastian, 8–9
Mommsen, Theodor, 4, 26, 41, 42, 43
Munier, Charles, 14

Nesselhauf, Herbert, 40, 41
Niederwimmer, Kurt, 135

Osborn, Eric, 16, 21, 84, 85
Von Otto, J. C. Th., 14, 117

Parvis, Paul, 3, 4, 10, 14, 38, 42, 43, 46, 48
Parvis, Sara, 7
Pautigny, Louis, 14
Pilhofer, Peter, 106, 107–8, 110, 112
Pouderon, Bernard, 115
Prigent, Pierre, 15
Pryor, John, 88, 89

Quasten, Johannes, 24

Rajak, Tessa, 79–80, 163, 164
Ratcliff, Edward, 156
Rist, John, 15
Robinson, James M., 69
Rudolph, Anette, 17
Rutherford, Will, 8, 10

Said, Edward, 161
Sanders, E. P., 18, 109
Schmid, Wolfgang, 24, 39, 40, 48, 49
Schoeps, Hans Joachim, 18
Schwartz, Eduard, 24, 43
Segal, Alan, 2, 18
Sibinga, Joost Smit, 16
Simon, Marcel, 18
Skarsaune, Oskar, 2, 4, 5, 8, 14, 16–17, 20, 34,
       77, 78, 85, 95, 137, 138, 139, 144
Slusser, Michael, 2, 3
Spanneut, Michel, 15
Spivak, Gayati, 161
Stanton, Graham, 87, 88, 95, 107
Stark, Rodney, 19
Stylianopoulos, Theodore, 83
Swain, Simon, 162, 163, 165
Swete, H. B., 106, 108, 109–10

Thirlby, S., 23
Trobisch, David, 4, 53, 54, 75
Tuckett, Christopher, 104

Varner, William, 141
Veil, H., 23, 42, 47, 48

de Vogel, Cornelia J., 15

Wartelle, André, 14
Wendel, Susan, 6
Werline, Rodney, 84

Whitmarsh, Tim, 162, 167
van Winden, J. C. M., 15, 165
Young, Frances, 118, 163

Zahn, Theodor, 23, 108

Index of Ancient Sources

Bible

Old Testament

Genesis
             57, 58, 63
1   140
1:1   142, 143
1:26-28   8, 140
1:26   140, 141, 143
3   140
3:22   8, 140,
           141, 143
4:23   62
6   34
17   84
18–19   138
18:1—19:28   62
18:1—19:24   144
18   62
18:1, 17-26   144
19:24   8, 62, 63, 138,
         140, 142,
         143, 144
22   86
28   138
31–32   138
35   138
49:8-12   55
49:8   84
49:10-11 55, 60, 65, 79
49:10   60
49:11   65, 66

Exodus   57, 63
3   138
23:20   129, 130

Leviticus   57
26:40-41   57

Numbers   57
13:16   130
24:17   60

Deuteronomy   57
12:11   129
14:23   129

Joshua   57, 58
5:2-3   130

Judges   57

1 Samuel
5–6   131

2 Samuel
7:13-14   80

2 Kings   57

1 Chronicles
16:23-31   60

Ezra   63, 64

Psalms[1] 58, 64
2:7   139, 143

19   133
22   58, 61, 66,
         70, 90,
         91, 130
22:7   91
22:15c-18   91
22:16   90, 91, 92
22:18   90, 92
22:22   130
45:6-7 (44:7-8 LXX)
         8, 138,
       139, 142,
       143, 144
45:7 (44:8 LXX) 142, 143
45:7-8   62
68:18 (67:19 LXX) 101
72 (71 LXX) 132
72 (71 LXX):17-19 132
96 (95 LXX) 129
96 (95 LXX):10 129
96 (95 LXX) 60, 134
96 (95 LXX):1 134
96 (95 LXX):1-3 134
99:1-7   132
99:3   132
102:25-27
 (101:26-28 LXX) 139
110 (109 LXX):1 8, 62,
      138, 139,
     142, 143,
         144
110 (109 LXX):1-4 143
110 (109 LXX):2 100

---

1. Cited by Hebrew/English numbering, with LXX numeration added in parentheses where appropriate.

Proverbs	58, 85	2:28-29		28:20	66	
8	140, 143, 144	(3:1-2 LXX)	6, 101–3			
8:21-36	58, 140			Mark	65, 68, 72, 74,	
8:22-36	8	Amos			88, 91, 92, 93,	
8:22-31	142	2:4	80		94, 107, 123	
8:22-25	140	5:6-15	80	6:13	129	
8:22	140	9:11	80	6:14	111	
8:25	142			12:35-37	139	
8:26-31	140	Micah		15:24	67	
8:27	142, 143	4:2b	69			
8:30	142, 143			Luke	65, 68, 71,	
		Zechariah			72, 74, 88,	
Isaiah		3:1-10	131		91, 92, 93,	
	58, 62, 64	9:9	65		98, 105, 150	
2:3	69, 100	12:10-12	68	1:31-32	72	
11:1-10	80			1:46-55	96	
11:1	60	Malachi		1:68-79	96	
32:15	100	1:11	157, 158, 159	2:29-32	96	
35	93			3–4	96, 97	
35:1-7	93			3:18-22	97	
42	133	*Apocrypha*		3:22	96, 97	
42:1	100, 133			4:14	98	
42:4	133			4:18-19	98	
42:5-13	133	1 Maccabees		7:16-17	98	
42:6-8	133	4:43	83	9:8	98	
42:8	8, 133			11:53	47	
42:9	133	4 Maccabees		16:16	83	
42:10	134	5:22-25	85	20:42-43	139	
43:10-12	100			22:44	72	
45:1	139	*New Testament*		23:6-12	111	
49:6	100			24	69, 96	
51:4	83	Matthew	64–65, 67,	24:19	98	
51:5	60		68, 70, 71,	24:22	79	
55:3-4	83		72, 88, 91,	24:27	79	
58:2	91		92, 93,	24:32	86	
63:15	84		105, 111	24:44-48	96, 100	
		1:21	72, 129	24:47-48	100	
Jeremiah	58, 62, 64	11:13	83	24:48	100	
31:31	83	11:27	71	24:49	100	
		13:2	84			
Ezekiel	58	13:36	84	John	5–6, 68,	
		14:1	111		72, 85,	
Daniel	58	21:1-7	66		88–94, 109	
7:9-28	58	21:43	84	1:1	71	
		22:43-44	139	1:1-3	134	
Joel		27:35	67	1:13	71, 89	
2 (3 LXX)	101–3	27:64ff.	111	1:14	70, 71, 89	
2:28 (3:1 LXX)	102	28	69	1:18	70	

3:5, 7	5, 88
3:16, 18	70
9	93
9:1, 19, 20, 32	93
19:13	91, 109
19:23	67
19:24	67, 92
19:34-37	68
20:10	111
20:25	67, 92
20:27	92
Acts	54, 74, 75, 158
1–2	64, 96
1:1-8	100
1:4	100
1:8	100
2	99, 102
2:17-42	96
2:17-36	99
2:17-21	96, 101
2:17-18	101
2:18	102
2:21-36	129
2:22	102
2:32-36	139
2:36	102
2:37-38	102
2:38	102
2:39	102
2:40-41	102
3:6, 16	129
13:15	84
13:46	84
15	80
15:16-18	96
15:19-21	81
17	81
Luke-Acts	6, 84, 96, 100
Romans	60, 71, 74, 75, 158
10:9-13	129
11:26	83

1 Corinthians	
1:2	129
2:16	82
8:5-6	134
12:1-3	129
2 Corinthians	
3:12-18	82
Galatians	71, 74
3–4	95
Ephesians	
4:8	101
Philippians	
2:9-11	128
Colossians	
1:15-16	134
Hebrews	54, 75
1	139
1:13	139
1 Peter	75
1 John	75
Revelation	54, 75

Works of Justin Martyr

Apology (both or nonspecific) — 2–4, 7–8, 13–17, 19, 23–24, 27, 29–30, 38, 39, 44–45, 47–48, 55–56, 59, 64–66, 70, 72, 77, 80, 116, 127, 145–51, 158, 166

1 Apology	3–4, 8–9, 15, 23–24, 26–32, 34–35, 38–40, 47–49, 92, 106, 123, 145–46, 158, 163
1	26, 30
1.1	24
2	85
2.1	24, 166
2.2	24
3.1	26
3.2	24
5.3-4	34, 81
7.1-4	47
7.4	26
7.5	47
9	81
12ff.	47
13.3	90
14.1	27
15-17	64, 65
15.6	155
16.14	26
21.1	89
22.2	89
23.1	79
23.2	89
27.1-3	126
28.1-4	34
28.1	89
28.2	33
31–52	65
31.1-8	78
31.7	56
32–52	56, 63
32	55, 56, 59, 60
32.1	55, 79
32.5	65
32.9	89
32.10	89
33.5	72, 73, 89
33.9	85
35	90, 92
35.4	91
35.5-8	67, 92

1 Apology (cont.)

35.6	7, 108
35.7	91
35.9	89, 91, 93
35.10	65
36.1	85
38	90, 91
38.4	92
38.7	89, 92
39–50	100
39.2	100
39.3	69
40	108
40.1	79
41.4	60
42.4	69
44	79
44.8	81
44.9	81
45.1	33
45.5	69, 100
46.1	90
46.2	85
46.3	85
47–49	95
47	84
48.2-3	93
48.3	89, 90
49	84
49.5	69
50	111
52.10-12	68
50.12	68, 69, 70
53	100
53.3	69
59–60	81
61	155, 156
61.4	5, 88
61.13	90
61.34	93
63.2	89
65.1	156, 157
65.3	157
66	155, 157
66.2	86
66.3	71, 89, 93, 105, 129
67.3	79, 88, 89, 93
67.7	69, 70
68.1-2	39
68.2	40, 48
68.3	26, 30
68.6-10	39
68.8	42
68.10	39
108	111

2 Apology — 3–4, 22–24, 26–32, 34–36, 39–40, 47–48, 165

1.1	39
2	28
2.1-8	123
2.2-16	48
2.11	32
2.13	33
3(4).1	23, 34
4(5).1	23, 34
4(5).3	34
5(6).1	33
5(6).2	33
5(6).3-6	33
5(6).6	90
6(7).1	33
6(7).5-9	34
7(8).1-3	34
8(3)	31
8(3).1-6	29
9.1	23, 34
10:1-2	80
10.4-6	34
11	30
11.2-5	35
11:3-5	72
12.5	125
13	49, 168
14–15	48
14	28
14.1	25, 26, 49
15	28
15.1	48
15.5	28

Dialogue with Trypho — 2, 4, 8, 13–17, 19–20, 28, 32, 34, 55–56, 58–59, 63–66, 70, 73, 77, 79–80, 82, 88, 95–96, 106, 116, 118, 131, 136–37, 140–41, 143–44, 151, 158, 166

1–47	79
1	167
1.3	79
3–8	77
3.1	77
6	78
7	78
8.1	86
8.2	73
8.4	98
10.2	71
11:2-3	83
11.5	6, 93, 95
14.8	68
16	84
16.1-4	95
16.1	57
16.3	18
17.1-2	100
23.3	85
25.1	84
25.5	95
28.5	157
29.1	157
29.2	82
30.3	90, 129
31:2-7	58
32.2	68, 82
32.3	102
35	81
35.5-6	32
38.2	80, 102
39.2	33, 156
41	157
41.2	157
42.1	69
43.3, 4	102
48–108	79

49.1	98	65.1	133	100.4	89
49.3-5	98	65.3	133	101.1-4	91
49.6	102	67.5-6	83	101.1-2	61
51.1—52.4	83	68.5	85	101.2	61
52–54	55	69	93	102.1-2	61
52	55, 56	69.6	93	102.3-4	61
52.1	84	71–73	63	102.5	61
52.2	55	73–74	129, 134	102.6	61
53.1	66	74.1	134	103.1-4	61, 111
53.2	66	75	130, 131	103.8	72
53.4	102	76	7, 129	103.9	61
55.1	102, 139	76.6	69, 90, 129	104.1-2	61, 92
55.3	84	77.3	102	105–107	108
56–62	8, 63, 138	82	84	105	107
56–60	8, 61, 137,	82.1	6, 95	105.1	5, 70,
	138, 140, 144	83	6, 100		88–89, 93
56–57	62, 138	83.2	100	105.2	61
56	85, 139	84.2	102	105.3	61
56.4	139	85.1-3	129	105.4-6	61
56.5	102	85.2	90	106	107
56.9	138	87–88	96	106.1-2	61
56.10	138	87	6, 96, 99,	106.1	69
56.11-15	138		100, 101, 103	106.2-3	130
56.11	139	87.1-2	97	106.3	6, 72, 107
56.12-15	62	87.2, 3, 4	97	106.4	84
56.12	138	87.3—88.2	98	108.3	95
56.14	139	87.3-6	99	109–136	798
56.15-23	138	87.3	98	109–110	69
58	138	87.5	99, 102	109	84
59–60	57, 138	87.6	96, 99, 101	109.1	69
61–62	8, 63, 138,	88	84	110.2	69
	140, 143	88.1-2	97	111–113	130
61.1—62.4	137, 140,	88.1	98	111.1	130
	144	88.3-8	97	112.2	130
61	85	88.3	72, 93, 97	113	130
61.2	86, 140	88.7	93	113.1-3	130
61:3-5	58	88.8	97	113.4-7	130
62	85	89.1	130	113.6	130
62.1	140	90.4	130	114.4	69
62.2-3	140	91.3	130	115	130
62.2	140	91.4	102	116.3	6, 95, 157
63.2	89	97–107	61, 66, 70	117	158
64	132, 133	97	6, 110	117.4	157
64.1	132	97.3	92	118.1	68
64.4	132	98–107	58	119.6	69
64.6	132	99.2-3	61	120.3-5	56
64.7	68	100	107	120.5	63, 80
65	8, 132	100.2	70, 71, 89	120.6	32

Dialogue with Trypho (cont.)
123.9   6, 95
126—128.1   138, 139
126   57
126.1   84
126.6   57
127.5   62
128.1   131
128.2—129   138
131.4-5   131
132   131
132.3   131
139.1   102
141   85

De resurrectione   15

*Syntagma against
the Heresies*   15

*Syntagma against
Marcion*   63

**Classical, Rabbinic, and
Patristic Texts**

Acts of Pilate   89

Aristeas, Letter of   77

Aristides
Apologia   118, 119
*Athanasius and
Zacchaeus*   141–44

Athenagoras
*Supplicatio pro
Christianis*   116, 118,
    123, 124–25
1–2   124
14.1   124
15.1   124
16.3   124
24.5   124
24.6—25.1   124
25.2   124
26.1   124
26.3-5   124

32.5   125
34.1   125
34.3   125
35   125
36   125

*Barlaam and
Josaphat*   16

Barnabas, Letter of   56
12:10-11   139

Clement of Alexandria
Excerpta ex Theodoto   33
26.1   33
26.3   33
41.1-2   33
43.1   33
Hypotyposeis   30
Paedagogus (Tutor)   116
*Protrepticus
(Exhortation)*   116
Quis Dives Salvetur
36.3   33

Clement of Rome
(and Ps.-Clement)
1 Clement   121, 158
58.1   134
59.2   134
59.3   134
59.3—61.3   134
63   156
2 Clement   121
Homilies   3, 20, 64
Recognitions   3, 16, 20

Codex Iustinianus
9.47.12   57

Constantine
Oration to the Saints, 117

Cyprian
Testimonia, 141

Damascus Document   80
7:15-20   80
7:15-17   80

Didache   14, 153, 154
10:2   135

Diognetus, Letter to
    13, 117,
    118, 119, 127

Eusebius
Chronicon   119, 120
Contra Hieroclem   116
Contra Marcellum   117
*De Ecclesiastica
Theologia*   117
Historia Ecclesiastica
    3, 4, 23, 31,
    36, 38, 42, 43,
    44, 45, 116, 118
II.2.4   36, 116, 127
II.13.2   29, 31, 36
III.24   90
III.37.1
121
III.39.15   90
IV.Pinax 17, 18   30
IV.1.1-3   116
IV.3.1-2   121
IV.3.1   35, 118
IV.3.3   35, 120
IV.8.6   46
IV.8.8   42
IV.9.1-3   38
IV.11.11   30, 31, 36, 127
IV.13.8   36, 127
IV.16.1   29
IV.16.2   29, 31, 32
IV.16.7-9   29–30
IV.16.7   29
IV.17   29
IV.17.2-13   28
IV.18.2   29, 30, 31,
    36, 116, 127
IV.18.9   30
IV.23.3   120
IV.26.1, 2   30, 116,
IV.26.2   122
IV.26.5   45
IV.26.6   45
IV.26.10   45

V.5.5	116	Irenaeus of Lyon		Plato		
V.7.5	116	*Adversus Haereses*	8, 13	*Timaeus*		81
V.15.3—17.4	121	*Demonstration of*				
V.17.4	121	*the Apostolic Preaching*		Pliny		
V.21.2-5	36		14	*Epistulae*		
V.24.2-5	121			X.38		47
VIII.13.2	36	*Jasonis et Papisci,*		X.82		45
IX.6.3	36	*Altercatio*	8, 16,	*Panegyricus,*		45
Martyrs of Old	35		63, 75, 117,			
Praeparatio Evangelica	116	chap. 11 (*passim*)		*Psalms of Solomon*		
				17:21-43		80
Gospel of the Ebionites	67	Jerome				
		De Viris Illustribus		Qumran		
Gospel of Nicodemus	90	19	120	4Q174 3:10-13		80
				4QTestim175		63
Gospel of Peter	6, 7,	John of Damascus				
	67, 91,	*Sacra Parallela*	31	*Simon and*		
chap. 8 (*passim*)				*Theophilus*	141–44	
1.1	108	Josephus				
1.2	111	*Antiquitates*		*Songs of Joshua*		63
3.6-7	7, 108	18.5.2	111			
4.12	7, 92, 110	*Contra Apionem*	117	Talmud		
8.30ff.	111			Bavli		
		Kerygma of Peter	56, 69,	Yoma		
Gospel of Truth	33, 34		70, 75	39b		83
38.7-24	33			*Sanhedrin*		
39.30—40.1	33	Lucian		38b		62
		Somnium				
Hadrian		6–17	35	Yerushalmi		
Rescript	3, 4, 7,			*Sota*		
	24–26,	*Martyrdom of Isaiah*	63	6:13		83
chap. 3 (*passim*),						
	119–22	*Martyrdom of Pionius*	36	Tanchuma		
				Y. Titissa		
Hermias		*Martyrdom of Polycarp*		34		87
Irrisio	116	10.1	123			
				Targum Jonathan	84, 85	
Historia Augusta	27	*Mekilta*	80			
Vita Hadriani				Targum Onqelos	59, 60	
20.8	27	Melito of Sardis				
		Apology (Address		Tatian		
Ignatius		*to the Emperor)*	3, 7,	*Ad Graecos*	7, 116	
Ad Magnesios			38, 45,	*Diatesseron*	67, 94	
11.1	90		116, 126			
Ad Smyrnaeos				Tertullian		
1.2	90	Philo		*Ad Scapulam*		118
Ad Trallianos		*De aeternitate mundi*		*Adv. Judaeos*	95, 141	
9.1	90	17–19	81	*Adv. Marcionem*		54

Adv. Valentinianos, 5   31   17.1—18.3   126   Theophilus
Apologeticus   30, 116,   21.1-16   126   Ad Autolycum   7, 116,
                          126   21.14-31   126   127
1.1   126, 127   22.1—23.19   126
1.4—3.8   126   25.1—27.1   126–27   Timothy and Aquila
2.10-17   126   28.1—38.5   127   141–44
7.1—9.20   126   39.1-21   127
8.1-2   126   40.1—55.7   127   Tripartite Tractate   33–34
8.3   126   46.1—47.11   127   123.11-18   33–34
9.5   126   47.12—59.4   127
9.11-12   126   49.5—50.16   127   Ulpian
9.17   126   De Idololatria   De Proconsule   44
9.18   126   20.5   47
10.1-2   126   To Scapula   118   Xenophon
10.10   126   Memorabilia   72, 73
11.10-13   126   Testaments of the Twelve   2.1.21-33   72
12.2-7   126   Patriarchs   16
15.8   126

A page from the fourteenth-century manuscript Parisinus graecus 450, completed on September 11, 1364 (fol 193 verso). This is the only independent manuscript of Justin's writings. Photo courtesy Bibliothèque nationale de France.